# CURRICULUM ALTERNATIVES

## Experiments in School Library Media Education

Robert N. Case
*Director*

Anna Mary Lowrey
*Associate Director*

SCHOOL LIBRARY MANPOWER PROJECT
*Funded by the* KNAPP FOUNDATION OF NORTH CAROLINA, INC.
*Administered by the* AMERICAN ASSOCIATION OF SCHOOL LIBRARIANS
*A Division of the* AMERICAN LIBRARY ASSOCIATION

AMERICAN LIBRARY ASSOCIATION
*Chicago 1974*

**Library of Congress Cataloging in Publication Data**

School Library Manpower Project.
    Curriculum alternatives; experiments in school library
media education.

    1.  School Library Manpower Project.  2.  Library
education--United States--Case studies.  3.  School
librarians.  I.  Case, Robert N., 1931-    II.  Lowrey,
Anna Mary.  III.  Title.
Z675.S3S356  1974          020'.7          74-12070
ISBN 0-8389-3154-5

Printed in the United States of America

# Contents

# Advisory Committee

LESLIE H. JANKE,  Chairman 1968-1973
University of California at San Jose
San Jose, California

ELEANOR E. AHLERS,  1968-1973
  University of Washington
  Seattle, Washington

THOMAS BUCHTA,  1970-1971
  Skokie School District #68
  Skokie, Illinois

RICHARD L. DARLING,  1968-1970
  Columbia University
  New York, New York

RUTH M. ERSTED,  1970-1973
  Minnesota Department of Education
  St. Paul, Minnesota

SARA I. FENWICK,  1968-1973
  University of Chicago
  Chicago, Illinois

BERNARD FRANCKOWIAK,  Ex Officio 1973
  Wisconsin Department of Public Instruction
  Madison, Wisconsin

MARGARET H. GRAZIER,  1972-1973
  Wayne State University
  Detroit, Michigan

FRANCES HATFIELD,  Ex Officio 1971-72, Member 1972-73
  Broward County Board of Public Instruction
  Ft. Lauderdale, Florida

PHYLLIS HOCHSTETTLER,  Ex Officio 1968-1969
  Portland State College
  Portland, Oregon

VIRGINIA OWENS,  1971-1973
  Oklahoma Department of Libraries
  Oklahoma City, Oklahoma

MIRIAM E. PETERSON,  1968-1973
  Chicago Board of Education
  Chicago, Illinois

ELNORA M. PORTTEUS,  Ex Officio 1972-1973
  Cleveland Public Schools
  Cleveland, Ohio

JOHN REBENAK,  1968-1973
  Akron Public Library
  Akron, Ohio

JOHN ROWELL,  Ex Officio 1969-1970
  Case Western Reserve University
  Cleveland, Ohio

ALICE C. RUSK,  1968-1972
  Baltimore City Public Schools
  Baltimore, Maryland

RUSSELL SHANK,  1968-1970
  Smithsonian Institution Library
  Washington, D. C.

LU OUIDA VINSON,  Ex Officio 1968-1973
  American Association of School Librarians
  Chicago, Illinois

CAROLYN WHITENACK,  Ex Officio 1967-1968
  Purdue University
  LaFayette, Indiana

EDWARD A. WIGHT,  1968-1970
  University of California
  Berkeley, California

ROBERTA YOUNG,  Ex Officio 1970-1971
  Colorado Department of Education
  Denver, Colorado

# Foreword

This report, a summary of the activities of the School Library Manpower Project during the past five years, reveals the many significant contributions the Project has made to Twentieth Century library education. As a result of the generous funding by the Knapp Foundation of North Carolina, Inc. the Project staff has been able to carry out all phases of the Project as envisioned in the original proposal approved by the American Library Association in 1967. The Phase I study of the role of media specialists in America's schools and the Phase II development of the six experimental programs in library education, have provided milestones that will have lasting influence upon the kinds of library media programs made available for young people in schools across the nation.

Throughout the course of the Project hundreds of specialists in all areas of education have been associated with the endeavor. Their efforts have been fruitful as a result of the able direction given to the Project by Director Robert N. Case; Associate Director Anna Mary Lowrey; and Lu Ouida Vinson, Executive Secretary of the American Association of School Librarians. The efforts of the staff have been enhanced by the strong support provided by the American Library Association, and especially by three of its divisions: The American Association of School Librarians, the Library Education Division and the Library Administration Division; all of which have provided representatives to serve on the Project's Advisory Committee.

Success of the Project has also been dependent upon the cooperation of the administrations and faculties of the experimental library education programs in the six institutions participating in the undertaking. The many innovations these institutions developed will undoubtedly become the prototypes for other colleges and universities as they develop or adapt their library education programs to adjust to the changes now taking place in American education. The information being shared by these institutions and the many outstanding publications that have been compiled by the Project staff will assuredly continue to serve as catalysts for the future improvements in library education as well as for the entire librarianship profession.

LESLIE H. JANKE, Chairman
Advisory Committee
School Library Manpower Project

# Preface

The School Library Manpower Project was initiated in 1968 as a five year effort to study vital questions leading to the redefinition of the concept of school librarianship and to support the effective utilization of professional school library media personnel through implementation and evaluation of a variety of new and innovative educational approaches. This document is a report of that study. The report is developed in two distinct parts—Part One: The Project, and Part Two: The Programs.

In Part One, a brief introductory summary of the Project's Phase I activities and accomplishments is included to provide the reader with the necessary background to the foundation and processes utilized in the initial years of the study. This review will serve as a transition into the Phase II endeavors. More detailed reports of Phase I findings are documented in *School Library Manpower Project, Phase I—Final Report* published in 1970, as well as in a number of publications and additional journal articles which appeared in the library and education press between 1969 and 1971.

The major emphasis in Part One of this publication relates specifically to the activities conducted during Phase II. A knowledge of the Project's requirements, the institution's responsibilities and the criteria of selection developed by the Project's Advisory Committee are essential for the reader to have if he is to understand the purpose and framework of the six experimental programs. The reader should give particular attention to the overview of the processes used in developing and implementing the curriculum, the interface between program staff and students, and the various steps employed in developing the guidelines for program evaluation through the use of nine evaluation topics. The conclusion of the Phase II report summarizes and brings into focus the major issues and recommendations set forth as a result of the Project's findings.

Part Two of this document includes the individual evaluative reports of the six Phase II experimental programs. All reports are developed within a similar structure with adaptability to the specific nature and special features of each program. The reports support the nine evaluation topics identified and developed during Phase II and are indicative of the status of these programs as of August 1973. The uniqueness of each program's proposal, objectives, institutional environment, program methodology and total resources affected the outcome of each program's experimentation. The six reports relate to individual programs with no effort made to compare one program with another. After studying the six individual reports of the experimental programs in Part Two, the reader may wish to return to Part One, Phase II for a review of the Project's conclusions and recommendations. As the profession moves toward a more comprehensive approach to the broad areas of instructional communication and technology, the reader of this document will see the relevance of these recommendations for his own leadership role in advancing new curricular design in education.

This publication brings to a close the original five-year study as proposed by the American Association of School Librarians and financed by the Knapp Foundation of North Carolina, Inc. The reader will recognize the need for a more definitive evaluation effort of the results of these experimental programs. A similar need was identified by the Project's Advisory Committee which took steps early in Phase I to implement plans for a Phase III summative evaluation study. The Phase III extension has been supported by funds from the Knapp Foundation and will conclude in 1974. An overview of the purpose and procedures to be utilized in this one-year extension is included in Part One. A final report of the Phase III findings and a status report of the six experimental programs will be published in early 1975.

# Acknowledgments

During the past five years hundreds of specialists in a variety of fields and disciplines have become involved in the School Library Manpower Project. The success of the Project and the contents of this published report are the results of the contribution and efforts of these people during Phase I and Phase II.

We are most grateful to the Knapp Foundation of North Carolina, Inc. for the generous grant which provided the library profession with the opportunity and subsequent responsibility to fulfill the stated goals of the Project. During the past five years the interest and trust of Mr. C. E. Stouch, President of the Knapp Foundation of North Carolina, Inc. has offered much encouragement to the Project staff. An additional foundation grant for a Phase III evaluation study during 1973-74 reflects this growing trust and continued relationship with the school library profession which began over a decade ago.

During the initial task analysis activities of Phase I, the Project received helpful direction from Dr. Glen Robinson and Mrs. Jo Ann Stenstrom of the Research Division of the National Education Association. The contribution and artistry of John O'Toole of the Smithsonian Motion Picture Group is reflected in his direction of the Project film *At the Center*. Though previously identified in the *School Library Manpower Project, Phase I—Final Report,* the Project staff wishes to recognize the members of the Task Analysis Committee and the Curriculum Content Committee who willingly shared their professional expertise and contributed to the foundations of the Phase II experimental programs.

The lasting results of the Project did not come from Chicago however, but from the six institutions selected to implement the Phase II experimental programs. Following Project guidelines the Program Directors and staff personnel of these institutions designed, modified and executed innovations in school library media education. The results of their endeavors have left a challenging impact upon the student participants, who by this time have scattered into hundreds of schools across the country putting new media concepts and theories into relevant practice. Special appreciation goes to Dr. Frank R. Birmingham, Mankato State College; Joseph F. Blake, Millersville State College; Miss Lucile Hatch and Dr. Chow Loy Tom, University of Denver; Dr. William E. Hug, Auburn University; Dr. Helen Lloyd, University of Michigan; and Dr. Howard Sullivan, Arizona State University. The abilities of the Program Directors to combine their professional expertise and awareness with their personal qualities and leadership strategies were what made all the difference in moving a proposed program to its final objectives as described in this report. The Project staff also recognizes the contributions made by Dr. C. Dennis Fink and Dr. Harold Wagner of the Human Resources Research Organization whose understanding of program analysis and evaluation design were valuable not only to the Phase II activities, but were instrumental in the formulation of the summative evaluation proposal to be implemented during Phase III.

The Project staff owes a great deal of gratitude to the individual members of the Advisory Committee, who under the chairmanship of Leslie H. Janke provided continuous professional direction and understanding. Most important of all we are grateful for the personal encouragement and support they gave us every step of the way. Our deep appreciation is also extended to three staff members—Miss Lu Ouida Vinson, Executive Secretary, American Association of School Librarians, for the sound guidance and key liaison functions she provided over the past five years, and to our girls Monday through Friday, Mrs. Cathryn Stachura and Miss Betty Szkodzinski, whose office skills and expertise kept us on time, on schedule and on target.

To all of you we say, "Thank you for your ideas, suggestions and encouragement." We were fortunate to be two people passing through in a particular era of great educational change. Our personal associations with all of you and the hope that we have in part achieved some measure of your expectations have made this experience personally and professionally most rewarding.

ROBERT N. CASE
ANNA MARY LOWREY

*Part One*

# THE PROJECT

Phase I
Phase II
Phase III

# Phase I

The decade of the sixties was a period of great educational change in response to societal upheavals and technological advances. Thrust into the center of this revolutionary movement, the definition of school librarianship needed to be redefined and the educational role of the school librarian resolved. Changing school curriculum, new applications of teaching methodologies and learning strategies, the impact of federal programs, and new methods of storage, retrieval and dissemination of information, to name but a few, were having a direct effect upon the school librarian's role in meeting informational, educational, and research needs. The diversity of job responsibilities in school library programs, the proliferation of media and their extensive use in library programs required by educational innovations and recommended in the *Standards for School Library Programs*[1] mandated the need for school media specialists to have the mastery of new concepts in the profession to meet these changing responsibilities. Nearly a decade has passed since the *National Inventory of Library Needs,*[2] published by the American Library Association in 1965, revealed the special concerns of school librarianship in providing sufficient well-qualified personnel to insure quality library service in every school. There was an urgent need to recognize and define the services, the different levels of responsibility, and the variety of job functions and tasks to be performed in school libraries. Following close behind these basic concerns was the recognition that a new approach to school library media education would be required if theory was ever to be put into relevant practice and if school library media specialists were ever to have the required knowledge, skills and competencies for

effective on-the-job performance. Thus it was that the national concerns of school librarianship in the areas of task analysis, recruitment, education and utilization of manpower became enmeshed in the evolution of new approaches for quality school media programs.

As more questions began to emerge, it became increasingly clear to the profession that these approaches called for thoughtful study and dramatic action on a number of points which would include expertise from a variety of disciplines in the broad fields of media, education and the behavioral sciences. The more these ideas began to formulate in the minds of key leaders in the school library profession, the more convinced they were that the time was ripe to advance into the seventies with a national, action-oriented program to address these issues. By early 1967 the Ad Hoc Recruitment Committee of the American Association of School Librarians had developed the major components for a long-range program proposal to study these major concerns. This proposal was to become the School Library Manpower Project. Additional support and refinements were gathered from the Library Education Division and the Library Administration Division of the American Library Association. The Executive Board of the American Library Association gave final approval to the proposal on July 1, 1967. The basic question of how the proposed study could be implemented was answered five months later through a generous grant of $1,163,718 from the Knapp Foundation of North Carolina, Inc.

The School Library Manpower Project itself evolved from needs identified in the earlier Knapp School Libraries Demonstration Project, namely, that it was essential that the library profession seek new ways to recruit school library personnel, study and implement more effective ways to educate them in their field of specialization, and determine how these persons could best be utilized in education. The five

---

1. American Association of School Librarians, American Library Association, *Standards for School Library Programs* (Chicago: American Library Association, 1960).

2. U.S. Office of Education, Library Services Branch, *National Inventory of Library Needs* (Chicago: American Library Association, 1965).

year School Library Manpower Project study, administered by the American Association of School Librarians, provided not only the school library profession, but the total field of librarianship with an opportunity to study vital questions and seek solutions through the implementation and evaluation of a variety of new and innovative approaches in school library media education. A nine-member Advisory Committee with representation from the American Association of School Librarians, the Library Administration Division and the Library Education Division, all divisions of the American Library Association, was appointed by the President of AASL to monitor the Project.

The School Library Manpower Project was developed in two distinct phases. During the two years of Phase I, 1968-1970, the Project was concerned with educational change and its effect upon school librarianship. The first purpose of Phase I was to study the roles and job functions of school library personnel to support the development of new occupational definitions. The second purpose was to provide recommendations for implementing six experimental school library media education programs in Phase II.

Throughout the various stages of Phase I and in the special study activities, every effort was made to assure that the Project would receive the highest level of input from consultants and leaders in the fields related to school librarianship. Increasingly during Phase I the Project recognized the valuable contribution from other disciplines and specialty fields such as public personnel, management, technology, communication, curriculum design, education, administration, and research. Representatives from these and other fields not only served as reactors to Phase I findings, but many offered initial and vital direction to the Project as members of special study committees.

Shortly after the School Library Manpower Project was activated, the American Association of School Librarians and the Department of Audiovisual Instruction adopted the *Standards for School Media Programs*.[3] While the new terminology of "media specialist," "media centers," and "media programs" was being used increasingly in education, the Advisory Committee believed that during this initial period of transition the terms "school library" and "school librarian" were more universally understood by the total community. In an effort to bridge the transition from one terminology to another and to foster effective recruitment programs to target audiences, the term "school library media" was used in Phase I definitions, discussions and publications which related to the Project. During the five-year period of the Project, the American Association of School Librarians and the Association for Educational Communications and Technology initiated procedures for the revision of the 1969 *Standards*. Early discussion indicated a growing national acceptance and use of the media terminology. As a result, later Project publications reflect this trend in terminology and are less precise in adherence to the term "school library."

The initial activity leading to the development of new definitions for school library media personnel was the Task Analysis Survey which was conducted under contract for the Project by the Research Division of the National Education Association. Guidelines established by the Project and the "Criteria of Excellence Checklist"[4] developed with the Research Division were used to identify the 694 outstanding school library media programs in the national purposive sample. The *Task Analysis Survey Instrument*[5] developed for the research study was used in the survey to identify the tasks performed by a wide variety of staff positions in school library media centers throughout the country. In October 1969 the published report *School Library Personnel: Task Analysis Survey*[6] was made available and served as a working paper to advance Phase I toward the development of new definitions for school librarianship.

In anticipation that an in-depth analysis of the survey's findings was necessary, a special Task Analysis Committee was appointed composed of ten members who represented a wide variety of position levels and disciplines in the fields of school librarianship, library education, library and education administration, technology, and public personnel.

The role of the Task Analysis Committee was to analyze the tasks performed by school library personnel as reported in the final report of the survey. In

3. American Association of School Librarians, American Library Association, and the Department of Audiovisual Instruction, National Education Association, *Standards for School Media Programs* (Chicago: American Library Association, and Washington, D.C.: National Education Association, 1969).

4. School Library Manpower Project, "Criteria of Excellence Checklist," *School Library Personnel: Task Analysis Survey* (Chicago: American Library Association, 1969), p. 8.

5. School Library Manpower Project, *Task Analysis Survey Instrument* (Chicago: American Library Association, 1969).

6. School Library Manpower Project, *School Library Personnel: Task Analysis Survey* (Chicago: American Library Association, 1969).

the analysis process, the Task Analysis Committee had to determine what tasks should be performed by a variety of school library media personnel in a building level school library media center to meet the personnel requirements of the 1969 *Standards for School Media Programs*. The study of these tasks resulted in many tasks and responsibilities being reassigned upward or downward to other school library media staff positions to effect a more meaningful approach to the development of occupational definitions.

In fulfilling its assignment to the Project, the Task Analysis Committee was charged with two major concerns—that of developing occupational definitions which would provide a career lattice approach for mobility within the positions, and, secondly, to identify in a series of statements the role and impact the positions would have on the development of the six experimental programs during Phase II.

The four occupational definitions that resulted from the work of this committee were: School Library Media Specialist, Head of the School Library Media Center, District School Library Media Director, and the School Library Media Technician. The major components of the occupational definitions included the nature and scope of the position, major duties, and the knowledges and abilities required for the position. The definitions were published in a 1971 Project publication *Occupational Definitions for School Library Media Personnel*.[7]

One of the main outcomes of the development of the occupational definitions and goals identified for the Project during Phase I was the focus and emphasis given these job functions in the Project's color sound recruitment film *At the Center*.[8] The purpose of the film was to motivate an interest in school librarianship as a career in education. The two major film goals identified by the Advisory Committee were: (1) to present the role of the school library media specialist as a changing, exciting and dynamic force in education and (2) to aid personnel in educational institutions and agencies and community education groups to gain a fuller understanding of the future role of school librarianship and its contribution to education. The Project's overall recruitment objective was to be clearly established in the film. Its message spoke to the quality and exper-

tise that was needed by school library personnel to be able to cope and understand, act and react, and to become directly involved in initiating and implementing plans to improve the learning process.

In October 1969 the Advisory Committee selected the Smithsonian Motion Picture Group Office of Public Affairs of the Smithsonian Institution as producer of the 28-minute film. Following this decision, film production activities moved rapidly. Location sites were identified, visited and selected in the late fall of 1969 and the shooting script was approved by the Advisory Committee in January 1970. Emphasis on national recruitment plans and the desire to include the wide variety of newly identified functions contributed to the final decision to use a number of film locations. *At the Center* was filmed at a college campus, a state media professional conference and in seven school districts during the early spring of 1970. The following locations were used:

> Baltimore City Schools, Maryland
> Montgomery County Public Schools, Maryland
> Oak Park-River Forest High School District,
>    Illinois
> Glencoe Elementary School District #35,
>    Illinois
> Fountain Valley School District, California
> Compton City Schools, California
> East Side Union High School District, California
> San Jose State College, California
> CASL-AVEAC Joint Conference, California

*At the Center* was premiered in July 1970 at the Detroit Conference of the American Library Association, with over 700 persons attending the premiere at the state assembly breakfast of the American Association of School Librarians. At the conclusion of Phase II, 225 prints of *At the Center* had been sold to library and education agencies. In addition to sales distribution, *At the Center* was made available for free bookings through a film distribution contract with Modern Talking Picture Service Incorporated. Through this contractual agreement covering the period August 1970 through August 1973, *At the Center* was shown 3,730 times to a total viewing audience of 137,923 persons. In addition to the bookings made to school, university, and community groups, *At the Center* had 110 telecasts to an estimated audience of 2,805,400 viewers.

Coterminous with the development of the occupational definitions and the recruitment film, an eleven member Curriculum Content Committee was appointed to study the new definitions and to de-

7. School Library Manpower Project, *Occupational Definitions for School Library Media Personnel* (Chicago: American Library Association, 1971).

8. School Library Manpower Project, *At the Center*. 16mm, 28:45 minute color/sound film (Chicago: American Library Association, 1970).

velop objectives and recommend guidelines for new curriculum programs in school library media education.

The Curriculum Content Committee was representative of schools of education, library school administration, undergraduate and graduate library and audiovisual education programs, district school library media supervisors, practicing elementary and secondary school librarians and recent library school graduates. Through its discussions and deliberations the Curriculum Content Committee was cognizant of the broad implications the recommendations would have for the Phase II experimental programs and for library education as a whole. Following the agreement of objectives for a school library media education program, the committee analyzed occupational definitions and identified "Major Areas of Competencies for the Education of the School Library Media Specialist."[9] The seven major areas of competencies identified were: Media; Human Behavior; Development and Interaction; Learning and Learning Environment; Planning and Evaluation; Management; Research; and Professionalism. Each major competency area was defined and supported by a series of behavioral objectives. The study of the Curriculum Content Committee was further detailed in its report "Suggestions for Curriculum Content Within Major Areas of Competencies."[10] This report, together with the document "Major Areas of Competencies for the Education of School Library Media Specialist," was forwarded to the Project's Advisory Committee for its deliberations and subsequent action.

Both the Task Analysis Committee and the Curriculum Content Committee recognized that within the limited time period of their assignments it was not possible to develop full and complete documents. In an effort to gain a broad base for reactions to these findings the Advisory Committee submitted the two working papers to a series of regional conferences. Three invitational regional conferences were held in the spring of 1970 in San Francisco, Pittsburgh, and New Orleans. A study of the reports of the Task Analysis Committee and the Curriculum Content Committee by the partici-

pants at the regional conferences led to specific recommendations for the Phase II experimental programs. Reactions from the field were instrumental in refining the work of the Project study committees as the participants in the regional conferences identified the proper order and sequence of the Phase I findings. The Regional Conferences involved 105 participants with thirty-five persons attending each meeting. Participants who attended the regional meetings represented school library and teacher education, audiovisual education, school libraries, and state certification offices. Representatives from general education, school administration and state education agencies were also included. Selected members from the Task Analysis Committee and Curriculum Content Committee attended the Regional Conferences and provided liaison functions from the special study committees.

In addition to the reactions to Phase I activities, the regional conferences provided an opportunity for leaders in special fields related to school librarianship to meet face to face in a full discussion of the future direction for the role and education of school library media personnel. As a result, new education demands for new job functions contributed to discussions on innovations in school library media education. Recruitment and manpower ideas were incorporated in discussions of national trends in certification. Throughout the regional conferences, the participants, Project staff and Advisory Committee liaison found that the regional concerns were similar to national concerns. The results of all three meetings emphasized the need for innovative practices in the education process to meet the mandates for change.

Recommendations from the regional conferences encompassed the following broad areas of concern in the education of the school library media specialist: avenues of entry, curriculum design, and program support. Each broad category included many specific recommendations which were later incorporated in plans for implementing Phase II.

*Avenues of Entry*

1. The preparation of the school library media specialist may begin with the undergraduate level, but the undergraduate degree will lead only to a provisional professional status.
2. The minimum program for a full professional status is a five-year program, preferably culminating in a master's degree.
3. The sixth year and doctoral program are desirable to provide specialization and additional

9. School Library Manpower Project, "Major Areas of Competencies for the Education of the School Library Media Specialist," *School Library Manpower Project, Phase I—Final Report* (Chicago: American Library Association, 1970), pp. 37-52.

10. School Library Manpower Project, "Suggestions for Curriculum Content Within Major Areas of Competencies," ibid., pp. 53-69.

competencies beyond those of the school library media specialist.

4. Both the fifth and sixth year programs should be learner-oriented and designed to meet the specific goals of each student.
5. A high degree of flexibility should be encouraged for timing of entry and entrance requirements in the school library media education program.
6. Entrance and in-program competencies should be recognized through proficiency measurements acceptable to the institution for equivalent credit hours thus fostering more effective articulation between the undergraduate and graduate school library media programs.

*Curriculum Design*

1. Plans for new curriculum design should encompass the development of behavioral objectives and methods for measuring competencies.
2. Individualization of instruction and interdisciplinary approaches should be utilized incorporating varieties of teaching and learning methodologies.
3. New curriculum design should be flexible and lend itself to continuous evaluation and modification.
4. Teaching methodology should be continuously reviewed for effectiveness in attaining stated program goals and should assure that individual student experiences are relevant and appropriately supervised.
5. The education program should provide an opportunity for appropriate electives outside the media field to meet individual students' program needs.
6. The education should be action-oriented to encourage decision making and should present a broad media point of view.
7. Selected components of the education program may be modularized into multimedia self-instructional packages.
8. Early and continuous fieldwork experience in all K-12 levels in settings that reflect a diversity of social, economic and ethnic backgrounds and learning experiences which would be most beneficial to the education program for the school library media specialist.
9. Fieldwork or internship should be designed which would provide opportunities for a number of modules, both structured and unstructured, to meet individual student needs.
10. While it is desirable for the school library media specialist to have classroom teaching experience,

fieldwork and/or internship are a minimal requirement of school library media education programs.
11. There must be a commitment from the administration of cooperating schools to lend support in planning, coordinating, and implementing fieldwork experiences.
12. The education program should be designed to allow for continuous feedback, assessment and evaluation to permit modification.

*Program Support*

1. The education program should have a dynamic, creative staff reflecting a variety of strengths in the media field.
2. The education program staff should be willing and encouraged to implement a variety of educational techniques, instructional methodologies and organizational patterns.
3. The education program should encourage and implement an interdisciplinary approach in the utilization of the total institution faculty with expertise in other fields.
4. The education program should recognize the value and contribution of human resources available outside the institution.
5. Faculty-student ratio should reflect consideration for the time spent in guidance and counseling to meet individual needs of students.
6. The education program faculty should establish and maintain a close liaison with state certification officers to facilitate certification of program graduates in as many states as possible.
7. The education program should recognize and utilize the essential role of support personnel in effecting the highest level of performance of the faculty and the successful utilization of materials, equipment and facilities within the instructional program.
8. Effective program implementation requires facilities, equipment and materials to accommodate the innovations and flexibility expected of the program.
9. The education program should explore the possibilities for using facilities, equipment and materials available within the total institution and local area.
10. The education program should utilize the expertise and input provided through an advisory board which represents a variety of education levels and disciplines.
11. The education program should show evidence that programs are provided for continuing edu-

cation and professional development of the faculty.

At the conclusion of Phase I the above recommendations from the regional conferences and the Phase I activities, including the working papers of the Task Analysis Committee and the Curriculum Content Committee, were compiled in *School Library Manpower Project, Phase I—Final Report*. This report was distributed to all participants attending the regional conferences and to members of all Phase I special study committees. Additional copies of the final report were forwarded to all library education programs offering at least 12 semester hours in school library competencies. Finally, the Phase I final report was deposited with all state departments of education and state libraries.

Phase I of the School Library Manpower Project concluded in August 1970. In fulfilling the objectives of the Project proposal, in meeting the direction given by its Advisory Committee, and in following a prescribed process of activities, Phase I brought many people together with many questions and many ideas. The process of Phase I drew upon a growing national interest and response to school library education and began to change attitudes of a large number of leaders in the library profession and key persons from specialty areas related to librarianship. Phase I sought answers to questions which have long been verbalized and it provided the library profession with recommendations to be implemented and tested during Phase II. The varied processes that led to these recommendations generated the momentum required to break away from the traditional holding patterns—a momentum necessary prior to initiating plans and designs for change. The process involved in this change, especially as it addresses the future of school library media education, became the Project's major focus during Phase II.

# Phase II

Phase II of the School Library Manpower Project was designed to build upon the results and recommendations of Phase I. Its primary goal was to provide six experimental program models in school library media education which would be a relevant and intelligent response to the needs identified in Phase I. The original proposal of the School Library Manpower Project stated that "all institutions or departments of institutions in the United States having at least 12 semester hours of library courses during the regular school year"[1] should be invited to submit a proposal for an innovative program. The proposed programs were to be oriented to present and future needs, task and personnel potentials, and focused on the specialized field of school librarianship within the broader realms of librarianship and teaching. The proposal placed no constraints upon the geographical location or the program level in the selection of the six experimental programs.

To assure that all qualified institutions would receive the information pertinent to Phase II of the Project a national survey of school library education programs was made early in January 1970 with assistance from the State School Library Supervisors. The survey questionnaire was developed to glean quantitative information and made no effort to ascertain the quality of a program. There were 306 institutions identified as meeting the requirement of offering twelve or more semester hours during the regular academic school year. Compilation of the results of the survey revealed that: (1) there were more undergraduate than graduate programs in the business of educating school librarians, (2) there was a great divergence in the numbers of full-time and part-time faculty staffing the programs, (3) there was evidence of a broad range of requirements in terms of credit hours, (4) fieldwork and/or internship was a recognized requirement, and (5) the inclusion of education in the utilization of all media was acknowledged by approximately 50 percent of the programs.

## PROPOSAL APPLICATION AND REQUIREMENTS

Three planning clinics were held in the fall of 1970 to which the 306 qualifying institutions were invited. Each institution was urged to send a library education faculty member and an appropriate member of the administrative staff. In addition to the twelve or more semester hour program, the eligibility for attendance at the planning clinics included an interest in designing and implementing an experimental program for the education of professional school library media personnel and at least one full-time teacher of school library education courses.

The planning clinics, held in Denver, Cleveland and Atlanta, focused on the goals for the Phase II experimental programs. The format and structure of the sessions were designed to encourage a dialogue between the Project staff and representatives from the 111 institutions interested in submitting a proposal. Participants in the planning clinics received copies of the "Proposal Format and Guidelines"[2] and through discussion gained a clearer understanding of the varieties of program change which could be activated in the experimental programs. The above mentioned document was developed by the Project

1. A Proposal for a School Library Manpower Project . . . . Submitted by the American Association of School Librarians and approved by the Executive Board, American Library Association, July 1967.

2. School Library Manpower Project, "Proposal Format and Guidelines for Experimental Programs in School Library Media Education, Phase II," *School Library Manpower Project, Phase I—Final Report* (Chicago: American Library Association, 1970), pp. 98-123.

staff with the assistance of special consultants from the fields of audiovisual education, library education and teacher education.

Criteria for grant participation encompassed the following four areas:

*Applicant Requirements.* The proposal applicant must have: the previously noted twelve or more semester hours of school library education courses, at least one full-time faculty on permanent appointment, state certification of the existing program which had been fully operational for a year, and graduates of that program active in the field.

*Operational Requirements.* The institution must: agree to participate for three years from the date of the award, accept the responsibility for dissemination of information about the experimental program, be responsible for self-evaluating its own program, agree to on-site observation and requested meetings by the Project staff, and submit periodic written and financial reports to the Project office.

*Time Requirements.* The funded program must: begin some phase of activity by September 1971 with instructional aspects beginning no later than January 1972 and program time must be sufficient to graduate at least one group of full-time students no later than January 1973.

*Program Requirements.* The experimental program must: have the equivalent of at least three full-time faculty with experience and competence in school library media education; offer a balance of content which included components in media and their associated technology, administration and/or management and guided field experience; demonstrate its relationship to general education, teacher education and other appropriate interdisciplinary fields, show evidence that state certification is assured for graduates of the program; include plans for staff development, recruitment and scholarship development, research and evaluation design; and have an Advisory Board. There were two financial constraints imposed upon the applicants. Funds could not be designated or expended from the award for scholarship grants or for capital outlay.

Forty-six proposals were submitted for award consideration and funding. Two were filed jointly by cooperating institutions. The proposal breakdown by program level was eighteen undergraduate, four combined undergraduate and graduate, twenty-three graduate, and one postgraduate.

## SELECTION CRITERIA AND AWARDS

The proposals were evaluated by a team of nine readers who were selected by the Project Advisory Committee on the basis of their broad background in school librarianship, library and audiovisual education, and evidence of previous experience in evaluating proposals for higher education programs. Eleven proposals were recommended for Advisory Committee consideration.

In the final selection, the first priority was the excellence of the content of the proposed programs, including components in media and their associated technology, administration and management, and guided field experiences. Recognizing that these could not stand alone in the education of a school library media specialist, a balanced relationship with general education, teacher education, and other disciplines was needed to support the program objectives. Evidence of articulation among schools and between levels of school library media education was also a contributing factor. Central to the criteria were innovative and experimental practices of the programs, with methodology appropriate to meet the goals to be attained. As the programs were to be experimental, program design had to show innovation and provide enough flexibility for continuous modification.

Evaluation criteria for the program's research and evaluation plans were analyzed closely with their objectives, immediate and long-range, stated in behavioral terms and related to one of the three Phase I professional occupational definitions. The two-year time limitation required that both the objectives and the evaluation techniques be realistic.

As the programs all stressed an interdisciplinary approach, careful attention was given to plans for staff development, providing opportunities for articulation, professional improvement, and program modification. Most proposals indicated a need for additional staff and it was necessary to ascertain their availability with respect to the range of expertise needed for the program. Evidence that the program director's specialty and understanding of the problems qualified him to direct the program was a principal selection criteria.

Additional criteria focused on questions relating to facilities and resources, program budget and institutional support, the relationship of the fieldwork component to the total program, and the development of recruitment plans and scholarship programs. As financial aid in the form of scholarships and loans was not authorized from grant funds, the evaluators looked to the proposals for the identification of new approaches for obtaining additional sources for scholarship program support. The predominant concern through all evaluation steps was the attention and understanding given to the role of the students. Flexible admission policies and assurances that the number of admitted participants could be accommodated by the proposed program method were needed. Finally, while assurances were required from state education agencies that the students graduating from the experimental program would be awarded certification, the evaluators sought additional evidence that the competencies of the students would match the program objectives. Many of the proposals indicated that much preplanning had been done prior to the submission of the proposal and that the institution proposed to mount these programs in a slower pattern even if the award was not received.

The six institutions selected by the Project Advisory Committee received $100,000 each to develop, implement and evaluate new curriculum design and innovative approaches for the education of professional school library media personnel. An additional $2,000 planning grant was awarded to each institution to support staff development activities prior to the implementation of the programs. The institutions approved for awards were: Arizona State University, Tempe; Auburn University, Alabama; Mankato State College, Minnesota; Millersville State College, Pennsylvania; University of Denver, Colorado; and the University of Michigan, Ann Arbor. Each experimental program began some phase of operation in September 1971.

During the two years of experimentation, each of the six programs—one at the undergraduate level, one at the post-master's level, one at both the undergraduate and graduate levels, and three at the graduate level—pursued its own program objectives explicated for training personnel identified in one or more of the occupational definitions. Each program was involved also in research and evaluation relevant to its own unique objectives. The Project staff, with the assistance of each institution and the Human Resources Research Organization, developed a plan to coordinate the research and evaluation for all six programs. A more detailed account of the evaluation is presented later in this chapter and in Part II of this report.

## PROJECT/PROGRAM COMMUNICATION

Communication between the experimental programs and the Project staff was deemed highly important by the staff and the Project Advisory Committee. Immediately following the award announcements the Director and Associate Director of the Project visited each of the six selected institutions. The purposes of these visits were twofold: (1) to relay certain concerns of the Advisory Committee and to receive assurance that these concerns would be given consideration, and (2) to establish a personal line of communication between the Project and the six experimental programs.

This line of communication proved to be a positive and successful element throughout the two years of experimentation. Visible aspects of the liaison between the experimental programs, the Project Advisory Committee, and the Project staff took a variety of forms. While phone calls and written communications played an important role, monitoring of the programs was most effective through personal visits to the institutions by one or both members of the Project staff. These visitations provided the opportunity for personal dialogue with the total staff, students in the program, interdisciplinary faculty, the appropriate administrative personnel and members of the program's Advisory Board. A total of forty visits was made to the six institutions which represented a period of seventy-nine days of visitation and observation. Written records of all visitations were made and submitted by the Project staff to the appropriate Program Director and to all members of the Project Advisory Committee.

In addition to the written reports relayed to members of the Advisory Committee, that group chose to hold three of its regularly scheduled meetings at the site of an experimental program. This procedure served to bring a better understanding of the written reports of the Project staff and to provide the opportunity for personal communication with those persons involved in the experimental programs.

Communication between the six experimental programs evolved throughout the two years. To support the exchange of ideas and the sharing of both successful practices and areas of concern, meetings of all six Program Directors were arranged by the Project staff. One of these was scheduled in Chicago and three were held at an experimental program location concurrently with the Project's Advisory Committee meetings. The Program Directors were provided opportunities to meet with the Project staff and the Project Advisory Committee at the Midwinter and Annual Conferences of the American Library Association.

Immediately following the grant award, the experimental programs were required to appoint representatives to an Advisory Board who would represent a variety of state and local educational agencies and the students enrolled in the program. The composition of these boards is delineated at the beginning of each program report in Part II of this publication. The Advisory Boards played a significant role in the experimental programs. Although the policies for each Board differed, those contributions most frequently noted were: to serve as a reactor panel; to give assistance in formulating policy and setting priorities; to function as an editorial board; to offer suggestions on recruitment, research and evaluation; to refer feedback from the field, and to act as a liaison between the experimental program and the external community.

The periodic written reports and personal interaction among all of those people involved with the implementation of the six experimental programs assured an understanding of the objectives of the programs, the ways and means selected to achieve the objectives, and the complexities within individual institutions which effect the administration and implementation of new programs.

Throughout the second phase, the Project and the six experimental programs received high visibility primarily through progress reports in periodicals and presentations at state and national meetings. The developmental nature of the programs and the continued modification which took place during the two years were not conducive to demonstration and visitation. Therefore, no specific program for public visitation was mandated or encouraged by the Project. Despite this, there existed many individual requests for information which were met by Program Directors and Project staff.

Dissemination of information concerning the progress and status of the programs was done by the Program Directors through a variety of media presentations at local, state and national meetings. The Project staff, frequently with the assistance of experimental program personnel, presented Project-related programs at national, regional and state meetings representing library education; audiovisual education; educational administration, research, curriculum, personnel and guidance; and other educational agencies.

## STUDENT PROFILE

Students enrolled in the six experimental programs began their training in September 1971, with the exception of the University of Michigan where student pursuits began in January 1972. The graduate programs experienced few problems in recruitment. The post-master's program experienced difficulty in recruitment, particularly during the first year. At the undergraduate program, however, the large number of applicants required a limitation on enrollees.

The Project staff developed a Student Profile form which was completed by each student enrolled in the experimental programs. The tabulation of the data from these forms was analyzed in an effort to present a general description of students in the programs. The results stated here represent a composite of all students during the two-year period.

There were 162 students enrolled in the experimental programs, representing 143 women and 19 men. Approximately two-thirds of the students were under 30 years of age. Half of these students had previous experience in libraries or education related fields and only 8 had been out of the field for more than 5 years.

Over 50 percent of the students learned about the experimental programs through word of mouth. The next two most frequent methods were printed medium and the students' search for certification requirements. Students entered the experimental programs for a variety of reasons but the five most consistently offered were: (1) the flexibility of a modularized program, (2) the opportunity to work within the broader scope of all media, (3) the opportunity to work more effectively as an educator with students, (4) the opportunity to participate in field-work experiences, and (5) to improve and update previously learned skills.

Fifty-seven of the 162 students were working toward their first degree with the remaining 105 students holding prior degrees. These prior degrees indicated some previous library education for 35 students. This previous training was obtained by 9 of these students at ALA accredited library schools.

Financial assistance was obtained by 42 students through graduate assistantships, university or alumni scholarships, federal and state loans, state scholarships and library school alumni scholarships. Eighteen students were on sabbatical leave or leave of absence from their present positions.

In response to what area, level and type of service the student hoped to enter, several expressed interest in more than one level, but more wanted to work in elementary school library media centers than in secondary school library media centers. About a third of the students eventually hoped to work at the college level. Fifty students aspired to district level positions and 29 students eventually hoped to work at the state level. Over one half of the students indicated a preference for locating in an urban area.

More than two-thirds of the students indicated no immediate interest in specializing in a particular area of school library media services. An analysis of the responses revealed that they believed experience in the field was necessary before moving into an area of specialization. The most frequently mentioned response for future study was the pursuance of a higher degree.

The students in the experimental programs were unanimous in only one response — none of them wanted to work completely alone. Twenty-nine responded that they would prefer to work actively with others, with the remaining 133 students indicating that they would prefer a balance between working by themselves and with others.

These 162 graduates of the experimental programs will be contacted during Phase III of the Project. The field follow-up and evaluation will provide the necessary data to permit a comparison of the Student Profile responses with on-the-job responses. At the time of this report the geographical location of the graduates represented approximately 23 states and 3 countries.

## CURRICULUM DEVELOPMENT AND IMPLEMENTATION

Reading the reports of each of the six experimental programs in Part Two will reveal a competency-based, field-centered approach to curriculum development. This similarity resulted from the influence of the work accomplished during Phase I of the School Library Manpower Project. The task analysis study and its results, the publication of occupational definitions and the identification of seven major areas of competencies by the School Library Manpower Project all served as guidelines to the experimental programs which were awarded a two year grant. There was strong evidence in the six experimental program proposals that steps had been taken prior to proposal submission to move the existing library education programs toward a merged media curriculum. Department and institution-wide study committees were in process and two of the institutions had achieved the recommendation by these groups to unite the library department and the audiovisual department into a department of educational media. In instances where department mergers had not occurred—a curriculum which encompassed a unified media approach was set forth in the proposals.

A heavy expenditure of faculty time was designated for preplanning prior to the start of the experimental program at each institution. Time was designated during the summer of 1971 for faculty members to exert a team effort toward the initiation of competency-based objectives or the refinement of earlier developed objectives. Work was also done on the writing of modules, blocks, or course structures to support the achievement of the identified objectives. Some time benefits were allocated for this work either in the form of reduced faculty load or extra assignment time supported by an equitable financial compensation. In the institutions which utilized the summer preplanning, the experimental programs started in the fall of 1971. The University of Michigan was the one exception to this pattern. Program preplanning at that institution was carried out during the first semester of the 1971-72 school year, with the first students enrolling in the experimental program in January 1972.

Another very important part of the preplanning efforts was the recruitment of staff. The School Library Manpower Project award allowed the financial support necessary to enlarge the staff, particularly in those areas where specialized expertise was necessary to implement the program. The needs included not only faculty areas of specialization, but also supportive staff, particularly in the production technology realm.

Recruitment of students to the experimental programs was not unique from those patterns generally followed by institutions. Brochures, specifically germane to the experimental programs, were prepared and distributed. These brochures and the word of mouth communication appeared to be effective recruitment efforts except at the University of Denver. The postmasters level of that program required a leave of absence for most students, which in turn required a stronger recruitment effort through personal contact and communication.

By electing to follow the guidelines which emerged from Phase I of the School Library Manpower Project, the experimental programs chose to pursue the competency-based, field-centered program in their efforts to achieve an efficient and effective educational system for preparing professional school library media personnel. This was dependent upon a systems design or process which would incorporate clear statements of expected behaviors, a task analysis followed by an ordered sequencing of learning experiences, a systematic assessment of the learner's achievement in the program, and a flexible curriculum structure to permit modification of the program.

Coming to grips with the above process was a time-consuming, difficult and sometimes volatile task for the six experimental programs. To achieve a workable agreement among faculty it became necessary to develop a team approach and rapport which encouraged differences of opinion but at the same time fostered a united effort toward a common goal. An objective reading of the six experimental program reports will disclose that a primary purpose existed among the six programs. They wanted to prepare professional school library media personnel with an understanding of their predominantly educational role and the ability to share a joint accountability with teachers in the learning process through receiving and transmitting media resources in the educational context.

The curriculum content to support this goal and to achieve the objectives within each program mandated content changes in the existing programs and an increased range of interactions with other disciplines. While the specific curriculum content was the prerogative of those responsible for its development in each experimental program, a general pattern of interdisciplinary extension was evident. There were varied contributions from the fields of sociology, business, management, research, psychology, finance, law and architecture. The programs drew most heavily upon the education department or school to provide the content for competencies in areas such as curriculum, instructional planning, learning theory, and human growth and development. The cooperation and understanding of these interdisciplinary departments was a crucial factor in the programs and required a continuous and open pattern of communication between them and the experimental programs. There was a strong evidence of growth in this area, particularly with the education divisions, and most particularly for those experimental programs sponsored by a department within the division of education. The practice of an interdisciplinary approach can operate advantageously to prevent the library faculty from becoming self-serving and to provide students with content which is relevant to job performance. The total program can then become an effort to educate school library media specialists who are prepared to function in the field as delimiting, rather than limiting contributors to the educational process.

Curriculum content and design was built upon the objectives generated to meet the goals for a particular program level and specific position focus. School library media education is faced with the same problem of other disciplines—the expanse of knowledge being so great that no one program can hope to provide more than a partial representation of what is known in the field. It became necessary, therefore, for curriculum priorities to be established which would succeed in providing the students with the basic knowledge necessary to perform effectively

in the position for which they were being prepared. The broad range of curriculum content needed to be assessed in terms of the established objectives and decisions made on deletions, additions and reorganization. In general, the configuration which evolved demonstrated the removal of some core requirements such as advanced cataloging and bibliography. The programs continued to address the traditional print materials but acquired an additional emphasis on all other media and the production aspects of certain media. Added to the requirements were those interdisciplinary fields consistent with the needs and prior experiences of the student. The reorganization and/or resequencing of content already in the curriculum and applicable to the experimental program was most evident in the areas of materials selection, cataloging and classification, reference, and principles of librarianship.

## FIELDWORK COMPONENT

Fieldwork is not a new term or new concept in the field of school library education although fieldwork is not universally required in all programs. The problems associated with the fieldwork component in the past were: (1) its planning and supervision varied in quality, (2) it was not developed as an integral part of the curriculum, and (3) there was little if any true communication between the field and the university beyond assignment schedules.

Requirements established by the School Library Manpower Project stated that the variety and extent of the practicum, internship, and/or fieldwork experience and their methods of supervision should be defined and described. A mutual commitment was expected between the institution and cooperating school administrators in planning, coordinating, implementing and supervising the fieldwork component. All of the proposals submitted to the Project contained this information along with letters of acceptance to participate from the cooperating school districts.

In Part Two of this report devoted to the six experimental programs, it will be noted that differences in terminology existed to designate the fieldwork activity, such as: practicum, internship, field observation, happenings, and field experiences—but all of these made up a sequence of activities in the field. Incorporated in all programs as part of the fieldwork component were: real and simulated observations, attendance at professional meetings, and short term and/or long term in-depth work in a media center under the supervision of university faculty and field supervisors.

In all six experimental programs some aspect of the fieldwork component came before the end of the program. The time determined for entry into fieldwork activities differed among the programs and extended from the first week to the last semester or quarter. Fieldwork assignments were made at a variety of levels and settings and gave the experimental program student a variety of experiences and contacts with teachers and students in the assigned schools. Such planning and sequencing of activities in the fieldwork component gave the intern a sense of reality of an on-going media program and permitted him to apply experimental program content and theory to reinforce newly acquired competencies. Early and continuous fieldwork practices were flexible in structure to allow the intern to travel back and forth between the university and the fieldwork centers in the resolution of problems.

Mounting a full program of fieldwork required university supervision with time allocated for that responsibility as part of the teaching load. The commitment and willingness of the university supervisors to devote additional time to orientation prior to fieldwork assignments was essential. Equally important was the willingness and commitment of supervisory personnel in the field media center. The fieldwork component called for an extensive number of media centers which could provide the kinds of experiences to support the student's objectives. Problems of control were difficult because of the widespread geographical locations of some selected centers and the logistics of time and scheduling.

It was frequently during field experiences, however, that students were able to bring the total program into focus. Personal student reactions to the fieldwork component were that it was one of the most valuable parts of the programs.

The curriculum design for each experimental program is best delineated in the reports found in Part Two of this report. However, some basic statements can be made about the different kinds of structures within which the programs operated to provide alternatives and choices. The undergraduate and two of the graduate programs elected to design programs on a modular base. The initial development of modules was a time-consuming and often painful process which required cooperative, constructive and supportive faculty interaction. It was the general consensus in these schools that agreement among the faculty upon a uniform module format and items for inclusion was advantageous to the process. Although the module formats differed in each experimental program, they all included spe-

cifically stated objectives, instructional techniques, learning activities, resources and some form of criterion measure. Another program, using a block approach for concentrated attention to one broad area of competency at a time, included similar items in its block development. Both the module and block design adapted well to the need for flexibility and modification. Each provided the means to relax the pace for some students and accelerate it for others, gave an opportunity for more options, and lent itself well to on-the-spot evaluation and modification by both faculty and students. Where the basic organizational pattern continued to rely on the traditional course structure, courses were designed to include objectives, activities, materials and criterion measures. It was notable that within the course structured curriculum, it was found possible to change curriculum design, to have content based on competencies described in course objectives without drastic change in the organizational pattern.

## PROGRAM STAFF

To bring about the changes described thus far required total staff involvement and support. In many instances it was necessary to include both professional and nonprofessional staff in certain levels of planning, since some aspects of program implementation were dependent upon the understanding and talents of supportive staff.

The experimental Program Directors looked objectively at the diversity of expertise within their faculties, identified the need to acquire additional kinds of talent and then attempted to coalesce the group through a shared planning and implementation process. More difficult than acquiring new staff, was the task of moving former faculty members toward the philosophical conception of the program. It would be erroneous to assume that the total field, or even all members of one faculty are committed totally to the same philosophy or endeavors. Where there was some hesitation to accept the concept at the beginning, two general routes emerged. The uncertain faculty member either moved into the process or moved out of the university of his own volition. This does not imply that no philosophical differences remained—but rather that they did not denigrate cooperative efforts to help students to succeed in their objectives and attain their potential goals.

There are certain professional and personal characteristics of staff in an experimental program which contribute to its success. A knowledge and expertise in the field is important, but almost equally as important is an understanding of how the faculty of other disciplines can contribute to the program. A strong commitment to education and to the unified media concept is essential to programs in school library media education. Recent, successful practitioners from the field are able to add a practical note to the program. Those faculty in an experimental program with a willingness to go beyond the normal teaching load will adjust more readily, particularly if they have developed a tolerance for ambiguity and the uncertainness that goes with experimentation. The courage to expose ideas and the risk of having these ideas challenged are frequently elusive characteristics among individuals. To do this—and at the same time maintain the integrity of personal convictions—is no easy task.

The staff development aspect of the six experimental programs was of primary importance if a fine line of communication among faculty possessing a diversity of talents and opinions was to emerge. Planning sessions, retreats, consultants, faculty meetings and increased use of informal methods of communication were employed. As the programs progressed it became evident that staff development, in actuality, permeated the total program. The curriculum development for the competency-based programs revealed the necessity for striving for a delicate balance between theory and practice. This required a rethinking by faculty on content and instructional strategies to be employed. There came from this a faculty concern with how the student learned as well as what he learned. The principle that students should be well informed about what they should be able to do moved the faculty-student relationship into a shared program responsibility. In many instances, staff development was supported by these shared responsibilities as the staff learned with the students. In all six institutions the programs relied heavily on a frequent interface between faculty members and between faculty member and student. In general, the development of staff generated a consensus on goals and content, methods of attainment and the ways and means of measuring attainment. It resulted also in an early agreement between students and faculty on the methods to be used for competency achievement.

## PROGRAM STUDENTS

The students in the six experimental programs discovered that they were more actively engaged in the education process than in their prior educational experiences. The Student Profile, previously discussed, substantiates that students in the programs represented heterogeneous educational backgrounds and experience. It was this heterogeneity which re-emphasized the need for a high degree of individualization. All of the programs were individualized, although individualized to a greater degree in some than in others. The constraints apparent in individualization included the amount of time required for program development, the limitations on counseling and guidance time, the required time necessary for the development of learning programs or packages and the inability of some students to adapt readily to their role in a competency-based, field-centered program. However, when the student discovered that he did have a voice in his education and that he was in fact an important contributor to it, he realized the advantages to him over the traditional course of learning.

For learning to become the personal experience envisioned in the experimental programs the best utilization of time became an important variable. Time was expended by the faculty beyond the normal teaching load traditionally tied to the credit-hour course structure. The faculty and students spent many hours in counseling and guidance dialogues when faculty could become more aware of the diversity of student backgrounds and needs for direction—and when students could gain direction and advice for pursuing the solution to problems.

Modules of study were available to the students with specifically stated objectives to point the way. Within the curriculum were alternative routes to pursue, with options on content selection and methods of instruction. Much of the feedback instrumental in program modification was the result of student evaluation of modules, methods and content emphasis. To maintain a program on this basis required a low ratio of faculty to students which was acquired in some instances through the addition of staff and in others through a redesigning of time priorities.

Students were selected for the experimental programs within the normal selection criteria expected by the institution. Flexibility within these criteria was evident, however, with the greatest leeway permitted through proficiency testing and program faculty judgmental decisions following interviews. Selection procedures and grading practices resulted in the query of whether or not traditional practices in these areas might be subject to some very fundamental questions such as: (1) to what extent are alternatives and options provided, (2) are the latent or potential characteristics of a student at entry level more important than specified competencies, (3) how are attitudes and values changed, and (4) how can progress in the affective domain be measured?

Some programs gave direct attention to the teaching or assessing of attitudes and values—and the high percentage of time devoted to counseling in all programs coped successfully with these personal and professional problems. Although frequently non-measurable, it is the professional opinion of the faculties that graduates of the programs will exhibit positive growth in these areas—and will be likely to create similar kinds of environments and learning experiences on the job.

Students graduating from the programs possessed some homogeneity in competencies—but in the end process, students finished at different levels of development based upon criterion measurement and individualized programs. The experimental programs endeavored to integrate learned experiences into the concepts of librarianship, thus providing students with the capabilities of resolving problems and innovating on the job to fulfill their responsibilities in the professional field.

## EVALUATION

Evaluation is deeply entrenched in education as something that is done to students, rather than for students. Student evaluation, however, must benefit the student so that that which he knows and that which he can do is critically and honestly assessed. In the six experimental programs the purpose of student evaluation was to gain as much insight into a student as possible so that his learning activities could be better directed. It was necessary to appraise his progress throughout the program to determine what he could do that he was unable to do before entering the program. Equally important was the emphasis on guided practice in self-evaluation for the student.

Criterion measurement, as opposed to norm-referenced testing, was frequently employed to assess student progress. This required some reconciliation with the grading status quo, since programs which encourage original decision making by students are less adaptable to objective assessment than those which require uniform results for all students. The programs did experiment, however, with modular credits, pass-fail, and A-incomplete, as well as variations within the standard grading procedures. The development and/or adoption of diagnostic tests, proficiency tests and indices of measurement received concentrated attention. Evaluation techniques such as audit reports, student and faculty diaries, performance testing and counseling also played an important role. While each program differed in its methods of assessment, there was emphasis in all six

institutions on oral and visual communication. The nature of the experimental programs thus required faculty and student adjustment to more fluid types of assessment procedures.

Student evaluation was not the only part of the evaluation process in the experimental programs. Equally important was the evaluation of the program in which the student was enrolled. The formative evaluation which was an integral part of the six experimental programs was based upon nine evaluation areas developed by the Project staff, the Project Advisory Committee, the directors of the six programs and the Human Resources Research Organization. The difficult part of developing a formative evaluation plan was to select the most critical topics, to describe for each topic the indices or specific elements of data which would be collected and to determine how they would be interpreted. The cooperative process of identification and selection of evaluation topics for the six experimental programs began by building from the three broad categories of general education, program support and educational objectives. From an initial compilation of eighty-eight topics a process was implemented to determine the major importance of each topic. Once the ranking was done and agreement reached, the formative evaluation indices and procedures were identified and selected. An analysis and review were made of the evaluation plans from each experimental program to ensure that each institution would be able to meet the requirements of the final evaluation plans for the Project.

*Nine Evaluation Areas for Experimental Programs*

1. Preparation of lists of specifically stated job-relevant training/education objectives.
2. Communication of program goals to students, staff, outside institutions, etc.
3. Development of procedures for assessing student proficiency.
4. Development of procedures for implementing individualized and/or modularized instruction.
5. Evaluating effectiveness of methods, media, and special program features.
6. Development of quality control procedures.
7. Development and/or utilization of field experiences and practicums.
8. Determining transportability of experimental programs.
9. Assessing probability of program continuance after end of Project funds.

The above nine topics were used by the six experimental programs to test the program objectives during the initial program development. This formative evaluation provided a basis for action whereby continuous program assessment could lead to constructive program development, could facilitate self-correction and modification and could permit accountability for program quality. It was not the intent of this formative evaluation to establish any arbitrary comparisons among programs, but rather to discover what was appropriate for the attainment of specific goals based on clearly stated objectives within an individual institution. Each experimental program conducted its own formative evaluation using the indices, measuring devices, and data gathering activities that appeared to be most applicable to each evaluation topic. In some instances, the research was of a sophisticated design, while in others the type of program experimentation was best assessed by informal, action research. Much of the data gathering was standardized for all six programs, while still other findings were reported which related specifically to a unique aspect of a singular program. No attempt was made to compare the six experimental programs, but rather a uniform structure was applied to evaluate the success of each program in meeting its own objectives.

The final evaluation-related activity undertaken in the latter part of Phase II was the compilation of approximately 700 tasks to be performed by school library media personnel. This instrument, entitled *Behavioral Requirements Analysis Checklist,*[3] will be used as the data-gathering device during the Phase III summative evaluation. The BRAC instrument is further detailed in the next chapter of this report.

CONCLUSIONS

The impact of the School Library Manpower Project and the work of the six experimental programs will have a positive effect on school library media education and school library media centers throughout the country. The grant money awarded to the six institutions was the means for providing improved programs over the former ones, which in turn sent media specialists into the field who will influence the school library media program under their direction. The monies provided additional staffing, resources, motivation, and the moral support to make change possible and also encouraged strong reinforcement from administrative units within the insti-

tutions. Each of the six experimental programs had done considerable program planning prior to the submission of a proposal, but the grant from the School Library Manpower Project accelerated progress to an extent that could not have been accomplished alone.

The models developed in the six experimental programs can serve as guidelines for the initiation of other programs. Readers of this report are cautioned, however, that no single model can be transported in its entirety, since programs must vary to fit the individual needs. The models should be studied carefully to acertain their adaptability before initiating change based upon them. The dangers in seeking to design a program before clearly establishing precise goals and objectives and identifying the functional behaviors to be attained are self-evident.

Perhaps the key element in the success of any program is the people who design it and the people for whom it is designed. Some very pertinent questions must first be resolved in terms of the faculty. How can we improve ourselves as faculty members and how much commitment do we have to the profession, ourselves and students? The faculties of the six experimental programs were willing to take the leadership and carry the added burdens of the programs. They were agreeable to relinquishing the traditional structure to explore other kinds of alternatives. Students, too, needed to adjust to the amount of flexibility and self-direction in sharing the responsibility for their education. The kind of self-renewal required in the process of program change frequently causes an inner conflict between the risks of change and the security of the status quo.

Curriculum design was found by the programs to be an everlasting process calling for group inquiry into a shared concern. It was discovered that in all instances the proposals promised too much in this area within the two year time limitation. There was total agreement that program redesign and implementation requires a multi-year effort built around well-formulated objectives that will yield high student satisfaction and attainment. Time was also needed to have faculties evolve as a team rather than as individuals who reflected only segregated thinking within their own areas of specialization.

Students played an important role in the program planning. They participated in module development and evaluation, frequently contributing the most significant changes through their responses. Student-faculty program planning sessions were one of the most valuable assets of the programs and individual conferences were found to be the best device

3. School Library Manpower Project, *Behavioral Requirements Analysis Checklist: A Compilation of Competency-Based Job Functions and Task Statements for School Library Media Personnel* (Chicago: American Library Association, 1973).

to communicate with students. Students participated in the decision making process and appreciated the amount of counseling and guidance time provided by the staff. Success in these areas could be traced partly to the informality visible in the programs. Perhaps it was not the informality itself—but rather that an environment of this type helped to break down the barriers often found in interpersonal relationships. It is highly probable that graduates of the experimental programs will provide similar kinds of flexibility and personal attention in their own media center programs.

There was a decided shift of emphasis to the field where authentic environment complimentary to the acquisition of competencies existed. Fieldwork, in its many forms, helped to develop a positive relationship between the school district, the university and the profession. The fieldwork component placed all students in a variety of situations closely related to opportunities for applying theory to practice. Consisting of observations, simulated visitations, participation in professional meetings and actual short or extended time blocks in media centers—the fieldwork put students in direct, working contact with many professionals and school students. Because of the changes involved in the experimental programs it was deemed necessary to provide orientation and in-service for media center field supervisors. To achieve the objectives of the program, the field center supervisors needed an understanding of the program's goals, its philosophy and its instructional practices. Fieldwork experiences do have an important influence on the student and at their best can reinforce the objectives of the school library media education program or at their worst can contribute to the imitation of mediocre and outmoded practices. Students in the experimental programs viewed their fieldwork experiences as being of primary importance and showed a preference for the option to serve at more than one level during the fieldwork time.

There was an increased awareness of the unified media approach in both the instructional patterns of the experimental program and in the utilization of varied media by the program students. The availability of professional and support personnel in the areas of nonprint media was an inducement to faculty and students in the programs and also to faculty in other departments to increase the use of a variety of media.

Flexibility was a particular need in the programs, especially for those students with prior experience. This, and the fact that the graduate level programs called for prerequisites in education and media, is once again cause for reiterating the need

to analyze and acknowledge the place and quality of undergraduate programs in the articulation process. It becomes constantly more evident that a one year graduate program will not suffice to prepare the school library media specialist and that the lack of undergraduate preparation penalizes the graduate level student by too great a loss of options.

There were other issues which appeared and remain unresolved. Competency-based programs, for instance, have their share of both supporters and critics. There are those who believe that a competency-based program is based upon objectives that clearly identify the purpose of the program, that they can be more honestly assessed, and that they provide the means for program flexibility. The critics maintain that there is the danger in competency-based programs that education will become too restrictive and prescriptive. The experimental programs would deny the latter premise based upon the resilience in the programs for alternatives, student self-pacing, cooperative program planning and modification, and a greater degree of attention to the affective change in students.

The six experimental programs were faced with a common problem related to time. The tremendous amount of time required for faculty planning, added counseling and guidance responsibilities, and program development and modification was difficult to equate with the accepted university pattern of teaching loads. Students also were faced with the pressure of time limitations: time to adjust to the flexibility inherent in the program, time to pursue independent study and time to spend in field-based learning experiences. Closely allied to the time problem is the question of how to assign credit hours to a program structured around modules and experiences to meet individual needs. The implementation of the fieldwork component in the six programs was faced with the problems of locating field centers within feasible geographical locations which were willing and able to support the objectives of the university-based program.

It is evident that there still remain questions to be answered—and that to maintain vigorous and viable programs of school library media education will require a continued self-renewal of both faculty and curriculum. Technology will continue to effect society and its educational pursuits, and the effects of new technologies can best be controlled by a wise change in instructional procedures and in the use of appropriate technology. For in the final analysis, it is what media educators do that will make the difference.

There is little doubt that the work of the School Library Manpower Project will have a degree of permanence upon future programs of school library media education. It is up to the professional educators, however, to prevent the petrification of this work, and to assume the leadership for continual evaluation and change to meet the contemporary needs of students and society. It must be recognized that those who assume the leadership roles will lose a degree of tranquility in exchange for some conflict and friction. There will need to be a continued reaffirmation by professionals to search for a better way. Unfortunately, there are many barriers built into the system that discourage this kind of leadership. But the work of the six experimental programs and other programs throughout the country have proved that there is a potential in the school library media field to redesign programs of education for school library media personnel.

The very existence of the School Library Manpower Project was indicative of a dissatisfaction with existing programs and indirectly a dissatisfaction within the profession. Most of all it was indicative of a desire to achieve the ultimate goal of providing media center programs which will meet the educational needs of students more effectively.

The achievements of Phase II of the School Library Manpower Project generally support the Phase I recommendations identified in Chapter One of this report. More explicitly, the work of the six experimental programs has assisted in the attainment of the Project's objectives to: (1) identify program strengths and weaknesses within a framework of modification; (2) evaluate successful, innovative practices; (3) evaluate the capabilities of each level of training; (4) encourage and support research and evaluation; (5) coordinate the findings of all six experimental programs; (6) disseminate Project information to the field; and (7) develop and recommend guidelines for school library media education.

The reports of the six experimental programs which follow in Part Two lay no claim to simple solutions for the complex problems inherent in change. They do, however, through the uniqueness of each program—address the work that has been accomplished, point out what remains to be done and display implications for the total field of library education as well as for the specialized area of school library media education.

## RECOMMENDATIONS

The reports and recommendations of each of the six experimental programs should be read by educators in departments of library science, audiovisual education, educational technology, and teacher education for a further understanding of change possibilities and capabilities. The following recommendations have emerged from Phases I and II of the School Library Manpower Project and are presented as guidelines to the total field of librarianship as well as to the specialized field of school library media education. It is the hope of the Project Staff and its Advisory Committee that the entire scope of the Project's efforts and these recommendations will provide direction for continued critical analysis and reform in the field of librarianship.

Education programs for professional school library media personnel should:

1. Be continually evaluated and modified to meet the present and future information needs of society.
2. Be submitted to intensive critical analysis to identify areas of program weakness and build upon existing program potential.
3. Provide a curriculum based upon the premise that all media can contribute to the learning process.
4. Incorporate a multidisciplinary approach to curriculum content.
5. Pursue curriculum development and staff development as an integrated and continuous process.
6. Place high priority on the development of learning objectives in behavioral terms prior to program development and during program implementation.
7. Encourage and acquire administrative support from the appropriate university unit prior to program planning and implementation.
8. Provide opportunities for individualization of student programs through entry proficiency testing, alternative routes of study, a variety of teaching and learning techniques and a personalized counseling program.
9. Contain a fieldwork component at a variety of levels and settings which reinforces and supports the objectives of the university-based program and exhibits a high degree of communication between the field and the university.
10. Allocate high priority to the development of communication channels between other departments, faculty, students and community units.

11. Demonstrate the required strengths of staff through addition or realignment to effectively utilize time, resources and facilities of the program.
12. Design a feedback system from faculty, students and the field for the purpose of planning, evaluation and modification.
13. Develop quality control procedures to document all aspects of the program.
14. Provide opportunities for students to contribute and participate in the development of their own programs.
15. Explore more opportunities to assess student competency through criterion measure and performance testing in the field.
16. Explore additional ways beyond class hours and course credits for equating the teaching load.
17. Pursue the possibilities for dealing more effectively with learning in the affective domain.
18. Provide students with the understanding that they are a part of the educational process.
19. Explore the value of faculty exchange programs with other programs of media education and the periodic return of faculty to actual practice in the field.
20. Recognize and encourage the program contribution which can be made through effective utilization of a variety of levels and types of support personnel.
21. Establish Advisory Boards to serve as reactors and consultants to the program.
22. Maintain a close liaison and working relationship with state certification personnel.
23. Evaluate the contribution of the traditional librarianship "core" to the school library media specialization.

Some of the recommendations set forth reiterate those stated at the end of Phase I of the Project. This repetition supports the fact that there is still a need for total professional effort before a broad impact can be achieved.

To reach the solutions that are required the profession itself must:

1. Encourage and honor the diversity of goals, personalities and backgrounds of the faculty and students involved in school library media education.
2. Be willing and able to adjust to change when necessary, develop a tolerance for failure, and recognize alternative methods of education.
3. Exhibit an open enthusiasm for its goals and a continued reaffirmation for providing inspiring teaching and learning experiences.
4. Demonstrate leadership to improve instruction with a commitment to the present and future information needs of society.
5. Actively and systematically engage in a national program effort which will recognize and permit upward mobility in quality education programs for all levels of school library media personnel.

# Phase III

Midway through Phase I, it became increasingly evident to the Advisory Committee, Project staff, and members of the various special study committees that a very serious time limitation at the conclusion of the five-year study would directly effect the final outcomes and total impact of the School Library Manpower Project. In the process of developing time schedules and detailing plans for Phase II, the Project staff and Advisory Committee identified a weakness in the Project's proposal: it provided only a three-month time period from the end of the experimental programs to the completion of the Project. This brief period did not provide time for a detailed study and analysis of each experimental program. While each experimental program was to develop its own evaluation report, the Project itself needed a plan, along with the time and means, to develop a full research study to test the validity of all the experimental programs.

As the Advisory Committee began to study this problem further, they were supported by expressions from members of the Task Analysis Committee, Curriculum Content Committee and from participants who attended the regional conferences. ALA staff liaison and the consultants who aided the Project staff in the development of the "Proposal Format and Guidelines"[1] for the Phase II experimental programs expressed similar concerns. The initial proposal of the Project called for recommendations to the library profession for a follow-up study at the conclusion of Phase II which would be based on the Project's findings. The need for a follow-up study had been clearly identified by the end of Phase I.

The Advisory Committee believed that additional time was required immediately following the experimental programs to do a comprehensive research study of the experimental programs and its graduates. As a result of the Advisory Committee's investigations and discussions, a subcommittee was appointed to work with the Project staff and ALA staff liaison and the Human Resources Research Organization to initiate an exploration of time, method, manpower and cost to support the purpose for an immediate extension of the Project. The proposal *A Summative Evaluation of Six Experimental School Library Media Educational Programs*[2] to extend the Project into a sixth year Phase III study was finally approved by the Advisory Committee, the American Association of School Librarians and the American Library Association in the winter and spring of 1972. During these deliberations the Knapp Foundation of North Carolina, Inc. was continuously apprised of the progress and development of identifying new and additional sources of support. The heavy investment by the Foundation and the six colleges and universities resulted in the development of occupationally relevant educational programs. The Foundation, recognizing the value and potential of the summative evaluation process and its wide application to the total field of education, awarded a grant of $150,000 to fund the Phase III extension in March 1973. Though the grant was not announced until June 1973 and the Phase III funding would not commence until August 1973, the Advisory Committee and Project staff were already preparing for the methodology to be utilized.

1. School Library Manpower Project, "Proposal Format and Guidelines," *School Library Manpower Project, Phase I — Final Report* (Chicago: American Library Association, 1970).

2. *A Summative Evaluation of Six Experimental School Library Media Educational Programs* (Chicago: School Library Manpower Project with the assistance of Human Resources Research Organization, 1972).

The first goal of the Phase III extension, then, is to assess the validity of the experimental programs and to give guidance for the future direction of library education programs. A second and equally important goal is to demonstrate the value of a quality control system for the continued evaluation and improvement of education programs.

The major objectives of Phase III are to conduct a summative evaluation of the six experimental programs and to develop and field test survey procedures for obtaining information from the experimental program directors and staff, in-program students, and from experimental program graduates and their supervisors on the job. Procedures will be developed for using survey information to evaluate and modify educational programs on a continuing basis. The six Phase II experimental programs, utilizing the survey information for program modification and revision, will also prepare status reports of their experimental programs three years after their inception.

In the early planning stages for Phase III, a study of the literature supported the need for a special inventory of competencies for school library media personnel to be used in educational program development. As the Project looked toward summative evaluation plans for Phase III, it recognized the need not only for an instrument to test the performance of the program graduates on the job, but also to assess the capabilities of an education program to produce competent school library media personnel. The efforts of the Project staff, with direction and input from the Advisory Committee and the directors of the six experimental programs, resulted in the publication of *Behavioral Requirements Analysis Checklist*.[3] The BRAC publication will be used during Phase III as the basic data collecting device.

The *Behavioral Requirements Analysis Checklist* is a compilation of approximately 700 tasks to be performed by school library media personnel. The job functions and task statements were developed not only from the occupational definitions and seven major competency areas identified and described during Phase I, but also from the behavioral objectives developed by the experimental programs during Phase II. During Phase III the BRAC instrument will provide the basis for four questionnaires. A separate questionnaire will be developed for collecting data from: students in or about to graduate from the experimental programs; supervi-

sors of recent graduates; program graduates; and experimental program directors and their staffs. The four questionnaires will all be based on the BRAC, differing only with respect to the specific questions relating to the job activity statements.

The development of the BRAC questionnaire, tabulation of data and initial analysis will be done in cooperation with the Human Resources Research Organization which will provide contractual services to the Project during the Phase III evaluation study. As questionnaires seldom provide much information as to why respondents respond in certain ways, the Project will conduct on-site interviews with a sample of persons who complete the questionnaires. Approximately 25 percent of the respondents will be selected for follow-up interviews to be conducted by the Project staff in the spring of 1974.

Phase III will include two major survey periods. The 1972 experimental program graduates will be surveyed in the fall of 1973. The 1973 experimental program graduates will be surveyed in the early spring of 1974. Following each of the major survey periods computer printouts will display the survey results for each experimental program. Copies of these displays will be forwarded to the appropriate experimental program director for use in developing his own comparative studies.

During Phase III a number of techniques will be developed and information obtained on the evaluation of competency-based education programs which will be of interest to those concerned with the education of professional school library media personnel. Three regional workshops are planned for the spring of 1974 in San Francisco, Chicago, and Atlanta for the purpose of discussing and disseminating information about the work of the six experimental programs and the results of the Phase III evaluation study.

A final report will be published at the conclusion of Phase III which will describe and interpret the survey findings. The final report will give special emphasis to the following evaluations of the experimental programs: (1) the degree to which the training programs prepared students to perform those activities which they are actually required to perform on the job, and (2) the degree to which the graduates could capably perform in the field those activities which were covered in the experimental programs. In addition, the final report will contain a status report provided by the program directors for each of the six experimental programs as of June 1974. The final report of Phase III will be available for distribution from the American Library Association in December 1974.

3. School Library Manpower Project, *Behavioral Requirements Analysis Checklist* (Chicago: American Library Association, 1973).

*Part Two*

# THE PROGRAMS

Arizona State University

Auburn University

Mankato State College

Millersville State College

University of Denver

University of Michigan

# ARIZONA STATE UNIVERSITY

COLLEGE OF EDUCATION

Dr. Del Weber, Dean

## AN EXPERIMENTAL PROGRAM IN
# SCHOOL LIBRARY MEDIA EDUCATION
## 1971–1973

*Final Report by*
HOWARD J. SULLIVAN

## Contents

# DEPARTMENT OF EDUCATIONAL TECHNOLOGY AND LIBRARY SCIENCE
## Dr. Howard J. Sullivan, Chairman

*Experimental Program Staff, 1971-1973*
Dr. Howard J. Sullivan, Program Director

Dr. Joel Benedict
Mrs. Emma Ruth Christine, 1972-73
Dr. Michal C. Clark, 1971-72
Mrs. Grace Dunkley, 1972-73
Dr. Vernon S. Gerlach
Dr. Norman Higgins
Dr. Craig Locatis, 1972-73
Mrs. Mabel Macdonald

Mr. David Mamalis
Mrs. Inez Moffit
Dr. Lester Satterthwaite
Mr. Patrick Smith, Graduate Assistant
Dr. C. Walter Stone, 1971-72
Miss Barbara Tenpas, Graduate Assistant
Dr. John Vergis

*Advisory Board*

Mrs. Georgeanna Chancellor, 1971-72
Grauate Student Member
Arizona State University

Miss Mary Choncoff
Director, Library Services
Arizona State Department of Education

Miss Lucille Crane
Librarian
Phoenix Union High School District

Dr. Jeanette DePriest
Director, Library Technician Program
Mesa Community College

Dr. Roy Doyle, 1971-72
Associate Dean, College of Education
Arizona State University

Shirley Dresbach, 1972-73
Graduate Student Member
Arizona State University

Mr. Gary Fadely
Representative
Arizona Association for Audiovisual Education

Mr. Ralph Ferguson
Director, Audiovisual Services
Arizona State Department of Education

Mr. Ace Flake
Principal
Mesa Public Schools

Mrs. Marilyn Fry, 1971-72
Undergraduate Student Member
Arizona State University

Mr. Warren Fry, 1972-73
Audiovisual Coordinator
Phoenix Union High School District

Dr. William Fullerton
Associate Dean, College of Education
Arizona State University

Dr. Norman Higgins
Associate Professor
College of Education
Arizona State University

Mrs. Shirley King
Library Coordinator
Tempe Public Schools

Mrs. Kate MacMullin
Media Specialist
Mesa Public Schools

Mrs. Mary Mathes, 1971-72
Media Specialist
Scottsdale Public Schools

Mr. Zak Moser, 1972-73
Teacher-Supervisor, Resource Services
Phoenix Indian School

Mr. Patrick Pomeroy, 1972-73
Personnel Director
Mesa Public Schools

Dr. William Poston, 1971-72
Personnel Director
Mesa Public Schools

Dr. Robert Strom
Chairman, Department of Elementary Education
Arizona State University

Mrs. Vera Vanderloo
Librarian
Mesa Public Schools

Dr. Del Weber
Dean, College of Education
Arizona State University

Mrs. Ida West, 1972-73
Undergraduate Student Member
Arizona State University

Miss Mae Wiita
Library Specialist
Phoenix Union High School District

# Overview

## DESCRIPTION OF THE INSTITUTION

Arizona State University is one of three state universities in Arizona. The three state universities are governed by a single Board of Regents who are appointed by the Governor of Arizona for an eight-year term. The president of each university is appointed by the regents and is directly responsible to them.

Arizona State is located in the residential and university community of Tempe in the metropolitan Phoenix area. The metropolitan area has a population of approximately 1,100,000, and the majority of the students at the University are metropolitan area residents who live at home and commute to the University. Arizona State is the only major university in the Phoenix area, and the University faculty are very heavily involved in educational and service activities throughout the area.

The growth of Arizona State since it attained university status in 1958 has paralleled the rapid population increase in the state of Arizona during the past two decades. The University enrollment for the fall semester of the 1972-73 school year was 27,322 students. Of this number, 20,508 were undergraduates and 6,814 were graduate students.

The College of Education is the second largest of nine colleges at Arizona State. The 1972-73 fall enrollment in the College of Education was 2,779 undergraduate students and 2,704 graduate students. In recent years it has produced the second largest number of certificated teachers of any institution in the United States.

The Arizona State experimental program was intentionally initiated and conducted primarily as a development project as opposed to a two-year training project or a demonstration project. This proposed program under the School Library Manpower Project was planned and operated in the Department of Educational Technology and Library Science, one of the seven academic departments in the College of Education. Comprising the Department of Educational Technology and Library Science are three curriculum areas: Audiovisual Education, Educational Technology, and Library Science. The M.A. Degree in Education is offered in all three areas, and the Ph.D. and Ed.D. degrees are offered only in Educa-

tional Technology. The only undergraduate program offered in the Department prior to the Arizona State experimental program was an eighteen-semester hour minor in Library Science. The Department has a total of 9.5 full-time faculty members distributed among the three curriculum areas.

## RATIONALE FOR THE EXPERIMENTAL PROGRAM

The rationale for the experimental program at Arizona State was based upon the increasing need, both nationally and in Arizona, for professional personnel who are capable of developing and operating instructional materials centers that are highly effective in helping children learn from both print and audiovisual media. In recent years the demand for a broad scope of media to support education programs and the dramatic increase in the number of high quality audiovisual learning materials has resulted in a movement away from the traditional, heavily book-oriented libraries in schools. Modern media centers contain a wide variety of instructional media for use by children. Yet, most higher education programs which prepare personnel to work in such centers have retained an extremely heavy emphasis on books, while generally neglecting the selection and use of newer media. Thus, professional personnel in the school library media field are not being well trained in many of the skills needed either to operate a well-balanced instructional materials center or to convert a traditional school library into a more modern and effective center.

The three curriculum areas in the Department of Educational Technology and Library Science represented a unique combination for developing an effective program for training students in the skills needed to develop and operate a successful school library media center. The Library Science programs at both the B.A. and M.A. levels emphasized almost exclusively the preparation of students to work in school libraries, as contrasted with public libraries. The Audiovisual Education program prepared students for work as coordinators or directors of media services at the school or district levels. Thus, existing within the Department was the potential for combining aspects of the Library Science and Audiovisual Education programs in order to provide students with the balance of library media skills needed to perform most effectively as directors or staff members in school library media centers. Further complementing this potential was the instructional research and development emphasis in the Educational Technology area within the Department. A major focus in this area is the identification of specific skills needed by learners and the development of effective means for enabling the learners to acquire these skills. The major strength in the Educational Technology area, therefore, resided in its potential for working with faculty from the other areas in the Department to help identify the precise skills needed by school library media specialists and to develop a program that was effective in enabling students to acquire these skills. An additional planned contribution from the Educational Technology area was the training of school library media specialists in skills related to the development and evaluation of instruction.

The financial resources available to the Department of Educational Technology and Library Science at Arizona State University were a critical element in enabling the Department to develop and operate the experimental program. In addition to the integration of library and media skills in the program, other important desired characteristics of the program were exportability and the capability for enabling students to participate in activities appropriate to their individual abilities and interests. Additional personnel and financial resources were required for the development period in order to develop a new program with characteristics of this type while at the same time maintaining a normal departmental load. The School Library Manpower Project provided both the resources and the motivational impetus to develop the experimental program at Arizona State over a two-year period. Without this support, several additional years would have been required to develop a program similar to the experimental program in its characteristics and degree of refinement.

# Program Goals and Objectives

## PROGRAM GOALS

Four major goals for the Arizona State experimental program were outlined in the original proposal for the program.

1. Training of a minimum of fifteen school library media personnel per year for the two-year period of the program.
2. Development of an individuated, modularized program.
3. Effecting of systematic change with respect to the number and size of school library media centers in Arizona and to the Arizona endorsement requirements for school librarianship.
4. Packaging of the program components for exportability to other colleges and universities.

A better overall understanding of the rationale underlying the four major goals can be achieved from additional knowledge about the Library Science program at Arizona State University and the status of school library media centers in Arizona at the beginning of the experimental program. Relevant background factors related to each program goal are briefly discussed below under each listed goal.

*Goal 1: Training of School Library Media Personnel.* The existing Library Science programs at Arizona State University at the beginning of the experimental program in the fall of 1971 were (1) the minor in Library Science for students taking the B.A. degree in either Elementary Education or Secondary Education and (2) the Library Science area of specialization for the M.A. degree in Education. Both programs reflected the strong book orientation common to Library Science programs generally, but this orientation was not balanced with an equally strong emphasis on other instructional media.

The Arizona State University proposal established as one goal the training of at least fifteen school library media personnel per year for the 1971-72 and 1972-73 school years. The fifteen students per year represented a combination of graduates from the B.A. and M.A. school library media programs planned and developed under the experimental program. Library Science students who did not participate in the experimental program continued to complete their program of studies under the existing Library Science programs.

The occupational definition focus specified in the Arizona State proposal differed for the B.A. and M.A. programs. Graduates of the B.A. program with a minor in school library media were to be trained as school library media specialists, capable of performing general professional duties in the school library media center. Students completing the M.A. program were to be trained as heads of school library media centers who would be capable of assuming the administrative responsibilities for operating a successful school library media center.

*Goal 2: Development of an Individuated, Modularized Program.* The plans outlined in the Arizona State proposal for the experimental program called for individuation of the program consistent with the needs and prior experiences of each student. Individuation of the program was to be achieved largely through modularization of the program of instruction.

Plans for modularization, as outlined in the proposal, called for offering of at least forty-eight modules during the first year of the program. Each module was to represent a five-week segment of instruction for which a student would earn one semester hour of credit, as contrasted with the eighteen-week, three-credit-hour courses in the regular University program. The content for forty-five separate curriculum modules covering a wide range of subject matter from Audiovisual Education, Educational Technology and Library Science was briefly described in the proposal. Modules appropriate for each individual student were to be identified by the student and a faculty advisor on the basis of the student's goals, needs, interests and skills.

*Goal 3: Effecting of Systemic Change.* This goal was identified in the proposal as a long-range goal of the Arizona State program. Arizona schools have not been as progressive as many other schools in installing newer educational innovations. When contrasted with the more innovative states, Arizona had relatively few school library media centers in 1971 with a good supply of print and audiovisual learning materials and a professional staff trained in selection and use of such materials. Through the combination of training of school library media personnel at Arizona State and increased emphasis on library media centers resulting from the experimental program, it was hoped that both the number and quality of such centers would be increased.

The only form of certification for school librarians in Arizona in 1971 involved endorsement as a school librarian after the student had completed eighteen semester hours of a prescribed set of Library Science courses. These courses included principles of librarianship; administration; cataloging, classification and organization; materials selection; reference; and literature for children or adolescents. The Arizona State Department of Education agreed prior to the beginning of the experimental program to endorse graduates as school librarians during its two-year duration of the program. The proposal for the experimental program also identified as desirable a plan for seeking a change in the Arizona State Department of Education endorsement procedures to permit permanent endorsement of future graduates of the Arizona program as school library media specialists.

*Goal 4: Packaging of the Program.* This goal related to organizing and packaging of components of the program in a form that would make them usable by colleges and universities lacking the resources to develop a similar program. The emphasis on instructional development in the Educational Technology area at Arizona State was cited in the proposal as making this goal particularly relevant to the Arizona State program.

## EDUCATIONAL OBJECTIVES

Instructional objectives relevant to training students in the skills needed to successfully operate a school library media center were derived from (1) the specialized competence of the instructor for each module and course and (2) the knowledges and abilities emerging from Phase I of the School Library Manpower Project as being required for School Library Media Specialists and Heads of School Library Media Centers. Each instructor in the program developed specific instructional objectives to indicate the skills that a student was to acquire from his particular modules and courses. During the first year of the experimental program, each objective was referenced to the knowledges and abilities from Phase I of the School Library Manpower Project, with the particular knowledges or abilities to which the objective was relevant being listed with the objective. However, the nature of many of the Phase I knowledges and abilities was general enough that several objectives often were referenced to a single knowledge or ability and several knowledges and abilities were often referenced to a single instructional objective.

The method of obtaining consensual validation of the relevance of each objective to the training of school library media personnel varied over the two-year period of the experimental program. During the first year, three-member teams, consisting of one faculty member each from Audiovisual Education, Educational Technology and Library Science, reviewed each module and objective. Thus, the final listing of modules and instructional objectives within a module was the product of an initial development effort by the instructor and a subsequent review by a three-member, interdisciplinary team. During the second year of the program, responsibility for the development of the objectives for a particular module and course was assigned to at least two faculty members working cooperatively. The listing of modules and objectives developed by these individuals was then circulated among the entire faculty and, when necessary, was edited for technical adequacy by a faculty member from the Educational Technology area.

Examples of specific instructional objectives from the Arizona State experimental program are presented in a later section of this report.

# Program Participants

## STUDENTS

Criteria for admission of students to the experimental program included minimum achievement and aptitude scores and enrollment for a specified number of semester credit hours. Candidates for the B.A. Degree were required to have a grade-point average (GPA) of 2.5 or higher on a 4.0 grading system. Students were admitted to the M.A. program on the basis of either (1) a minimum undergraduate GPA of 3.0 combined with a Miller Analogies Test (MAT) score of 41 or above, or a Graduate Record Examination (GRE) combined score of 799 or above, or (2) a minimum undergraduate GPA of 2.5 and either a MAT score of 46 or above or a GRE combined score of 849 or higher. Admissions during the 1971-72 school year were limited to full-time students taking twelve or more credit hours per semester who would be able to complete their B.A. or M.A. programs by the end of the academic year. During 1972-73, a plan was developed to allow more students to participate in the experimental program. Upper-division and graduate students taking six or more credit hours per semester and meeting the aptitude and achievement requirements were allowed to enroll in the program. (See Table 1.)

Students were recruited for the experimental program in a number of ways. A brief announcement describing the program was distributed to all instructors in the Elementary Education and Secondary Education Departments for reading in their classes. In addition, program faculty visited many of the larger classes in these departments to describe the program and to encourage further student inquiries. A program faculty member met individually with each student who entered the B.A. program in Library Science or applied for admission to the M.A. program, described the experimental program to him, and offered each qualified student the opportunity to enroll in the program. More than 4000 brochures describing the program and encouraging student inquiries and applications were mailed in the spring of 1971 and again in 1972 to academic departments and placement offices in approximately 1000 universities and colleges throughout the country.

Arizona State University Tuition Scholarships were available to out-of-state residents in the M.A. program who had an undergraduate GPA of 3.0 or higher. The total academic-year value of such a scholarship was $890. One student in the experimental program received a University Tuition Scholarship during the first year of the program, and 2 students were awarded scholarships during the second year.

Data on program enrollments for the two-year period are summarized in Table 1. It can be seen from the table that a total of 16 students was enrolled in the experimental program during the 1971-72 school year. Six of the 16 students were in the B.A. program, 5 in Elementary Education and 1 in Secondary Education. Ten students were in the M.A. Degree program. The mean cumulative grade-point average for the 6 B.A. candidates at the end of the 1971-72 school year was 3.31. The mean undergraduate grade-point average for the 10 graduate students was 3.13. All 16 participants during 1971-72 were full-time students.

Table 1 also reveals that a total of 29 new students enrolled in the program during the 1972-73 school year. Of these participants, 25 were full-time students, and the remaining 4 were enrolled for at least six hours of course work per semester. There were 17 students in the B.A. program, 14 in Elementary Education and 3 in Secondary Education, and 12 in the M.A. program. The mean cumulative

TABLE 1. PROGRAM ENROLLMENT SUMMARY

| YEAR | PROGRAM | | | | |
| | B.A. | | M.A. | | |
| | NO. | GPA | NO. | UNDER-GRADUATE GPA | TOTAL ENROLLMENT |
| --- | --- | --- | --- | --- | --- |
| 1971-72 | 6 | 3.31 | 10 | 3.13 | 16 |
| *1972-73 | 17 | 3.27 | 12 | 3.21 | **29 |
| Two-year totals | 23 | 3.28 | 22 | 3.17 | 45 (41 full-time) |

*Includes new enrollees only, and not students continuing from 1971-72.
**25 full-time and 4 with between 6 and 13 hours per semester.

GPA of students in the B.A. program was 3.27; the mean undergraduate GPA for students in the M.A. program was 3.21.

STAFF

Because of the interdisciplinary nature of the program-development activity and of the experimental program itself, it was planned that all faculty members in the Department of Educational Technology and Library Science would participate in the program. There were 9.5 regular faculty members in the Department at the beginning of the 1971-72 school year. Four faculty members were in the Educational Technology area, 2.5 in Audiovisual Education and 2 in Library Science. The remaining regular faculty member taught courses in the evaluation of children's and adolescents' literature within the College of Education. A number of characteristics of the faculty are summarized in Table 2.

To supplement the regular Departmental faculty, 5 additional faculty members were hired for one or both of the two years of the experimental program. Selected characteristics of the faculty hired specifically for the program are also summarized in Table 2. Four of these 5 individuals had Library Science as their curriculum area, and the remaining member was an educational technologist.

Two graduate assistants enrolled in the Ph.D. program in Educational Technology were assigned to the program on a half-time basis during both school years. Their major responsibilities focused primarily on the analysis of technical adequacies of various materials developed within the experimental program. It seems fair to assess the overall level of capability of the faculty for the experimental program at Arizona State as very high. Several members of the regular departmental faculty have achieved national prominence in their fields through publications, research and development activities,

and leadership of professional organizations. The Department faculty is particularly influential in Arizona in the field of audiovisual education. The Department received a total of approximately $350,000 from federal and private funding agencies for special research or development projects during the two-year period of the experimental program.

A potential weakness within the Department was the small number of regular faculty members in each curriculum area. This was particularly true in Library Science, in which there were only two regular faculty members at the beginning of the experimental program. However, the experimental program funding enabled the Arizona State Program Director to hire very competent additional Library Science faculty for the program. One faculty member employed especially for the program during 1971-72 had had a distinguished career in librarianship that included the directorship of libraries at a major university. Each of the other three Library Science faculty members employed for the program had been active leaders in professional school library organizations and had had several years of successful experience as school library media center directors at the school or district levels.

There were several changes with respect to the directorship of the experimental program during its two-year period. The first Program Director served from spring of 1971 until the beginning of the fall semester of 1971. During the fall semester, he was on sabbatical leave from the University and was replaced by a new staff member serving in the role of Acting Director. The original Director resumed the directorship upon his return in January of 1972, and he retained this position until November 1972. At this time he was replaced for the remainder of the program until August 1973 by the former Acting Director. Both Directors were from the Educational Technology curriculum area.

TABLE 2. Summary of Faculty Characteristics

| | REGULAR DEPARTMENTAL FACULTY | | | |
| CURRICULUM AREA | FACULTY RANK | HIGHEST DEGREE | DEGREE INSTITUTION | DATE OF DEGREE |
| --- | --- | --- | --- | --- |
| Audiovisual | *Professor | Ed.D. | Stanford | 1955 |
| Education | Professor | Ed.D. | USC | 1954 |
| | Associate Professor | Ed.D. | Indiana | 1965 |
| | | | | |
| Educational | Professor | Ed.D. | ASU | 1963 |
| Technology | Professor | Ph.D. | Oregon | 1964 |
| | Associate Professor | Ph.D. | Syracuse | 1970 |
| | **Assistant Professor | Ph.D. | Stanford | 1969 |
| | | | | |
| Library Science | Assistant Professor | M.A. | Denver | 1950 |
| | Assistant Professor | M.L.S. | Denver | 1968 |
| | | | | |
| General | Assistant Professor | M.A. | ASU | 1945 |

| | FACULTY HIRED FOR EXPERIMENTAL PROGRAM | | | |
| CURRICULUM AREA | PREVIOUS JOB | HIGHEST DEGREE | DEGREE INSTITUTION | DATE OF DEGREE |
| --- | --- | --- | --- | --- |
| Library Science | **Indust. & Educ. Consultant | Ed.D. | Columbia | 1949 |
| Library Science | IMC Director | B.S. | ASU | 1961 |
| Library Science | ***Dist. Curr. & Lib. Superv. | M.S. | USC | 1953 |
| Library Science | ***Inst. Res. Center Director | M.A. | San Jose | 1960 |
| Educational Technology | ***Research Fellow | Ph.D. | Syracuse | 1973 |

*Half time in Department
**Faculty member for 1971-72 only
***Faculty member for 1972-73 only

All members of the Department of Educational Technology and Library Science participated in activities related to the program. Twelve of the 15 faculty members listed in Table 2 taught one or more courses or modules in the experimental program during the two-year period. Each of the 15 faculty members also had the responsibility for development of particular modules for the program. Faculty meetings were held on approximately a bi-weekly basis during the first year of the program and on a weekly basis during the second year. The original Program Director normally held each regular meeting for the total experimental program faculty. The replacement Director scheduled most meetings for smaller faculty groups working on a common problem. The documents produced by these working groups were then reviewed by the entire faculty in meetings held for that specific purpose. A more detailed description of procedures employed by the faculty in advisement of students, course development, and instructions is presented in the later section on program components and procedures.

## ADVISORY BOARD

There was a nineteen-member Advisory Board for the experimental program at Arizona State. Seventeen of the members agreed to serve on the Board in response to a request made of each member by the first Program Director. One B.A. student and one M.A. student in the program were elected to the Board each year by their fellow participants. The Board was composed primarily of individuals in key library or audiovisual positions at a school, school district, or state level.

Four Advisory Board meetings were held during the two-year duration of the experimental program. The meetings were structured primarily to inform the Board about the progress of the program. Recommendations and assistance were sought from the Board particularly with respect to dissemination of information about the program and to placement of graduates. Specific contributions at the Board meetings resulted in publication of several journal and newsletter articles describing the program and in placement contacts for several students.

# Program Components

The nature of any comprehensive new instructional program can be expected to vary considerably over the early years of its development. Because of the amount of work required to formulate and develop such a program, the program components and procedures will, of course, normally be much more completely developed in the second year of development than during the first year. Feedback gathered from those involved in the program during its first year also permitted its developers to make improvements in the program.

During the two years of the experimental program at Arizona State, the variations in several aspects of the program appeared to be even greater than the typical variations in instructional programs during their first two years of development. There were several factors contributing to the changes in program development procedures and in organization of the courses over the two-year period. Perhaps the most important factors were the three changes in program directorship (although only two persons were involved) during the two-year period and the employment of two additional key faculty members in the Library Science area for the second year of the program. As is typically the case in development of a new program, the experience and insights gained during the first year also led to a number of modifications.

This section of the report describes the components of the experimental program at Arizona State and the procedures used in the program and in its development. Also described, when appropriate, are the major changes in each component over the two-year period and the reasons for these changes.

## CURRICULUM FORMULATION

The proposal for the Arizona State program specified the development of programs at both the B.A. and M.A. levels. The B.A. program would enable Elementary Education and Secondary Education majors to earn a twenty-four-hour Library Science minor and would prepare them for positions as school library media specialists. The M.A. program would enable students to earn a Master of Arts in Education degree with a specialization in Library Science.

The basic unit of curriculum for the two programs was to be the module, with at least forty-eight modules to be offered during the first year of the program. Each module was to carry one semester hour of credit.

Prior to development of the program, it was necessary for the faculty to make a number of important formulation decisions shortly after funding was approved in May 1971. Issues of particular importance included (1) whether the basic administrative unit for course registration and credit purposes should be the one-credit-hour module (or course) or the three-credit-hour course, (2) determination of the curriculum components and of a schedule for development of courses and modules, and (3) procedures for providing and integrating training related to print and non-print materials.

One of the initial formulation decisions was to make the three-credit-hour course, rather than the one-credit-hour module, the basic administrative unit for registration and credit-hour purposes. This decision was based on a number of factors. Under the three-hour system, courses in the experimental program could still be organized into modules, but could be offered under existing course numbers and titles which would meet the Arizona State Department of Education requirements for endorsement as a School Librarian K-12, the only official endorsement or certification in Arizona in either the school librarianship or media fields. Since students were required by the University to register for all courses at the beginning of the semester and because it is normally easier to vary content for individual students in a three-credit-hour block than in a one-hour block, the opportunity for flexibility of scheduling and manipulation of course content within a course was also as great or greater in, say, five three-hour courses in a semester as in fifteen one-hour courses. Other factors contributing to the decision to use the three-credit-hour course as the basic administrative unit were the beliefs that (1) offering a large number of courses in a new program that was still in an early stage of development would result in more scheduling problems and confusion among both faculty and students in planning and monitoring student programs, and (2) the limited number of faculty members in the Library

Science and Audiovisual Education areas could do a better job of fielding both their regular courses and the courses in the experimental program if the latter courses were fewer in number but more comprehensive in amount of content.

The decision that the three-credit-hour course would be the basic administrative unit for the program was made with the understanding that each course would consist of modules. A module was conceptualized as one or more instructional objectives covering a homogeneous block of content. The instructional objectives for a module were to be accompanied by specification of the instructional materials and procedures necessary for student attainment of the objective and by sample assessment items for determining whether students had attained the objectives. The degree to which students could work independently to master the skills for a module would, of course, vary with the particular skills included in that module. The proposal called for inclusion of three modules of approximately five weeks duration each into each one-semester, three-hour course.

The development schedule for the program called for increasingly greater development and use of the modules over the two-year period. Essentially, it was planned that during the first year the required and elective courses would be identified for both the B.A. and M.A. programs, the objectives for each course would be written and organized into modules, assessment items would be written for each objective, and appropriate existing instructional materials would be keyed to the modules. The tasks of writing the objectives and assessment items for each course and module would be accomplished by a team of two or three persons, including representatives of each curriculum area in the Educational Technology and Library Science Department to which the course content was relevant. These tasks were to be completed during the first semester in which the course was offered in the 1971-72 school year. Instructional materials and procedures would subsequently be identified and keyed to each module, so that the completely developed program could be tried out with students during 1972-73.

There are several potential alternatives in a school library media training program for attempting to ensure that a student acquires the desired skills related to both print and non-print materials. One such alternative is to divide the program into print-related courses and non-print-related courses, with the former taught by Library Science faculty and the latter by faculty skilled in other media. A second alternative is the inclusion of a balance of print and

non-print content within each appropriate course under a team-teaching arrangement in which the print-related content is taught by an individual skilled in print materials and the non-print content by a specialist in non-print materials. Still another alternative involves inclusion of a balance of print and non-print content within each appropriate course, with the course being taught by a single individual skilled in both areas.

In 1971, the skills of the experimental program faculty members in the Library Science and Audiovisual Education areas were to a large extent specific to their own subject-matter areas. That is, the Library Science faculty members were skilled with respect to selection, processing, evaluation, and utilization of materials, particularly those of the print variety, while the Audiovisual Education faculty members were skilled in selection, processing, evaluation and utilization of non-print materials. The Library Science faculty was able to teach the courses and modules dealing with the selection and utilization of materials and management of a school library media center without assistance from the Audiovisual Education faculty, while some outside assistance was useful with respect to coverage of non-print materials in the selection course. There was, of course, greater skill and emphasis on production of non-print materials in the Audiovisual Education area than in Library Science.

The decision was made prior to the fall semester of 1971-72 to have the Library Science faculty teach the courses related to collections development, cataloging and classification, and management of school library media centers. Special emphasis in these courses would be given to non-print materials, with assistance in planning this aspect of each course to be provided by members of the Audiovisual Education faculty. Media production courses were to be taught by the Audiovisual Education faculty members. Thus, direct training in the selection, processing, evaluation and utilization of both print and non-print materials was to be provided in courses taught by the Library Science faculty with out-of-class planning assistance from the Audiovisual Education area, while the production of non-print materials would be taught in separate courses by the Audiovisual Education faculty.

## DEVELOPMENT PROCEDURES

Development of the curricula for the experimental program was accomplished in several stages. Initially, the programs of study, as defined by the required and elective courses for both the B.A. and the M.A. programs, were determined. The modules comprising each course and the essential components of each module were then specified. Finally, outlines were constructed for each course in the program.

The original determination of the B.A. and M.A. programs of study was accomplished primarily in meetings involving the entire faculty of the experimental program. Both programs of study were developed during 1971-72, the first year of the program. Minor revisions were made in the B.A. program during the second year, and more extensive revisions were made in the M.A. program. Initial versions of these revised programs were formulated and developed in meetings involving only the program Director and the Library Science faculty. Subsequently, these versions were presented and discussed at meetings of the entire faculty, and the programs were adopted after suggestions made at the general faculty meetings were incorporated into them.

Following determination of the original programs of study in 1971-72, groups of required courses from the programs were assigned to teams of two or three persons who represented each subject area relevant to the particular groups of courses. Each team included individuals from at least two of the three curriculum areas in the Department. The tasks for each team were to write the instructional objectives for their particular courses, cluster the objectives within each course into modules, and write assessment items for each objective. The components for each course including module topics, objectives, and assessment items were to be reviewed by a selected panel of faculty members after their development. Appropriate instructional materials were also to be keyed to each module.

During the early summer of 1972, the concept of the module specification was conceived and a format was developed. Throughout the remainder of this report the term "mod specs" is frequently used to refer to module specifications. The development tasks actually completed to this date for all required courses included the development of instructional objectives for each course, the clustering of objectives into modules, and the writing of assessment items for each objective in a majority of the courses. Since the mod specs were to include instructional objectives and assessment items, as well as a listing of the instructional materials and activities for the module, the objectives and assessment items that had been developed for each course and module during 1971-72 served as a base from which the mod specs could be developed into their prescribed format.

The task of developing a completed set of mod specs for each course during the second year of the program was assigned to the instructor for that particular course. At least one other faculty member agreed to assist with this task for each course by being available to the instructor for planning and consultation and by reviewing the instructional materials generated by the instructor. After development of each mod spec, it was reproduced and distributed to each faculty member.

Course outlines were developed for each course after development of the mod specs. The course outline for each course was developed by the faculty member with primary responsibility for development of the mod specs for the course.

The sets of course outlines and module specifications for all courses were edited for final copy by a single faculty member. The course outlines were edited primarily for consistency of format and appropriateness of content. Editing of the mod specs concentrated on improving the technical adequacy of their components and on achieving consistency of format and a relatively standard amount of detail in the various specifications. This final editing process was used with all materials prepared for distribution at the end of the program.

## CURRICULUM COMPONENTS

There were two basic curriculum components for the experimental school library media programs at Arizona State University. The program of study, or list of required and elective courses for each program, represented a very general curriculum listing. The sets of module specifications developed for the courses in each program constituted a much more specific designation of curricula for each program. These two basic sets of curriculum documents were supplemented by the course outlines for each course in the program.

The complete curriculum outline developed for the Arizona State University program contains the programs of study for the B.A. and M.A. programs, the course outline for each course in each program, and the set of module specifications for each required course. These materials were compiled into a 190-page document published in June 1973.[1]

1. *A Curriculum Outline for Training School Library Media Specialists* (Tempe: Arizona State University, Department of Educational Technology and Library Science, 1973). Available from the Department, Box FLS, College of Education, Arizona State University, Tempe, AZ. 85281. $7.

The programs of study in effect at the conclusion of the experimental program and for the continuing school library media programs at Arizona State University are shown as Appendices A and B. The titles of the courses in both the B.A. and M.A. programs are the titles that existed at the beginning of the experimental program. Changes of titles of several courses to make the titles more consistent with the unified emphasis in the courses are planned for the time that new University catalog copy is adopted in 1974.

As shown in Appendix A the program for the B.A. Minor in Library Science for students majoring in either Elementary Education or Secondary Education requires a total of twenty-four semester credit hours. Eighteen of these hours for the Elementary Education major are in Library Science-related courses, which were carefully planned by the second year of the experimental program to emphasize both print and non-print materials. Fifteen of the twenty-four hours are in Library Science-related courses plus three additional hours in a basic Audiovisual Education course are required for the Secondary Education major. The basic Audiovisual Education course is required of all Elementary Education majors by the Elementary Education Department. The remaining six credit hours for both Elementary Education and Secondary Education majors involve student teaching in a school library media center. The twelve hours of required Library Science courses in both the Elementary Education program and the Secondary Education program are included in the requirements of the Arizona State Department of Education for endorsement of an individual as a School Librarian K-12, the only type of endorsement or certification presently available in Arizona in the library or media fields.

The program of study shown in Appendix B for the M.A. degree in education with a Specialization in School Library Media is a thirty-semester-hour program, excluding prerequisite courses. Included in the program are twelve hours in the student's major area of school library media, a twelve-hour professional education core which is required by the College of Education of all master's degree students in the College (Information Science, a course listed in the professional education core, is actually a Library Science course which has been accepted as a substitute for a general education course in the College's twelve-hour core), and six hours of approved electives.

A student who enters the M.A. program with no background in the school library media field must take five three-hour prerequisite courses. These five courses are required courses in the program for the B.A. minor. The fifteen hours of credit for these courses added directly to the thirty hours in the M.A. program would constitute a forty-five semester-hour requirement for a student entering with no prior school library media course work. However, a student who takes the prerequisite courses after receiving his B.A. degree may use two of the courses to satisfy the six-hour elective requirement for the M.A. degree. Thus, graduate students with no prior school library media course work may earn the M.A. degree in Education with a School Library Media Specialization by successfully completing a minimum of thirty-nine hours of graduate work.

Several changes were made in the programs of study for the B.A. and M.A. programs over the two-year period. In the B.A. program, most of the original required courses were retained as requirements throughout the period, partly because of Arizona state endorsement requirements. Within the individual courses in this program, however, the original emphasis on print materials in school libraries was progressively increased to a more balanced emphasis on both print and non-print materials. Similarly, at the beginning of the program the course work related to the school library media center dealt almost exclusively with the print-oriented library. The nature of this content was modified so that it concentrated on integrated media services and functions. In addition to the changes within courses, an Audiovisual Education course (Audiovisual Materials and Procedures in Education) was added to the list of required courses for Secondary Education majors. Consolidation of two courses (Selection of Library Materials, and Library Materials for Children and Adolescents) required at the beginning of the program permitted the addition of an elective course for Elementary Education majors and of the Audiovisual Education course for Secondary Education majors without an increase in the total number of hours.

In the M.A. program, the specific course requirements were modified considerably over the two-year period. A production course in Audiovisual Education (Photography and Graphics) was added as a required course in the fall of the second year of the program but was later dropped from the program and replaced by inclusion of a similar course as one of three alternatives acceptable for a three-hour requirement. These alternatives were: (1) Practicum: Production of Instructional Media, (2) Seminar: Reading and Communication, and (3) Internship:

School Library Media. The latter was required if students had not interned during undergraduate years or if they had no work experience in school libraries. Two Educational Technology courses (Instructional Development and Evaluation, Technology and Instruction) were added as required courses in the fall of the second year, but were subsequently dropped as requirements because of concern over the small amount of library-related content in the program during the fall of 1972-73 and over the relevance of these two particular Educational Technology courses to the school library media field. An Educational Technology course is currently being designed to cover the development and presentation of effective instruction and will be added to both the B.A. and M.A. programs in school library media when this course is offered for the first time in the spring of the 1973-74 school year.

A course outline was developed for each course in the program to provide students and other interested individuals with a brief overview of the requirements, content and objectives of the course. The course outlines were simply a rather standard form of summary useful for such purposes as student review prior to making a decision about enrollment in a course, providing students with a course description at the beginning of the course, and facilitating communication among appropriate faculty members about the content of each course.

Each course outline was a one- to three-page document listing the following information about the particular course:

1. Course number and title
2. Requirement or elective status of the course
3. Prerequisite courses
4. Textbooks and materials required
5. Module topics covered in the course
6. Instructional objectives for the course

The instructional objectives were stated in terms of the specific skills that students were expected to acquire from the course. These objectives were, of course, the same objectives contained in the various module specifications for the course.

The course outline developed for Library Administration is presented as a sample course outline in Appendix C to illustrate the format used in the outlines and the length and amount of detail typical of most outlines. Examination of this sample course outline will also reveal the topics and instructional objectives for the management course in the B.A. program, as well as indicating other pertinent information about the course.

A module, as noted earlier, was conceptualized as one or more instructional objectives covering a homogeneous block of content. Original plans as outlined in the proposal for the program called for development of modules of five weeks' duration. However, early experiences in planning and developing modules revealed that it was inappropriate from the standpoint of sound instructional design both to establish a fixed time period for mastery of the objectives of a module and to attempt to include relatively equal amount of content in each module. During the first year of the program a module often included several objectives and the number of modules typically included in a course ranged from three to five. However, when the concept of the module specification was introduced prior to the beginning of the second year, the amount of content in individual modules was modified so that a module most frequently included only one instructional objective and its other components related to that objective. Thus, the number of modules included in most courses during the second year of the program was relatively large, averaging about eight modules per course.

The module specification for each module contained basic information relevant to appropriate instruction for the module and to assessment of student performance on the instructional objective of the module. The mod spec had three components:

1. *Objectives*—Statements of each skill that students were expected to acquire from the instruction related to the module.
2. *Mastery Items*—One or more sample items for each objective. The mastery items could be used to (1) provide students with an opportunity to practice the skill called for in the objective, and (2) pre-assess and/or post-assess student performance of this skill.
3. *Activities, Information and Materials*—A list specifying materials and activities appropriate for use in instruction related to the objectives for the module and presenting other information pertinent to the instruction, when such additional information was available.

A sample specification for a module on planning district media centers is presented in Appendix D. This module is one of ten modules from Library Administration, the same course for which the sample course outline was presented in Appendix C.

Examination of the sample mod spec in Appendix D will reveal the relationship between the components of a module specification. It can be seen from the objective that this particular mod spec is designed for use in teaching students to be able to construct a plan for a district media center, a relatively sophisticated and complex task when contrasted with most other instructional objectives. Because of the complexity of this task, the number of activities in the sample mod spec is larger than the number normally included in a mod spec.

A procedure for tryout of each mod spec and for incorporating appropriate revisions based upon its use was developed for use during the second year of the program. Course instructors were assigned the responsibility of maintaining records of the use of each mod spec and of documenting suggested and actual revisions. Most of the final mod specs for the various courses have undergone at least one classroom tryout in the courses for which they were developed, and many of them have been revised from earlier versions as a result of their use in the school library media program.

INSTRUCTIONAL PROCEDURES

Two of the most important characteristics of a curriculum are its content and the methods by which it is implemented in instruction. The proposal for the experimental program called for development and implementation of an "individuated, modularized training program" to train professional personnel for work in school library media centers. The mod specs served as the planning documents for implementing the training program.

The mod specs were developed by course instructors for the purpose of serving as guides to their instruction for each module. Each instructor used the mod specs for instructional purposes in his particular courses in whatever manner he found most appropriate. Explicit requests made of the faculty with respect to development and use of the mod specs did not specify direct procedures for use of the specs during instruction. However, the faculty was directed during the second year of the program to (1) be sure that mod specs were prepared for each course before teaching the course, (2) record results on the mastery items for each module and (3) note the modifications to be made in each mod spec as a result of its use in the course.

The use of specifications as guides for planning and presenting instruction increased progressively over the two-year period. The development pace was much slower during the first year of the program than initially projected, and the basic components (instructional objectives and assessment items) developed for most modules during the first year did not explicitly

indicate appropriate instructional activities and materials. Thus, use of specifications for the modules as a basis for instruction was much more extensive during the second year of the program when the mod specs listed instructional materials and activities and were designed as more detailed guides to instruction.

The responsibility for assessment of student performance related to each module and objective within a course was assigned to the course instructor employing his own mod specs. The sample mastery item in each mod spec served as a prototype item for use in generating additional assessment items for an objective or module. No organized procedures were employed at the end of a semester or at the end of the program for assessing and recording student competencies across a number of courses or across the entire program. A compilation of assessment items for the total program was in the developmental stage at the end of the two year experimentation. As with many other aspects of the experimental program, procedures for individualization varied considerably over the two-year period. During 1971-72, individualization procedures did not vary appreciably from the procedures previously employed in the Library Science program. In 1972-73, a conscientious effort was made to provide as much individualization as feasible within students' programs.

One method of providing individualization was to include elective courses in programs of study. The fifteen semester hours of requirements for endorsement as a school librarian (the credit hours for this requirement were reduced to twelve in the program by consolidating two courses) in Arizona plus the six-hour internship left little room for electives in the twenty-four-hour B.A. Minor program. Similarly, the twelve-hour Professional Education core required by the College of Education of all students in Master's degree programs in the College greatly reduced the opportunity for elective courses in the thirty-hour M.A. program. Students majoring in Elementary Education in the B.A. program could choose six hours of electives in their twenty-four-hour program from among a limited number of courses, while Secondary Education majors were able to take only three hours of electives. The thirty-hour M.A. program included six hours of approved electives from among any courses offered in the University, and three additional hours from among a limited number of courses in the student's major field.

During the second year of the program, individualization was available to a greater degree within the individual courses than in the form of elective courses. Within most of the courses in the B.A. program and one of the three required M.A. courses in school library media, students were permitted to by-pass some modules or objectives within modules on the basis of either their performance on a pretest for the module or their reported prior experience with the content of the module. This was not the usual practice for all modules within most courses, but it was employed by several instructors with modules in which one or more students were judged to have a relatively high probability of already being able to perform the skills to be taught in the module.

A frequently employed form of individualization for more complex instructional objectives was to allow each student to conduct a guided in-depth study or intensive development effort with a topic of his own choice in order to attain the particular objective. That is, the objective was the same for all students but the content area on which the student concentrated for his learning activities was selected by each individual student. Several examples of objectives from the program for which each individual student selected his own topic or area of concentration are listed below:

1. Design and develop audiovisual instructional products which require use of a number of media skills and are desgned according to given principles of instructional and media design;
2. Demonstrate the ability to conduct in-depth research on topics of historical or social significance in the library media field by preparing a written report on a topic of the student's choice;
3. Prepare annotated bibliographies for units of instruction. Each bibliography will be accompanied by a description of its potential use and limitations and will include a wide variety of media available to the teacher or media specialist;
4. Compile and organize, according to criteria presented in class, all instructional materials for units of instruction which incorporate a wide range of print and non-print media. (The particular grade level and topic for the sample unit constructed by each student as a learning activity will be selected by the student.)

Another form of individualization was to allow students to pursue learning activities for modules or objectives on an independent study basis without class attendance. Although the program proposal indicated that this procedure would be used extensively in the experimental program, it actually was em-

ployed sparingly. While there was a considerable amount of student work done independently, in most cases, faculty felt that frequent class attendance was required for students to obtain objectives.

FIELD EXPERIENCE

Formal field experiences constituted an important part of both the B.A. and the M.A. programs. The field experience in each program was based upon supervised practice in a school library media center. The University supervisor of all student interns in the experimental program was hired for the two-year period on leave of absence from her position as the Director of an Instructional Materials Center in a large high school. The responsibilities and coordinating functions assigned to the fieldwork supervisor added a capability the former program did not have previously.

The interns in the B.A. program received six semester hours' credit for approximately 288 clock hours of supervised practice and related activities in a school library media center. These students were also required to enroll for six credit hours of supervised classroom teaching as a part of their program in Elementary Education or Secondary Education. Whenever it was possible, the student's school library media internship was scheduled concurrently with or after his classroom teaching, because of the potential value of his classroom experience for his work in the school library media center. The internship involved required participation in scheduled seminar meetings with the University supervisor and other interns, visitations by the University supervisor at least three times during the internship and evaluation of the intern's performance by a team composed of the intern, the school library media center supervisor, and the University supervisor. The evaluation was accomplished through (1) activity checklist, (2) midterm evaluation report, (3) time card, (4) record kept on personnel card, (5) observation of the intern in the school library media center, (6) seminar meeting participation, (7) conferences with interns during internship, (8) final evaluation report, and (9) consultations with the supervising librarian.

The intern program at the M.A. level was designed for graduate students who had neither interned nor been employed in a school library media center. Students in the M.A. program could enroll for either three semester hours of credit involving approximately 144 clock hours in a school library media center or six semester hours of credit and 288 clock hours. A student enrolling for six credit hours of internship was able to intern for three credit hours each in an elementary school center and in a secondary school. The split-level internship had several advantages. It provided exposure on two or more levels in curriculum, materials, and services. Having gained experience working with students and faculty on two or more levels, the graduate intern was able to make an intelligent career choice. This expanded experience increased the possibility that the student could be considered for a position on any level.

While both the undergraduate and graduate intern programs were designed to provide a wide variety of real experiences in the school library media center, the graduate program placed an emphasis on administrative responsibilities and practices. Procedures involving seminars, visitations and student evaluation were similar to those in the B.A. program.

# Program Results

The most straightforward way of assessing the effects of an experimental program is to examine the results as they relate to whether the stated goals of the program were attained. Also of importance, of course, are the judgments of participants in the program with respect to its value. Data relating to the attainment of the four goals of the Arizona State program and to student evaluation of the program are presented in this section.

## ATTAINMENT OF PROGRAM GOALS

*Goal 1: Training of School Library Media Personnel.* One of the four goals of the program stated in the original proposal was the training of at least fifteen school library media personnel per year. These individuals were to be enrolled as full-time students in the experimental program.

During 1971-72, the first year of the program, 16 full-time students were enrolled. Twelve of the 16 students actually completed the program during this year, 6 at the B.A. level and 6 at the graduate level. Three of the 4 1971-72 students who did not complete the program during that year finished during the 1972-73 school year. Thus, 15 students who were enrolled during the first year completed the program, although 3 of the 15 did not complete the program until the second year.

All 12 of the students who completed the program during 1971-72 were employed in school library media centers during 1972-73. Eight students accepted positions in elementary schools, 2 in junior high schools, and 2 in high schools.

During 1972-73, 25 full-time students and 4 part-time students were enrolled in the program. Not included in these figures are the students who were enrolled during 1971-72 and continued during 1972-73. Fifteen students, 8 in the M.A. program and 7 in the B.A. program, completed their programs in

June 1973. Three additional students completed their work during the summer of 1973. Three of the 15 students who completed their programs during the 1972-73 academic year were the 3 continuing students from 1971-72 who did not complete the program at that time.

In summary, a total of 45 students was enrolled in the experimental program over its two year duration. Thirty full-time students completed the program by the end of the 1973 summer session, 16 at the graduate level and 14 with B.A. degrees. Thus, the stated program goal of training 15 full-time school library media personnel per year was essentially realized, although 3 of the 15 1971-72 students who completed the program did not actually do so until 1972-73.

*Goal 2: Development of an Individuated, Modularized Program.* This goal called for individuation of the program consistent with the needs and prior experiences of each student and for modularization of the program, including the offering of at least forty-eight modules during the first year of the program.

Modules were not developed during the first year of the program to the degree described in the program proposal. Module specifications were ultimately developed for the entire program, but the modules were of a different nature than had been described in the proposal. In general, the amount of flexibility of student use of the modules and the accuracy of assessment implied in the proposal were not achieved in the program itself. Thus, although modules that were very useful in instruction were developed, field tested and revised for future use, the goal of modularization was not achieved to the extent described in the proposal.

The results obtained with respect to individualization were similar to those reported for modularization. A conscientious, successful effort was made during the second year of the program to provide for an extensive amount of individualization within courses, whereas a considerably lesser amount was provided during the first year. However, the proposal described the modules as a basis for individualization that would allow students to select rather freely from among a wide choice of options and implied that the students would work quite independently through the modules. This degree of individualization was not achieved in the program.

In December of 1972, a report describing the successes and problems experienced in the first year of the Arizona State program and outlining plans and objectives for the remainder of the second year was submitted to the School Library Manpower Project office. This report described objectives for the remainder of the program with respect to modularization and individualization that were more modest and realistic than those outlined in the proposal. The efforts described in the December report were, in fact, implemented during the second year. The original goal stated in the proposal with respect to individualization and modularization was not successfully attained, however.

*Goal 3: Effecting of Systemic Change.* This goal was described in the proposal as a long-range goal with implications for the number of school media centers in Arizona and for endorsement requirements in the state, which currently has the school librarian endorsement as its only form of certification in the library and media fields.

One significant factor related to the goal of systemic change is that the school library media education programs developed at Arizona State over the two-year period will now become the regular programs in the Department of Educational Technology and Library Science for training school library media center personnel. The new programs will replace the former, more traditional school library program at Arizona State. In the future, therefore, the training for all students in the Library Science program will emphasize both print and non-print materials and will be designed to prepare students for successful employment in a school library media center. Since the Department of Educational Technology and Library Science at Arizona State trains many more students for school librarianship and media center positions in Arizona than does any other Arizona institution, this change in the Arizona State program should have an increasing impact on the nature of school library media centers in the state.

Other important occurrences related to the goal

of systemic change were also noted during the program. In May of 1973, the Director of Library Services for the Arizona State Department of Education, a member of the program's Advisory Board, met with the program faculty to describe plans for the establishment of a new School Library Media Specialist Certificate in Arizona. Another notable occurrence has been the considerable interest shown by Arizona school administrators in the program and in the employment of students capable of developing a total media program. The concept of the school library media center has received a considerable amount of favorable publicity in Arizona during the past year as a result of several articles about the program in professional publications.

The goal of effecting systemic change is rather general and a difficult one on which to obtain reliable short-range data. The available evidence indicates, however, that the program was successful with respect to attainment of this goal.

*Goal 4: Packaging of the Program.* This goal called for packaging the components of the program so that they would be exportable to other colleges and universities. The basic components of the program were compiled in *A Curriculum Outline for Training School Library Media Specialists,* the 190-page publication cited earlier. Thus, the goal of packaging of the program for exportability was achieved through compilation and publication of the curriculum outline containing the programs of study, course outlines and all module specifications for the experimental program.

## STUDENT ATTITUDES

Although comments and suggestions about the program were obtained from students both informally and in several meetings, objective data on student attitudes were collected on only one occasion. In May of 1973, near the end of the second year of the program, students were asked to complete an evaluation form on the 1972-73 program. This form contained 15 five-choice Likert-type items and 2 additional items which solicited suggestions for improvement of the field experience and of the total program. Student responses to the evaluation form are summarized on a copy of the actual form in Appendix E. Each of the 15 statements included on the form was a positive statement about the program. For 13 of the 15 statements (including one tie), the response choice selected most frequently by the 22 students who completed the form was Choice 2, indicating agreement with the statement. The choice selected most frequently for the other

2 items was Choice 1, indicating strong agreement with the statement.

Several items were included in the evaluation form for the explicit purpose of determining student attitudes or judgments toward particular areas of concern in the program. Responses to Item 3, written to assess student opinion about the balance of print and non-print materials, reveal only a mildly favorable reaction. Responses to this item combined with student comments on Item 17 suggest that several students would prefer a somewhat greater non-print emphasis than their program contained. Re-

sponses to Items 6 and 11, which were designed to assess student attitudes toward faculty-student rapport and interaction, indicate generally favorable attitudes on these issues. The summarized responses for Item 8 reveal slightly favorable attitudes toward individualization opportunities in the program. The most positive student responses were registered toward the field experience (Item 9).

Student evaluation of the overall program, as indicated both by responses to Items 12-15 and to the entire form, was generally favorable.

# Program Conclusions

An overall analysis of the results related to attainment of the program goals and to student evaluation provides a general indication of the success of the program with respect to these items. Of the four major goals set forth in the proposal, three were successfully attained at the level stated or implied in the proposal. The fourth goal relating to individualization and modularization was not achieved at this level.

Student evaluation of the experimental program during its second year, as indicated by an end-of-year evaluation form, was generally favorable. No similar evaluation data were collected during the first year of the program. However, since much of the development effort was not implemented until the second year, it seems unlikely that student evaluation would have been as favorable during the first year as it was during the second.

Consideration of only the data that is directly relevant to whether the program goals were attained and to student evaluation of the program obscures or ignores other important issues related to the program. Several such issues having implications for the Arizona State program or for the broad field of school library media education are discussed in the remaining portion of this report.

## DIFFICULTY OF THE PROPOSED EFFORT

Educators who have attempted to develop their own courses—or especially courses to be taught by others—to the point where a set of important and well-formulated instructional objectives exist for the course, where valid assessment items are prepared

for each objective, and where high student achievement levels are obtained on the objectives, realize that this is a very difficult and time-consuming task. The difficulty of the task is normally increased when an attempt is made to treat worthwhile instructional objectives on essentially an independent study basis, because appropriate self-contained instructional materials (i.e., materials that effectively produce attainment of the objective with little guidance or direct instruction from a competent instructor) do not exist for most such objectives. An intensive, multi-year effort is required if a departmental faculty, including many who are not trained or skilled with respect to objectives-based instruction, is to develop and implement a competency-based curriculum that is organized around well-formulated objectives and that yields high student attainment of the objectives.

The difficulty of the development effort described in the proposal was greatly underestimated in that document. An enormous amount of faculty effort was expended on the experimental program over its two-year duration at Arizona State. Although significant progress was made toward development of an effective, integrated objectives-based program, a considerable amount of additional work remains to be done in order for the program to yield the ideal balance of skills and highly efficient student achievement envisioned in the proposal.

## INDIVIDUALIZATION OF INSTRUCTION

The goal in which the Arizona State experimental program was least successful was the goal related to modularization and individualization of instruction. There are essentially only four means for varying the objectives and content to which a student is exposed in his program of study (1) placement in given courses on the basis of program-relevant skills that the student lacks, (2) elective courses, (3) assignment of objectives within a course on the basis of course-relevant skills that the student lacks, and (4) student selection of objectives or topics within a course.

There are a substantial number of basic competencies that are essential to successful performance in a school library media center. Certain course work must be required of students so that they will master these skills, irrespective of whether state certification policy requires that students complete specified courses. Prior to taking the required courses, few students at the undergraduate level already possess many of the basic competencies taught in these courses. Thus, unless a school library media education program includes a relatively large number of credit hours in the library media field, it seems highly unlikely that students will have many important opportunities in a well-designed program to select very freely among courses and objectives. It simply was not possible to give students many such options in the Arizona State programs, especially in the B.A. program, in which students with no prior school library media experience enrolled for only eighteen semester hours of course work and six hours of field experience.

In contrast with allowing a student to select many courses or objectives of his own choice in a program that contains a limited number of credit hours, it is often possible and desirable to permit a student to work on a topic of his own choice while in the process of attempting to attain certain objectives. For example, the student who is learning the skill of developing an instructional unit or a particular type of audiovisual product may be allowed to select the particular topic on which he develops his unit or product. It was this form of individualization that was most often feasible for the majority of the students in the Arizona State program.

## SELECTION AND RETENTION OF STUDENTS

There was a considerable amount of good fortune with respect to the types of students enrolled in the experimental program. Students entering the B.A. program were initially screened through guidance and counseling procedures within the College of Education with limited screening by the Library Science faculty. Despite this procedure the average undergraduate cumulative grade-point average of students enrolled in both the B.A. and M.A. programs during each of the two years was above 3.00 on a 4.00 grade scale. Moreover, the majority of the students in the experimental program were skilled socially as well as academically.

The limited problems related to selection and retention in the Arizona State program became most serious at the time that students were to be placed in school library media centers for their fieldwork experience. Each year there was a student or two who, in the opinion of the faculty, simply did not belong in a center. Yet, the faculty had previously adopted no formal review procedure that would permit them to retain such students.

The faculty agreed during the spring of 1973 to adopt a guidance and counseling procedure for reviewing and formally approving or denying the application of each student for the internship experience, so that approval for the internship would be treated as an objective for which the student must qualify, rather than as a relatively automatic part of his program. It is hoped that this procedure will lead to better retention of students who are judged to be poorly qualified for professional work in the school library media field.

## DEVELOPMENT PROJECTS IN EDUCATION

The Arizona State program was implemented as a development project rather than a two-year training project or a demonstration project. The importance of this distinction relates to the short-term and long-term effects of the different types of projects. Training programs of limited duration, such as the two-year period of Phase II of the School Library Manpower Project, normally are intended to have their greatest effects on students who are enrolled in the program during the period of their funding. Faculty effort and funds can be expended exclusively on efforts to make the operating program as effective as possible. Demonstration projects are normally planned to provide high short-term visibility for one or more existing programs, with the potential longer-term effects to be derived from the ideas and imitative behaviors that the project stimulates in other people. Well-planned development projects involve an attempt to produce programs of a more permanent nature that can continue to be used with reliable effects after the termination of the project. Because the planned program is intended for use over a relatively longer time period, greater faculty effort goes into the initial formulation of the programs and into the development and revision of appropriate materials for long-term use. Less faculty time is available for direct efforts in the operation of the instructional program in a development project, because of the greater amount of time expended on formulation, development, field testing and revision of materials. However, if the development effort is successful, this handicap with respect to short-term effects on the operating program during the funding period should be more than offset by the greater long-term effects resulting from relative permanence of the program and from its continued use after the termination of funding.

Because the Arizona State program was operated primarily as a development project, it was not possible to devote the full resources of the program to the training of students during the two-year period of the experimental program. Considerable effort was directed toward the development of materials and procedures that would continue to serve as the basis for a more effective curriculum following the termination of the experimental program. The project was conducted so that it would have a relatively permanent effect, rather than having its major effect only during the two-year period. Consequently, the training aspect of the program was not as effective as it might have been, particularly during the first year, if the full resources of the program had been expended on the training function. The training process became progressively more effective during the two-year period with the increased development and field testing of materials and procedures to serve as the basis for the continuing Arizona State program.

In development of a relatively substantial and permanent program, the most positive results are seldom, if ever, realized during the first two years. The potential long-term effects resulting from the use of a program development procedure at Arizona State, rather than of a training effort for only the two-year period, would appear to justify the type of strategy that was employed.

CONTINUATION OF THE PROGRAM

The school library media programs developed during the two-year experimentation at Arizona State will become the University's training programs in the school library media field. Additional work with respect to development and refinement of the

programs is planned for the 1973-74 school year and thereafter.

Based on data and observations from the second year of the experimental program, two types of modifications in the Arizona State school library media programs appear to be most appropriate for the immediate future. One such modification is the development of an additional course in Audiovisual Education that teaches students to produce prints, slides, filmstrips and audiotapes (these skills are now taught in several different courses, rather than in a single course); and of a course in Educational Technology that teaches students the basic skills related to development of effective objectives-based instruction and to assessment of student attainment of instructional objectives. Both of these courses will be offered during the 1973-74 school year. It is probable that the school library media programs of study will be revised during 1973-74 to include these two courses.

A second desirable modification in the school library media program is the further development of valid end-of-module or end-of-course tests for use in the various courses. These tests would permit better identification of weaknesses in the program itself and in the skills of individual students. Development of assessment materials of this type, most likely for use as cumulative end-of-course tests, is planned for the 1973-74 school year.

The Arizona State program that was developed under the support of the School Library Manpower Project is a vastly improved program over the one that it replaced. Students who formerly would have been trained as school librarians now are being trained as school library media specialists at Arizona State University which trains more students for work in school library media centers in Arizona than does any other institution. The graduates of the experimental program and the publicity it has received represent a very positive force for improving school library media centers throughout the state. Continuation and further refinement of the program developed under the School Library Manpower Project should contribute significantly to better training of school library media specialists in Arizona and to the growth in the number and quality of school library media centers in the state.

Appendix A

Course List, B.A. Minor
in Library Science


This program is for all students desiring endorsement as a School Librarian K-12.
All Courses include both print and non-print media.

Elementary Education Majors

*Required Courses

| | | |
|---|---|---|
| LS 440 | Cataloging and Classification | 3 hours |
| LS 463 | Library Materials for Children | 3 hours |
| LS 471 | Basic Reference Resources | 3 hours |
| **LS 481 | Library Administration | 3 hours |
| **EE 478 | Student Teaching in the Elementary School | ***6 hours |

Electives - Any two of the following:                                6 hours

    IM 311  Children's Liturature (3 hours)
    LS 423  Books, Libraries and Society (3 hours)
    LS 464  Library Materials for Adolescents (3 hours)

                                              Total:  24 hours


Secondary Education Majors

Required Courses

| | | |
|---|---|---|
| AV 411 | Audiovisual Materials and Procedures in Education | 3 hours |
| LS 440 | Cataloging and Classification | 3 hours |
| LS 464 | Library Materials for Adolescents | 3 hours |
| LS 471 | Basic Reference Resources | 3 hours |
| **LS 481 | Library Administration | 3 hours |
| **SE 433 | Student Teaching in the Secondary School | ***6 hours |

Electives - Any one of the following:

    LS 423  Books, Libraries and Society (3 hours)
    LS 463  Library Materials for Children (3 hours)

                                              Total:  24 hours


  * If AV 411 is not required in the student's program for a major in
    Elementary Education, it must be added as a required course for the
    minor.  In this case, he may take only one elective course instead
    of two.

 ** LS 440, LS 463 or LS 464, and LS 471 are prerequisites for LS 481 and for
    student teaching in the school library (EE 478 or SE 433).  Concurrent
    enrollment in LS 481 and student teaching in the library is recommended.

*** These 6 hours refer to student teaching in the school library or school
    library media center.  They must be taken in addition to the 6 hours
    of student teaching in an elementary or secondary school classroom.

Appendix B

Master of Arts in Education

School Library Media Specialization

This program prepares teachers to serve as school media librarians.  All courses in the major area include both print and non-print media.

Major Area:      12 hours

| | | |
|---|---|---|
| Required: | LS 511  Cataloging II | 3 hours |
| | LS 522  Reference Resources II | 3 hours |
| | LS 531  Instructional Materials Centers | 3 hours |

| | | |
|---|---|---|
| Electives: | AV 580  Practicum:  Production of Instructional | |
| (Choose one) | Media | 3 hours |
| | *LS 584  Internship:  School Library Media | |
| | LS 591  Seminar:  Reading and Communication | |

Professional Education Core:      12 hours

| | | |
|---|---|---|
| | EP 510  Educational Psychology | 3 hours |
| | EE 511  Elementary Curriculum or | |
| | SE 522  Secondary Curriculum | 3 hours |
| | ET 510  Information Science (or LS 498) | 3 hours |
| | EF 500  Educational Research | 3 hours |

Electives:      6 hours to be selected from any university courses numbered 400 and above and included in the student's approved graduate program.

--------------------------------------------------------------------------

**Prerequisites:      15 hours, as listed below.  Six of these 15 hours may be used to satisfy the six-hour elective requirement, if they are taken after receiving the Bachelor's degree.

| | | |
|---|---|---|
| | AV 411  Audiovisual Materials and Procedures | |
| | in Education | 3 hours |
| | LS 440  Cataloging and Classification | 3 hours |
| | LS 463  Library Materials for Children or | |
| | LS 464  Library Materials for Adolescents | 3 hours |
| | LS 471  Basic Reference Resources | 3 hours |
| | ***LS 481  Library Administration | 3 hours |

* LS 584 is required if the student has neither interned nor been employed for at least a semester in a school library.

** The prerequisites for AV 411, LS 440, LS 471 and LS 481 may be satisfied by attaining acceptable scores on examinations covering the content in each of these courses.  On the approval of the student's M.A. committee, equivalent courses taken at other universities may be substituted for AV 411, LS 440, LS 471 and LS 481, but not for LS 463 or LS 464.

*** LS 440, LS 463 or LS 464, and LS 471 are prerequisites for LS 481.

Appendix C

SAMPLE COURSE OUTLINE

COURSE NO. AND TITLE:  LS 481  Library Administration

REQUIRED IN:  LS minor  (elementary and secondary education majors)

PREREQUISITE COURSES:  LS 463 or LS 464, LS 440, and LS 471

TEXTBOOKS, MATERIALS REQUIRED:
    Gaver, M.  Services of Secondary School Media Centers; Evaluation and
       Development.  Chicago:  American Library Association, 1971

    School Library Personnel Task Analysis Survey (and) Task Analysis Survey
       Instrument.  Chicago:  American Library Association, 1969.

-------------------------------------------------------------------------------

MODULE TOPICS:

    I.   Functions of a school library media center
        A.  Program of services
        B.  Curriculum development
        C.  Instruction
        D.  In-service Training
        E.  Acquisition, processing, circulation
        F.  Miscellaneous other functions

   II.   Organizational patterns
        A.  Internal relationships
           1.  line and staff
           2.  personnel utilization
           3.  effective completion of all tasks
           4.  responsibility/accountability

        B.  External relationships
           1.  district office
           2.  in-school personnel
           3.  state or other governmental officials/departments
           4.  professional organizations

  III.   Facilities for effective programs
        A.  Architectural considerations in relationship with program
        B.  Internal specifications (furniture, equipment, space allocations,
           etc.) for effective program.
        C.  Scheduling for maximum utilization

   IV.   Policies and procedures
        A.  Budget preparation
        B.  Other record-keeping
        C.  Selection policies
        D.  Acquisition, processing, circulation
        E.  Miscellaneous other policies and procedures

Appendix C (cont.)

COURSE OBJECTIVES:

Completion of the management/administration course should provide the student with background information and experiences needed to develop skills required to (1) identify and fulfill the primary service responsibilities of a school library media center;  (2) establish necessary organizational structures and optimal administrative arrangements;  (3) plan and maintain the physical facilities required;  and (4) develop and administer essential policies and procedures to carry out school library media center functions.

The specific skills that the student will be able to perform upon completion of the course are listed below:

1. Describe specific functions related to aims and objectives, curriculum development, instruction, inservice training, and public relations, when presented with situations where he must present the program for a school library media center.

2. Describe the organizational structures which represent functional relationships that should exist within a SLMC staff, including processing, instruction, research, special services, administration, development of educational program, selection, production, collections development, etc.

3. Describe decision-making relationships that should exist between a school library media center staff and the district library officers, the school principal, the teachers, the students, state education officials and other librarians.

4. Describe the functions and organization of a district library media center in providing services to the school library media centers, to teachers, and other district personnel.

5. Given a description of curricular goals, number of students, and instructional activities, write performance specifications that describe characteristics of the environment needed for the instructional activities to occur.

6. Describe key functions and activities of media centers that must be accounted for in writing performance specifications for these centers.

7. Describe general kinds of ventilation, lighting, acoustics, etc. that should be specified in performance specifications and identify examples of each.

8. Identify examples of acceptable performance specifications and describe their role in client communication with architects.

Appendix C (cont.)

LS 481

9. Construct a plan for a district media center. The plan must include: a) a description of the functions the center would perform to meet the district's own peculiar needs, b) a description of activities and processes that would have to occur in order to perform these functions, c) a description of staff and their working relationships, d) a description of the line and staff relationships of the district center director with other professionals within the district, and e) suggested strategies for implementing the plan.

10. Name and briefly describe the major policies that should be covered in a school library media center policy manual. An acceptable performance should meet the checklist requirements included in the course.

11. Describe procedures for selection and acquiring of materials to be purchased.

12. Develop an acceptable system for circulation of materials.

13. Develop procedures which correlate time to given needs of the program, students, and other personnel in scheduling the use of facilities.

A number of optional objectives are also included in the course. Each student is to select the optional objective of his choice and complete the activities related to it.

Appendix D


SAMPLE MODULE SPECIFICATION


SLMP Module Specification                                    LS 481-6


Area:      Management
Module #6: Planning district media centers


I.   Objective:

     Construct a plan for a district media center.  The plan must
     include:  a) a description of the functions the center would perform
     to meet the district's own peculiar needs, b) a description of activities
     and processes that would have to occur in order to perform these functions,
     c) a description of staff and their working relationships, d) a descrip-
     tion of the line and staff relationships of the district center director
     with other professionals within the district, and e) suggested strategies
     for implementing the plan.


II.  Example of Master Item:

     1.   You have been asked to help plan a district media center for
          the Pushover School District.  Read the attached description
          of the district, job descriptions of key district personnel
          outside the media center, and budget.  (These would be provided.)
          Then complete the following tasks.

          a).   List the functions and activities the media center might
                perform to meet the needs of the district.
          b).   List the kinds and numbers of personnel needed in the
                center to perform these functions and describe the jobs
                they would perform.
          c).   Construct an organization chart that indicates line and
                staff relationships within the center.
          d).   Describe the staff and line relationships of the district
                media center's director to other district personnel.
          e).   Tell how decisions regarding specific functions (e.g.,
                textbook selection) would be made.

     2.   A district media center performs the following functions:
          central purchasing, central processing and cataloging,
          inventorying maintaining AV equipment, coordinating selection
          and evaluation of materials, storage and distribution of 16mm
          films, coordination of TV services, and production of TV lessons
          working in concert with teachers and curriculum specialists.

          a).   Construct a flow chart for each process performed by the
                center.

Appendix D (cont.)

LS 481-6

b). Write job descriptions for personnel needed to perform these functions.

c). Construct an organization chart indicating authority relationships within the organization and describe how decisions related to the articulation of different functions would be made.

III. Activities:

1. Have students observe, monitor or participate in any local planning studies for central centers that may be underway.

2. Give students organization charts and job descriptions of personnel. Have students identify those personnel with whom a district center director would most likely have either staff or line relationships.

3. Give the students a list of school district personnel similar to the one below and have students indicate the personnel with which a center director usually has an authority or line relationship and those persons with which he usually has a staff or consultative relationship.

   a). Graphic artist
   b). Director of television
   c). Principals
   d). Teachers
   e). School media center librarians
   f). District director of curriculum
   g). District director of guidance and research
   h). District coordinator of music
   i). Supervisor of data processing

4. Give the students descriptions of central media center director work relationships (like the ones below) and have them tell whether or not they are staff or line.

   a). A central media center director works with a team of English teachers and the District Curriculum Specialists in selecting new textbooks. Duties include identifying potential texts and related materials and rendering a professional opinion of their quality.

   b). A central media center director presents a budget to the Board of Education. Duties include explaining essential features of the budget and modifying the budget in accordance with Board decisions.

   c). A central media center director works with center staff to develop film distribution procedures. Duties include approving final procedures, monitoring problems, and making changes in procedures when necessary.

Appendix D (cont.)

LS 481-6

5.  Give students lists of functions of district and school media centers
and have them tell which are typically performed at the district level
and which are not.  Given functions may include the following:

    a).  Purchasing of materials for entire district
    b).  Catalogs and materials
    c).  Distributes equipment and 16mm films
    d).  Selects and stores materials for each school
    e).  Coordinates with data processing.

6.  Give students definitions of staff and line relationships like the
ones below and have them indicate whether they are staff or line.

    a).  A relationship where one has authority over others and
    is directly responsible to others.

    b).  A relationship where one has not direct authority, but
    is expected to work with others on an informal, consul-
    tative basis.

7.  Have students visit a district media center and write a short
description of the tasks performed by each individual within the
center.

8.  Have students draw a "flow of work" diagram for buying, cataloging,
processing, distribution and other central center functions that
would indicate a study of "time and motion" components.

IV.  Information and Materials:

Read:

Davies, Ruth Ann.  The School Library:  A Force for Excellence.
    R. R. Bowker, New York:  1969, Ch. 2, "The School Library Supervisor,"
    pp. 227-242.

Association for Supervision and Curriculum Development:  N.E.A.
    The Supervisor:  New Demands-New Dimensions, ed. William H. Lucio.
    Washington, D.C.:  1969.

Appendix E

SUMMARY OF STUDENT RESPONSES

SLMP EVALUATION FORM: 1972-73

Program (check one) B.A. _12_ M.A. _8_ (No response 2)        May, 1973

This form will be used as a basis for evaluating the SLMP program during 1972-73 and for making improvements in it. All responses and comments will be typed before they are reviewed by any faculty members. Please do not write your name on the form.

For items 1-15, mark each item by circling one of the numbers as follows:
   1 = strong agree with statement        4 = disagree with statement
   2 = agree with statement               5 = strongly disagree with statement
   3 = neither agree nor disagree

1. The content of the program was relevant to what I hope to accomplish professionally.
   1   2   3   4   5   No Response
   *(6) (14) (1) (1) (0)   (1)

2. Considering my background and ability, the things that I was expected to learn were at about the right difficulty level.
   1   2   3   4   5
   (6) (13) (2) (1) (0)

3. There was a good balance between the amount of course work devoted to print materials and the amount devoted to non-print materials.
   1   2   3   4   5
   (5) (7) (7) (3) (0)

4. The faculty members had good knowledge of their subject matter.
   1   2   3   4   5
   (10) (9) (4) (1) (0)

5. The quality of instruction was above average.
   1   2   3   4   5
   (6) (8) (6) (1) (1)   (1)

6. There was good rapport between the faculty and the students.
   1   2   3   4   5
   (5) (13) (5) (0) (0)

7. The course content was presented in an interesting manner.
   1   2   3   4   5
   (3) (13) (6) (1) (0)

8. I had sufficient opportunities in the program to work on projects or tasks of my own choice.
   1   2   3   4   5
   (5) (9) (5) (4) (0)

9. My field experience was a good one.
   1   2   3   4   5
   (12) (3) (3) (0) (1)   (3)

(Please complete other side of sheet)

*Numbers in parentheses indicate the number of students marking each response choice. Numbers do not always total to 22 because students occasionally marked more than one choice for an item.

Appendix E (cont.)

SUMMARY OF STUDENT RESPONSES

SLMP EVALUATION FORM:  1972-73

| | 1 | 2 | 3 | 4 | 5 | No Response |
|---|---|---|---|---|---|---|
| 10. In general, the faculty was available for advisement and individual help. | (7) | (11) | (2) | (2) | (0) | (1) |
| 11. Sufficient opportunities were available in the program for faculty-student interaction. | (6) | (13) | (3) | (0) | (0) | |
| 12. Overall, I would rate the SLMP program as a good program. | (4) | (15) | (2) | (1) | (0) | (1) |
| 13. I would advise a friend with similar interests to enroll in this program. | (5) | (13) | (2) | (1) | (0) | (1) |
| 14. Considering the number of credit hours in my school library media program, I feel that I was well trained for work in a library media center. | (7) | (11) | (2) | (1) | (0) | (1) |
| 15. I have a positive attitude toward the program. | (8) | (13) | (2) | (0) | (0) | |

---

16. What specific things could be done to improve the internship or field experience in a library media center?

    (Responses to this item were summarized on a separate sheet. The most common suggestion by students was that they have the opportunity to intern in more than one center.)

17. What specific things could be done to improve the school library media program in which you were enrolled?

    (Responses to this item were summarized on a separate sheet. The most common suggestion related to offering more non-print content, either through additional Audiovisual courses or through greater emphasis on non-print materials in one specified Library Science course.)

# AUBURN UNIVERSITY

SCHOOL OF EDUCATION

Dr. Truman M. Pierce, Dean

## AN EXPERIMENTAL PROGRAM IN
# SCHOOL LIBRARY MEDIA EDUCATION
## 1971–1973

*Final Report by*

WILLIAM E. HUG

## Contents

# DEPARTMENT OF EDUCATIONAL MEDIA

## Dr. William E. Hug, Head

*Experimental Program Staff, 1971-1973*

Dr. William E. Hug, Director

Mrs. Patricia F. Beilke, Associate Director

Mrs. Jacqueline M. Abney, 1972-73
Mrs. Carol M. Anthony
Mrs. Mary R. Klontz
Mrs. Anna M. Knight, 1972-73
Dr. Thomas E. Miller
Dr. James A. Nemsik, 1971-72
Mrs. Joan S. Nist

Mrs. Carrie C. Robinson, 1972-73
Mrs. Estelle Shaw, 1972-73
Dr. Allen N. Sheppard, 1971-72
Dr. Clarence D. Wright
Miss Linda Miner, Secretary
Miss Jane C. Cobb, Graphics
Mr. Robert A. Borzak, Photographer

*Advisory Board*

Mrs. Patricia F. Beilke, ex officio
Assistant Professor
Department of Educational Media
Auburn University

Dr. Kenneth A. Cadenhead
Director, TTT Project
Auburn University

Mrs. Mozelle Cummings
Assistant Director
Alabama Public Library Service

Dr. William E. Hug
Head, Department of Educational Media
Auburn University

Mr. John E. Marcinowski
Instructor
Opelika State Vocational Technical Institute

Mr. James E. Owen
Superintendent of Schools
Phenix City

Mrs. Carrie C. Robinson
Library Media Supervisor
Alabama Department of Education

Mrs. Gloria Jean Sanders
Library Media Specialist
Auburn Public Schools

Mrs. Estelle Shaw, 1971-72
Student Member
Auburn University

Mrs. Kathleen Strickland, 1972-73
Student Member
Auburn University

Mrs. Ruth Williamson, 1971-72
Teacher
Auburn Public Schools

# Overview

Auburn University's experimental graduate program for the preparation of media specialists was field-centered and competency-based. The program defined media specialist as the basic professional managing a media program in an elementary or secondary school. The role of the media specialist incorporated competencies formerly associated with librarianship, the audiovisual field, and curriculum theory and development especially as curriculum related to instructional design. The field-centered thrust of Auburn's program related to the extensive number of field experiences in which students were required to participate during their academic program. The competency-based aspect of the program reflected the belief that many professional activities had to be learned, observed, and evaluated as the student performed in a simulated or actual working situation. Each student's program of study was individually planned and under the supervision of an assigned advisor. Upon completion of the program, the student earned the Master of Education or the Master of Science degree and certification as a media specialist by the State of Alabama. Graduates from the Auburn program have been employed in the states of Alabama, Maryland, Virginia, North Carolina, Georgia, Florida, and Mississippi.

The Department of Educational Media was contacted in writing, by telephone, and through personal interviews (sometimes all three) by employers seeking graduates from the program. About ten such requests were made for every graduate available. Most students were employed before graduation. Positions accepted were varied and included administrative positions in media programs on the college and junior college level, media specialists' positions in small and large school districts, and production positions in industry and government. Eight students during the 1971-1973 period continued to pursue the doctorate at Auburn, Florida State University, and Indiana University.

## DESCRIPTION OF THE INSTITUTION

Auburn University, Auburn, Alabama, is one of two land grand institutions in the state. Auburn University seeks to discharge its responsibilities through its three divisions of Instruction, Research, and Extension. The University's instructional programs stimulate the student to reach his full potential as a human being and to provide him with knowledge and skills that will allow him to develop competencies for successful participation in a demanding and practical world. The University conducts research programs that push forward the frontiers of knowledge in all areas as well as the more practical aspects of research that endeavor to discover new and better ways of performing the many tasks that society demands. In the University's extension and service programs, Auburn continually strives to reach out to the people, to the communities, and to the industries of Alabama by designing programs that respond to the needs of the State and the Southeast.

Auburn University has a student body of approximately 16,000 students. The City of Auburn has a population of 22,767, and adjoins the County Seat of Lee County, Opelika. Auburn is located sixty miles northeast of Montgomery, 120 miles southeast of Birmingham, 125 miles southwest of Atlanta, and 30 miles northwest of Columbus, Georgia.

The School of Education offers programs for graduate study in six areas. One hundred twenty-one graduate programs are offered University wide. The School of Education at Auburn University is accredited by the National Council for Accreditation of Teacher Education for the preparation of elementary and secondary teachers and school service personnel. Programs lead to degrees of Master of Science, Master of Education, and Doctor of Education. Departments in the School of Education include Administration and Supervision; Counselor Education; Educational Media; Elementary Education; Foundations of Education; Health, Physical Education and Recreation; Secondary Education; and Vocational and Adult Education.

The School of Education prepared school library personnel over ten years prior to State Department of Education approval of the media specialist program in September 1971. The Department of Educational Media was established July 1, 1970, for the education of school media personnel. Auburn University became the first institution in the state to qualify students for certification as media specialists.

The Department of Educational Media serves several functions. The instructional program provides, through its sixteen upper division and graduate courses, an area of concentration for candidates for graduate degrees and a minor for students seeking their bachelor's degrees. The Learning Resources Center serves as a learning laboratory to students and faculty of the School of Education as well as a training facility for media personnel. The functions of research and public service include departmental research, graduate research, and experimental projects and programs. The department strives to keep a balance between instruction, research, and service so that each contributes to the other and at the same time advances the purposes of the School of Education and Auburn University.

The department maintains a close working relationship with national and state agencies and committees studying the role of the media specialist. During the development of Auburn's school media program, the department contacted the School Library Manpower Project for advice and assistance. Competencies identified by the School Library Manpower Project, by Teaching Research, a Division of the Oregon State System of Higher Education, and *The Big M in Education—Media Specialist: A Role Defined*[1] provided the Department with a content base for building Auburn University's program.

Faculty members of the department became interested in the work of the School Library Manpower Project as they assisted the State of Alabama's Committee for the Preparation of Educational Media Personnel to develop competencies for media personnel in that state. *School Library Personnel: Task Analysis Survey*[2] provided a comprehensive list which was used to check and validate the work of the Alabama Committee. The report of the committee was published as *The Big M in Education—Media Specialist: A Role Defined*. The work of this committee influenced the State Department of Education in the establishment of media specialist certification in Alabama.

Auburn's association with the School Library Manpower Project developed an appreciation of the Project's goals and prompted the department to sub-

mit a proposal for participation as an experimental training program of the Project. Auburn's proposed program became identified as "Project LIBRA." The term LIBRA symbolized the dual and balanced thrust of the program which emphasized field-centered and competency-based activities built upon thirteen global objectives.

## UNIVERSITY RESOURCES

The Learning Resources Center of the School of Education, which serves as a learning laboratory for students and faculty of the Department of Educational Media as well as the School of Education, was utilized as a training facility during the experimental graduate program for the preparation of media specialists. Spaces and materials were provided for large and small groups, traditional classes, and independent study. The Learning Resources Center afforded a wide variety of equipment and included both photographic and graphic personnel.

The Ralph Brown Draughon Library of Auburn University offered its staff, facilities, and materials for the experimental program. The library contains nearly a million volumes, more than 10,000 serials and other materials, including microphotographic reproductions. During the 1971-72 academic year five students of the experimental program performed fieldwork in this library under the guidance of library personnel and the faculty of the Department of Educational Media.

## DESCRIPTION OF THE EXPERIMENTAL PROGRAM

Students were admitted to the experimental graduate program for the preparation of media specialists after they met screening standards set by the Graduate School and the Department of Educational Media. Students were required to complete the Graduate Record Examination Aptitude Test and the Advanced Test in Education. These tests, in conjunction with the last 100 hours of course work, were combined in a formula to determine admission. Screening reports were sent from the Graduate School to the Department of Educational Media where admission was determined. The department requested a personal interview and a minimum of twelve hours in media as part of entrance requirements. Students having no formal training or experience in media were required to complete twelve hours of qualifying work. After a student was admitted, an advisor was assigned and the student was scheduled for a comprehensive written examination, which was designed by the Department of Educa-

1. *The Big M in Education—Media Specialist: A Role Defined* (Montgomery: Alabama State Department of Education, 1970). ERIC Ed 044025

2. School Library Manpower Project, *School Library Personnel: Task Analysis Survey* (Washington, D.C.: National Education Association, 1969).

tional Media to help assess the entrance capabilities of the student, but was not used as part of the entrance requirements. The comprehensive examination included test items on materials selection and preparation, media for children and young adults, reference materials and services, organization and administration, classification and cataloging, principles of systems design, and instructional design.

The individual nature of the experimental program does not lend itself to a description of a typical course of study for any one student. Each student's program included course work, fieldwork, and participation in events. The amount of course work depended upon the experience and academic background of the individual student. Courses such as Research in Education, Technology in Education (basic principles of instructional design), Modes of Mediated Instruction (producing and field-testing of teaching-learning module), and electives or requirements taken from departments other than the Department of Educational Media were typically part of each student's program of study. Educational Psychology, Research in Education, and a course in general curriculum or social or philosophical foundations were required by the School of Education for all Master's degrees awarded.

Four graduate courses were designated as field courses—Problems in the Administration of Media Services, Media Services in School and Community, Studies in Education, and Evaluation of Media Programs. Students enrolled in these field courses were engaged in the identification and resolution of problems that existed in field centers surrounding Auburn University. Students enrolled in Problems in the Administration of Media Services were engaged in activities such as setting up and field-testing procedures for technical processing, short- and long-range planning, and facilities design. Students enrolled in Media Services in School and Community were engaged in activities such as setting up a community resources file, producing a manual for field trips, and establishing working relationships among resources available in a particular community. Students engaged in Studies in Education worked on problems selected by students and advisors in order to concentrate on a dimension not otherwise covered in their programs. Activities of students enrolled in Studies in Education included reading programs designed to strengthen individual backgrounds, production of teaching-learning modules and slide-tape presentations, and the design and execution of educational events such as film festivals, book fairs, or in-service activities for the faculty, students, and/or administrators of a par-

ticular school district. Students in Evaluation of Media Programs utilized checklists and other instruments available in the literature as well as designed procedures for collecting information and making judgments about media programs that existed in the Auburn area. Fieldwork involving program evaluation varied from comprehensive views of basic functions to detailed assessments of a particular operation.

Students participated in educational events occurring at Auburn University, in the field centers, as well as elsewhere in Alabama and throughout the nation. Events at Auburn University included such activities as orientation sessions for new students (students with some experience in the program conducted many of these sessions), materials displays, guest speakers and consultants, conventions, and workshops. Students participated in events frequently designed by other students in conjunction with field courses that took place in one of the field centers cooperating with Auburn's program. These events included groups of students visiting field centers in the surrounding area, attending seminars and discussions concerning media services with teachers and administrators of a particular school district, and puppet shows and story-telling demonstrations. The meetings and conventions of the Alabama Library Association as well as the national conferences of the Association for Educational Communication and Technology, American Educational Research Association, and the American Library Association provided students with the opportunity to participate in additional events.

The student's advisor was responsible for designing and submitting an individual's program to the Graduate School, coordinating and monitoring a student's progress, and scheduling as well as participating in the final oral examination. A team of two or three faculty members working with each student identified and designed work to be accomplished in the field-related courses. Each graduate student had a mailbox where information about required and optional events could be obtained. Course work, fieldwork, and the participation in events were individually orchestrated in order to build the best possible program for each student.

## PHILOSOPHY AND ASSUMPTIONS FOR CHANGE

The importance of the school library media specialist's newly defined role in education has had considerable impact in Alabama. Auburn University's administrators and faculty have contributed to the work of state-wide committees in the development of the emerging role of the school library media specialist.

Auburn University's President provided leadership for the Alabama Education Study Commission which met in 1968. The commission sounded the need for a new kind of professional in school libraries:

> It is recommended (a) that state universities and colleges institute formal programs of study at the graduate level for preparation of media specialists and (b) that teacher education programs include adequate preparation in media utilization.[3]

The Alabama committee for the Preparation of Media Personnel, a fifty-six member committee, met over a sixteen-month period (February 1969-April 1970) entirely at the expense of the individual members who were convinced of the necessity for and potential of this type of trained personnel in the field of education. The published recommendations of this series of meetings further defined the media specialist's role in the public school.

The commitment of Auburn University and the School of Education to the new concept of the school library media specialist has been demonstrated. Three new faculty positions were added to the educational media program just prior to the establishment of a new department, the Department of Educational Media, in the School of Education (July 1, 1970). In the same period the entire maintenance increase allocated to the School of Education (1969) was awarded to the new department.

The experimental graduate program endeavored to establish the frequently neglected but necessary balance between on-the-job training and the more theoretical university-based experiences. Practicing school library media personnel and full-time University students were enrolled in the experimental program. The field-centered experiences provided students with multiple learning environments. The fact that the field center participant (part-time student from a cooperating school library media program)

was enrolled also as a student in the experimental program made on-the-job training and experience more relevant to the new concept of the school library media specialist and his role in today's education. The competency-based aspect was partially the result of task analysis studies of media specialists. A field-centered, competency-based program for the training of media specialists was in direct response to the kind of professional needed in schools as well as to the more basic need to establish an equitable and effective balance between the practical and the theoretical aspects for the education of professionals at all levels.

Few school media centers were operational models of what the School Library Manpower Project or *Standards for School Media Programs*[4] describe. Consequently, most field experience ran the danger of perpetuating out-moded practices and attitudes rather than providing experiences applicable to the new concept of the media specialist and his role in modern education. The Auburn program incorporated a number of field centers and their key personnel into a unified, goal-oriented program that complemented and gave direction to university-based experiences.

The commitment of the staff to the experimental program was more than an expression of attitude toward instruction. The staff believed that projects or departments sincerely seeking change had to utilize a new system for generating, managing, and monitoring programs. The staff believed that the new program at Auburn demanded content mastery by participants in order for them to perform competently rather than to simply demand content mastery with the hope that the student would eventually see a relationship between content and practice. The media specialist must be a fully functioning human who understands the process of which he is a part. The staff therefore ascribed to the old axiom that it is not what you know that counts, but what you can do with what you know.

---

3. Alabama Education Study Commission, *Report of Task Force I: The Role of Public Education in the State of Alabama* (Montgomery: Alabama Study Commission, 1968), p. 123.

4. American Association of School Librarians, American Library Association, and the Department of Audiovisual Instruction, National Education Association, *Standards for School Media Programs* (Chicago: American Library Association, and Washington, D.C.: National Education Association, 1969).

# Program Goals and Objectives

Thirteen global objectives were identified by the experimental program for the preparation of media specialists. These global objectives established the comprehensive scope of the experimental program. The development process is shown in Figure 1. Each student was expected to demonstrate competency in:

1. Selecting teaching and learning materials,
2. Producing and re-packaging media to meet specific user demands,
3. Contributing as a member of a teaching-learning team,
4. Assisting in curriculum planning,
5. Guiding students in forming appropriate study habits,
6. Designing, implementing, and evaluating systems for media storage and retrieval,
7. Applying physical, mental, emotional, and social processes as they relate to learning in the library media program,
8. Determining and implementing purposes, functions, and components of the library media center necessary to support the total school program,
9. Interpreting the media program as it relates to the school and community,
10. Expressing a commitment to continued professional growth,
11. Conducting workshops, in-service instruction, discussions, demonstrations, and other activities that assist users to better utilize the school media center,
12. Evaluating and encouraging promising innovative practices as they relate to the media program, and
13. Developing and implementing methods for utilizing community resources in the school media program.

## DEVELOPMENT OF PROGRAM OBJECTIVES

After the global objectives were identified and before performance objectives were constructed, related content was assembled for each of the thirteen areas. The content for each objective indicated appropriate experiences in terms of courses, fieldwork, participation in events, and independent study modules. In cases where ends or terminal behavior were clearly defined, independent learning modules were designed. Figure 2, entitled A Systems Approach to Curriculum Design, outlines the procedure utilized for module development.

The content for global objective number one (select teaching and learning materials) encompassed resources treating the selection of library media, including criteria for (1) formulating selection policies, (2) identifying materials, (3) assessing purpose-need-demand relationships, (4) controlling and assessing quality of content and format, (5) matching learning materials with learning styles, and (6) maintaining balance in selection. The primary thrust of the content supporting this objective revolved around the philosophy, procedure, and evaluation for collections development. Emphasis was placed on the unique presentation forms and the theoretical potential afforded by each media and by media-mixes. The selection resources contained criteria for managing controversial media and for withdrawing and discarding materials. Another emphasis related to the process media specialists use in suggesting media to individuals as well as groups. The materials provided students with information which they were expected to translate into a program to develop and implement a selection and acquisition plan for a specific educational program and a specified user population.

The content identified for objective number one (select teaching and learning materials) was broken down into performance objectives. Examples of these performance objectives were:

1. The student will prepare a bibliography of tools essential for selection of media. Criterion: work judged against a prepared model.
2. Given a series of information requests, the student will locate and select resources providing the requested information. Criterion: work judged against a prepared model.
3. Given the objectives of a learning sequence, the student will classify the objectives and select media appropriate to the class (verbal, discrimination, motor performance, affective). Criterion: objective measure.

Competencies were developed using the Learning Resources Center, demonstrations, self-checklists,

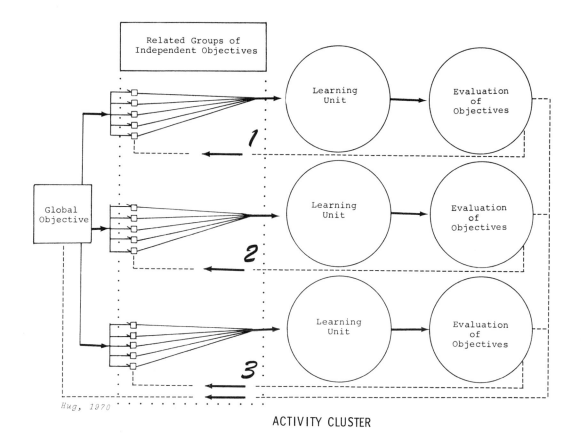

Figure 1. Process for the Development of Global Objectives

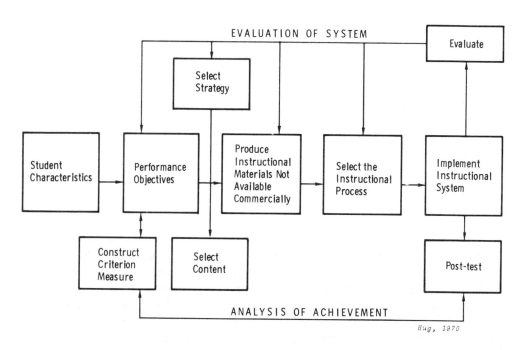

Figure 2. A Systems Approach to Curriculum Design

independent study, small group discussion, simulation, and prepared independent study modules.

Global objective number two (produce and repackage media to meet specific user demands) was designed to develop competencies which enabled students to produce and repackage information utilizing the characteristics of specific user groups and the knowledge of strengths and weaknesses of specific media and media-mixes. This content included the principles and practices of instructional design and communication theory and the means of translating these principles, practices, and theories into mediated instructional materials. Samples of performance objectives developed from global objective number two were:

1. Given a problem and the criteria for repackaging media, the student will devise three appropriate plans, choose one of the three, and develop the materials. Criterion: media produced evaluated against identified criteria.

2. The student will select one of the media listed and prepare an in-service experience for teachers. Each student must select a different category until all are taken. Criterion: student-teacher evaluation of videotaped in-service experience.

These objectives required the use of graphics and production laboratories, independent study space, demonstrations, and a variety of machines and materials. The micro-teaching (VTR) units were also utilized.

Global objective number three (contribute as a member of a teaching learning team) assembled content to help media specialists (1) diagnose needs (level, learning requirements, learning styles, appropriate media, etc.), (2) advise teachers regarding materials, (3) order materials, (4) make bibliographies, (5) set up displays, (6) produce and repackage materials with students and teachers, and (7) act as resource persons. Materials were also provided that assisted media specialists in helping teachers provide learning environments requiring a constant use of materials in the media center and in helping students utilize machines and materials. The major thrust in this content area was on interaction of the teacher and the media specialist as each contributes to the solution of a curriculum development and implementation problem. Examples of performance objectives for global objective number three were:

1. Given a unit of study and various materials describing display techniques, the student will arrange a learning environment appropriate to the topics. Criterion: subjective appraisal by peers.

2. Utilizing a specific field center, the student will attend and participate in a series of curriculum development meetings within the particular school. Criterion: interaction analysis based on checklist provided.

3. Working with a field center supervisor, the student will select a teacher in this school and develop an instructional package with the teacher and students concerned. Criterion: work judged against principles and practices of instructional technology which includes methodology for validation and revision.

These sample performance objectives utilized techniques mastered in courses developing competencies in instructional design. The objectives incorporated techniques of problem identification and resolution in the field center. The University tended to be the safe planning ground whereas the field centers were the testing sites.

In global objective number four (assist in curriculum planning) content was utilized to develop the various educational strategies necessary for well developed, multi-level curricula. Materials that explicated the technique and appropriate use of strategies such as interpersonal communications, inquiry, demonstrations, sensitivity training, questioning techniques, and case studies were collected. Since the appropriateness of media is dependent upon the strategy employed as well as the content and level of the learner, the content developed skills in matching modes of inquiry to instructional purposes. Materials also focused on the process of curriculum development, including how to (1) specify entry behavior, (2) formulate operational or performance objectives, (3) test for objectives, (4) use media in conjunction with individual and group activities as a means of obtaining performance objectives, and (5) evaluate the instructional system employed. Objective number four concentrated on modes of inquiry whereas the preceding global objective concentrated on more disciplined approaches to instructional design. The two global objectives could easily merge. Sample performance objectives for global objective number four were:

1. Given a content outline and a general description of desired learning outcomes, the student will suggest appropriate learning strategies (e.g., small-group problem solving, research and reporting, inductive inquiry, etc.). Criterion: work judged against model descriptions.

2. Given a series of uses of the media center for various disciplines, the student will draft a plan

to develop activities related to these disciplines that comprise the curriculum of the field center school. The plan will be presented before a simulated curriculum planning committee of the student's peers. Criterion: self-peer and faculty evaluation of presentation.

Materials and general modes of inquiry were considered as each related to the other. Seminar and previewing space as well as materials gathered from the field centers were used extensively in the realization of these objectives.

The content concentration of global objective number five (guide students in forming appropriate study habits) provided information that assisted media specialists as they attempted to improve students' listening, viewing, and reading skills. Sample performance objectives were:

1. After reading materials identified, the student will prepare a list of ways he can assist learners in forming appropriate study habits. Criterion: group discussion and consensus.
2. The student will prepare a display or bulletin board of appropriate study habits and materials for a specific field center. Criterion: field supervisor, peer, and University faculty evaluation.
3. After identifying a field-center pupil who needs help in one of the skill areas listed, the university student will formulate a plan and work with the pupil for a two-week period in order to help him overcome his weakness. Criterion: achievement of a target identified by university student and a pupil.

The general emphasis of this global objective was to provide the information to university students so they could move into field centers and work with pupils on the improvement of study habits.

Global objective number six (design, implement, and evaluate systems for media storage and retrieval) drew upon content that developed an understanding and proficiency in classification systems for all media. Classification systems, subject headings, descriptive cataloging, card cataloging, and shelf listings were utilized in relation to a total system for media storage and retrieval appropriate for a specific educational program. Examples of performance objectives in this area were:

1. The student will demonstrate a knowledge and comprehension of the principles and practices of selected classification systems. Criterion: objective measure.
2. The student will classify a sample collection of media according to the Dewey Decimal System. Criterion: check against model.
3. The student will prepare an index for the sample collection. Criterion: check against model.
4. The student will establish policies and procedures for circulation in a given field center. Criterion: subjective appraisal of prepared policy manual by student-faculty group.
5. The student will establish and execute a plan for user orientation in a field center. Criterion: subjective appraisal of a plan by student, faculty, user group.

As in other global objectives, objective number six tended to be developed in a theoretical sense at the University with competencies being applied to an actual field center. These kinds of activities demanded a close working relationship between the faculty and students of the field center and the faculty and students of the University.

Global objective number seven (apply physical, mental, emotional, and social processes as they relate to learning in the media program) was formulated to develop content that related to (1) readiness, (2) entry behavior, (3) learning styles, (4) encoding, (5) decoding, (6) learning conditions, (7) motivation, (8) pacing, (9) reinforcement, (10) retention, (11) sequencing, (12) evaluation, (13) presentation forms, and (14) media-mixes. Typical performance objectives for global objective number seven were:

1. Given the reading assignment, the student will list three principles of best practice for readiness, pacing, reinforcement, and retention. Criterion: student-teacher evaluation of accuracy of interpretation.
2. Given clinical knowledge about attitudinal and emotional states (fear, anger, love, joy, as well as compensation, sublimation, compulsion, etc.), the student will list how these states may influence the use and/or design of media. Criterion: objective measure.
3. Given the unique characteristics of social-philosophical populations (Mexican-Thomist, Negro-Idealist, working white-realist, etc.), the student will list ways the social-philosophical background may influence the rejection or acceptance of specified school activities. Criterion: objective measure.

Sensitizing students to and accounting for the many variables that can impinge upon educational programs tended to be centered at the University. Lectures, films, and discussions aided students in understanding the complexity of the total educational endeavor. Emphasis was on the need for working with children through applying principles developed. Information gained from this global objective emerged in the discussions of activities throughout the students' participation in the experimental program. The faculty perceived that these discussions tended to be more knowledgeable and objective and less dogmatic than discussions prior to the students exposure to the content of objective number seven.

Global objective number eight (determine and implement purposes, functions, and components of the library media center necessary to support the total school program) drew heavily from content of general systems theory. Consequently, the content assembled was concerned with a systems approach to management and administration which included the formulation and implementation of a system for identifying purposes, functions, and components of the media program necessary to support a school program. These materials developed evaluation criteria and techniques for applying minimal standards of achievement to the criteria identified. Information relating to functions such as management and administration, design, information, and consultative were collected as each function cut across typical operations—collections development, technical processing, utilization, maintenance, etc. Sample performance objectives for global objective number eight:

1. Given a series of matrices with functions identified on another, list interfacings that you can identify and feel are important. Criterion: active participation in a small group discussion.
2. Given a slide-tape presentation on best educational practice and technological responsibility as each relates to the management function, the student will identify and list principles of best educational practice and indicators of technological responsibility for each operation identified. Criterion: student-teacher evaluation of completeness and appropriateness.
3. Given a specific field center and its operational manual, the student will make a functional and component analysis of that center. Criterion: work judged against accuracy of following identified procedures.

Students were introduced to matrices as a method for accounting for the needed functions and operations of media and educational programs and flow charting for the purpose of short- and long-range planning of media programs. Several schools where students worked were in the planning stages of development which afforded a unique experience for these students. In other words, students and faculty of the Auburn program helped some schools develop the basic concept of a media program that later materialized.

Global objective number nine (interpret the media program as it relates to the school and community) centers around the public information function of the media program. Methods for informing the community of the function of the media program as it operates within the school program were assembled. Methodologies for stimulating community interests and understanding were collected. Sample performance objectives included:

1. Given a field center, the student will plan several activities designed to acquaint the community with the media porgram. After consultation with faculty, the student will select and implement one design. Criterion: appraisal of the activity against stated objectives by the student, field center supervisor, and community participants.
2. Given the standard operational procedure for a particular field center, the student will prepare a 15 minute slide-tape presentation outlining what the media center can do for the education program, the student, and the community. Criterion: appraisal of presentation against student stated objectives.

Eliciting school and community support for the media program was a problem in many of the field centers working with the Auburn program. Students organized in-service programs for community people and faculty members on the use and value of media programs and conducted open house activities for the community, students, and faculty in several field centers.

Global objective number ten (express a commitment to continued professional growth) assembled content that developed factors which contributed to the formulation of a positive philosophy of self as well as a philosophy for the media center. Five areas were developed: (1) an understanding of the necessity for adaptation to change, (2) a belief in the necessity for respect of the individual, (3) a commitment to a humane and open society, (4) an understanding of the issues of the professions, and (5) an examination and re-examination of professional goals. Professionalism incorporated a detailed study of appropriate codes of ethics which included ethical practice in the use of media. Materials considering professional responsibilities were collected. Sample performance objectives for global objective number ten were:

1. Given a film, a case study, and a required reading list, the student will identify, list, and explain ten issues related to the media professions. Criterion: Student-teacher evaluation of work accomplished.
2. Given an agenda of professional meetings in the State, the student will attend one each quarter and submit a summary of the issues and actions taken. Criterion: subjective evaluation of the substance and effect of the report by students and faculty.

The use of many events seemed to be the most viable strategy for developing global objective number ten. Students engaged in events such as the Alabama Instructional Media Association workshops, meetings, and conventions. Some attended meetings of the American Library Association and reported back the concerns and issues as well as insights into new technologies that they found at the national conferences. In other words, many of the valued learning outcomes provided by the Auburn program were not structured in terms of tight performance objectives but rather were experiences that were required of students in the form of events.

Global objective number eleven (conduct workshops, in-service instruction, discussions, demonstrations, and other activities that assist users to better utilize the school media center) collected materials that developed techniques suggested for in-service education including working with individuals, small groups, and large groups. The system utilized for the development of in-service instruction and workshops consisted of the preparation of objectives, the translation of objectives into viable systems of in-service education, and follow up and evaluation of the effectiveness of the experience. Sample performance objectives were:

1. Given the videotaping equipment of a particular field center, the student will provide a training session for students and teachers of that field center in order to orient them to the use of this equipment. Criterion: in-service instruction will result in a 25% increase in VTR utilization by staff and students of the field center.
2. Given the materials preparation equipment for a particular field center, the student will design and implement an in-service education program for students and teachers of a particular field center for the purpose of increasing student and teacher preparation of media. Criterion: a demonstrated increase of 25% in the utilization of materials preparation equipment.

3. After completing the reading assignment, develop a list of principles to be utilized in the design and evaluation of in-service programs. Criterion: participation in a small-group discussion evaluated by students and faculty members.

Involvement of students in planning and conducting workshops, in-service instruction, demonstrations, and other activities in field centers was considerable. Sometimes students organized groups within the field center to conduct their own in-service, other times students worked individually in a particular field center, and still other times groups of University students conducted in-service activities in the field.

Global objective number twelve (evaluate and encourage promising innovative practices as they relate to the media program) was based upon content relating to change strategies and the role of the change agent. Sample performance objectives included:

1. Using the resources listed, the student will identify ten critical incidents which result in the acceptance or rejection of an innovation. Criterion: approval of instructor.
2. Using the materials listed, the student will identify seven characteristics of a successful change agent. Criterion: successful completion of task as evaluated by instructor.
3. Given a list and a description of ten innovations, the student will pick five and discuss them in terms of how they might move forward principles of best educational practice. Criterion: principles identified evaluated against criteria for best educational practice.

Strategies which tended to be University-based frequently were associated with independent study units produced for the development of concepts of change and change theory. Students read extensively from the bibliographies provided for this global objective.

Global objective number thirteen (develop and implement methods for utilizing community resources in the school media program) collected information to develop ways and means of accessing informational resources outside the school media program. Content included (1) identification of resources, (2) rationale for developing and utilizing community resources, (3) basic principles in using community resources, and (4) formulation of criteria for selecting community resources. In addition, techniques were developed for outlining procedures utilized in field trips and community experiences by students. Sample performance objectives were:

1. The student will design a plan for identifying resources available in the community of a particular field center. Criterion: plan checked against a model.
2. Using an approved plan, the student will make a survey and prepare findings and procedures for utilizing community resources. Criterion: appraisal by administrators of field center.

Most experiences of students as they related to acquiring community resources for the school media program were developed in the field. Numerous resource guides, procedures, and manuals were produced by students during the two years of the experimental program.

Over fifty learning modules were produced by faculty and students to develop the global objectives indicated. These modules were sometimes prescriptive and sometimes elective. Each module consisted of an identification and description of the global objective, a specification of performance objectives, a description of the terminal behavior required, and a strategy for gaining the terminal behavior identified. These modules were printed in groups relating to each of thirteen global objectives. For example, global objective number one (select teaching and learning materials) has five modules developed by staff and students and utilized in students' programs. The learning modules were printed and kept in file cabinets so they could be selected by students and staff as they moved through various experiences provided in the program—formal course work, fieldwork, and the participation in events. Students were encouraged to design their own modules and to redesign existing modules to fit the specific learning purposes of the student. In other words, the aggregate of modules served as a resource which provided alternative

ways to learn needed competencies identified by the student during his quarterly conferences with faculty. The control, direction, and redirection of a particular student's program formally resided with the two quarterly conferences each student had with two or more faculty in the program. Informal conferences were scheduled throughout the student's program as needed.

Approximately eight of the students enrolled in the experimental program at Auburn were practitioners in field centers. These individuals, as well as many other students, had considerable experience and formal preparation in librarianship. Consequently, a dramatic difference in individual programs existed. Students with extensive experience worked with problems such as the design and evaluation of media programs in field centers. Other students' programs were filled with basic skills development in organization and administration, production and utilization of media, reference, cataloging, instructional design, etc. Global objectives that were the most prescriptive related to principles and practices of instructional design because few students possessed experience in that area. Students and faculty saw the instructional design process as a positive point of entry of the media specialist into the curriculum design and development process. During one student's oral examination these remarks were recorded:

Teaching (University) students principles and practices of instructional design and affording the opportunity for students to develop and field test modules is "where it's at." If a media specialist can do this, he will be involved in curriculum development, he will become involved with helping students and working with teachers.

# Program Participants

During the first year of the experimental program, participating field centers in schools surrounding Auburn University were required to have a professional from the field center enrolled in the program before Auburn would formally assign students to that center. These professionals were designated as field center participants. Two general purposes existed for this configuration. First, schools interested enough to encourage professionals within their schools to engage in graduate training were believed

to possess the kind of attitude toward media programs that would increase the probability of transforming traditional school libraries into media programs that would penetrate all aspects of the school program. Second, having professionals in the field centers enrolled in the experimental program facilitated the communication of program goals. The field center participants enrolled in the program, full- and part-time University students, and faculty of the University were considered as one operational group.

Field center participants enrolled full time for summer quarters and for six hours credit during the school year. Although three basic kinds of students existed—field center participants, part time and full time University students—the greater variance existed in the background of students rather than in their association with a field center or in their part-time or full-time status.

Two students in the experimental program were principals of elementary schools in Alabama, two students were supervisors of large district media programs, and at least twenty students were employed in schools with media programs over five years old. One student possessed a commercial art background, approximately eight students possessed academic baccalaureate degrees, six students had Master of Science degrees in Library Science. Approximately one third of the students had no library media experience and were attempting to earn a degree in Educational Media before they began practice. The planning session with the student and designated faculty was the most successful programming strategy employed to meet the various time constraints and backgrounds of the individual student.

Because of the variation in students and their requirements for field experience (e.g., some were already employed in junior colleges and wanted to focus on media services at that level) and also because of the impracticality of locating new field centers with professionals who would volunteer to enroll in the experimental program, the requirement that a field center had to have a professional in the program was dropped during the second year. The result was an increase in the number of field centers that were utilized for one or two activities and a decrease in the number of field centers that were continuously utilized. Many of the field centers initially identified were continued. However, the actual number of schools providing experiences for students expanded and fluctuated in number from quarter to quarter. Although not insurmountable, this did present some problems in the areas of geographical logistics and the need for stronger orientation for fieldwork supervisors who were not enrolled in the Auburn program.

At the beginning of each quarter each student conferred with two assigned faculty members to outline, discuss, and plan evaluation procedures for the quarter. During these hour planning sessions courses were discussed, the student's past performance was reviewed, quarter objectives were outlined, methodologies for monitoring the student (especially in the fieldwork) were agreed upon, and rationales were

agreed upon for both the staff and the student as they attempted to understand and build purpose into a specific student's program. Without exception, students and staff felt these planning sessions were one of the most valuable aspects of the experimental program. The second planning session that each student had each quarter was conducted near the end of the quarter to summarize problems and progress in order to ascertain if the student accomplished what he initially set out to do.

Since the majority of the course work was taken within the Department of Educational Media and since the total staff of the department was involved in the individualized student planning sessions, all aspects of the curriculum were modified during the planning sessions to fit a particular student's needs. For example, some students needed to review certain aspects of classification and cataloging. They enrolled in this course but took only those aspects they needed and built in other related experiences which were not normally associated with this course. Several other students who had a great deal of experience in the administration of media centers enrolled for courses in administration and management but were assigned the preparation of modules or already prepared modules that developed specific competencies identified beyond what might be considered basic to this area. For example, one student with an extensive background, both academically and in terms of practical experience, was assigned the task of organizing all in-service instruction for a particular school during the 1971-1972 academic year. This field center participant, during full-time work in the summer of 1971, planned a series of in-service activities to take place the following year with the help of students who would be assigned to that center. The field center participant earned six hours of University credit each quarter during that academic year for planning, supervising, and evaluating many kinds of in-service activities conducted in the field center school. In this case, faculty from the University, full- and part-time students from the University, and the field center participant managed to bring the media program into a leadership position in that particular school.

## COMMUNICATION OF PROGRAM GOALS

As far as the students and faculty were concerned, individual conferences were the best device for clarifying, modifying, adding, and eliminating objectives for any particular student. Global objectives were available to all students. During student-faculty conferences activities were assessed as they contributed to the thirteen global objectives. In other words, in order to maintain some balance in an individual's program, experiences were compared with the thirteen global objectives to avoid omitting important aspects or overemphasizing other aspects of an individual's program. All course work, modules, events, and fieldwork were classified according to the objectives they supported. Many activities in the field related to several global objectives. For example, two students organized and classified a record collection in a junior high school and planned and conducted in-service meetings to promote the utilization of this collection. During this process these students identified strengths and weaknesses in the collection as it related to the particular junior high school program. Thus they were involved with some aspects of global objective number one (selecting teaching and learning materials). The records had to be packaged in such a way that they could be utilized by the student and teacher population of the school, which related to aspects of global objective number two (producing and repackaging media to meet specific user demands). The primary thrust of the activity related to global objectives number six (designing, implementing, and evaluating systems for media storage and retrieval) and number eleven (conducting workshops, in-service instruction, discussions, demonstrations, and other activities that assisted users in utilizing the school library media center more effectively). The way each activity related both primarily and secondarily to the global objectives frequently occupied a significant portion of the time during student-teacher planning and evaluation conferences.

Short- and long-range performance objectives were written down for field experiences in the folders maintained for each student in the program. Each field-centered activity module listed the primary Auburn faculty consultant, the field center, the student, the date the activity was approved, the starting date, and the expected date of completion. The student and staff, during individual conferences, formulated the problem, listed the global objectives that were to be achieved, and identified prerequisites in terms of reading, modules, or courses that should be taken at the same time the experience was approached. In addition, the student was expected to identify the content that related to this problem, formulate specific performance objectives that could be observed, work with the faculty consultant or with the members present during the planning periods in order to determine appropriate criterion measures, and outline specific strategies that were going to be utilized in the field activity. Evaluation conferences between students and faculty held at the end of the quarter generally centered around an analysis of achievement and a consideration of how the activity could be modified if other students were to engage in a similar activity. The field-centered module form is shown in Appendix A.

Communication of program goals to the faculty of the School of Education, educational personnel in the state of Alabama, and individuals and groups across the nation took the form of formal presentations, literature printed and available upon request, and visitations to Auburn by various interested groups. A slide-tape presentation depicting the experimental program was made and available upon request and two informational programs were carried by the local educational television station. Presentations were made at national conferences as well as state and local conferences, workshops, and meetings. Two articles were published in national journals and several others in local association publications.

## STUDENT ADMISSION CRITERIA AND SCHOLARSHIP PROGRAM

As mentioned earlier, a formula utilizing the student's last 100 hours of academic work, scores on the Graduate Record Examination, and the advanced test in education were utilized for initial screening. If, by formula, the student scored 500 or more, he was asked for a personal interview in order to assess his transcripts and to determine if he needed qualifying work. The department requested at least twelve quarter hours in educational media prior to full admission. In some instances, extensive experience was considered in lieu of formal course work. In all cases the students enrolled in the program had a Bachelor's degree and in many cases had already earned a Master's degree in a different area.

Six one-third time graduate assistantships were awarded at the beginning of each academic year. Six one-third time assistantships were also awarded separately for the summer quarter. In order to be eligible for a graduate assistantship in the department, students had to be fully admitted to a graduate degree program at Auburn University. The work-study program afforded financial assistance for graduate students who could qualify. Scholarships per se were not available.

## STAFF DEVELOPMENT AND ROLE OF INTER-DISCIPLINARY PERSONNEL

The Department of Educational Media employed twenty-seven staff members during the 1971-1973 period. Sixteen staff members were directly involved with the experimental program. The Auburn program made use of work-study students, clerks, secretaries, technicians, graduate student assistants, graphic artists, media specialists and University professors. The staff believed that each member of the Department of Educational Media, as well as the different members of the staffs of field centers, could contribute to the educational program in at least two ways. First, specialists such as graphic artists and technicians could assist students and faculty in the production of materials and could help them keep equipment in good working order. Secondly, the staff believed students working with all kinds of personnel tended to develop an appreciation for their contribution and consequently would have a better perception of how these personnel could be utilized and managed when the students graduated and became employed. Often work-study students could be observed teaching a student how to operate a VTR unit or how to change a bulb in a particular projector or where to locate materials in the Learning Resources Center. The duplicating clerk provided information about the potential uses of various reproduction processes in the Learning Resources Center. Graduate assistants worked in field centers and conducted small group workshops, seminars, and laboratories. The autotutorial laboratory for materials production and machine operation was exclusively managed by graduate student assistants. Media specialists from participating field centers took time to teach students operations that were unique to their particular programs. Students worked with graphic artists to solve design problems; with photographers to make and develop pictures; with technicians to make minor repairs and to become familiar with general maintenance needs; with work-study students to schedule, deliver, and set up equipment; and with graduate teaching assistants to work with faculty on special projects, materials preparation, and many other kinds of learning activities.

The staff of the Department of Educational Media was encouraged to participate in professional organizations locally and nationally. Part of their voluntarily in-service development occurred as staff members monitored each other's courses. When student conferences were organized, care was taken that a balance in competencies existed in the staff members present. The perceptions and insights presented by staff members representing different backgrounds resulted in an increased sensitivity to the total field of media.

Consultants were invited to help the staff and students better understand *Standards for School Media Programs* and media programming to meet the individual needs of students. Resource persons within the area were invited to contribute to class projects and events. For example, one class invited a couple who possessed extraordinary expertise in puppetry to make a presentation to students enrolled in the Media for Children course. In another instance, a commercial distributor was invited to display materials and to explain their unique place in the school curriculum. In still another instance, a commercial distributor conducted a workshop on the repair and maintenance of learning resources.

Staff growth and development were identified as major program objectives. As in all experimental programs, the staff learned along with the students. Each faculty member was afforded opportunities for professional interaction at local, state, and national levels. The Staff was provided financial support and time allocations to attend workshops, conferences, and to visit exemplary programs. Recommended materials were also purchased for staff development. The close working relationship between the staff and field centers kept the staff in constant contact with the realities of the field. This contact provided information that assisted in the professional growth and development of the staff.

## ADVISORY BOARD

The Advisory Board of the experimental program was composed of educational leaders from the State of Alabama. They represented the school and public library fields and included (1) a school superintendent, (2) a supervisor from Alabama Public Library Service, (3) a classroom teacher, (4) a State Department of Education school library supervisor, (5) an instructor from a technical school, (6) a University professor from the Department of Elementary Education, and (7) a student from Auburn University's experimental program who was appointed by the program faculty.

The principal responsibilities of the Advisory Board were (1) to formulate policies, (2) to set priorities, (3) to assist the research and evaluation process, (4) to serve as an editorial board for publicational and news releases, and (5) to serve as a liaison between the program and the greater community.

Ten selected activities of the Advisory Board during the two years of the experimental program serve as an example of work performed by this body. The Advisory Board initiated and/or supported the following activities:

1. Advocated that information about the experimental program should be disseminated at state

and national meetings and approved the literature to be disseminated.

2. Suggested and approved ways and means of communicating the role of the media specialist in individualized instructional programs to local school administrators.

3. Received reports and modules as they were produced and suggested modifications for improvement.

4. Supported the move through verbal communication to the Department of Education for granting a teacher unit to the media specialist in the State of Alabama (needed to secure State monies).

5. Suggested consultants for the experimental program.

6. Invited students to discuss the experimental program with the Advisory Board.

7. Participated in the evaluation of the School Library Manpower Project's 1973 publication, *Behavioral Requirements Analysis Checklist* (BRAC).

8. Approved and made recommendations for the comprehensive examination of program graduates.

9. Approved the production of a presentation made to the faculty of the School of Education about the experimental program. This presentation was later utilized at the national conferences of the American Library Association and the Association for Educational Communications and Technology.

10. Invited a representative from the Millersville (Pennsylvania) State College experimental program to gain insight into ways the Auburn experimental program could be improved.

# Program Components

Each student's program, as well as most of his individual experiences, all modules, and much course work, contained a general structural organization. In both total program planning for specific activities, entering capabilities were assessed (examinations, records inspection, interview, self-assessment), objectives were identified, strategies for achievement were formulated, and monitoring and evaluation procedures were agreed upon. Some parts of this structure were tightly controlled (e.g., field-tested modules) while other activities dramatically changed the structure as work progressed (e.g., fieldwork). Admission to the graduate program for the preparation of media specialists was rigidly adhered to in all except one case. The exception was an individual already possessing a Master's degree, thereby having demonstrated his capacity for graduate work. A special request was submitted to the graduate school, and this student was admitted to the program. The comprehensive exam taken after admission to the program was also a formal way of assessing knowledge, comprehension, and skills in order to identify strengths and weaknesses in a student's background for the purpose of program planning. In experiences designed for an individual student (e.g., field project, event) the assessment of entering capabilities might simply have taken the form of a discussion between the faculty and the student. In field experiences designed specifically for the student, objectives were formulated but modified as the realities of the field came into focus. For example, three students were to produce a videotaped program for one field center to use on closed circuit television. After looking at the needs and the capabilities within that field center, students, staff, and field center administrators decided to develop a plan for producing a number of programs during the following academic year rather than to produce one program. The activity shifted from producing and packaging a program to an exercise in planning. None of the students involved had planned an educational television program but each had used VTR units. Consequently, the experience turned out to be one that was more appropriate than the experience initially conceived.

The general process outlined applied to program planning as well as individual exercises. Activities were grouped into three generic categories—course work, fieldwork, and participation in events. Modules were utilized to some extent in all three experiences.

## COURSE WORK

All courses of the Department of Educational Media changed during the time of the experimental program. Traditional course work was, to a large degree, supplemented or replaced with such activities as programmed instruction (Classification and Cataloging), elective and required individualized learning modules (Learning Resources), fieldwork (Problems in the Administration of Media Services, Media Services in School and Community, Studies in Education, and Evaluation of Media Programs), and events (especially Media for Children, Media for Young Adults, and Practicum). Students in the program for the preparation of media specialists spent an average of thirty-two quarter hours in media. The department has less control of requirements made by the School of Education which are (1) eight hours in administration and supervision courses taught in the Department of Educational Administration, and (2) a minimum of eight quarter hours from the Department of Foundations in Education including a basic graduate course in educational research. The University stipulates that at least fifty percent of the course work toward the Master's degree be on the 600 level (graduate students only). Certification of media specialists in Alabama includes 400 level (upperdivision and graduate) courses in Learning Resources, Media for Children, Media for Young Adults, Reference Materials and Services, Organization and Administration, Classification and Cataloging, and Practicum in addition to the Master's degree in media from a state approved program of study. The Practicum carries variable credit from one to ten hours and is used in a variety of ways. The first time a student enrolls for Practicum he works in the Learning Resources Center, training in a number of specific operations. After the basic Practicum has been taken the student may enroll for Practicum again and work in a field center, in the University library, or in junior college libraries in the State of Alabama. A student having considerable practical experience may be excused from the basic Practicum and proceed directly to more advanced work. Course work in the Department of Educational Media on the 600 level includes Technology in Education, Modes of Mediated Instruction, Principles of Media Services, Problems in the Administration of Media Services (F), Information Resources in the School and Community (F), Individual Studies (F), Seminar, Research in Media, Evaluation of Media Programs (F), Field Project, and Thesis. Courses designated as (F) are field-centered, i.e., the content is individually designed and monitored by three members of the faculty and focuses upon experience in one or more field centers at a variety of school and academic levels.

Some concern was expressed that the structure of the curriculum might result in some students graduating without needed competencies. When student folders were examined, basic areas seemed to be missing from many students' programs. A more careful examination usually disclosed that the student in question had undergraduate work in librarianship or media and already had acquired needed competencies. The average student had at least twenty-eight quarter hours course work in media prior to entering the experimental program. Students without formal training and/or experience were the exception rather than the rule.

The students and faculty of the program were quick to realize that what courses purported to teach and what students could do were two different things. The students continually reminded the staff that they didn't feel confident in processing materials until they worked in the Practicum, that they didn't know how to conduct a film festival until they managed one at a field center, that they didn't fully understand how to apply principles of instructional design until they began working with teachers on design problems, and that they didn't appreciate the importance of media specialists becoming involved in the total instructional program until they worked in various centers and were able to see the benefit to the media program that involvement can produce.

## FIELDWORK

Although fieldwork could be introduced in conjunction with any course in the curriculum offered by the Department of Educational Media, it more familiarly was planned in conjunction with graduate courses already identified. During the first year the experimental program attempted to bring two faculty members together with each student for the initial planning conference and to schedule the same two faculty in the evaluation conference taking place at the end of the quarter. Although there were no particular objections to this plan, during the second year of the experimental program the design was altered. During the winter quarter of the second year it was decided that a faculty committee of three be established to serve on student-faculty planning conferences and that a chairman be assigned to serve two consecutive quarters in order to monitor the whole procedure. This procedure aided in reporting faculty load to the University. All faculty could be requested to serve in any particular student-faculty planning conference as well as in the evaluation conference at the end of the quarter. And, all faculty were available to students as they worked on field-centered activities. In other words, even though a given faculty member was not a member of the field committee for any particular quarter, he could have been asked to direct a specific field experience because of his expertise in that area. In addition, even though several members of the faculty might work with the student on a particular field problem, one faculty member was usually assigned and assumed the responsibility for coordination. The new design produced a better comprehension of all of the field experiences in which students were engaged. Before, it was necessary to review all student folders in order to ascertain the many kinds of field experiences that were going on in a particular quarter. After the change, the committee chairman maintained a composite of all field experiences. An example of the extensiveness of field experience is cited for the spring quarter of 1973. During that time fifteen students spent over 2,400 clock hours working on projects in the field.

Time constraints and the geographic location of field centers were lessened by the liberal use of the telephone. Students as well as staff were encouraged to call the department collect before they wrote or made a trip to Auburn. Many problems were resolved in this way in an efficient and effective manner. The time of student and staff was considered a resource too important to spend waiting in an office or behind the wheel of a car when a telephone call could provide the means for communicating.

Generally speaking, a procedure was followed during student-faculty planning conferences. Records were reviewed by the team before the conference. During the conference the student's experiences prior to entering the program as well as the experiences the student had during the program were discussed. Because of the close working relationship between graduate students and the staff, after the first quarter had passed, the student was known as an individual, and faculty could easily discuss the student's experiences, needs, and professional aspirations. During the student-faculty conferences students were encouraged to identify their own weaknesses and to specify experiences that they believed would build competencies they needed. Field centers were identified after an appropriate experience for a particular student was isolated. The student-faculty conference frequently identified independent study modules that the student needed to complete. If modules were unavailable for the development of the competency the student and faculty members felt important modules were designed immediately for the required experience.

One important spinoff from student-faculty conferences resulted in the formation of teams of students to approach problems. Many of the activities identified as essential involved several students. These students were then brought together and plans were

made for the execution of the activity identified. For example, the in-service program developed earlier in this report met the needs of many University students who needed experience in conducting in-service for teachers and students. Other activities were designed and executed by individuals. For instance, one student worked with a junior college mathematics teacher in redesigning a basic mathematics course. This activity incorporated a total look at the curriculum of the course, the production of behavioral objectives, the design and production of numerous visual aids, and the production of tests that were congruent with the course objectives.

Benefits to the field centers were communicated to the staff in the form of letters, visits to the department by field center personnel, and telephone conversations. One principal of a field center stated in a letter that "we could not have been ready to open the media center when school began this fall without the help of your students." A superintendent said that the graduate program in educational media "has at long last developed a relationship between the public schools and the University that truly benefits both concerned." The reason for this positive reaction from the field centers was believed to center around the policy (1) that students entered fieldwork in order to work on the solution to a problem that developed competencies needed by that student and (2) that the field center had the problem and both needed and wanted it resolved. Students were assigned to field centers when these two criteria were met.

## EVENTS

Although course work and fieldwork incorporated the use of teacher-made as well as student-made modules of instruction, the participation in events rarely included modular experiences. More typically, events included participation at professional meetings; attendance at lectures provided by visiting scholars; field trips; assistance at workshops; film festivals; materials displays; and informal social functions. The purpose of participation in events was to develop professionalism as well as esprit de corps.

At all stages of a student's development in the program, he was encouraged to contact faculty and other students for help and assistance. The faculty of the Department of Educational Media believed that working with people was an essential competency that both the faculty and students must encourage and develop. Because of the belief that an effective media specialist must have good working relations with his staff, the students, faculty, and administration of his school, a three-day workship in interpersonal communications was offered to program faculty and students at the beginning of each academic year. The workshop, designed by Northwest Regional Laboratories, was unanimously accepted by both students and faculty, and was the only tightly constructed experience (module) that was considered an event. This workshop was later modified in order to relate specifically to the role of the media specialist in elementary and secondary school programs.

Students frequently engaged in ten or more events during any one particular quarter. Each student was required to complete a form indicating the events in which he participated each quarter. During student-faculty planning conferences events were discussed and students were further encouraged to expand their participation. The final oral examination given to each student upon completion of the formal program of study indicated enthusiasm and complete cooperation of students in educational events. Negative reactions always centered around a particular experience, and students with such complaints quickly underscored the value of participation in events as a general thrust of the program.

An example of a report of an event by a student was the participation in a national conference in instructional technology held at Auburn. The student identified the activity and explained how he participated in the conference. He said, "I took an active part in small group discussions, in general sessions, and in discussions with individuals between sessions." When asked what he had learned, the student replied that he learned many perceptions professionals held concerning the field of instructional technology and shared in the excitement of seeing a newly emerging field being defined.

## PHILOSOPHY OF EVALUATION

From the beginning of the experimental program the Department of Educational Media would not allow evaluation procedures to restrict or predict the experiences that staff felt students ought to be engaged in. In other words, even though many events and other activities were not assessed in any formal sense, this lack of assessment did not suggest to the staff that the activity was inappropriate. The program was determined that any kind of evaluation must go beyond the content students managed to assimilate. Perhaps the most beneficial of all evaluation procedures was the close working relationship that existed between staff and students. The faculty observed that prior to the initiation of this program

they frequently struggled to write something substantial on a letter of recommendation. The staff further commented on how well they knew the recent graduates' philosophies, capabilities, particular strengths and weaknesses and how much easier and confidently they could recommend a particular student for a specific job. This does not mean to say that the many and varied evaluation procedures did not contribute to the understanding of students in the program. This posture resulted in a faculty that was as concerned with how students learn as well as what they learn. Students frequently expressed that they would turn to the Department of Educational Media for help after they entered the field to resolve problems that they felt were beyond their comprehension or ability. The purpose, then, of evaluation in this program was to gain as much insight as possible into the individual student in order to better direct his learning activities.

## ASSESSMENT OF STUDENT COMPETENCIES

Because faculty and students worked together virtually every step of the way, the assessment of learning activities was a continual process. Terminal activities required by field-centered modules were indicated by criterion measures determined with the assistance of the faculty team. In the case of field-centered modules, two or more encounters with the field situation were sometimes needed before criterion measures were refined and verified. On-going assessment of learning activities and student progress during field activities was made through the use of audit reports. These reports were required at two week intervals and were always available for student-faculty conferences. Audit reports, as shown in Appendix B, contained the following requests for information.

1. A description of the objectives toward which the student is working.
2. A list of the activities, contacts with persons and contacts with materials in which the student has been involved in relation to the student's objectives.
3. A description of new insights, meaningful experiences and any problems concerning the student's work toward objectives.
4. A description of ways by which faculty members may assist the student in achieving objectives.

Assessment of student competencies was considered under two general categories—formative and summative evaluation. Audit reports of field experiences tended to be formative whereas criterion measures, written examinations, and student-faculty conferences at the end of the quarter tended to be summative in nature. The principal strength of the audit report was to formalize a procedure and time when the student had to report about what he was doing and to make a contact with the faculty member supervising the field activity. Some students complained that filling out audit reports tended to be a nuisance and time consuming. Yet, these same students agreed that thinking out procedures saved them from proceeding in unproductive directions as well as clarifying the tasks in which they were engaged. For example, one student had as his objective for a field experience to explore and learn the potentials and limitations of videotaping equipment in a school situation. The periodic audit reports and conferences initiated by the student with individual faculty members kept the student in contact with the faculty directing and redirecting his progress during this investigation. The audit reports for this project reflected the kind of equipment that the student utilized, the schools that he worked in, and the contacts with people that he made. In this case, the student worked with over eleven teachers, media specialists, and principals in order to discuss ways VTR units were used as well as ways that these personnel would like to use videotaping equipment. Contacts were made in three different school settings. After the student experimented extensively with the equipment at the University, assessed the kinds of projects that the field schools were anxious for him to investigate, and formulated a plan for videotaping activities within the school, the student proceeded to work on a number of projects in the field. This student's audit reports reflected problems that he encountered as he progressed with this activity as well as ways and means for resolving the problems identified. In addition, the audit reports reflected the reading and research that the student had done as well as the specific videotaping sessions he conducted.

The audit reports were reviewed by the faculty members who attended the student-faculty conferences at the end of each quarter. The student-faculty conferences conducted for field experiences at the end of each quarter tended to be summative in nature. Generally speaking, faculty members requested the student to summarize the activity in his own words, outlining some of his successes and some of his problems. Specific items (reported directly to faculty members, reflected in the audit reports, or in written materials that the student presented) were frequently discussed in detail. Questions from the faculty asking the student to recall something that he had read, to describe a procedure, or to summarize an event tended to verify the student's activity as well as provide an opportunity for the student to summarize, synthesize, and evaluate his field experiences.

Many kinds of summative evaluations were found in the fieldwork, class work, independent learning modules and events. The evaluation of class work within the Department of Educational Media took the form of validated criterion measures in some instances and of presentation of projects in other cases. Course work in Learning Resources and Media for Children and Young Adults tended to be project oriented. Course work in Classification and Cataloging, Cybernetic Principles of Learning Systems, and Technology in Education utilized criterion measures.

Three faculty and two students were trained in CIPP (Context, Input, Process, Product) evaluation techniques in workshops developed and implemented by the Evaluation Center of the Ohio State University. Originally, the staff believed that the model might serve as an organizational frame for the department to evaluate its program. A consultant from the Ohio State University came to Auburn to explore this possibility. There were two reasons for not continuing this plan. First, the faculty argued that any evaluation must take into consideration each student's individual objectives, his program for achieving these objectives, and his entering competencies. The CIPP model did not seem to have the potential to evaluate each student independently. More confidence was expressed in the use of the School Library Manpower Project's publication, *Behavioral Requirements Analysis Checklist* (BRAC). Second, the CIPP model began to provide processes that were being utilized to teach students how to conduct a needs assessment of a specific educational program. All faculty in the Department of Educational Media concluded that the CIPP model was better used in this way, at least for the time being.

Many kinds of assessment techniques were utilized in the independent study learning modules constructed by the staff. Examples of some of these techniques follow to demonstrate their application within specific global objectives. For example, under global objective number one (select teaching and learning materials) one of the modules introduced the student to the variety of information resources available. In this sample module all performance objectives were evaluated during student-faculty conferences. During these conferences the student and faculty member arrived at one of four conclusions (1) objective was not completed, grade incomplete,

(2) objective was completed in a satisfactory manner, grade C, (3) objective was completed in a good manner, grade B, and (4) objective was completed in an exceptional manner, grade A. Another module developed for global objective number one assessed the quality of interaction among students as related to specific research questions. This module had as its objective the matching of information resources to specific student populations. For example, in the first performance objective outlined, the student was asked to clarify and develop five concepts orally for student and faculty groups (1) the nature of learning, (2) education as a fixed curriculum, (3) the nature of instruction, (4) the purpose of validation, and (5) principles of instructional technology. The quality of the contribution each student made was determined by his peers based upon questions posed in the module. The evaluation was formulated on such points as:

1. Did he provide new information?
2. Did he examine information from a new viewpoint?
3. Did he clarify ideas through review of the logic involved.
4. Did he offer appropriate examples to illustrate topics under discussion?
5. Did he ask questions on assumptions which discussion members held to help focus the discussion?

For global objective number two (produce and repackage media to meet specific user demands) a number of modules were prepared by the staff. A module on graphic and audio production illustrated a different dimension to the evaluation of students in the program. This module incorporated a self-instructional package for the machine operation necessary in the production and display of materials. In this module all operations were checked out by graduate assistants after the student performed the task. A sample criterion was the production of a color lift transparency. Another criterion was to properly set up and operate a piece of communications equipment.

Assessment techniques can also be illustrated from the criterion measures developed for global objective number four (assist in curriculum planning). One of the modules developed for this global objective utilized a field-tested criterion measure assessing the student's comprehension of the cognitive domain. A sample criterion item was:

Putting together elements and parts so as to form a whole is identified as

_____A. Knowledge  _____D. Analysis
_____B. Comprehension  _____E. Synthesis
_____C. Application  _____F. Evaluation

The directions of another part of this same criterion measure illustrate a second technique used in this module. Given an educational objective the student was directed to classify the objective according to categories in the cognitive domain—knowledge, comprehension, application, analysis, synthesis, or evaluation. In addition, the student was to determine if the objective was stated in behavioral terms and if the conditions and a standard of performance were indicated.

In another module developed for global objective number four the student was given reprints of articles that developed perceptions for the participation of media specialists in curriculum planning and development teams. The criterion for this module took the form of a written analysis of the articles reviewed.

Another technique was utilized in modules developed for global objective number twelve (evaluate and encourage promising innovative practices as they relate to the media program). One of the modules for global objective number twelve exposed the student to a large number of terms that he needed to know— continuous progress, DATRIX, ERIC, IGE, IPI, learning contract, MARC tapes, NICEM, PI, PLAN, PLATO. In order to familiarize himself with the acronyms and other terms introduced in this module, the student was asked to complete a series of charts in order to identify information sources about each of the terms identified, to give a description of the term, and to state the implications for the media center. Another module developing global objective number twelve exposed the student to the vast amount of literature on innovation and change. The student was provided with note cards bearing the bibliographic entry of a book or article as well as where it was located. The student read many of these resources, made copies of reviews and attached them to the cards, and engaged in a number of discussions with fellow students and faculty about the concepts represented in the readings. Many students worked on and discussed this module for more than a year. Because of the quality and high interest of the materials represented and because of the open-endedness of the module itself, students reacted favorably to this particular design. The retention of information was disclosed in final oral examinations when students continually referred to those materials that they were introduced to in this module.

Evaluation procedures for events were least well defined. The exception to this was the interpersonal communications experience designed by Northwest Regional Laboratories. Even though this was generally classified by the program as an event, it could also be considered a group module. Events such as film festivals and the attendance at conferences sometimes were accompanied by checklists that reflected judgments. Conversations during conferences, student discussions, and oral examinations reflected many benefits that students realized from attending events.

The final examination a student underwent was the oral comprehensive examination taken the last quarter of his program. Examination schedules were set up, students were notified, and participants in the examination were identified. Each student was examined by at least two faculty members of the Department of Educational Media. Before the examination each student's folder containing all of the completed modules, field experiences, courses, and events were studied by the faculty participants. Cassette tapes were made of each comprehensive examination. Through a faculty review of these tapes, strengths and weaknesses in the program were identified and made available to the faculty in order to

improve the program in the future. For example, several students complained that their experience in instructional design was not what it could be. Upon examination of these students as well as questioning others, the faculty found that the instructional design sequence required students to complete forty hours of programmed instruction independently in the carrels in the Learning Resources Center. The students found this to be time consuming and boring. On the basis of this student feedback the sequence changed so that the students viewed the program materials in groups with a faculty member present who introduced enrichment material and discussed the content. The following quarter this new approach was enthusiastically supported by students.

Assessment techniques took many forms. The audit report used to track and monitor field experiences was considered to be formative in nature. The comprehensive examination taken at the end of the first quarter was diagnostic. Class work and modules reflected a wide variety of assessment techniques including validated criterion measures, structured group encounters, projects, observed performance of a task, and research and reporting. The final oral examination concentrated on questions that would cause the student to synthesize his experience in the program.

# Program Results

The thirteen global objectives represented problem areas which, in a sense, associated this competency-based approach with a problem-centered approach. In any case, the content was treated in terms of what the student needed to know in order to prepare himself to solve a particular problem or to play a particular professional role. Specified content areas rarely constituted an appropriate organizational pattern for competency-based curricula emphasizing the identification and resolution of problems in field centers. In other words, what the student knew and how he approached the resolution of a problem in the field center seemed to be two different skills. The focus of the Auburn experimental program was to integrate a program of field experiences with other activities in order to develop both skills.

In regard to content, much of the time of the students and faculty during curriculum planning sessions was spent in adjusting content that would facili-

tate performance. Faculty members frequently defended specific content as well as the sequencing of content that seemed to be eroding as the actualities of the field became evident. In other areas, the faculty and students working in the field found knowledge and skills that were not clearly defined in the experimental program that were needed by field practitioners.

## PROGRAM MODIFICATION

Identification of and agreement on purpose were the most powerful tools for restructuring experiences and priorities. Although philosophical discussions were numerous, they rarely resolved the specific issues. For example, a continuing dialogue existed that revolved around whether or not best practice related to learning principles at the University and then applying the principles in practice or whether best practice related to first providing field experience that would vest the principles with meaning when they were developed at the University. This kind of discussion frequently grew from a faculty member's belief that a particular course or module was prerequisite to a given field experience. When problems of this nature occurred, every effort was made to identify the purpose of the activity in order to reorder priorities, change sequencing, and match staff with the problem and the students engaged in the problem resolution. In one such case, the contention was that two students needed to complete a structured exercise on scripting and story-boarding before putting a slide tape presentation together. Because of time and other logistics involved it was impossible for these two students to do one experience and then another. As a result, the students were allowed to engage in the theoretical at the same time they were developing the presentation. In another case, some faculty believed that two students working on an in-service program in media utilization ought to first complete several modules related to this area. The discussion that followed revealed that the purpose of the in-service activity and the content advocated were only slightly related. Again, as the purpose for the field activity became apparent the kinds of prerequisites that were appropriate in the minds of the faculty frequently changed.

## PROCESS AS THE COMMON ELEMENT

Redirection of program elements became closely associated with the perceived needs of a particular student. The process utilized as faculty worked with a particular student revealed to the satisfaction of both the faculty and the student those activities from which each student would benefit. Every effort was made to keep the staff constantly in contact with personnel nationwide involved with defining and redefining the field. One student explained during the final oral examination that the program had changed dramatically since entering graduate study in Educational Media in 1971. At this time the program in Educational Media consisted of doing many interesting but isolated things that were described as "rewarding, creative, and challenging." The student continued to explain that "everything now is much more related. You know what you must do in order to move programs forward. There seems to be a real consensus of the faculty concerning what we're about."

The common concept developed concerning the nature of a media program and the role of the media specialist as perceived by this student developed after professionals with different backgrounds started functioning as teams engaged in planning individual programs. Before the experimental program faculty members perceived their roles in relation to advising students assigned to them and developing courses that reflected their own academic preparation. One course in the department was book-oriented, the next course machine-oriented, the next course production-oriented, and so forth. Work in instructional design and general systems theory seemed to be tacked on to everything else and began as a nice-to-have-but-not-necessary-to-have experience. As the program progressed, principles of general systems theory and the application of the practices in instructional design permeated the thinking of all individuals as they worked together to plan the best possible program for each individual student. Faculty members monitored each other's courses and frequently crossed areas of expertise in order to assist and gain perspective. The most significant result was the complete breakdown of four graduate courses as formal lecture experiences. Because of the nature of the content and because of the characteristic competencies that are associated with each area, courses in Problems in the Administration of Media Services, Informational Resources in the School and Community, Studies in Education, and Evaluation of Media Programs became a collection of competencies that were developed theoretically at the University and applied in the field.

Although the modules prepared by both faculty and students were always reviewed by faculty and rewritten to incorporate suggested changes, the real test of a module came when the student attempted the teaching-learning sequence. In other words, the most significant restructuring of modules was the result of student response. Students frequently tore a module apart and put it back together to meet their specific needs. On the other hand, some students revised faculty modules which were then utilized by other students.

## PROGRAM IMPACT ON THE UNIVERSITY

The impact the experimental program made on the University can be listed under two headings. First, the department assumed a leadership role in the development of a competency-based program within the School of Education. Second, the Department of Educational Media assisted in the development of media programs in the School of Veterinary Medicine, the School of Pharmacy, the School of Business, and the School of Industrial Engineering. Although only faculty members from the Department of Educational Media were involved with redesigning the

Teacher Education Program within the School of Education, students as well as faculty worked with the development of media programs in other schools within the University.

As the School of Pharmacy began planning a media program, students of the program for the preparation of media specialists became directly involved. Specific activities were identified after the Dean of the School of Pharmacy and the Director of the experimental program explored the contributions the School of Pharmacy could make to the experimental program as well as the contributions students could make to the emerging media program in pharmacy. Activities included (1) identifying information resources related to curricular needs, (2) interviewing, surveying, and discussing faculty (pharmacy) perceptions of media program potential, (3) conducting in-service activities on machine and materials usage and media preparation, and (4) making short- and long-range plans for facilities, resources, and programs. During this time the School of Pharmacy supported one experimental program student as he attended conferences about pharmacy and visited other schools of pharmacy in order to learn about media programs of these schools. This student was eventually employed by the School of Pharmacy to build its media program.

In contrast to the School of Pharmacy, the School of Veterinary Medicine had a well developed media program, including a library and autotutorial laboratory supported by librarians, media personnel, medical illustrators, and photographers. Program students visited the facility in order to understand the complex operation of such a program (event) and participated in several projects within the media program of the School of Veterinary Medicine. For example, a slide-tape presentation was made by students in the experimental program to explain the color coded card catalog. Three faculty members of the School of Veterinary Medicine enrolled in courses in instructional design in the department to produce materials for the school's autotutorial laboratory. One of these professors was the joint author of a text in veterinary medicine organized around principles and practices of instructional design.

Program faculty were involved as the School of Business and the School of Industrial Engineering began to develop media programs. The Director of the experimental program addressed both faculties and secured a consultant to assist the School of Business in initial planning. The Department of Educational Media faculty worked with the Learning Resources Committee of the School of Industrial Engineering in making plans for its program. The Director of the experimental program assisted the School of Industrial Engineering in locating an appropriate professional for coordinating the development of its program.

# Program Conclusions

The most powerful procedure used for change related to the persistence of the University faculty to build a program for each individual, taking into consideration both the direction media programs are moving and the realities of the field. Continual comparison of the student's program with the thirteen global objectives helped maintain a balance and served as a check on the kinds of experiences that students needed. The belief that the graduate program for the preparation of media specialists should be a beginning rather than an end was summarized by one student during a planning session.

The program has done more to increase my interest and awareness in all of the things I need to know than I ever thought it could. I know I must continue to attend classes and workshops to help increase my ability to integrate my media program with all programs of the school. I guess I would say that the program doesn't give you a set of facts and principles good for all times as much as it opens the door to what the future could hold.

## PROBLEMS ENCOUNTERED IN PROGRAM PLANNING

Since the planning of each student's program always presented new problems, agreeing on procedures was of high priority. In general terms the procedure included four basic steps. First, every effort was made to know the student, to know his professional goals, and to gain his confidence. Second, specific program elements for each student in terms of course work, fieldwork, learning modules, and events were logged. Third, methods, which included timing and sequencing, were drafted on a tentative basis in order to bring into focus to both the staff and the students how competencies were to be gained. Fourth, the staff and students agreed in writing to the ways and means competencies were to be evaluated.

Five problems were encountered in this process. First, the philosophy of individual staff members tended to reflect their academic preparation and experience. Because of the diverse number of individuals on the professional staff—librarians, instructional programmers, materials production specialists, administrators, and curriculum personnel—the media program and the role of the media specialist were perceived in many ways. An interesting point was observed during departmental faculty meetings in this regard. As decisions were made, especially those related to essential as opposed to enrichment content, the somewhat dogmatic positions of various faculty members tended to support a possible incorrect observation that no unified program existed. These same individuals, when working with a student on ways and means of resolving a problem, rarely reflected the divergence of opinion that sometimes existed in faculty meetings. The point was that even though there were differences in perception of a media program and the role a media specialist should play in the educational program, these differences seemed to stay on the philosophical level and to disappear when working together on problem identification and resolution. In other words, the very process of cooperative decision making engaged in during program planning developed a working philosophy which transcended the differences among faculty.

Second, the program demanded that faculty and students spend many days in school field centers. The program also demanded involved methodologies for contacting students and for scheduling conferences, events, module evaluation sessions, orientation sessions, and so on. The secretary of the experimental program spent at least one-half of her assigned time with such logistics. Appointments, meetings, and classes were continually being rescheduled, demanding an exceptional amount of tolerance on the part of the staff. The students seemed to take this process in stride and exhibited little frustration with the frequently bizarre schedules that they followed.

Third, matching faculty with tasks to be accomplished proved to be a difficult matter. What the staff members perceived that they could do sometimes did not work out that way. For example, one staff member who felt little confidence in programmed instruction turned out to be a proficient

programmer. Another professional employed as a programmer found great difficulty in applying this competence to the curriculum. Another example of role shift occurred when one member of the faculty began to develop interpersonal communication experiences for the experimental program. Although trained as an audiovisual specialist, this faculty member developed considerable expertise and found much gratification in working on interpersonal communication problems. In this sense, faculty members were encouraged to explore new ways in which they could function within the program. Nevertheless, two members saw this as deleterious to the program and their professional goals and tended to isolate themselves. They eventually left the program.

Fourth, the concept of accountability in any normative sense was difficult. Seeing what an individual student's experience in the program was as well as reading why students engaged in particular activities demanded that the investigator look into the records of the individual student. Ways and means of describing the competencies of the typical graduate of the Auburn program for the preparation of media specialists were largely undeveloped. Knowing the capacities and limitations of an individual was given a higher ranking than being able to make normative statements concerning performance on standardized measures.

Fifth, during the program, staff, students, and professionals in the field centers continually expressed the fear that the experimental program might become too prescriptive in the future. This stems from the general belief that the process of planning and building a student's program remains the most important experience provided. This posture severely limits the development of any definitive lists of required competencies as well as the transportability of the program. The philosophy of the program is transportable; however, the close relationships and dependence upon field centers would permit only bits and pieces of the program to be utilized by other institutions. Task analysis and program descriptions were used as resources to check the balance in an individual's program rather than indicators of content and competencies that had to be taught.

## RECOMMENDATIONS

The experimental program as initiated at Auburn University will continue to be the pattern for the education of the school library media specialist. The emphasis on individual program needs, however, will demand continuous change and modification in program development. Change in the Auburn program was closely associated with an attempt to build more purposeful programs. In this context, purposes were tied to the individual and his potential and actual contribution to the development of school media programs. The conclusions drawn after two years of the experimental program were stated in terms of seven recommendations.

1. Students, instructional staff, and field center personnel should agree upon procedures for program planning and participate in the process.

2. Planning sessions should result in a consensus about goals, methods for attaining goals, and ways and means of measuring attainment.

3. Diagnostic efforts, regardless of the strengths or weaknesses, should be employed wherever practical.

4. Programs should concentrate on competencies that relate to the role media specialists play in the field. If this role is to be developed in a graduate program the staff must work with students in field centers that provide the environment for role development.

5. School resources, University resources, and community resources should be accessible to students. This accessibility is related to the quality of interpersonal relations developed among these agencies.

6. A way should be provided for various staff members—graphic artists, photographers, technicians, etc.—to contribute to program planning and implementation. This will revitalize and redirect programs for the preparation of media specialists in many positive ways.

7. The student should be the key to program improvement. If the instructional team knows each student well, sample information will become available for continuous program improvement.

The introduction to the booklet entitled *The Shape of a Curriculum*,[5] produced to describe Auburn's experimental program for the preparation of media specialists, summarized the general concern of this program.

> Confining students to the classroom when they are increasingly aware of local, state, and world problems handicaps the university as well as its students. Mass media keep students instantly informed and constantly frustrated by articulating problems to which most classroom activities bear little relationship. The university must learn to capitalize on the enthusiasm and commitment of its most valuable resource—the student—by providing ways for students to confront problems that make a difference.

> The focus on commitment places a high priority on the formulation of objectives. Students who are committed because they see the relevance and personal meaning of their programs of study will more likely achieve. This does not mean that we should decrease our efforts to provide more and better ways to learn, but rather that we should encourage the expending of additional energy toward identifying concerns and capitalizing on one of the most potent of all human characteristics—the desire to contribute, to vest life with meaning, to be able to say "I made a difference."

5. *The Shape of a Curriculum:* An Experimental Program for the Training of Library Media Specialists (Auburn: Dept. of Educational Media, School of Education, 1971).

Appendix A

PROJECT LIBRA
FIELD-CENTERED MODULE

---

Auburn Faculty Consultant                    Student(s)

_____    _____

Field Center                                 _____

_____    _____

Date Approved _____    Starting Date _____

Expected Completion Date _____

---

PROBLEM STATEMENT _____

_____

_____

GLOBAL OBJECTIVES _____

_____

_____

_____

_____

_____

IDENTIFIED PREREQUISITES _____

_____

_____

COMPLETE THE FOLLOWING AND ATTACH TO THIS COVER SHEET

---

1.  Identify content mass (locate possible sources of information--books, films, filmstrips, articles, etc.).
2.  Formulate performance objectives (spell out exactly what you expect to do and how your faculty consultant will know it has been done).
3.  Construct criterion measure (base it on identified objectives).
4.  Specify strategies (present detailed plans for activities in which you will engage in order to attain your objectives).
5.  Analyze achievement (base analysis on stated objectives).
6.  Describe strengths and weaknesses (write a brief description of your solution of this problem).

Appendix B

DEPARTMENT OF EDUCATIONAL MEDIA
*Graduate Student Audit Report*
Auburn University, Auburn, Alabama

Field Work Only

Student's Name_____ Date_____

Title of Activity_____

Faculty Advisor(s)_____

Date Activity Began_____ Expected Completion Date
_____

1. *Describe the objectives toward which you are working.*
   _____
   _____
   _____
   _____

2. *List the activities, contacts with persons and contacts
   with materials in which you have been involved in relation to your objectives.*
   _____
   _____
   _____
   _____
   _____

3. *Describe new insights or meaningful experiences and any
   problems concerning your work toward objectives.*
   _____
   _____
   _____
   _____
   _____

4. *Describe ways by which faculty members may assist you in
   achieving your objectives.*
   _____
   _____
   _____
   _____
   _____
   _____
   _____

# MANKATO STATE COLLEGE

SCHOOL OF EDUCATION

Dr. Benjamin A. Buck, Dean

## AN EXPERIMENTAL PROGRAM IN
# SCHOOL LIBRARY MEDIA EDUCATION
### 1971–1973

*Final Report by*

FRANK R. BIRMINGHAM and DALE CARRISON

---

## Contents

# INSTRUCTIONAL MEDIA AND TECHNOLOGY PROGRAM
## Dr. Frank R. Birmingham, Program Leader

*Experimental Program Staff, 1971-1973*

Dr. Frank R. Birmingham, Director

Mr. Dale K. Carrison
Dr. Edmund Colby
Miss Myrna K. Folkers
Dr. Bettie R. Helzer, 1971-72
Mr. Gary Hughes, 1972-73

Mr. Daniel W. Lester
Mrs. Frances M. McDonald
Mr. James T. McKenzie, 1972-73
Mr. Kenneth C. Pengelly
Dr. Dennis Sarenpa

*Advisory Board*

Mr. Robert W. Anderson
Audiovisual Supervisor
Minnesota Department of Education

Mr. James H. Bacon, 1971-72
President
Minnesota Association of School Librarians

Dr. Winston Benson, 1972-73
Dean, Graduate School
Mankato State College

Miss Marcella M. Bertrand
Director, School Libraries
Independent School District No. 77, Mankato

Dr. Frank R. Birmingham
Program Leader, Instructional Media and Technology Program
Mankato State College

Dr. Luther Brown
Chairman, Department of Library and Audiovisual Education
St. Cloud State College

Dr. Benjamin A. Buck
Dean, School of Education
Mankato State College

Mr. Dale K. Carrison
Executive Director of Libraries
Mankato State College

Dr. Edmund K. Colby, 1972-73
Director, Audiovisual Services
Mankato State College

Mr. Thomas E. Collins, 1971-72
President
Audiovisual Coordinators Association of Minnesota

Miss Ruth M. Ersted
School Libraries Supervisor
Minnesota Department of Education

Mr. Eldm D. Flatten
Principal, Oak Grove Elementary School
Bloomington Public Schools

Dr. Donald E. Glines
Director, Program for Educational Alternatives
School of Education
Mankato State College

Dr. Patricia J. Goralski
Director, Profesions Development Section
Minnesota Department of Education

Mr. Clyde L. Greve, 1971-72
Chairman, Department of Library Science
University of Northern Iowa

Dr. Donal M. Holden, 1972-73
Director, Center for Curriculum and Learning Strategies
School of Education
Mankato State College

Mr. Gene R. Hugelen
Librarian, Valley Junior High School
Rosemount School District No. 196

Mr. Gary A. Lundin, 1971-72
Chairman, Department of Laboratory Science
Mankato State College

Dr. Gabriel D. Ofiesh
Director, Center of Educational Technology
American University
Washington, D. C.

Mrs. Diane Olson, 1972-73
Librarian, Fairmont Senior High School
Fairmont Public Schools

Miss Marcia S. Paulsen, 1971-72
Student Member
Mankato State College

Dr. Neville P. Pearson
Professor of Education
University of Minnesota

Mr. Willard Phillipson, 1972-73
President
Audiovisual Coordinators Association of Minnesota

Mrs. Phyllis Thornley, 1972-73
President
Minnesota Association of School Librarians

Dr. Robert B. Vanderwilt
Director, Experimental Studies Program
Mankato State College

# Overview

## DESCRIPTION OF THE INSTITUTION

Mankato State College is a multi-purpose institution of higher education. The College asserts this responsibility by pursuing the purposes that correspond to such institutions: to preserve the several kinds and areas of knowledge, expand knowledge, disseminate knowledge, apply knowledge, and demonstrate the principled use of knowledge in the enrichment of the culture, the society, and the intellectual, cultural, artistic, and emotional growth of the individual. Mankato is a public college within a state-supported college system; therefore the College has implicit responsibility to be of special utility to the people of the State of Minnesota and more particularly to those in the southern half of the State and the contiguous portions of neighboring states. Together these institutional purposes constitute the touchstone for determining the merit of more specific goals and judging the worth of specific activities. These basic purposes guide the manner in which Mankato State College undertakes to select the most suitable activities of instruction, research, demonstration, and public service and to establish criteria and assign priorities.

The instructional activities of Mankato State College are intended to assist students to be self-directed individuals, good citizens, and capable workers. Therefore, the instructional efforts of the institution provide liberalized general education, as well as more specialized education and training in the several academic disciplines, professions, and vocational fields. To achieve these purposes, instructional efforts include pre-service, in-service, mid-career, and highly specialized opportunities. The College serves students of the usual undergraduate age and those from older age groups. The College has the opportunity to assist students in adapting to the changing circumstances in the economy and remaining abreast of advances in their disciplines, professions, and other fields.

As a public educational institution, Mankato State College makes all possible effort to meet and support its obligation. It undertakes to provide students with experiences which transcend academic study and formal preparation for job and career. Students are given from one to six years of living and learning under limited supervision, and increased opportunity to experience self-determination, as well as having a voice in shaping the college environment. Mankato State College proposes both to make education relevant to the future life of the student, and assist him in accurately perceiving what is relevant in a rapidly changing culture. It seeks to innovate and change patterns and content of instruction to afford and demonstrate a flexibility of approach and adaptability which the future will require of college graduates.

## DESCRIPTION OF THE DEPARTMENTS SUBMITTING THE PROPOSAL

The proposal submitted to the School Library Manpower Project for a graduate level school library media education program at Mankato State College was developed jointly by the Audiovisual Education and Library Science Departments during the summer and fall of 1970. Extensive planning involved each member of the two departments. The resulting proposal was created so that the graduate program could be individualized easily and organized in learning blocks as needed to provide the greatest learning and teaching efficiency and effectiveness. The block structure as defined in the proposal refers to blocks as major curriculum content areas based upon competency categorization. Competency is defined as the level of knowledge attainment necessary to work self sufficiently on the job.

At the time the proposal was developed, the Departments of Audiovisual Education and Library Science offered multi-purpose program courses at both the undergraduate and graduate levels, including special programs leading to Minnesota certification, sixth year specialist degrees, and support courses for other subject area majors and minors on campus. The primary function of the Departments was to build a strong cultural and professional foundation for effective contribution to the media profession and to prepare personnel for both general and special positions within the profession.

The Department of Audiovisual Education, administratively located within the School of Education, and the Department of Library Science, administratively located within the School of Arts and Sciences, had operated since 1968 in the provision of the graduate program in media leading to a Master's degree. This cooperation in program development was extended in the fall of 1970 to the provision of a media-oriented minor at the undergraduate level.

The merger of the Departments of Audiovisual Education and Library Science became a reality in 1971, with the new Instructional Media and Technology Program administratively located in the School of Education. The combined departments have operated most efficiently since their official merger and have been able to significantly ease the implementation of the experimental program goals and objectives while continuing the on-going programs at the undergraduate and graduate levels.

## RATIONALE FOR CHANGE

The demands being made by society upon our schools are concentrated in the area of the improvement of instruction and accountability. This fact makes it imperative that the media programs in our schools be broadened and further developed and that the media professional become more competent to implement and administer necessary changes. The added complexity of subject matter and the increasing need for specialization, force school personnel to seek additional education as well as enforce the demand for media personnel with contemporary media education. The experimental program was designed to provide the flexibility necessary to meet the needs of the students involved, while at the same time to establish high standards to insure a quality product. Every media professional must have adequate preparation to best fit him for his performance as an educational leader. This should include research and theory, functional subject matter in professional courses and the chance for specialization. In the experimental model, persons completing the course of study would be able to assume an active role in the media profession at both a practitioner and an administrative level. The objectives of the program were to develop the competencies and attitudes in students required for designing, selecting, acquiring, organizing and evaluating media; for serving as responsible mediators with potential users; and for planning and managing a total media program related to general educational goals and specific school objectives.

Mankato State College has a long tradition of providing for the educational needs of the area which it serves. Certification requirements, interest in the content emphasis expressed through students and practitioners in surveys, structure of school staffing, salary schedules, and sabbatical leave policies, as well as large numbers of informal reactions of interest from students in the upper Midwest area, clearly demonstrate the need and student demand for a program of the nature proposed. Because of changing patterns, certification requirements in particular reflect the necessity to employ new curriculum levels and designs for the education of media professionals.

Mankato State College is unique in the development of its graduate media program by virtue of the open climate for change and the faculty and facility support. The size and diversity of the teaching staff contributed heavily to the establishment of a solid base for the program. In addition, there were numerous other staff throughout the College who made significant and timely contributions to the media education program. The structure of the experimental curriculum was organized to maximize the educational impact of the total program for the students involved and, through them, the media profession as a whole.

The present graduate program requires a minimum of fifty one quarter hours, consisting of audiovisual instruction, curriculum and instruction, library science, and media-oriented administration, management, and services coursework. This program, which meets the certification requirements in both the areas of audiovisual director and of school librarian, as well as the new Minnesota media generalist and supervisor requirements, is designed to prepare people for positions in all types of media centers, particularly those positions requiring competencies in administration and management.

The experimental program replaced the regular graduate program for a selected group of eighteen full-time students. In addition, regular graduate courses were retained to meet the needs of the more than 300 full-time and part-time students currently enrolled in the departmental graduate program. The experimental program differed from the regular course of study in the structure of content areas and the consequent use of staff preparation and instruction time. Arbitrary course delimitations were avoided and sequenced, in-depth content area blocks were developed for instructional purposes. These blocks facilitated more efficient and effective use of an instructor's time and abilities than did the traditional course-oriented structure. The curriculum design was inherently flexible and lent itself to evaluation and modification.

The experimental program was evaluated continuously during the course of the two-year grant to determine which portions of it should be integrated into the regular on-going graduate program.

## IMPLEMENTATION REQUIREMENTS

Institutional support of the experimental program included the approval and support of the Vice President for Academic Affairs and the Graduate Dean, who granted special permission to adjust the normal course load requirements and other on-campus graduate regulations in order for the block concept of course programming to be implemented. To provide the curriculum and instruction component, the necessary backing from the Curriculum and Instruction Program in the School of Education was secured. Those of the Curriculum and Instruction faculty members who were willing to work within the methodology of the experimental program, were incorporated into the experimental program to provide the curriculum-related competencies. Without the support of various areas of the institution, and particularly the media system, the experimental program could not have been as flexible and comprehensive in its subject area coverage, nor would the appropriate materials, equipment, and facilities have been available for use.

Staff requirements for the program included one full-time faculty member to serve as coordinator and liaison between the students and other program faculty members. The coordinator also served as a counselor and security symbol by providing program continuity and by bringing together the loose ends of learning which occurred due to the program block structure. A full-time technician to aid the faculty and students in the development of instructional materials and a full-time secretary to assist with the clerical duties were provided also. Numerous persons (clerical, technical, and instructional) were associated with the program over the two-year period—some for an entire block and others for short lecturer/consultant periods. The program staffing, although complex from a managerial standpoint, was a strong feature of the program because it was able to draw on the best expertise available from a large number of people. Staff development was an on-going activity carried out primarily on an individualized basis under the direction of the program director.

Curriculum development was most demanding before the program began and during the initial implementation of the curriculum blocks. Almost daily planning conferences were held during the summer before the program began. Weekly curriculum coordination and revision meetings were held during utilization of the first blocks. The most extensive curriculum revisions took place at the end of the first year during a two-day retreat. The program staff and three elected students reviewed every day of the program, by assessing sets of diaries kept by each student and faculty member during the year. Each field trip, visits to school media centers, conferences and conventions, etc., were carefully evaluated in terms of the program objectives. A complete re-organization of the curriculum for the 1972-73 school year was developed at that time.

Curriculum development for an experimental program of this type is of necessity a continuous activity to meet the needs of the students and to individualize instruction. The instructional staff must provide a curriculum flexible enough to accommodate change and meet specific needs and at the same time maintain the content at a level sufficient to cover all competencies considered essential. The program was able to accomplish this goal in curriculum development. A key factor was staff interest and involvement on a continuous basis before, during, and after participation in program blocks or segments of blocks.

# Program Goals and Objectives

The goals of the experimental program were: (1) to develop and implement the best possible program of education for the media professional, (2) to prepare media professionals to meet the demands of contemporary K-12 education, (3) to prepare professional school library media personnel at an entry level of competency, and (4) to graduate media professionals with master's degrees qualified to meet the Minnesota certification requirements for media generalist and media supervisor. These goals were developed on the basis of (1) past experience of the Instructional Media and Technology Program faculty (both media practitioner and media education experience), (2) the documentation resulting from Phase I of the School Library Manpower Project, (3) input from current students and graduates of the IMT Program, (4) input from practitioners in the field and state professional associations, and (5) the competency based Minnesota certification requirements for Media Generalist and Media Supervisor. The goals and consequent structure of the experimental program were a synthesis of the data derived from all of these sources.

Specific competency based objectives were developed to implement the basic goals of the program, using the documentation of task analysis and competency requirements developed from Phase I of the School Library Manpower Project and the competency checklists used for evaluation of Minnesota certification as media generalist and media supervisor. Following the guidelines set forth by the School Library Manpower Project during Phase I, the instructional staff of the experimental program at Mankato State College adapted and developed a competency checklist to implement the basic goals of the program. An example of the competency checklist designated to evaluate competencies in the media component is found in Appendix A. Similar checklists were developed for all of the other competency areas incorporated in the curriculum. Program participants were expected to demonstrate ability to perform within the major areas of competencies and attitudes required in a school media program with emphasis in the areas of: (1) designing, select-

ing, organizing, and evaluating media, (2) serving as a responsible mediator with users and potential users, and (3) planning and managing a total media program related to general educational goals and specific school objectives.

Program related objectives were developed to provide parameters for content and method inclusion and structure. These objectives were based on the collective experience of the IMT Program faculty, with additional input from current and past IMT students and from practitioners in the field. The experimental program was expected to: (1) foster articulation and eliminate repetition of content, (2) achieve maximum utilization of resources, including staff, facilities, equipment, materials, time and field experiences, (3) stimulate continuous curriculum revision and development, and (4) achieve the best possible media education program without expenditure of funds above a level which the College would be able to continue when the grant funds ended. The processes of interdisciplinary methods and approach, varied learning methodology, appropriate mediated instruction, individualization for instruction, varied teaching methodologies, development of behavioral objectives, and methods of measuring entrance and in-program competencies were used to work toward achievement of the experimental program objectives.

# Program Participants

## STUDENTS

Eighteen people were enrolled as full-time students during the experimental program; ten in the first year and eight in the second year. The program required one calendar year (four quarters) to complete and culminated in the awarding of a Master's Degree with a major area of concentration in media. A total of seventeen students received the graduate degree by the end of the second year of the experimental program.

The experimental program selection criteria included the following: (1) bachelor's degree from an accredited college or university; (2) undergraduate grade point average of 2.7 or higher on a 4.0 scale; (3) Graduate Record Examination Aptitude Test with a combined total score of 900 or an individual test score of 500; and (4) satisfactory recommendations. None of these criteria was absolute; any one

could be waived upon petition by a student showing extenuating circumstances or by the selection committee based on total evaluation of the applicant.

A selection committee of five consisting of the director, two assistant directors, one faculty member with expertise in library science and one with an audiovisual specialization made the final decision on the selection of participants in the experimental program for the first year. The director and the experimental program faculty made the decisions for the second year. This change in the selection process was implemented in order to utilize the expertise gained by the faculty during the first program year.

Individual counseling and guidance were an integral part of the experimental program starting with the initial interview. Periodic counseling appointments with the director and/or the two assistant directors were required. These interviews were used to chart and evaluate the student's progress and gave guidance to the student's program participation and direction. Individual interviews and proficiency measurements were also used for placement and curriculum exemption purposes throughout the student's year of study.

The processes of counseling and interviewing were documented through the development of comprehensive personnel folders for each student which were kept up to date by summary analysis of each direct contact with the student in a counseling and/or interviewing situation. This summarization was recorded by the experimental program staff member involved in the situation. Additional documentation was provided by personality and aptitude tests administered at the beginning of the program and competency checklists administered quarterly during the program. Students also wrote a statement of media service philosophy at the start of the program and at the end of the program. These two statements were compared and discussed with the student. The personnel folders were used to develop a total picture of the student's progress through the experimental program and to identify strengths, weaknesses, and needs which needed to be addressed by the students and/or the faculty.

Recruitment for the regular graduate program included annual distribution of descriptive brochures and leaflets to a regular mailing list of schools and colleges, association newsletters and conferences, and alumni of the undergraduate program. For the experimental program a descriptive brochure was mailed to all of the above and to all members of the Minnesota Association of School Librarians and the Audiovisual Coordinators Association of Minnesota. Contact was made with the state supervisors of audiovisual and library science in neighboring states and with their respective state association to obtain additional mailing lists. Publicity news releases were sent to *Audiovisual Instruction, School Library Journal, Today's Education,* and regional and state professional publications for teachers and media personnel.

The first year participant selection criteria included a Bachelor of Arts or Science degree with liberal arts emphasis, teacher certification, and some type of teaching experience. Although persons with library science and/or media coursework were not excluded, the emphasis in selection was on new entrants to the media field. These criteria were interpreted broadly in actual application in order to select the persons with the best overall qualifications for entry into the experimental program. This procedure resulted in a participant group which included one person without teacher certification, and persons with no teaching and/or media experience to fifteen years teaching and/or media experience. An evaluation of the first-year participant group resulted in a tightening of selection criteria for the second year, with emphasis on group homogenity. The reasons for this were (1) the first-year student without teacher certification was judged to have a distinct disadvantage in achieving the understandings and knowledges expected and in keeping pace with the rest of the group, and (2) the wide range in experience caused splits within the student group on both a philosophical basis and a work output basis. Another significant observation was that students with teaching experience but no media experience progressed most rapidly in all phases of the program, apparently because they could relate the content of the program to curriculum and instruction, but had no preconceived attitudes on the ways and means of a media program. Students with no teaching experience were also judged to be at a disadvantage. The changes in participant selection policy for the second year of the experimental program were desirable on the basis of evaluation results of the second year students. Fewer learning and peer group problems were identified, and the students generally progressed at a more even and rapid pace.

Financial aid and scholarships for the experimental program students were drastically reduced due to enrollment decline and financial pressures of the College. Prior to the experimental program eleven graduate assistantships were utilized by media graduate students. Seven to nine graduate assistantships were projected to be available for the students during 1971-73 when the proposal was written in 1970. In reality, only two graduate assistantships and one scholarship were available during the first year. The second year only one scholarship was available through institutional support. The scholarships for both years were made available from a commercial agency. One student during the first year and two during the second were supported by sabbatical leaves from their places of employment. Other students had various loans to help them through the year such as: two NDEA Loans, one student guaranteed loan, and one Mankato Campus Financial Aid Loan.

The very nature of the experimental program with evening and Saturday sessions, field trips, conferences and professional meetings, and internships made employment during the school year extremely difficult. The total Media System within Mankato

State College made student assistant jobs available within the library but most students were unable to take advantage of this opportunity because of the diversity of time schedules in the experimental program.

STAFF

A basic prerequisite for successful implementation of the experimental program was a staff who were flexible, dynamic, and creative in their approach to media education. The success of the program was due in great part to the staff members who participated and who had these personal qualities. The five core faculty members and seven part-time faculty members were open to new and varied methods of instruction (individualization, self-instruction, competency base, etc.) and curriculum organization (block, field base, team teaching, etc.). These people were knowledgeable and competent in both the subject areas of library science and audiovisual, as well as in educational technology. They were recognized as excellent teachers and had excellent rapport with students. All of the faculty members had teaching and/or consultant experience at the elementary or secondary school level and most had both practitioner and teaching experience, as well as higher education teaching experience. The average age of the staff was relatively young (30-35). Two of the full-time persons had moved from the practitioner level to teaching within the past two years and thus were able to draw upon recent experiences. Within the total program, the staff represented all of the content and competency areas covered, and individual faculty members complemented each other in terms of interests, education, and experiential backgrounds.

One new staff member was added for the purpose of coordinating the program during the course of the experimentation. This person also had the attributes previously described and fit well into the total staff picture. The enthusiasm and commitment of the experimental program staff was another significant factor for success of the program. At the beginning, one staff member was less eager to participate; however, the rest of the group soon built up the interest and enthusiasm and carried the person into the program with full participation.

The program faculty was supported by the interdisciplinary expertise of the entire College. Many members of the college-wide faculty were utilized as guest discussion leaders to cover special topics such as special education, interpersonal relationships, etc. School of Education Curriculum and Instruction faculty were involved directly as experimental program staff members and indirectly as guest lecturers and consultants. Educators from outside the college, particularly from the Minneapolis-St. Paul area, and State Department of Education personnel were utilized as consultants, lecturers, and counselors to provide additional expertise wherever relevant and necessary. These people served not only an instructional function, but also a reaction and evaluation function for modification and improvement of the program.

Media and production support personnel with expertise in both print and non-print materials and in both electronic and non-electronic production were readily accessible to the staff of the experimental program, as were the facilities and equipment for the use of both students and support personnel. Mankato State College has excellent personnel with a broad range of competencies to affect the maximum utilization of materials, equipment, and facilities by the staff of the experimental program.

A staff development program for all faculty directly involved in the experimental course of study was held during the spring and summer preceding the start of each program year in the fall. At the start of the program, two faculty retreats oriented all persons on the IMT faculty to the experimental program and developed the curriculum content areas included in the block program. These meetings enabled all persons to have input into the final content and structure of the program. One retreat was held at the start of the second year of the program for the purpose of making program modifications and improvements based on the first year's experience. Two students from the first-year program participated in this meeting. Other aspects of the staff development program included continuous involvement in and knowledge of program development and provision of background materials dealing with innovative methods of curriculum development and instructional methodology.

Provision was made for a reduced teaching load for the 1971 summer session for faculty who were directly participating in the experimental program. These courses were picked up by part-time instructors or dropped for that session. Provision was also made for these faculty members to have time and transportation to visit the schools which were to be used for observation and internship. Comprehensive syllabi for all content area blocks were developed during the summer of 1971 in preparation for the first year of implementation. The summer of 1972 was used to review and revise the curriculum for the second year.

Throughout the two years of the experimentation, staff overtime commitments were heavy because of the large blocks of time devoted to program instruction and because most of the program faculty continued to be involved in college and department governance and administration and in the regular undergraduate and graduate programs. Because of the block structure and irregular time periods of the experimental program, staff loads were difficult to equate with regular teaching loads. Consequently, staff morale was sometimes hard to maintain. The enthusiasm and drive of the students, however, served to offset this problem and to build and maintain the enthusiasm and drive of the staff. Whenever possible program faculty were relieved temporarily of responsibilities outside the program and occasionally were relieved of all responsibilities and sent home to rejuvenate.

At the start of the experimental program a position of media technician was added to provide production and technology support for the program faculty. The first year this person was not utilized to the fullest extent, principally because the faculty did not have their instructional programming developed far enough in advance to have special materials produced or they preferred to do the production themselves rather than supervise someone else. This situation changed the second year as faculty were better prepared ahead of time and because the media technician was utilized as an instructional team member rather than as a production assistant, a procedure that worked very well and enhanced the instructional process.

During the course of the experimental program, meetings conducted by the Program Director of all departmental faculty, program faculty and staff were held as needed to provide continuity and clarification as well as continuous evaluation and appraisal. During the first year, these meetings were almost weekly, then became less frequent as the program developed into the second year because less review was necessary and because coordination was handled differently.

A new position of coordinator was created to serve as the key link and stabilizing force to the students and program faculty. This person did not have administrative responsibilities, but instead acted as an instructional manager and curriculum coordinator. The coordinator had one less block teaching assignment to compensate for his additional counseling and coordinating activities. He attended all program instructional sessions and provided the linkage between blocks in subject content or relationships to the media profession as a whole. The consensus of all involved was that this position is imperative for this type of program to tie the segments of the various blocks and the curriculum content into a meaningful total school library media professional education program.

## ADVISORY BOARD

The Advisory Board, consisting of twenty persons representing media practitioners, audiovisual and library educators, graduate students in the media program, state consultants and school and college administrators, met with the program faculty and students during each quarter to evaluate the progress of the experimental program and appraise the skills, attitudes, and professional growth of the student. Each year two students were selected by the program faculty and served on the Advisory Board. A strength of the structural design of the program was its flexibility and emphasis on individualization of instruction. Consequently, modifications could be implemented in the program at any point when deemed necessary by the faculty and/or Advisory Board.

The contribution of the Advisory Board was mainly that of a reactor panel. Other contributions were made individually and collectively by Advisory Board members, including the identification of internship and job opportunities, guest lectures, student recruitment, and program publicity and public relations. On the basis of this role and the results of this adjunct part of the experimental program, the Advisory Board was considered to provide a useful function and should be continued as part of the regular undergraduate and graduate programs. The wide representation of educational backgrounds, experience, and positions was a valuable asset and should be built into the selection of future Advisory Board members.

# Program Components

## CURRICULUM BLOCKS

The curriculum of the experimental program was a modular, block-oriented approach to media edu-

cation. Each learning block included the major curriculum content area based upon competency categorization. The curriculum design was devised and developed by the faculty of the Instructional Media and Technology Program, formerly the Audiovisual Education and Library Science Departments, as an optimum approach to media education, ensuring maximum utilization of instructional time, materials, equipment, and facilities. The block curriculum structure provided for an inter-related, interdisciplinary instructional program representing basic media content areas and a wide range of media competencies as suggested and defined during Phase I of the School Library Manpower Project.

A unique characteristic of the experimental program and a key element to its inter-disciplinary utilization of college resources was the fact that the program represented the combined effort and expertise of three academic departments representing two schools within the College. Indirectly, through the use of various facilities and faculty to supplement the resources permanently available to the program, additional academic departments made contributions in the areas of education administration, curriculum, sociological and psychological backgrounds, and special education.

Individualization of instruction was obtained through the recognition of entrance and in-program competency attainment, as measured through the use of proficiency examinations, interviews, and observed field work behavior patterns. These measuring and evaluation devices were used to determine the strengths, weaknesses, and needs of each student, as well as to individualize instruction by identifying content areas where required competency levels had not been reached. Checklists of knowledges, behavioral patterns, and produced results were used as the basis for measurement and evaluation. These checklists were completed by the instructor, the student, and the field supervisor if appropriate, and then reviewed in a meeting of these persons.

The curriculum components, which were learner oriented, were organized to provide for maximum flexibility in terms of teaching and learning methodology, interdisciplinary and interrelated content, and competency measurement. Therefore, provision could be made at any time to change focus or provide remedial or supplementary instructional activities for any program student without effecting the integrity of the overall program of instruction. Theories and principles were translated into operational learning pathways for students during the process of curriculum block building. Each block structure was based on a pattern of (1) goal or purpose of block, (2) behavioral objectives to be met, (3) competency areas to be attained, (4) activities to be accomplished, and

(5) instructional methods, materials, and facilities to be used. The emphasis throughout the program was on learning by doing, on process rather than results, on systematic study of problems rather than "pat" answers, and on developing and fostering reflective thinking.

There were seventeen curriculum blocks developed for the experimental program. Each curriculum block was based upon a content resume which specified the content, objectives, teaching and learning strategies, time allotment, and the competencies to be obtained. An example of the curriculum content resume for the "Professional Resources" content area from which a block was developed is shown in Appendix B. An example of three days of the one week block structure for this content area is shown in Appendix C. In addition to the "Professional Resources" block, blocks were developed for the following content areas.

> Orientation and Communication
> Professional Resources
> Philosophy, Organization and Role of Media
>     Centers
> Media Selection and Acquisition
> Instructional Theory and Design
> Media Identification and Utilization
> Identification, Organization, and Retrieval of
>     Media
> Observation and Internship
> Administration and Management of Media
>     Programs
> Individual and Group Dynamics
> Instructional Systems Design and
>     Implementation
> Management Principles and Practice
> Automation and Data Processing
> Electronic Media Design and Utilization
> Interaction Analysis
> Research Design and Methodology
> Practicum in Media Design

The premise behind the modular approach to curriculum building was to make the most effective and efficient use of student and faculty instructional time. The curriculum blocks were individually developed and lasted for varying periods of time depending on the amount of content and experiences involved. The blocks were sequenced according to a pattern based on moving from the general to the specific, with each block relating to the preceding block and building on that content. The sequencing was changed the second year to better meet the needs of students for internship placement. The evaluation of the first year's program indicated that interning students lacked some competencies which were necessary for having a well-rounded, comprehensive internship experience. For example, students and their supervisors both identified a lack of knowledge in basic audiovisual production techniques.

All curriculum block faculty were full-time, enabling them to concentrate their efforts on developing and implementing new educational techniques and methodologies and identifying and packaging the best instructional materials. The faculty for each block worked as a team making joint presentations, participating in discussions, and being present at all block activities. Guest lecturers and consultants were involved as much as possible in the team approach and were expected to participate fully during the period of their involvement.

The time periods assigned to content areas were sufficiently flexible to permit modification before and during a segment in order to accommodate and implement new and/or varied methods, materials, or facilities. Students, faculty, and guest lecturers and consultants were given ample opportunity for input into block structure throughout the program. The continuous program evaluation during and after each block further provided input for change during the program. Several times block structural problems identified in one block were minimized in a later block because of this process.

During the full-time blocks students participated in no other course areas. During periods of less than full-time blocks, students were usually involved in two or more content areas and/or field experiences. The designation of a block as full-time or part-time depended on the content, the instructional methods used, and the amount of lab or field experience involved. The blocks utilized a combination of total group, small group, and individual meetings, depending on the best method of presentation and evaluation of prior competency attainment on the part of students.

A wide variety of teaching and learning strategies were used depending on the content of the particular subject area. The emphasis at all times was on the learner and his abilities and needs. Self-instruction through use of autotutorial, computer assisted instruction, programmed instruction, and contracts were used wherever possible. Both commercially produced and instructor produced self-instruction materials were utilized. The program media technician provided invaluable assistance in production and adaptation of these materials.

Student and faculty reactions to the curriculum

structure and content were very positive, as evidenced by the final evaluations of both years of the program. The most significant problem during the internship was student participation or non-participation in a particular block because of prior competency attainment. Students apparently felt strong peer group pressure to participate even though they could choose to utilize that time for other activities. The second year this problem was minimized by having fewer total group meetings and better student orientation to the block concept and purpose of self-instruction. Articulation of the program with past education and experience and with future education and experience was considered and was a basic criterion for evaluaton and modification of the continuing program.

## FIELD EXPERIENCES

Field experiences in the Mankato program were defined as all short term field activities such as tours, observations, attendance at professional meetings and conferences, seminars with professional leaders and field work in a specialized situation.

These experiences reflected a variety of social, economic, and ethnic backgrounds, and were provided throughout the experimental program to give program participants experiences with students in classrooms and media centers, with individual teachers and teacher terms, with varying school sizes and organizational patterns, and with types of libraries and resource centers other than in the school setting. All students and faculty attended an average of eight state and national professional association meetings each year. These activities provided an opportunity for students to enrich their knowledge and background by meeting people throughout the state and nation and talking with leaders of their chosen profession. Pre-planning of field experiences provided an opportunity for students to view displays of materials and equipment, and to observe how professional associations are organized and operated. Seminars were held during the Association for Educational Communications and Technology and the Ameircan Library Association national conferences each year at the conference sites to further utilize and maximize the availability of the resources at hand.

An internship consisting of an indepth on-the-job field experience under the guidance and supervision of a professional library media specialist was a program requirement for each student. The purpose of this experience was to enable the student to consolidate and apply the knowledge gained during the first half of his program and to identify areas where he lacked necessary competencies or an appropriate competency level. The internship also served to give the student a feel for the "real world" as opposed to the "classroom world." Internship locations were assigned on the basis of student choices of grade levels; type of instructional program; rural, city, or urban environment; and geographic location. Most students were assigned to two locations during their internship, with one location being their first choice of grade level and lasting for a four-week period and the second location being their second choice of grade level and lasting for a two-week period. Supervision of students was provided by both the program field supervisor, who visited each student at least once a week, and the professional library media person at the location. Most students were given a specific project to accomplish during the term of their internship, and were expected to participate as a media professional in the on-going activities of the library media center. Examples of special projects included production of a self-instruction unit, development of a student and faculty handbook, and assignment to a teacher or a department as a curriculum materials specialist.

Students were assisted in obtaining housing and finding transportation if needed. No stipend was paid to the internship students. However, a stipend was paid to the on-the-job supervisor.

Internship problems the first year centered around inadequate orientation of on-the-job supervisors and inadequate supervision. Students were often assigned non-professional tasks and/or were expected to perform as media professionals without any help or support from an on-site person. These problems were minimized the second year by thorough orientation of supervisors prior to the internship and by continued contact between the program supervisor and the on-site supervisor throughout the period of the internship. During the second year program faculty regularly visited internship students and advised and counseled with them on their experiences and problems. This procedure helped to give the student confidence in what he was doing, as well as providing another avenue of supervision and evaluation.

On the basis of post-internship and final program evaluations by all persons involved, the internship was rated very high as a desirable and indispensable part of the experimental program. All students felt the experience was a highlight of their academic program.

Enrichment for the instructional program was provided by Target Topic weekly evening seminars designed around special topics not covered in the curriculum block. These irregularly scheduled seminars were directed by guest discussion leaders and resource persons from on and off the campus who gave an in-depth look at topics needing special attention or focus and which were not covered adequately during the regular program. Wherever advantageous, the seminars were held off-campus to make use of special facilities, equipment and/or materials. Prior to the seminar, persons acting as discussion leaders and resource persons were required to submit a topical outline for the subject area to be explored, a brief bibliography of background information, and requirements for facilities, equipment, and materials needed during the seminar. Students were given this information and were required to read in the topic area before the Target Topic session.

Instruction on audiovisual production was handled the first year through Target Topic Seminars. The final evaluation indicated that the seminar blocks of time were not sufficient and that students preferred more in-depth, interrelated instruction in production techniques. A production block was developed for use during the second year and was scheduled in the first quarter of the academic program so that students could then use their production competencies throughout their program for assignments and experiences in the other curriculum content areas.

The concept of Target Topics did not work as well in practice as the theory behind the concept indicated. Because Target Topic Seminars were supplementary to the basic program, the students had a tendency not to take them seriously and to do little or no preparation. Several students stated in their final evaluations that because of the constant pressure of total involvement in the regular block program they could not mentally become involved in Target Topic Seminars. They had no capacity left to do so.

During the second year the number of Target Topic Seminars was greatly reduced and sessions were scheduled on days with minimal activity in the regular block program. This procedure, on the basis of the second year final evaluation, worked well. Examples of Target Topics were: professionalism, government publications and services, professional organizations, historical perspectives, governmental legislation, mass media, cable television, and discrimination in children's literature. The seminars varied in length from two to four hours depending on the scope of content.

## CURRICULUM CONTENT AND STRUCTURE

The curriculum structure of the experimental program was based on the premise that the most efficient and effective curriculum design was to package content according to functional relationships, thus covering related content together in a total context. For example, the media selection and acquisition block covered the aspects of selection and evaluation sources and processes, type of materials, general subject area materials, reference and bibliography, and purchasing sources and processes, i.e., the whole range of activities involved in obtaining materials for a library collection. For each block a document called a curriculum content resume was developed, which included content areas, behavioral objectives, instructional methods, facilities and materials needed, time period, and evaluation methods. A total of seventeen blocks and corresponding curriculum content resumes were developed. Each block was structured to interrelate with blocks already completed.

Supplementary activities, scheduled during the block, such as field trips, Target Topics, etc., were related to the block content insofar as possible. Provision was made for continuous evaluation by both students and faculty through use of evaluation forms, interviews, and periodic reviews. A final evaluation of each block emphasized content and structure and whether objectives had been achieved. Due to the flexibility of the program, modifications could be made during blocks if needed. Provision for individualized instruction based on identified needs enabled students to proceed at their own pace and to move ahead or back as desirable.

Block outlines and curriculum content resumes for each block were given to students at the beginning of each block. The entire schedule of activities for that time period were reviewed in order to allow students to set their own achievement goals and time deadlines. By this approach, feedback was received immediately concerning individual student needs and competency levels. Provision was made at this point for students to "test out" of all or parts of a block by demonstrated competency proficiency. This procedure, usually in a similated or actual work situation, emphasized knowledge and attitude as demonstrated by process and results.

Blocks varied in time structure and length, with some blocks consuming six to nine hours a day for three to five weeks. Other blocks were scheduled concurrently with other activities, such as the research design and methodology block, which was implemented over a period of eighteen weeks for three to five hours per week. The decision on time structure and length was based on content, method of instruction, amount and type of experience, and assignments required.

The major evaluation device used on a continuous basis was student and faculty diaries. These diaries, in which students and faculty were encouraged to make notes daily, reflected attitude, need, enthusiasm, disappointment, happiness, despair, etc, and proved to be the best source of continuous feedback information. The insights provided by these sources were invaluable for use in modifying the first year's program for use the second year. Modifications which resulted from diary comments included different sequencing of blocks, reduction of duplication of content, earlier field visits and experiences, and more attempts to individualize program components. The diaries also provided an excellent source of information by which to keep track of student progress and problems. Since the diaries were only read by the program directors, students and faculty felt free to put down real and complete attitudes and feelings, thus greatly increasing the usefulness of this source of data. Based on cross-checking information in the diaries with other types of feedback, the diaries seemed to have a high degree of validity and reliability.

# Program Results

## JOB-RELEVANT EDUCATION OBJECTIVES

The instructional objectives of the experimental program were based on the job descriptions in *Occupational Definitions for School Library Media Personnel*[1] and the competencies which were identified as a result of Phase I of the School Library Manpower Project. Also taken into consideration were the designated competency and certification requirements for media personnel in Minnesota and the surrounding states. This background data was used

1. School Library Manpower Project, *Occupational Definitions for School Library Media Personnel* (Chicago: American Library Association, 1971).

to develop curriculum content resumes for each subject area covered in the Mankato State program. From these resumes, daily program planning guides for each learning block were prepared for the use of students and faculty. During and at the end of each learning block, the progress of each student in meeting the behavioral objectives and attaining competencies was evaluated through continual contact between the students and instructors. This contact provided a means for the instructors to assess student achievement and identify areas needing remedial attention. The assessment was based on performance factors, i.e., the ability of the students to perform on the job in the same manner as would be expected if they were full-time professionals. An interim evaluation of each student occurred during the internship.

The final evaluation at the end of each year included a project-oriented demonstration of competency levels and individual interviews with each student. The project for each student was related to tasks which they would perform on a full-time job. Students and faculty rated the project-oriented activity high in both years of the program, in terms of usability, practicality, informational content, and implementation. The results of implementation indicated both reliability and validity.

## COMMUNICATION OF PROGRAM GOALS

The communication of program goals to students, staff, the college community and other persons was accomplished principally through personal contact and news releases. The staff of the experimental program made a major effort to communicate the function, purpose, and goals of the program to the students on a continuing basis at student and faculty meetings, in personal contact, and through instructional contact. The program director spent considerable time in disseminating information about the program to the college community, particularly those segments, such as the Graduate Dean and Council and the School of Education, which were directly related to the program. This process was evaluated through feedback in the form of personal contact, letters, and phone conversations obtained from various segments of the community, with the result that communication was generally rated as good to excellent. Breakdown in communication occurred the first year of the program with the on-site field supervisors, particularly in the pre-internship period. The on-site supervisors did not have sufficient background knowledge about the students to judge their capabilities and competency levels and consequently tended to either expect too much or too little from them. The

second year the supervisors were kept informed of overall program progress from the beginning through mail and phone contact. Efforts were made to have direct personal contact with supervisors several weeks in advance of internship, with special emphasis on a review of the program to date and the goals and objectives of the internship experience. This approach eliminated the problems of the first year.

One of the weak spots of the total program served to illustrate that adequate communication did not of itself guarantee a successful experience. Every effort was made to communicate with the School of Education and the Curriculum and Instruction Program concerning the goals and objectives of the experimental program from the time the proposal was written to the completion of the program. However, the curriculum block was the weakest subject segment of both program years, with little evidence that the School of Education faculty provided any individualization or recognition of the need for the students in the program to attain special competencies. This program block was restructured, and one person from the Curriculum and Instruction Program identified to work with the experimental program on this subject area during the second year. This approach provided for continuity between program components lacking during the first year, but did not overcome problems with appropriate content related to specific needs of experimental program students.

## STUDENT PROFICIENCY ASSESSMENT

The experimental program was designed to incorporate continuing assessment of student proficiency on a building block basis, i.e., each assessment would reveal a more comprehensive and sophisticated proficiency in areas previously covered in the program. This expectation was not totally realized, primarily for two reasons: (1) too little continuity between blocks and interrelating of blocks, and (2) ill-defined methods of proficiency assessment. More emphasis was placed on this aspect of the program during the second year, with faculty refining their techniques of measurement and attempting to build into them validity and reliability. Traditional methods of testing were not used, except as a pre-test situation to determine student needs. Testing was based on proficiency or competency attainment, using actual or simulated situations. Students were expected to produce output comparable to what would be expected of them on the job.

A major component of the proficiency assessment process was the Spring Quarter internship program. During this period the on-site supervisor and the program field supervisor were able to assess student strengths and weaknesses and provide on-the-spot developmental experiences to build up weak areas. This process was cited by both the students and faculty during the end of program evaluation in both years as a strength and a very useful component of the curriculum. This information was supplemented by an in-depth interview, involving the student, the field supervisor, and the on-site supervisor, at the completion of the internship to further identify student needs. Weaknesses revealed in this process were then built into the remaining instructional time. The interviews were valuable feedback experiences for all people involved.

The area of student proficiency assessment was one of the major trouble spots for the experimental program students the first year in terms of adjustment to the program structure and flexibility. The fact that the program included no tests or formal papers and that only a grade of "A" or "Incomplete" was given were interpreted by some students to mean no pursuit of anything that did not interest them. This attitude persisted until the internship period when these students finally learned how much they had missed along the way and why particular content areas were stressed. Unfortunately the world is not filled with students just waiting for the freedom to learn and hence motivation must sometimes be accomplished through the club of evaluation. However, the students during the second year had a maturity of purpose indicative of internal motivation from the beginning of the year, and the attitude described above did not exist. This attribute resulted from more homogeneous selection criteria the second year. Apparently, the tone set in the group from the beginning of the second year governed the attitude during the year with the contrasting results described.

## INSTRUCTIONAL PATTERNS

The curriculum structure of the experimental program was built around the block concept of subject coverage. Before the implementation of the experimental program, all competency areas were categorized into subject content blocks, which were in turn sequenced according to a logical progression of competency development. The sequence was from general to specific and from so-called basic or "prerequisite" areas to advanced application-oriented areas. The implementation of these blocks was carried out by the instructors assigned to each block. A lead instructor was identified for purposes of coordination and development of the blocks as needed. All instruction was carried out on a "team" basis, drawing upon the strengths of each team member.

The evaluation of instructional patterns was based upon group sessions of all program students and faculty at the end of each block, student and faculty interviews, diaries kept by each student and faculty member during the first year, and upon examination of student competency proficiency results. These activities provided a strong positive reaction to the instructional patterns used. A special strength identified in the evaluation was the flexibility of the block structure and the adaptability to make modification as needed during the period of emphasis for a particular block. Another major factor was the ability of students and faculty to accept changes in schedules without becoming apprehensive and abrasive. Without this acceptance, the program results would have been much less positive.

The modular block approach was, however, an early barrier for some students during the first program year. In spite of giving lip-service to individualization, some first-year students wanted to be treated exactly the same as the other students in the program with no recognition that some persons were capable of far more advanced activities than others. Some students must have structure to feel secure; unfortunately, they insist that other students should be structured also. Ways must be found to meet these diverse needs of all students and still maintain a coordinated program. The best solution seems to be more dedicated time on the part of faculty to meet with students individually and in small groups and to act as the structured security symbol.

## SPECIAL PROGRAM FEATURES

Special program features included (1) team instruction, (2) self-instruction, (3) Target Topic Seminars, (4) internship, (5) field experiences or observations, (6) professional meeting attendance, and (7) program informality and flexibility. Team instruction was generally very effective, as attested to by the reactions of students and faculty. The primary problems encountered during the first year were some lack of communication at critical times and some lack of coordination of content coverage. However, these areas were generally evaluated as not seriously effecting the total program and did not occur during the second year. Efforts were made to monitor more closely content coverage in blocks and the interrelationships of block content. The full-time experimental program coordinator coordinated all blocks and their content, utilizing the various staff, material, and facility resources as needed. More concentrated effort was made the second year to use the talents of persons with special expertise and to coordinate a true "team" approach to instruction rather than providing individual segments of instruction. This effort achieved more in-depth coverage, and also provided the program students with exposure to a variety of instructors.

Self-instruction was a primary objective of the experimental program. The general block instructional pattern included a general group introduction, individual activities, group and individual discussions, remedial developmental activities as needed, and group synthesis and review. At each of these stages the student was expected to work on his own, supplementing the group sessions and specified individual activities with other learning experiences related to his special needs and interests. Consequently, a major portion of the time in each block was nonstructured and free to be utilized by the student as needed. During the second year, however, the students preferred a group approach and did not seem to need or demand to work alone. An identified strong point of this aspect of the program was the availability of the instructional staff for students to consult and/or discuss with as needed. Here again, more time must be made available for program staff to meet with students and to individualize the self-instruction activities according to student background and experiences.

Target Topic Seminars were one of the downfalls of the experimental program in its first year. The concept upon which the Target Topic sessions were developed was valid and sound; however, due to student disinterest and scheduling problems, they were relegated to a low priority and consequently barely got off the ground. The sessions that were held were evaluated by the students and faculty involved as being good and valuable, thus leading to the conclusion that, with better coordination and management, the results might have been different. The Target Topic part of the program was modified the second year to have fewer, more tightly scheduled sessions, with more input from students in the selection of topics and speakers to be scheduled. An attempt was also made to more closely relate the topics to the learning blocks and other scheduled activities. Consequently, these Target Topic sessions occurred and were considered successful during the second year.

## FIELD EXPERIENCES

The internships were carefully planned to meet individual needs and to relate to career goals. Although students were consulted for preferences and asked for reasons why certain locations were desired, the final assignment was based on a variety of factors, including sequencing of experiences to assure maximum opportunity for growth. The supervisors' personalities and experience were also considered a factor in placement. A letter was written to each supervisor explaining the experimental nature of the program and an evaluative checklist was included for completion by the supervisor at the end of the student's internship. The cooperation of supervisors was excellent, with all of these persons viewing the opportunity as both a privilege and a professional responsibility.

Another major positive aspect of the experimental program was the broad variety of field experiences for students. Without exception, the field experience component was rated high by all people involved. The feeling was universal that the field experiences were the one most valuable aspect of the program. The faculty also noted that many of the field experiences represented excellent staff development activities for them as well. These experiences, including tours, trips to all types of media centers, observations, attendance at professional meetings and conferences, seminars with professional leaders, and field work activities, were scheduled to closely relate with the block content. An identified strength of this program component was the pre-field experience introduction and discussion and the post-field experience discussion and evaluation. Based on observations of staff and other program related personnel, there was no doubt that the program students became more sophisticated in knowledge gained from their field experiences than many people who have been in the field for years. Since this was one of the most costly experiences to provide, continued evaluation of this program area is planned. However, it may be several years before the cost effectiveness can be fully determined.

All student and faculty expenses incurred as a part of field experiences were paid through the experimental program grant, thus enabling all persons to participate equally without monetary considerations. Where possible, group rates for travel, lodging, and meals were secured. Careful itinerary planning also permitted cost savings. Reactions to the field experiences were so positive from students that the first year's group suggested that this part of the program should be continued even if the next year's students had to pay all or part of their own expenses.

The types of field experiences changed little from the first year to the second year. All students, and as many program related faculty as possible, were expected to participate. Evaluation, both individual and group, was carried out as part of the debriefing sessions held after each activity. A pre-activity session was held before each field experience to prepare the students in terms of background about the field site and what things to observe. A post-activity session was held to critique the field experience and review and evaluate student observations.

Program informality and flexibility were often cited by students in their program evaluations as a positive aspect in the total experimental program evaluation. All persons associated with the program felt that this informality and flexibility provided an atmosphere that was more conducive to learning than the more traditional classroom atmosphere. An example of the informality was the first name basis on which students and faculty talked with one another. Students were encouraged to talk with faculty as colleagues rather than as teachers. Other examples of the informality were students and faculty traveling and rooming together on trips and student activities scheduled in faculty homes.

## QUALITY CONTROL PROCEDURES

The evaluation of the experimental program was a continuing process with emphasis during the first year on immediate feedback and consequent program modification as needed. Students and faculty were given opportunities throughout the program to evaluate both formally and informally the content, structure, and other aspects of the program. The end of the first year evaluation was focused on identification of program areas needing specific changes during the second year and the methods by which these changes would be implemented. The end of the second year evaluation focused on program continuance and transportability. The next stage of evaluation will be a follow-up study with the program graduates which emphasizes the job relevancy of the experimental program and retrospective program evaluation. A review of the various components of the evaluation process to date indicates accomplishment of the stated goals and objectives, with the exception that the follow-up study has been delayed longer than anticipated due to pressures of time and

other commitments. Internal studies will complement the summative evaluation to be conducted by the School Library Manpower Project during Phase III.

Methods of evaluation during the first year included student and faculty diaries, individual interviews, observation of program activities and experiences, review sessions at the completion of each learning block, and feedback from persons outside the program who came in contact with program students and faculty. The diaries were of particular value in giving feedback upon which immediate changes could be made and problems solved. However, the diaries provided little evidence related to the transportability of a program. The overall effectiveness of the teaching methods for transportability are difficult to assess since methods relate to a specific person with a particular set of needs and interests.

## EXPERIMENTAL PROGRAM TRANSPORTABILITY

Transportability must be considered in terms of instructional program priorities at the receiving institution and how experimental program segments would fit into on-going programs. Initial review of the results of the various types of program evaluation at Mankato State would indicate that each institution considering an approach similar to this experimental program must develop its own program, unique to the institution's resources and capabilities. Concepts, structure, method, and content may be obtained from other institutions, but the final program design is a new entity.

Program continuance must be looked at not only structurally but also philosophically. The experimental program at Mankato State has affected the on-going program philosophically, particularly in terms of content emphasis and student awareness. Even if no structural parts of the experimental program were continued, the philosophical impact has been felt and will continue to be felt.

# Program Conclusions

In retrospect the experimental program at Mankato State College was successful (defining successful as being better than previous media education programs). The final evaluation by program students and faculty for both years indicated that, even though there were problem areas in both years, the experi-

mental curriculum was much improved over the traditional program of media graduate education and was well worth the investment of time, effort, and money. Both formative and summative evaluation supported this point of view, as did empirical data.

Strong points of the experimental program included: (1) informality between students and faculty, (2) block approach to curriculum content, (3) broad range of field experiences from visits to internships, (4) attendance at state and national media-related meetings and conferences, (5) personal dialogue in an informal setting between students and leaders in the media field, and (6) informal evaluation sessions throughout the program. The strengths of the program identified above relate specifically to the close interpersonal relationships of students and the persons with whom they came in contact and to an experimental curriculum which was based on a building block structure. The result was a personalized program of graduate education, a rare thing in higher education today.

Weak points of the experimental program included: (1) insufficient individualization of instruction to take into consideration the education and experience with which each student started the program, (2) curriculum content sequencing and coverage, and (3) professional education (curriculum and instruction) competency coverage. Although these weaknesses were considerably improved during the second year of the program, due to changes on the basis of the first year's continuing and final evaluation, students and faculty stated that further improvements could and should be made for better articulation and individualization of program content and instruction. One suggestion that was made and which should be pursued is that all total group class sessions be banned. All instruction should be small group and individual, using one or two faculty to act as full-time instructional facilitators and counselors.

Suggestions for improvement of curriculum content sequencing and coverage related to developing a more valid and reliable base of evidence concerning relative importance of various components of media education. This problem area could be resolved with another two year's implementation of the program, based on the substantial improvement empirically evident between the first and second year of the experimentation. Although the coverage of professional education competency areas showed improvement the second year based on student and faculty evaluations, the interrelation of this content area with the total program was cited by both students and faculty as a problem area. The best solution at this time appears to be to have a full-time program faculty member responsible for the professional education (curriculum and instruction) content area. School of Education faculty would then be utilized on a guest lecturer consultant basis. The practice of bringing full-time faculty from other disciplines into the pro-

gram for a temporary period did not work well during either year of the experimental program. This fact was true both in the professional education content area and in other content areas. The problem, as identified in student and faculty evaluations, was that temporary faculty could not assimilate well into the on-going program because of a lack of knowledge and information about what had happened and what was to happen. They could not interrelate with the total program.

Intensive and continuous program orientation for temporary staff may resolve this problem. However, the judgment at this time on the basis of time priorities would be that comprehensive orientation would have to come at the expense of other areas of the program and, therefore, another solution to the problem should be found.

The experimental program had a definite impact on both the College and on the media profession in Minnesota. The College, which had undergone a thorough re-examination of its goals and objectives used the experimental program as an example of curriculum and instructional change to better meet the needs of contemporary society. This resulted in much increased visibility of and knowledge about the Instructional Media and Technology Program. The effect of this process remains to be seen. The impact of the experimental program in the State is less tangible. The State Department of Education showed strong interest in the program and used it as an example for other disciplines. Some attitudes of media personnel throughout the State were effected positively, particularly as related to their viewpoints and knowledge about Mankato State and about school library media education. The program served as a focus to bring school audiovisual and library personnel together for discussion purposes. One other significant result of the experimental program was to emphasize the fact that Mankato State already had a good media education program and faculty before the experimental program was funded. Without this former foundation, the program would have been much more difficult to implement.

The experimental program at Mankato State College combined the ingredients of personalization, experiential instruction, and competency based content to formulate a different and improved approach to professional education for school library media personnel. The results were well worth the time and effort involved in the program and will provide a basis for further examination and change in media education.

Appendix A

Competency Checklist
for
Media Component

This checklist should be used to evaluate the level of student competency in the areas noted.  Please read the definition of each major component and then rate each competency using the definition as a frame of reference.  The levels of competency are defined below.  The line in the appropriate column should be checked for each individual competency.

Competency levels:

1. extraordinary proficiency

2. thorough competence, with capability of proceeding without supervision and guidance

3. beginning level competence, with need of supervision and guidance

4. some knowledge, without capability of implementing

5. no knowledge

MEDIA

Defined:  Media are the printed and audiovisual forms of communication and their accompanying technologies.  The media program provides a totality of services focused on the best utilization of these media to facilitate, improve and support the learning process.

| Competencies: | 1 | 2 | 3 | 4 | 5 |
|---|---|---|---|---|---|
| 1. To locate and select reliable sources of information about media. | — | — | — | — | — |
| 2. To develop a collection of bibliographic tools essential for keeping abreast of output in media and technology. | — | — | — | — | — |
| 3. To differentiate between the process of assessment based on professional judgment and evaluation based upon prescribed criteria and/or satisfaction of the user. | — | — | — | — | — |
| 4. To identify and apply appropriate criteria for assessment and evaluating materials and equipment in terms of their purported function and the needs (cognitive, physiological and affective) of the potential user. | — | — | — | — | — |
| 5. To provide accessibility to resources and equipment through processing and a systematic physical arrangement amenable to the user. | — | — | — | — | — |

|  |  | 1 | 2 | 3 | 4 | 5 |
|---|---|---|---|---|---|---|
| 6. | To apply and adapt principles of classifying, cataloging, and indexing to the media collection. | — | — | — | — | — |
| 7. | To appraise systems and aids for classifying and cataloging of resources available from other agencies. | — | — | — | — | — |
| 8. | To create produce and adapt resources, programs and/or technology to meet special needs. | — | — | — | — | — |
| 9. | To instruct students and teachers in the use of printed and auiovisual materials and equipment. | — | — | — | — | — |
| 10. | To interpret the content and intent of media and equipment to students and teachers. | — | — | — | — | — |
| 11. | To plan, arrange and conduct in-service education for teachers and school library media staff in the effective use of media. | — | — | — | — | — |
| 12. | To motivate and guide students and teachers in developing reading, viewing and listening competencies including skills, attitudes, and appreciation. | — | — | — | — | — |
| 13. | To demonstrate by example, effective ways to utilize media. | — | — | — | — | — |
| 14. | To apply instructional methodology and knowledge of instructional objectives to the place and utilization of media in the educational program. | — | — | — | — | — |

Appendix B

## INTRODUCTION TO PROFESSSIONAL RESOURCES BLOCK

This block covers professional resources, individual indexes, journals, and other pertinent publications.  The overall objective is to make you aware of their existence and interrelationship.   These resources will be of continuing value for your research and professional growth during the year and through-out your future career.

Content Areas:  Professional Resources

Specification:  Review, examination, and utilization of audiovisual and library facilities, collections, and services, with emphasis on bibliographic tools, professional literature, equipment op-eration and utilization, and facility arrangement and utilization, in order to develop awareness and familiarity with resources to be used throughout the program.

Teaching and Learning Strategies:  Tours, self-instruction programs, user exercises, small and large group instruction and discussion, and interaction with subject area media specialists.

Time Block:  One week, with continuing emphasis and instruction throughout the year.

Competency Areas:

To develop a collection of bibliographic tools essential for keeping abreast of output in media and technology.

To evaluate, utilize, and design media technology to facilitate learning.

To engage in continuous study for professional growth, including the study of current information and trends affecting message design and system analysis and contribution to the creation of such processes.

To support and play a constructive role in professional organizations and activities.

To identify and differentiate among research methods.

To locate pertinent research.

To interpret findings of existing research.

To instruct students and teachers in the use of printed and audio-visual materials and equipment.

Appendix C

MANKATO STATE COLLEGE SCHOOL LIBRARY MEDIA EDUCATION PROGRAM
Daily Program Planning Guide

DAY: Monday, Tuesday, Wednesday   DATE: Sept. 25,26,27   BLOCK: Professional Res.   1 Page of 1 Page

| Time | Faculty | Location | Activity | Objectives |
|---|---|---|---|---|
| Monday 9:00–12:00 noon | F.M. J.M. | ML 1023 | Meeting – Introductory Materials | 1. To explain goals and objectives of unit. 2. To outline assignments. 3. To introduce content. |
| 1:00 p.m. | F.M. J.M. K.P. | ML 1023 | ERC self-instructional unit | 4. To identify the location of the ERC and note the existence of the self-instructional tape which Knapp students will listen to on Tuesday. |
| Tuesday 9:00–11:30 a.m. | F.M. J.M. K.P. | | Audio-tutorial unit for: Education Index ERIC | 5. To be able to identify the basic professional tools you need to utilize for study during the remainder of the year. |
| 1:00–2:00 p.m. | F.M. J.M. K.P. | ML 1023 | Examine professional periodicals, noting the following: Publisher Intended Audience Features: Reoccurring column Reviews, print-non-print News notes Nature of the articles, i.e., scholarly, popular Types of ads Professional or commercial journal | 6. To compare AECT, ALA, Wilson and Bowker, Minn. State pubs, and professional teaching journals. |
| Wednesday 9:30 a.m. | J.M. | Minnea-polis | Bloomington field trip | 7. To discuss the professional colln. (what there, how selected, how used, and what professional readings done to keep up to date). 8. The professional colln. on the district level is discussed. How selected, utilized, etc. 9. Remainder of trip to serve as background for the Philosophy and Organization of a media Program. (Oct. 4th block) |
| Evening | J.M. | S.L. | Target Topic "Role Identification" | |

# MILLERSVILLE STATE COLLEGE

DIVISION OF EDUCATION

Dr. James E. Maurey, Dean

## AN EXPERIMENTAL PROGRAM IN
# SCHOOL LIBRARY MEDIA EDUCATION
## 1971–1973

*Final Report by*

JOSEPH F. BLAKE and KENNETH I. TAYLOR

## Contents

# DEPARTMENT OF EDUCATIONAL MEDIA

## Joseph F. Blake, Chairman

*Experimental Program Staff, 1971-1973*

Mr. Joseph F. Blake, Director

Dr. Kenneth I. Taylor, Associate Director

Mrs. Isabelle H. Binkley
Mr. Robert A. Greybill
Dr. Robin Kranz
Mrs. Mary Emma Llewellyn
Mrs. Minda M. Sanders

Miss Margaret R. Tassia
Miss Alice L. Wagner
Dr. Byron M. Wagner, 1972-73
Mr. Keith E. Yoder

*Consulting Members from Other Departments*

Dr. Ralph G. Anttonen, Director of Educational Research

Dr. Carl O. Schmidtke, Chairman of Secondary Education

*Advisory Board, 1971-1973*

Mr. Joseph F. Blake
Chairman, Department of Educational Media
Millersville State College

Miss Deborah K. Breiner
Student Member
Millersville State College

Miss Gwenn Brown
Supervisor of Libraries
Chester-Upland School District

Dr. Nicholas Brown
Vice President for Academic Affairs
Millersville State College

Mr. Ernest Doerschuk
State Librarian
Pennslyvania State Library

Dr. William H. Duncan
President
Millersville State College

Mrs. Linnea P. Frerichs
Student Member
Millersville State College

Dr. Harry K. Gerlach
Deputy Commissioner of Basic Education
Pennsylvania Department of Education

Dr. Donald S. Glass
Superintendent
Lancaster City Schools

Miss Katherine Green
Student Member
Millersville State College

Mrs. Elizabeth P. Hoffman
Chief, Division of School Libraries
Pennsylvania Department of Education

Miss Kathleen Kies
Chief, Division of Teacher Education
Pennsylvania Department of Education

Dr. James E. Maurey
Dean, Division of Education
Millersville State College

Mr. John S. Rees
Trustee
Millersville State College

Mr. Melvin Rosier
Superintendent
Lampeter-Strasburg School District

Dr. L. Lloyd Ruoss
Executive Director
Lancaster-Lebanon Intermediate Unit 13

Dr. Garold C. Wisor
Assistant Commissioner for Higher Education
Pennsylvania Department of Education

# Overview

## A PROGRAM FOR THE BEGINNING SCHOOL LIBRARY MEDIA SPECIALIST

Millersville State College is situated in southeastern Pennsylvania in the heart of rural Pennsylvania Dutch country. The historic borough of Millersville and its county of Lancaster combine the old and the new in an unusual blend of eighteenth-century architecture and contemporary industrial, business, and governmental facilities. The college capitalizes on cultural, social, and educational benefits of nearby Philadelphia, Baltimore, Washington, and New York City.

The history of the College spans more than a century. Founded as a private academy in 1854, it became the first teacher preparatory school in Pennsylvania in 1855 and was approved as the first state normal school in 1859. Teacher preparation remained as the College's single function for one hundred years. In 1959 its name was changed to Millersville State College, and it became a multi-purpose undergraduate and graduate institution. Today the campus covers 225 acres and contains fifty buildings. Approximately 330 full-time faculty members and administrators serve nearly 4,500 undergraduate and 1,200 full- and part-time graduate students.

The College is a member of the American Association of Colleges for Teacher Education and the Middle States Association of Colleges and Secondary Schools. It is also accredited by the National Council for Accreditation of Teacher Education.

The Department of Educational Media celebrated its fiftieth anniversary in 1973. Courses in the use of books and libraries and in children's literature were taught as early as 1912. Later, an instructional program in library science was developed, consisting of fifteen hours, of reference, classification, cataloging, book selection, children's literature, school library administration, and demonstration lessons. The first class was graduated in 1923. In September 1969, faculty members teaching audiovisual courses joined the Library Education Department to form the Department of Educational Media. The department is located in the Division of Education and offers a unified undergraduate program of pre-service preparation in educational media.

The Millersville program was designed for the beginning school library media specialist. It was the only totally undergraduate media program of the six experimental models in the School Library Manpower Project. The four-year program was in a stage of transition from traditional courses to a more flexible approach to learning. In this transition, the Department of Educational Media provided experiences that were personalized and more closely identified with responsibilities encountered by graduates in their first year of professional activity.

Occupational task analyses of practicing media specialists, including a locally conducted study of departmental graduates, were the basis of learning experiences developed in modular form which provided creative application of media principles to new situations on and off campus. These instructional modules advised students in advance of expectations to be required, held students accountable for attainment, provided them with feedback concerning progress, and emphasized terminal rather than entry performance.

Field experiences began in the freshman year. Occurring off campus, these experiences allowed students to observe and participate in classroom and media center activities of nearby schools. The experiences were designed to help students obtain a feel for the nature of media services as a profession before their senior semester of student teaching. Student teaching refers to supervised fieldwork performance for one semester in the senior year and places students in classrooms as well as media centers to gain practice in supervised pre-service teaching. A part of this semester time was spent in classrooms to dramatize the point that media services should be planned in relation to the processes of teaching and learning that occur within the school in classrooms and laboratories. Throughout the program, student evaluation of modules, field experiences, and student teaching responsibilities provided the staff with a new foundation for program review and revision.

A basic position of the department is that beginning school library media specialists should relate media services to teaching and learning requirements of all school personnel. This position is reflected in the department's two-fold interest in both media specialists and teachers. Needed in schools, according to

**111**

the department, are media specialists who are concerned with education first and media second. Also needed are classroom teachers who are proficient in basic media competencies that are vital to instruction. Common loyalties help both groups plan and develop programs together.

A prominent feature of the experimental program at Millersville was encouragement of total faculty involvement in program development and implementation. In this respect, the process by which faculty members learned to work together on common objectives was considered to be as important as the products that emerged from the joint endeavor.

## PHILOSOPHY AND ASSUMPTIONS FOR CHANGE

The School Library Manpower Project award to Millersville gave national recognition and support to an undergraduate program that was already being changed as a result of local planning. That change originated in an initial attempt to consolidate campus media services and teaching. In September, 1968, the President of the college established an ad hoc committee of faculty members, directors of programs, and administrators from library education, audio-visual instruction and services, the college library, computer programs and services, and teacher education. The committee studied all media programs and services of the college and made recommendations increasing their effectiveness and efficiency.

Three recommendations were made for refining and improving campus services. Resulting actions produced several organizational changes needed for modernizing pre-service preparation of school library media specialists. The first of these was reorganization of the Library Education Department into the Department of Educational Media to provide a unified program of media instruction. The second was that the Department of Educational Media should continue administration of the program of school library media services for the college's Elizabeth Jenkins School for Children. Managed by an educational media faculty member, this program is acknowledged as an advanced prototype of the modern media center for an elementary school. The media center functions as a model for school districts within the college's service area and as a laboratory for students of the Departments of Educational Media and Elementary Education.

A third recommendation resulted in a review by the department of the preservice curriculum for school library media specialists. This review supported the recognition that more emphasis should be placed on validated, occupationally-related competencies needed by the school library media specialist. It also indicated that variables seem to be present in traditional programs of library education which account for the persisting perception of school libraries as adjuncts to education. One of these variables is an interpretation of the multimedia concept that is concerned primarily with media as ends in themselves, i.e., media are viewed as objects to be ordered, accessioned, classified, cataloged, and stored rather than elements of the larger processes of teaching and learning. Another variable is heavy emphasis on professional identity with library history and other kinds of libraries having vastly different purposes and clientele. The result is minimal professional identity with educational goals of schools and college departments of education.

As a consequence of the above recommendations and actions, the Department of Educational Media was brought closer to all teacher preparation in the Division of Education. It is the position of this division that effective improvement in the total teacher preparation program is accomplished by means of interdepartmental participation. Formerly an assortment of independent professional education courses, the teacher preparation program is being restructured around a carefully specified set of occupationally-related competencies and responsibilities that cross course lines and are attained on and off campus.

The new Department of Educational Media was assigned a dual role in the preparation of media specialists and of teachers with other specialties. That role was intended to demonstrate to the campus and others that, as school library media education is brought toward the center of educational activities, three important outcomes may be anticipated. First, teacher candidates become more effectively equipped with essential media competencies. Second, beginning school library media specialists gain greater commitment to the teaching-learning process while meeting teaching competencies. Third, with education as a shared concern, teacher candidates and beginning media specialists learn to work more effectively together in designing productive learning environments.

The department's two-fold responsibility for school library media specialists and other teachers is justified on the basis of what is required by the schools in which Millersville's student teachers and graduates are placed. Both elementary and secondary schools are adopting newer approaches to teaching and learning that personalize instruction and relate programs to community activities. Young people are encouraged to examine topics of their choice, progress through subject matter at their own rates, draw upon a variety of media for reference, consult outside authorities as needed on matters of current interest, work together in processes of creative inquiry, and express original findings and ideas to others with and through locally produced media.[1] Teachers are planning programs and learning environments that are open, flexible, and subject to modification.

In these new approaches to teaching and learning school library media specialists are needed who understand the curriculum in a comprehensive way and participate in instructional planning that affects every area of the school. The media centers, in turn, must be planned and administered in relation to educational needs that originate outside their walls.

On the basis of these observations, the new program of the Department of Educational Media was

---

1. Kenneth I. Taylor, "Creative Inquiry and Instructional Media," *School Media Quarterly* I (Fall 1972):18-26.

designed to provide the following changes and improvements:

1. More thoughtful preservation of the best features of the department's original program.
2. Implementation of a competency-based, field-centered, and performance-oriented program which introduces job-related opportunities as early as possible in the curriculum.
3. More appropriate curricular integration of concepts from fields such as educational administration, psychology, research, and sociology by relating them to responsibilities of school library media specialists.
4. Availability of experiences known to be related to critical knowledges and skills and which are designed to allow application of those knowledges and skills.
5. More efficient use of learning resources and time in the development of professional skill, thereby allowing time for the pursuit of general education in greater depth.

# Program Goals and Objectives

## RESPONSE TO SCHOOL REQUIREMENTS

The Millersville program focused on three major objectives:

1. Development of a competency-based, field-centered, and performance-oriented undergraduate program for the beginning school library media specialist.
2. Provision of learning activities in a greater variety of modes and settings.
3. Education of beginning school library media specialists as teachers who function as instructional leaders in their schools.

Definitions of three terms in the first objective are as follows: "Competencies" are considered to be presently identifiable knowledges and skills that have been found to be essential to successful administration of school library media centers and programs. "Field-centered" means the curriculum is directed to media programs of the schools. "Performance-oriented" refers to professional activity that is greater than the sum of known, identifiable, occupationally-related competencies. It includes aspects of professional decision-making, educational philosophy, and

service that distinguish one individual from another. In particular, it goes beyond what is to be done in present schools by suggesting what "should" be done theoretically and idealistically. In this respect, it illustrates how departments of educational media may progress beyond the "status-quo" of occupational task-analyses.

These objectives identify two principles that have continued throughout curricular planning. First, the program is based upon education and media as its fields of study. Second, it is designed to prepare students first as *teachers* who plan instructional strategies and learning activities with others in their schools, and second as *media specialists* who draw upon media as elements that are used within strategies and activities.

Although the department encountered constraints that resulted from college tradition, progress was achieved through joint participation by students within the department, members of other departments of the Division of Education, and co-workers in surrounding schools. Results at the conclusion of the two-year experimentation indicated that evolution of a competency-based and performance-oriented program from infancy to maturity is primarily a long-term process of group inquiry into a shared concern, i.e., the design and development of a curriculum that is responsive to the requirements of schools in which graduates are placed.

On the basis of a transitional program that has been characterized from its beginning by staff involvement, members of the department believe that much of the curriculum can be stated in terms of competencies needed to begin working in a school library media center. These competencies can be identified from outside sources, e.g., the work of the School Library Manpower Project and locally conducted studies, as were done by Millersville. Once identified, these competencies may be incorporated into a curricular outline that cuts across traditional course offerings.

It also appears that a number of overt behaviors can be specified in terms that are acceptable as evidence of given competencies. Although the relationship between overt behavior and attainment of desired objectives is imperfect, Millersville believes that observation of overt behavior is one way by which attainment of some objectives can be assessed and evaluated. Initially, specification of behaviors is difficult to accomplish. The task becomes more definitive as faculty members gain experience and as the state of the art advances.

A competency-base can be structured to promote personalization with respect to point of entry into the curriculum, pacing, sequencing, and assessment. An advantage gained from a personalized program was that opportunities were found to encourage students to design their own instruction in lieu of that prescribed by the department. In general, students were able to design instruction more precisely in such a program than in a traditional course setting. A modularized approach to learning established optimal conditions for students, faculty, and local practitioners to collaborate in the undergraduate program, while developing offerings that were often appropriate, with minor modification, to in-service school library media specialists.

The performance orientation of the program, as defined by Millersville, focused on pre- and in-service professional activities in the schools. Performance was viewed as more than a body of identifiable competencies that were minimal in administering a program of media services. Performance includes those aspects of professional decision making, educational philosophy, and service that distinguish one individual from another. Aspects such as these are likely to arise out of association with one's professors and identification with the philosophy of a department. Evaluation of these aspects tends to be based on professional judgments by one's teachers and colleagues. Performance orientation is also related to the third major program objective to be discussed later in this section, i.e., the preparation of media specialists as teachers who function as educational leaders in their schools.

Although more opportunities for personalizing learning can be provided by the experimental program, personal learning is not equated with insular learning, nor is independent study seen as the only desired pattern of learning in the Millersville program. A variety of modes and settings is desirable. Significantly, instructional modules do not have to limit learning to activities that occur away from other people. They can be developed to bring students into contact with community members and agencies, such as public libraries and area schools. Modules can also provide ideal opportunities to have students report experiences and share ideas with other students in groups that are smaller than conventional classes. The possibilities for consultation between student and teacher on a one to one basis at any point are almost endless.

From observation of departmental students during field experiences, student teaching, and first-year teaching, Millersville anticipates that school library media specialists who have learned through appropriately diversified experiences will be more flexible in the programs they ultimately manage in their schools. It also anticipates that professionals who have had more care devoted to their own personal learning styles during preservice preparation will, in turn, give personal attention to students in their schools.

Performance orientation of the Millersville program signifies an emphasis on behavior of the school library media specialist as a professional teacher and co-worker in his work setting. The department believes school library media specialists must be active in the teaching-learning process by displaying a diagnosing, prescribing, treating, and evaluating style of inquiry. They must be able to practice and communicate the behavioral science concept of media services and instructional design. Early preparation of this nature can be similar or identical to that received by other teacher candidates and much of this preparation can be offered on the campus. An approach to instructional design, including identification of behaviors at higher degrees of precision, can be demonstrated by departmental staff and displayed in modules. Students may gain practice by planning parts of their own instruction. At Millersville, additional practice is provided by placing students of educational media in classrooms as teachers for a part of their student teaching experience.

Students must be knowledgeable also about capabilities and environmental aspects of human learning as it relates to selection and utilization of all kinds of media. Students should be encouraged to evaluate materials with reference to an outside target, namely learner characteristics, patterns of learning, and teaching strategies. Campus preparation is supplemented with observational and participatory experiences in area schools that begin as early as possible. Millersville is now attempting to establish a sequence of cumulative, off-campus experiences that begin in the freshman and continue through the senior year.

Students must be prepared to relate effectively to individuals in all fields of the educational community, to function in leadership roles as responsible enablers of educational change and development, and to be competent facilitators of curricular-related media programs and services. It is hoped that programs can be designed on campus to have media specialists work with other teacher candidates on current educational problems of interest to particular schools. An adoption of professional education blocks of preparation by the Departments of Elementary and Secondary Education in lieu of discrete courses anticipates this goal. With cooperating schools, the Department of Educational Media has begun the planning of representative media center and classroom-related experiences for its student teachers that place greater emphasis on instruction as it actually occurs.

## AN OCCUPATIONAL FOCUS

An occupational task analysis was conducted in 1971 at the beginning of the experimental program. A faculty committee studied task analyses and occupational definitions obtained from outside sources and then formulated a basic checklist of duties that

might be performed by beginning school library media specialists. The checklist was sent to persons who had graduated prior to the experimental program and then reviewed with each graduate at his school.

Detailed information on processes involved in the analysis, opinions sought from graduates, and the nature of the checklist is given later in the section, "Program Components." Only general observations concerning the early planning stages of the program will be given here.

Basically, it was found that the 1970 and 1971 graduates contacted in this study were pleased with the undergraduate training which they received in the Millersville program. Comments from the principals interviewed were favorable and complimentary to both the graduates and the program. In the opinion of the graduates, student teaching had been the most valuable preservice experience. They stated that their cooperating librarians, i.e., those who directed their student teaching in the school media centers, had a very significant influence on them. Over ninety percent of the graduates visited appeared to follow the practices that their cooperating librarian followed.

The majority recommended very strongly that student teachers be given experience at all three school levels. Nearly three-quarters of the graduates felt that classroom experience during student teaching would have made them better media specialists. A better knowledge of curriculum, especially at the elementary school level, also would have been helpful.

This task analysis benefited the department by providing evidence as to which tasks and knowledges should be included in the preservice program. It served as a base for providing more reliable instructional objectives in the curricular outline and its accompanying modules for the experimental program. It gave a clearer indication of which tasks and knowledges should be on campus and which in field situations.

# Program Participants

## STUDENTS

As an established undergraduate program with more than a fifty-year history, Millersville had no special recruiting problems. The major constraint was a commitment made by the department in its proposal to the School Library Manpower Project to

produce graduates by December, 1972.[2] This meant that all work for the Bachelor of Science degree had

2. *Proposal for an Experimental Program in School Library Media Education . . . December 1970* (Millersville: Millersville State College, Department of Educational Media, 1970).

to be completed by or before this date, and that students involved would, necessarily, enter the new program at various stages of preservice training.

It was originally planned to phase students into the program in three stages. Stage I, 1971-72: Twenty-five full time students would volunteer for this beginning stage. Stage II, 1972-73: Twenty-five more advanced students would be moved into the program along with all incoming first year students. Stage III, 1973-74: All students and faculty would be involved.

Stage I began in September 1971 when the staff and thirty student volunteers initiated the first learning activities of the experimental program. The students came with a wide range of abilities, motivation, and interests. Variety was added by including six elementary education majors who had planned initially to complete only a library education "area of interest." These six students were representative of a joint effort by the Departments of Elementary Education and Educational Media to design opportunities for achieving double majors in these fields.

These thirty students and the departmental staff launched a new program having the complexity of thirty individual sets of student needs. The faculty moved immediately from rhetoric on personalization to the reality of having to customize experiences for individuals and for groups of students. Twenty-nine students completed the semester, one resigned from the program to marry. The second semester of Stage I was devoted to designing, initiating, and field-testing a new approach to student teaching in collaboration with a local school district. Six of the students participated in this new approach by moving through a specified sequence of experiences in media centers, classrooms, and other parts of schools at elementary, middle, and senior high levels.

In September 1972 the original plans for Stage II were modified so that more time could be spent extending the new student teaching approach to other nearby school districts. Experimental program modules were introduced into the regular program to include teacher candidates in other subject fields. Thus modules were refined in class-like settings, a procedure that accelerated faculty and student involvement in a restructure of instructional activities throughout the department. Twenty students graduated from the experimental program by December 1972.

## STAFF

Staff requirements for a program like Millersville's can best be explained by identifying individual qualities and characteristics that were exhibited by members of the department and found to be important. These are: commitment to teacher education; commitment to the unified media concept in basic education; desire to move the learner to the center of the instructional stage; successful work experience in schools at elementary and secondary levels; tolerance for ambiguity, especially in the initial stages of the program; knowing *how* as well as knowing *about;* product-oriented work habits; sharing of expertise and knowledge; viewing program products as joint endeavors and a willingness to go beyond the "teaching load." Through funding from the School Library Manpower Project it was possible to add three new members to the staff. These new members represented preparation, respectively, in curriculum and instruction, instructional design and evaluation, and production techniques. Specialized contributions of these new members were used to supplement an existing body of departmental talents and promote staff development.

In transition toward a more flexible program, Millersville adopted the viewpoint that program development and staff development were essentially the same. It seemed that an experimental program had greater likelihood of success if it sought cooperative staff participation in all facets of development. These facets included early stages of planning, curricular decisions, learning activities, and evaluation.

The new program dictated a strong thrust toward cooperative planning, a need that grew as the program was refined. A Program Development Committee, composed of all members of the department and of consultants from other departments was instrumental in the advancement of the program. Regularly scheduled meetings provided each member with a comprehensive view of the program and informed him about progress on its essential parts. Members of other departments in the Division of Education assisted in planning interdepartmental approaches to broader blocks of experiences.

An important result of cooperative planning was an increased willingness of the faculty to share experiences with other departments as the college recognized, responded, and sometimes anticipated requirements of schools. Interdepartmental cooperation was extended to other departments of the Division of Education, principally to the Departments of English, Elementary Education, and Secondary Education. A new first-year introduction to the field of knowledge was developed with the Divisions of the Social Sciences, Humanities, and Sciences.

Recent commitment by the Commonwealth of Pennsylvania to competency-based programs has been influential in stimulating interest of other campus departments in the process by which the experimental program was initiated and implemented. A department manual on the writing of instructional modules was especially useful to outside departments.[3] Millersville's Division of Education will be the first in the commonwealth to be reviewed for progress in competency-based teacher education programs.

## ADVISORY BOARD

Members of the program's Advisory Board served as reactors and consultants to the experimental program. Progress of the program was communicated via printed reports, conferences with individual members, and presentations to the board as a whole. In turn, members of the Board were in positions to interpret the program to others.

The Board was composed of sixteen members,

3. *The Instructional Module: Specification, Design, Development* (Millersville: Millersville State College, Department of Educational Media, 1972).

four of whom represented students of the program. Other members included administrators of the college and the Division of Education, administrators of local school districts and one intermediate school unit, the president of the Pennsylvania School Librarians' Association, the state librarian, and representatives of the State Department of Education.

As consultants, members of the Board assisted on an individual basis. Student members interpreted program development to educational media majors on formal and informal occasions. Campus administrators lent continuing support and assisted in facilitating interdepartmental cooperation. Superintendents of local school districts enlarged opportunities for off-campus classroom and media center field experiences and were instrumental in the design of a new approach to student teaching. Other professional representatives reviewed the curricular outline, competencies, individual instructional modules, and student teaching activities. Members of the Board played an important role in obtaining local and state support of the program after discontinuance of funding from the School Library Manpower Project.

# Program Components

## GENERAL AND PROFESSIONAL EDUCATION

The undergraduate experimental program focused on the first level of professional responsibility, that of the school library media specialist in the individual school media center. This level of responsibility was outlined in the occupational definitions of the School Library Manpower Project.[4]

The media education core of the department and a teacher education core of the Departments of Elementary and Secondary Education constituted the professional component of the major in educational media. This professional component was complemented and strengthened by a strong program of general studies. Each student designed his own program by electing courses from the Divisions of Science and Mathematics, Social Sciences, and Humani-

4. School Library Manpower Project, *Occupational Definitions for School Library Media Personnel* (Chicago: American Library Association, 1971).

ties, while also exploring one area in depth outside the department. This area was designated as his "area of interest." Through general electives and the area of interest, departmental students devoted over sixty percent of their undergraduate time to general studies.

The relationship of general and professional preparation is illustrated in Figure 1.

Retaining Millersville's emphasis on general education, the experimental program was an attempt to include realistic and replicable elements in the preservice experiences of its students, insofar as these elements could be ascertained. These elements, namely occupationally-related competencies and performance-oriented responsibilities, were identified partly through analyses of work situations and partly on the basis of judgments by professional media specialists and other educators.

Competencies were considered to be presently identifiable knowledges and skills that were found to be essential to successful administration of school

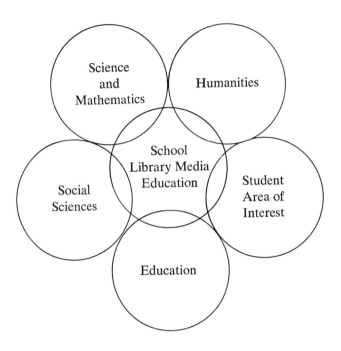

Figure 1. Department of Educational Media Program of General and Professional Education

library media centers and programs. Although no entirely satisfactory description of competency-based teacher education had yet been established, the American Association of Colleges for Teacher Education indicated that programs moving in this direction could be characterized as competency-based if:

1. Competencies (knowledges, skills, behaviors) to be demonstrated by the student are:
    a. derived from explicit conceptions of teachers' roles,
    b. stated so as to make possible assessment of a student's behavior in relation to specific competencies, and
    c. made public in advance;
2. Criteria to be employed in assessing competencies are:
    a. based upon, and in harmony with, specified competencies,
    b. explicit in stating expected levels of mastery under specified conditions, and

c. made public in advance;
3. Assessment of the student's competency
    a. uses his performance as the primary source of evidence,
    b. takes into account evidence of the student's knowledge relevant to planning for, analyzing, interpreting, or evaluating situations or behavior, and
    c. strives for objectivity;
4. The student's rate of progress through the program is determined by demonstrated competency rather than by time or course completion;
5. The instructional program is intended to facilitate the development and evaluation of the student's achievement of competencies specified.[5]

The American Association of Colleges for

5. Stanley Elam, ed., *Performance-Based Teacher Education; What is the State of the Art?* (Washington, D.C.: American Association of Colleges for Teacher Education, 1971), pp. 6-7.

Teacher Education equated the terms "competency-base" and "performance-base" in the document cited above. The term "performance-orientated" was employed in the Millersville program in another sense. As indicated earlier, the more elusive "performance-oriented responsibilities" of the media specialist refers to professional activities that represent more than the sum of known, identifiable, occupationally-related competencies. They included aspects of professional decision making, personal education philosophies, and qualities of service that distinguish one individual from another. In certain respects, these activities could be considered to go beyond what is being done in present schools by suggesting what "should" be done theoretically and idealistically. Consequently, they illustrated how departments of educational media might be able to progress beyond the status-quo of presently identifiable tasks to responsibilities that become essential as new situations arise. The emphasis in this instance was on the process of educational change rather than on the application of ready formulas.

## CURRICULAR DESIGN

Curricular development is commonly concerned with three questions: "What should students learn?", "How should students learn?", and "How can learning be made more effective?" Taken together, these questions established logical priorities for intra- and interdepartmental group study. The first question defined objectives at various levels of specificity that delineated behaviors and content. The second identified instructional strategies and learning activities. The third called for program revision as procedures of teaching and learning were modified. Departmental study of these questions was concerned with the inter-relationships of teaching, learning and media.

To the Department of Educational Media curricular change represented an effort to preserve the best features of its original program as it implemented an essentially personalized program of study that was based on identifiable competencies and oriented toward performance responsibilities. In its gradual transition, one that involved the entire staff, the process by which curricular change is brought about was considered to be of prime importance.

The process of curricular change may be described as a series of departmental tasks that are sequential solely on the basis of inception, not completion. Once begun, the tasks became concurrent staff responsibilities that were increasingly interrelated. They included identification of major objectives, examination of established course content, development of a new curricular outline, and occupational task analyses, all of which preceded utilization of educational media and development of teaching and learning methodologies. Each task is discussed in the next section to indicate the nature of program development at Millersville.

## PROCESS OF CURRICULAR CHANGE

The three major objectives of the program represented a behavioral science base in program design:

1. Development of a competency-based, field-centered, and performance-oriented undergraduate program for the beginning school library media specialist.
2. Provision of learning activities in a greater variety of modes and settings.
3. Education of beginning school library media specialists as teachers who function as instructional leaders in their schools.

This base included the behavioral science modes of inquiry in problem-solving as well as its modes of information retrieving and sharing. Inherent was a recognition that, although all branches of knowledge are important in the preparation of school library media specialists, the behavioral sciences contribute unusually important concepts and methods of inquiry that are needed in contemporary educational thought and practice. In relation to media services, the "behavioral concept" was considered more appropriate to the processes of teaching and learning than the traditional "physical science concept," i.e., the behavioral science concept holds that practice should be based on dynamics of human behavior, whereas the physical science concept stresses primacy of devices and procedures as adjuncts to the presentation of ideas.

This recognition of a behavioral science base was accompanied by a desire for new approaches in teaching and learning that are characteristic of the behavioral sciences, approaches that are concerned with the designation of identifiable competencies and responsibilities at high degrees of specificity. These approaches led to an increasingly complex cyclical process of describing, analyzing, proposing, prescribing, treating, and observing student behaviors as a consequence of learning activities. The process was seen as a means by which continuous program improvement could be implemented through joint efforts of students and teachers. Such a procedure insured that student problems were dealt with responsively and intelligently in human terms.

Following the indentification of major objectives, the faculty studied the first curricular question, i.e., the "what" of learning, by identifying topics covered in existing courses. The study indicated where duplication of content could be eliminated and where intentional redundancy might be desirable. Broad topics were identified which the staff believed should remain in the program. To these topics, new topics were added during the growth of the program.

The department believed that students should have command of knowledges, competencies, and professional responsibilities related to learning theory; student growth and development; human behavior; instructional strategies; instructional design; communication techniques; content of a broad range of audiovisual and printed media associated with school library media centers and classrooms; evaluation and selection criteria for all classes of media; materials related to literature for children and young people; reference materials and information retrieval; evaluation, selection, and utilization of instructional and production equipment; production techniques; reading, listening, and viewing abilities to assure proper guidance for utilizing media; theory and function of school library media programs; administration of school library media collections; and research techniques for consumers and disseminators of information.

These topics and a suggested curriculum content from the School Library Manpower Project[6] were used to prepare a departmental curricular outline that was in constant revision.[7] The outline is divided into five broad areas, called curricular "contexts," which cut across course structures:

100  Human Behavior: Development and Interaction
200  Learning Environment
300  Media
400  Administration
500  Research

Two further divisions of the outline, "sub-contexts" and "components", indicate content and program objectives in greater detail as an aid to the staff

6. School Library Manpower Project, "Suggestions for Curriculum Content within Major Areas of Competencies," *School Library Manpower Project, Phase I—Final Report* (Chicago: American Library Association, 1970), pp. 53-69.

7. *Performance-Based Curriculum, Library Science K-12* (Millersville: Millersville State College, Department of Educational Media, 1972).

in specifying competencies and writing expectations for instructional modules. Sub-contexts are broad and somewhat comparable in designation to traditional course offerings. For example, the first two sub-contexts in the Media Context are:

301  Selection of Media
302  Acquisitions—Materials and Equipment

Each sub-context is divided into components, i.e., program objectives, for which any desired number of instructional modules may be written. Two components for the sub-context, Selection of Media are:

301.01  Specify basic selection tools used in elementary, middle and senior high schools.
301.02  Apply appropriate selection criteria

The first section of the Media Context illustrates relationships of contexts, sub-contexts, and components:

300  Media
Defined: Media are the printed and audiovisual forms of communication and their accompanying technologies. The media program provides a totality of services focused on integrating the utilization of these media to facilitate, improve, and support the learning process.

301.  Selection of Media

The student will
301.01  Specify basic selection tools used in elementary, middle, and senior high schools.
301.02  Apply appropriate selection criteria.
301.03  Plan the involvement of staff, students and community in selection processes.

The Media Context is defined above. Other contexts of the curriculum are defined as follows:

100  Human Behavior: Development and Interaction

Human behavior is an evolving series of physical, mental, emotional, and social processes occurring in human beings. The total mode of learning, including the effective utilization of media, is dependent upon a knowledge of human behavior and the application of this knowledge to interaction with people.

200 Learning Environment

Learning environments may be viewed as those conditions under which knowledge, skills, attitudes and social behavior are acquired or restructured. These conditions include instructional strategies, media behavioral management techniques, interpersonal relationships and curriculum. This also recognizes the home and total community as contributing elements in the education of the individual.

400 Administration

Administration is a cooperative process which has as its purpose the optimum operation of the school library media program. Its functions include the management of media services and the establishment of related learning environments that support the entire instructional program of the school.

500 Research

Among the roles open to media specialists in the empirical research process are those of consumer, diffuser, developer, evaluator, and researcher. The beginning school library media specialist is primarily a consumer and diffuser concerned with logic, methods, techniques and presentation of data as employed in educational planning.

Local occupational task analysis was important in helping the department identify responsibilities of media specialists in real-work settings. To identify these responsibilities it was necessary to learn from the 1970 and 1971 Millersville educational media graduates what beginning media specialists needed to know in order to perform successfully on the job during their first year; how well Millersville graduates were prepared to perform tasks of beginning media specialists; in which areas they felt best prepared; and in which areas they should have had additional help or preparation; as beginning media specialists, did they find the work satisfying to them personally; and how important they felt these tasks were to a school media program.

To develop an instrument for use with these graduates a faculty committee studied task analyses and occupational definitions of the Illinois Library Association[8] and the School Library Manpower Proj-

ect.[9] The committee reviewed the studies, sorted, deleted, combined, and added some tasks to produce the "Millersville Checklist of Ninety Tasks Performed by Beginning Librarians in School Media Centers."[10] The ninety tasks of the Millersville checklist vary in specificity and levels of professional activity. The checklist was field-tested with seven experienced school library media specialists before being sent to graduates. It was then reviewed with the graduates at their schools. Of ninety-five students who completed majors in educational media in the two years before the study, seventy-three were employed in school library media centers. On-location interviews in fifty-two schools, twenty-six of which were elementary, resulted in a number of observations.

Basically, graduates were pleased with the undergraduate training obtained at Millersville, indicating that student teaching had been the most valuable preservice experience. The majority recommended that student teachers be given experience in school library media centers at all three school levels and that part of their time should be spent in classrooms. A better knowledge of curriculum would have been helpful, particularly at the elementary school level. They also recommended that the Department of Educational Media and other departments of education work together more effectively to familiarize prospective teachers with services of a media center.

The Millersville task analysis helped the faculty to revise present offerings and placed preservice preparation in line with occupational requirements. Recommendations made by the 1970 and 1971 graduates were incorporated into the program. With the aid of cooperating librarians in nearby school districts, the department adapted the checklist to assure that each student would be given a core of realistic field experiences at three school levels before graduation.

PROGRAM DEVELOPMENT

The curricular outline and the occupational task analysis were used by the staff to direct attention to a more comprehensive view of unified content and related competencies. For example, the Media Con-

8. Illinois Library Task Analysis Project, *A Task Analysis of Library Jobs in the State of Illinois* (Chicago: Illinois Library Association, 1970).

9. School Library Manpower Project, *School Library Personnel: Task Analysis Survey* (Washington, D.C.: National Education Association, 1969) and *Occupational Definitions for School Library Media Personnel* (1971).

10. "Millersville Checklist of Ninety Tasks Performed by Beginning Librarians in School Media Centers" (Millersville: Millersville State College, Department of Educational Media, 1972).

text illustrates where responsibilities for training in media competencies may be shared and coordinated by staff members. The task analysis indicated where occupational tasks could be incorporated into broader curricular contexts, e.g., Human Behavior and Learning Environment, instead of narrower course structures.

A Program Development Committee, composed of all members of the Department of Educational Media and several members of other departments, such as Elementary Education and Secondary Education, was an especially effective vehicle for continuing study of curricular principles and the instructional methodologies. Meeting on a regular basis, the committee included in its activities the review and revision of the curricular outline; review and adoption of individual and groups of instructional modules; identification of desired relationships among departmental offerings; design of field experiences; occasional resolution of college constraints, such as class hours, credits, teaching loads, and grading practices; and evaluation of the program. Minutes of the meetings furnished a continuing log of staff involvement and growth in curricular planning.

The Program Development Committee began with an overview of the curricular outline. The five broad contexts were found to be more useful than a greater number of course syllabi in identifying interrelationships among program offerings. This was immediately evident as each context was examined apart from other contexts. At an early point, the staff saw a need to identify more complex relationships among the contexts themselves. For example, review of the Media Context indicated that media could not realistically be considered or studied in isolation. Principles of evaluation and selection of media were likely to be comprehended most effectively if related to aspects of human behavior and learning environment, as represented by the two contexts that precede the Media Context. As a further consideration, research techniques, as found in the fifth context, should eventually be related to all four preceding contexts. It was agreed that effective instructional modules, a principal methodology of the new program, would often be identified with and draw upon more than one part of the outline.

As the program developed, the curricular outline underwent periodic revision. In earlier versions, the first context of the outline was Media. Later, it was moved to third position in order to give dominant consideration to teaching and learning, as reflected in the contexts of Human Behavior and

Learning Environment. The curricular outline also needed to be expanded. For example, it was agreed that professional foundations for the Library media fields should have greater representation in the outline, although many topics for this area were already displayed in instructional modules.

Much of the committee activity during its first year was centered on the development of instructional modules for review. It was the committee's position that because first stages of module writing were tentative attempts by individuals to bring instruction into public view, the faculty adopted a supportive and constructive role in its appraisal of modules. Significantly, no module was rejected by the committee. After field testing, revision, and review, modules were considered to be program products that represented the entire staff.

On the basis of these committee activities, it appeared that staff members learned more about the writing and the results of modules by examining efforts of their colleagues than by studying products from outside sources. Modules of other programs comprised many forms and differed in composite parts, e.g., audience, specificity of objectives, and duration of activities.

The committee spent more time during its second year critiquing modules that had been written jointly by two or more staff members. Modules for areas in which competencies were readily identified, e.g., cataloging, information retrieval, instructional design, and local production, were developed in the greatest number. Modules for areas in which student judgments and decisions were required, e.g., certain aspects of evaluation of media and administration of media centers, proceeded more slowly but with a considerable degree of care and revision.

Committee activities dramatized for the department that program development is a never-ending, time-consuming, and demanding intellectual process; that an individual staff member is likely to become dissatisfied with his own products soon after he makes them visible; and that evaluation in areas requiring original decision making by students is less open to objective assessment than areas requiring identical results from all students.

The committee included members of other departments of the Division of Education, some of whom attended regularly and others on a consultative basis. These members provided a two-way mode of communication. First, they were able to observe and participate in the department's process of curricular change. Second, they were able to suggest ways in which interdepartmental cooperation could be implemented. Progress in this latter respect was accomplished through cooperative planning of professional education "blocks" of experiences for teacher candidates, including educational media majors.

The committee gave assistance and received support in a recent plan of the Division of Education to develop teacher preparation programs that were competency-based and performance-oriented in all departments of education. A model for the division, Figure 2, indicates desired campus and off-campus experiences. The model designates knowledges and competencies, as represented by the Knowledge and Procedures components, that are to be developed primarily on the campus. Performances in the Action Component are developed primarily in school situations where persons interact in the process of teaching and learning. These are indicative of many professional activities and responsibilities that are needed

in decision making and problem-solving as new situations are encountered. Divisional efforts to become more field-centered reinforce comparable goals of the Department of Educational Media and will contribute to their continuation after the experimental period is completed.

## TEACHING STRATEGIES AND LEARNING ACTIVITIES

In its process of curricular change, the department devoted its attention first to curricular offerings, then to desired approaches to teaching and learning. Greater diversity in learning activities was reflected in the second major program objective, "Provision of learning activities in a greater variety of modes and settings."

The outcome of the objective resulted in the extension of experiences beyond classroom walls, as a result of cooperative rather than individual faculty endeavor. Experiences were designed for indepen-

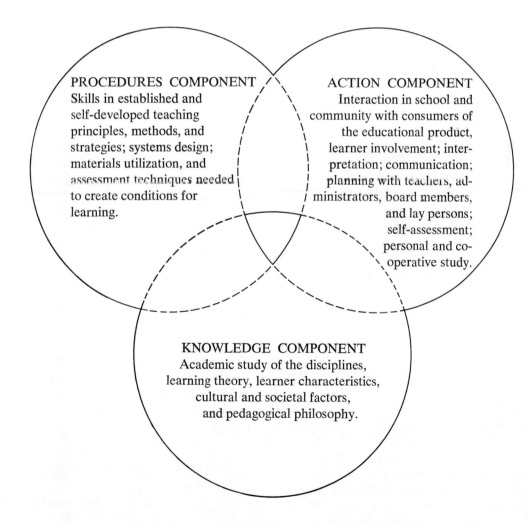

Figure 2. Model of a Competency-Based, Performance-Oriented Teacher Education Program

dence and personalization in learning, for small group sessions in which students shared ideas and reactions, and for school settings in which students worked with teachers and young people. These experiences were specified in instructional modules by the department.

No element in the Millersville program emerged so clearly as the instructional module to symbolize the principle that program development is staff development. Group participation in a modularized approach to instruction was enhanced by the fact that the module itself was not a new teaching strategy but an administrative technique or device whereby a department addressed itself openly to the second and third of the three questions common to curricular planning: "How should students learn?" and "How can learning be made more effective?" Modularized instruction furnished a visible means of identifying a variety of proposed instructional strategies (the "how" of learning) and revising those strategies (the "effectiveness" of learning) as the program evolved.

There is no universally accepted format for modules. Modules may be long or short and may be designed for use primarily by teachers or by students. If there is to be a productive sharing of modules among staff members of any one department, however, it seems advisable that all should agree on a common format for their written description. Such a format assures a measure of uniformity and standardization, while permitting flexibility.

The department produced a form that facilitated the writing of modules by staff members (see Appendix A). The form was of interest to members of other campus departments and to visitors from other campuses. The form consists of the following specifications: module number, curricular context, curricular subcontext, curricular component, students, expectations, prerequisites, activities, and evaluation. For reference in the discussion of these specifications, a representative module for the Media Context is shown in Appendix B.

The module number relates the module to the curricular outline. The terms, *context, subcontext,* and *component,* as sequential divisions of the curricular outline, have been defined earlier in this report.

An identification number for a particular module is added to the component number. For example, for the component "apply appropriate selection criteria," having number 301.02, any identification number from one to ninety-nine may be added to allow the staff to write a variety of modules for any single component. Program number 301.02.01 of the illustrative module is interpreted as follows:

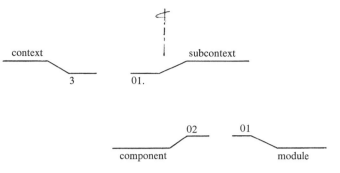

The "Students" section of the module identifies those persons for whom the module is intended, e.g., preservice majors, inservice majors, elementary majors, or all teacher candidates. Modules are designed for specific groups or various combinations of groups.

The "Expectations" section serves two functions. It communicates in advance to students, teachers, and others the goals of the module, and it assists module writers and other staff members in designing activities and assessment procedures that follow.

"Expectation" is a student-oriented term similar in purpose to performance objective. On the basis of two years of experience, Millersville believes that the writing of objectives should not become a stumbling block for the staff. The abundance of disparate definitions, specifications, and terminology for objectives, as found in educational literature, might justify reader conclusions that many authorities consider the writing of objectives to be all that is involved in program development. Although standardization in the writing of objectives should undoubtedly occur at some stage of program development, it is unlikely that this step needs highest priority at the beginning of a new program.

Obviously student behaviors should be stated more precisely than "understanding" or "appreciation" and should advance beyond recall of information. According to the Tyler rationale, behaviors should also be accompanied by an indication of the content to be studied.[11] Millersville suggests that beginning module writers specify the expectations of students as carefully as they can, then continue on to plan appropriate activities. Greater precision can be gained from experience as modules are pretested and submitted for review by one's colleagues.

Examples of expectations as presently found in the Millersville modules are listed with program numbers:

301.01.06. After examining recent issues of recommended professional periodicals important to

11. Ralph W. Tyler, *Basic Principles of Curriculum and Instruction* (Chicago: University of Chicago Press, 1950).

school media specialists, the student will cite distinctive characteristics of each, specifying one or more ways in which it may be employed as a professional tool.

303.01.09. Following some appropriate background reading, the student will identify some current examples of professional thinking on several aspects of the organization of materials in libraries or media centers by summarizing these ideas in a written or spoken presentation.

403.03.01. After reviewing principles of functional design, the student will apply recommended standards to a school of designated level and size in preplanning general space allocations for a school media center physical plant.

501.01.01. The student will define the following terms: experimental research, descriptive research, constant, variable, independent variable, dependent variable, statement of problem, hypothesis.

"Prerequisites" include either general background competencies needed to begin a module or specific competencies which were acquired in a preceding module. An attempt was made to hold prerequisites to a minimum to promote program flexibility.

"Activities" represents sequential tasks made available to the student with the intent that they will help him meet expectations of the module. Included are settings in which learning is to occur and materials are to be used. In this section, modules were designed to provide a variety of individual and group experiences, simulations, and observations. A wide range of media was often represented. Departmental modules usually indicated in this section that students could design their own instruction in lieu of that prescribed by the staff.

"Evaluation" may involve pretesting, post-testing, and remediation. For certain competencies, evaluation is objective and stated with a high degree of precision. For performances involving original decisions and solutions as students work with others, judgments by one or more staff members are usually needed.

To have opportunities for peer group discussion in the first year of the program, the twenty-nine students were divided into three Professional Awareness Teams. Each team included two members of the department. These teams met throughout the fall semester and brought out student ideas on the design, implementation, and evaluation of experiences. An

initial topic of discussion for several meetings was student responses to their new independence in the experimental program. Other topics included follow-up reactions to presentations by staff members from outside departments, discussion of modules calling for student ideas on topics such as selection policies for media centers, appraisals of tours at nearby schools, and exchange of observations in local school classrooms. These Professional Awareness Teams, or PAT groups, afforded one means of student-faculty interaction that was useful in guidance and counseling.

## FIELD EXPERIENCES

The field-centered theme of the program required more than the usual number of field experiences formerly provided in the campus elementary school and community schools. Field experiences were defined at Millersville as those obtained by students in schools before formal student teaching began in the senior year. These experiences had high priority in the program, inasmuch as the department emphasized uses of instructional media in realistic teaching-learning situations. This is based on the belief that it is crucial for undergraduate programs to help students become familiar with the nature of school library media programs and services well before their final year of preservice preparation.

The first group of students in the program visited media centers and classrooms of urban, suburban and rural schools. In most schools, they were given overviews and tours by school administrators. All students observed teachers and students in classrooms. On occasion, some were invited by teachers to participate in instruction. As a result of their experiences, a number of students made repeated visits to the schools.

A departmental goal, as yet unrealized in the experimental program, was to provide a cumulative sequence of field experiences that extended from the freshman year to the senior semester of student teaching. A similar goal was envisioned by other departments of the Division of Education but awaits resolution of administrative mechanics involving separate programs for large numbers of students. It is probable that the Department of Educational Media will begin by providing a sequential program of its own. It prefers eventually to relate its field experiences to broader aspects of educational preparation in schools on an interdepartmental basis.

A new approach to student teaching was initiated in the spring semester of 1972. Former practice assigned a student to one cooperating librarian for a semester, offering limited experiences in media centers, classrooms, and other parts of the school. Competencies were either vaguely stated or unspecified. Often it appeared that traditional library practices were passed on from in-service librarians and teachers to preservice candidates in a process that inhibited newer procedures advocated by the campus program. The reality of this process was confirmed by the department in on-site interviews of its 1970 and 1971 graduates.

A pilot project was began in 1972. Six students were assigned in teams of two to rotate within one school district through a specified sequence of experiences in media centers, classrooms, and other instructional areas at elementary, middle, and senior high school levels. A variety of classroom experiences brought student teachers out of media centers much of the time and offered new ways to apply media services to units of study during early stages of planning and implementation. "A Checklist of Tasks to Be Performed" was designed to assure that students performed basic media tasks at each school level.[12]

The three-level process was expanded from one school district to five in the fall, at the beginning of the second year of the program. Students continued to spend a portion of their time at three school levels, participating in media centers and in class rooms. In classrooms, they observed and acted as teacher-aides or teachers, as planned by the teacher in charge.

Prior to the experimental program, student teachers attended seminars designed by the field supervisor. These included meetings on the college campus and visits to new or renovated school media centers. In the experimental program, these seminars were conducted in schools and planned by the supervisor with the cooperating media specialists. Administrators, teachers, and representatives of specialized services contributed to the seminars to help student teachers see and understand the functions of media centers in relation to the entire school.

The new student teaching program will remain substantially the same in the immediate future. In a review of the program, student teachers and cooperating media specialists recommended continuation of classroom experiences in conjunction with those of media centers. They also recommended that the greater share of student teaching time be divided between two school levels instead of three so that students could have more involvement in school-wide

---

12. "Checklist of Tasks to Be Performed" (Millersville: Millersville State College, Department of Educational Media, 1972).

programs. These levels would include an elementary school and one of the two remaining school levels as selected by the student teacher. Participation at the third level would be limited to two weeks and consist of observation.

## SPECIAL PROGRAM FEATURES

A new departmental offering for freshmen who entered the department in the second year of the experimental program illustrates the degree of flexibility that was achieved by synthesizing content and adopting new methodologies. In an elective entitled "Inquiry, Education, and Media," students were introduced to the sciences, social sciences, and humanities as broad fields from which implications might be derived regarding patterns of inquiry for those who are concerned with the study of education and media. It was proposed that students of educational media would understand major fields better if they were knowledgeable about characteristic contributions and limitations of individual fields. Content was based on the broad spectrum of knowledge that has been discovered to date, unique efforts in major fields to acquire new knowledge, methods of ordering and preserving established knowledge, and ways of disseminating knowledge to others for the continuation of inquiry.

The offering supplemented a twelve-hour block on environmental studies that was originated by the Division of the Social Sciences, but which drew upon contributions at appropriate times from teachers in the Divisions of the Sciences and the Humanities. The three-hour offering of the Department of Educational Media also drew upon contributions of teachers on an interdivisional basis. Thus, by taking the full fifteen-hour block of coordinated studies, educational media freshmen observed teachers of many disciplines as those teachers approached a problem in common in the twelve-hour block; and they met with many of the same teachers personally as part of the Department of Educational Media's offering.

The synthesis of content achieved in this instance was consistent with the philosophy that was demonstrated by the departmental curricular outline, specifically in the manner that it crossed traditional course structures. Synthesis was augmented by drawing upon persons in and outside the department. Readings consisted of primary historical and contemporary source materials of the broad fields and representative disciplines within those fields. Students visited work settings of faculty members in other departments and discussed the nature of their work. Visits were made to local schools to determine the importance of general education for school library media specialists as consultants who must be prepared to work with teachers in all subject areas. Modules, small group sessions, meetings with experts, and field activities removed students from regular classroom procedures.

Although the departmental offering was approved and reviewed by the Program Development Committee, the experiences provided and the evaluation of those experiences were conducted by a nondepartmental member, the Director of Research for the College. Responses of the students were that such experiences would be valuable not only for all entering media majors, but for freshmen of other departments as well. The cooperation of teachers in many disciplines led the department to believe that offerings of this kind can play an important part in furthering interdepartmental and divisional participation in future planning.

## INSTRUCTIONAL MEDIA

If beginning school library media specialists are to be knowledgeable about all varieties of instructional media and competent in using media as elements within the teaching-learning process, it is evident that any education program must be designed to demonstrate effective utilization of media. The department was fortunate in being able to draw upon extensive resources to accomplish this end. On many occasions, it was possible to offer alternate approaches to students in their preferred uses of media. The department provided facilities and equipment for the production of media by departmental majors and other teacher candidates for their work with young people in field situations.

Facilities, equipment, and materials supporting the program were modern and extensive. The Department of Educational Media is housed in a wing of the College's Ganser Library, which is equipped with a dial-access system capable of delivering audio and video programs. Facilities with space for large group instruction, regular classrooms, and a production laboratory are connected with the dial-access system. There are an additional eighty other dial-access stations located throughout the building.

The curriculum materials center of the library provides a wide variety of contemporary instructional materials for examination and use. Included in the extensive collection were texts, courses of study, units of work, filmstrips, phonograph records, films, kits, transparencies, games, and other media, as well as equipment to use them. A large and representative collection of books for children and young adults was also housed in the center.

The department acquires and maintains for its students all of the current Books on Exhibit collections which are displayed and available in a seminar room. It also owns a collection of films and other media frequently used in the experimental program and has ready access to county school district and state university film libraries. A unique project of the department, the Vocational Education Information Network, provides immediate reference to the resources of local, state and national information systems. VEIN also provides on the job training for students and serves as a model demonstrating new ways of meeting the information needs of educational consumers.

Other supportive resources and services are provided by components of the College's Stayer Research and Learning Center. These include the Educational Development Center, which develops and implements collaborative pilot projects and renewal programs with local school districts; the Department of Elementary Education; the Office of Evaluation and Research; and the Elizabeth Jenkins School for Children. Unified media services for the Jenkins School are provided in a media center which also serves as a laboratory for students and faculty of the Departments of Elementary Education and Educational Media. These resources and services were of primary importance in establishing a departmental focus on teaching and learning as the first concern of the beginning school library media specialist.

## ASSESSMENT OF STUDENT COMPETENCIES

Some authorities claim that competency-based programs should be designed only for those student behaviors that may be measured with scientific precision. Pursuit of this idea to its logical end might mean that teacher preparation programs at present would be confined to limited numbers of readily identifiable and measurable behaviors in the psychomotor and at the lower levels of the cognitive domains. Given the present state of the art of competency identification and assessment, Millersville would be content if it could identify as high as, say, forty percent of needed occupational competencies that might presently be measured with some precision.

The performance orientation of the experimental program is needed to prepare media specialists for more elusive but essential professional responsibilities that are required in individual and collective inquiry into new problems as encountered in school settings. As professional workers know, evidence of satisfactory professional performance in these respects is still likely to be based, as a rule, on judgments made by one's colleagues.

In Millersville's modularized approach to teaching and learning, the department made assessment procedures known to students before instructional activities were begun. In each module, assessment was related directly to stated expectations of the student. The responsibility of module writers was to employ assessment procedures with as high a degree of objectivity and reliability as possible.

The difficulties of assessing behavior in this respect were well known by the staff. Nevertheless, several advantages were found as a result of this approach. Modules with activities for independent study, small groups, and field settings enabled the staff to assess student progress in situations that occurred outside classroom walls. Modules provided opportunities for more frequent assessment than in the former program and encouraged staff members to plan together in establishing policies and attempting new methods of assessment. It was necessary for students to furnish satisfactory evidence of completion of a module if it was a prerequisite for another related but more advanced module. As students progressed through modules at individual rates, the staff was able to follow their progress at various stages in a sequence or block of modules.

The department found that assessment was easiest for areas in which basic competencies were readily identifiable. These areas included operation of equipment and certain aspects of instructional design, local production, cataloging, and information retrieval. Assessment was more complex for areas in which original and personal solutions were sought. These areas included evaluation and selection of media for designated instructional purposes and activities for which a number and variety of materials may be equally appropriate. They also included solutions to problems of administering media centers, such as the planning and implementation of services for newer types of school programs. In these instances, decisions and solutions of students could not be said to be either right or wrong without consideration of supporting rationale and evidence. To provide a better standard of objectivity in assessing these behaviors, judgments by more than one staff member or by teachers and media specialists in schools were often required, as was personal consultation with the individual student.

In student teaching, assessment of basic tasks for the routine administration of media centers was relatively simple. For performance-oriented responsibilities in which student teachers interacted in the on-going instructional process with teachers and young people, collective professional judgments of the field supervisor, classroom teachers, and cooperating media specialists seemed to furnish the only available means of assessment.

A fundamental aim of Millersville's competency-based program was to make the time needed for completion of a program a variable rather than a constant for all students. Students were offered opportunities to repeat activities or to undertake alternate remedial activities until satisfactory achievement was demonstrated. The practice was to assess student behavior whenever possible on a pass-fail basis. In terms of customary college grading systems, this implied that all students would receive high grades upon satisfactory completion of the program. This policy is a matter of concern to many persons when appraising undergraduate programs, but not always of equal concern when considering graduate programs.

At the completion of the experimental program the policy of grading was unresolved in view of the fact that the body of competencies needed for successful administration of school library media programs has yet to be identified in its entirety. Nevertheless, staff gave more careful consideration to the matter than it did in the former program. It remains evident that the performance of preservice students and also of in-service school library media specialists varies considerably from one individual to another. The question still remains of whether or not a common standard of performance can be applied to individuals with original as opposed to routine solutions or to the individual who contributes well beyond minimal expectations of his campus department or his school.

On several occasions, Millersville built alternate levels of expectations into individual field-tested modules. In one instance, students were given the option of writing five separate annotations for materials on a designated topic or of synthesizing the content of the five annotations into a unified discussion in which the materials would be contrasted and compared. It was apparent that students who chose the latter task demonstrated a more complex set of behaviors than those who chose the former.

In retrospect, it appears that grading on a pass-fail basis may be sufficient for areas in which competencies are readily identified and specified, whereas grading on a relative basis may remain necessary for performances of a high professional order. If this is the case, then judgments by professionals are likely to remain necessary in the years ahead—at least until that time when scientific measures are found that can be applied to activities involving interaction in collective endeavor, decision-making and problem-solving in creative ways.

# Program Results

## RELATIONSHIP TO PROGRAM OBJECTIVES

The formative evaluation plan for the Millersville experimental program utilized the following nine evaluation topics suggested by the School Library Manpower Project:

1. Preparation of specifically stated job-related education objectives.
2. Communication of program goals to students, staff, outside institutions.
3. Establishment of procedures for assessing student proficiency.
4. Development of procedures for implementing individualized and/or modularized instruction.
5. Evaluation of methods, media and special program features.
6. Development of quality control procedures.
7. Establishment of field experiences and student teaching activities.
8. Determination of transportability of the program.
9. Assessment of probability of program continuance after experimentation ends.

Seven principal sources of data were established by Millersville to identify the persons who made these assessments. These assessments were made by (1) writers of modules, including the entire staff as modules were reviewed; (2) outside persons, e.g., directors of the School Library Manpower Project and members of the Commonwealth's Department of Education; (3) students, after completing modules; (4) students, after completing observations in classrooms and during student teaching; (5) field supervisors regarding student pre-professional and professional activities; (6) departmental staff regarding pre-professional and professional activities; and (7) the entire program staff.

Results of the program after two years were formative in nature and dependent upon judgments and recommendations by students, faculty members and teachers in the field. Summative assessment of a program that has been modified during growth probably should be deferred until a greater degree of program maturity is attained.

Results provided here are structured around the three major objectives of the program. In general it was found that a competency-based, field-centered, and performance-oriented program that was flexible and personalized could function compatibly with customary college requirements. For example, modules could provide diversity in experiences on and off campus. Groups of modules could be associated with course numbers, titles, and hours; be assigned as blocks to be administered by individual faculty members and yet release students from regularly scheduled classes. Course offerings could be crossed and synthesized interdepartmentally, and field experiences could occur well before the senior semester of student-teaching.

The first major objective of the experimental program was three-fold: "Development of a competency-based, field-centered, and performance-oriented program for the beginning school library media specialist." A number of competencies were identified for all aspects of the curriculum and were stated in general terms as components of the five contexts of the curricular outline, i.e., Human Behavior, Learning Environment, Media, Administration and Research.

As modules were developed by the staff, increasingly complex relationships were established among the five contexts. As modules grew in complexity and sophistication, the curricular outline was revised accordingly.

Competencies stated in modules became more specific and were accompanied by greater diversity in experiences and uses of media. Competencies in media utilization are unlikely to be developed satisfactorily without realistic reference to principles of human growth and development. The competencies of the Human Behavior Context were difficult to incorporate into operational modules. As a result these principles of human growth and development were reflected in the experimental program little more than in the traditional programs. Unanswered is the question of whether or not the staff can obtain the assistance it needs from educational psychologists or whether it should develop modules in this area. The staff may be justified in deferring its decision until existing campus psychology courses are incorporated into larger blocks of professional experiences for all teacher candidates. The Department of Educational Media may then be in a position to select elements pertaining to human growth and development that need particular emphasis when developing competencies for media specialists.

Clarity of competencies as stated in instructional modules and adequacy of accompanying activities was determined principally in the field-testing of modules with students. These aspects of modular assessments were achieved with increasing success as modules were introduced to a greater number of students. Student evaluation of modules was obtained by means of the module evaluation form given in Appendix C. Although students evaluated every module during the two years of the program, it became evident that the information might be obtained equally well by having them assess groups of modules instead.

Upon their introduction to the instructional module, students required more attention from instructors than for traditional assignments. Instructors were obliged to see that basic media were indeed accessible to students to assure efficient progress. As students gained experience and became accustomed to independence outside the classroom, they needed less staff attention to details and exhibited more originality. Originality was encouraged in modules by inclusion of the statement that students could design their own instruction, with staff assistance if desired, in lieu of activities proposed by the module writers. All students in the first year of the experimental program "agreed" or "strongly agreed" to the continuation of the modularized approach to instruction.

The field-centered emphasis of the program, as reflected in the first objective, brought students into classrooms and media centers of nearby schools before student teaching began, a practice seldom followed in the former program. These experiences offered a realistic base from which departmental students related campus instruction to characteristics of young people, classroom activities, and media services. Observation and participation in classrooms enabled students to identify essential ties between classroom instruction and media programs. A goal of the department was to structure field experiences from the freshman to the senior year in a sequential and cumulative sequence. A student teaching program that placed prospective media specialists in classrooms and media centers at three school levels was favorably accepted by the students. A distinguishing feature of this aspect of student teaching was the extent to which teachers, media specialists, and administrators in the field were involved in planning experiences for departmental students. Involvement of these persons brought students into contact with more professionals than in previous years.

The performance orientation of the experimental program covered capabilities of the professional worker that cannot as yet be identified as basic competencies. Admittedly elusive, these involve processes of interaction with others, decision making in new situations, and performance at a high professional level that are gained primarily by working with active participants in the field. This focus, the third part of the first major objective, was relatively new in definition for the department. Its immediate appeal to many people lay in its clarity regarding the role of the body of competencies presently identified in the program and its admission that total professional performance seemed to involve qualities that could not be adequately specified in terms of minute, progressive tasks. It appears that assessment of these qualities must continue to be based on judgments by professionals in the fields of media and education.

The second major program objective focused on the provision of learning activities in a greater variety of modes and settings. Evidence of change in this direction was available to students, faculty members and others in the display of activities as found in modules. It was directly observed also in activities that occurred on and off campus. More attention was given by the staff to independent study, small group examination of materials and discussion of educational problems, student projects that were applicable to current school settings, and original studies that involved joint planning with the campus instructor and the school library media specialist or classroom teacher.

A high percentage of systematically programmed activities for independent work was developed first for cataloging, information retrieval and production of materials. The latter area was particularly successful in adapting instruction to the personal needs of preservice teaching candidates in their respective subject fields. Students, as a rule, appreciated opportunities to see planned sequences of specific tasks at the beginning of their study and to be able to complete them at almost any desired time. Conferences between student and instructor occurred more frequently than in the traditional program and rates of progress became increasingly individualized.

The lecture was used less as instructors discussed ideas with smaller groups of students. Original projects requiring longer periods of time were more common than before. Field experiences, previously confined to the campus laboratory school, took place in urban, suburban, and rural schools. Collaboration between campus instructors and professional workers in nearby schools occurred as they helped students to design materials and conduct original studies related to the present school needs and problems. Greater use was made of materials from the department, the library's curriculum collection, and the campus laboratory school as they were tried out in local schools under the direction of classroom teachers. Student teaching seminars, originally held on campus, were conducted in schools and involved contributions by teachers and administrators from those schools.

As the department became involved with professional preparation offered by the Departments of Elementary and Secondary Education, it provided experiences that involved media specialists and teachers of other fields in larger blocks of time than afforded by traditional class schedules. Experiences offered by these departments are become modularized in kind. An experimental tie-in with the Division of Social Science in a fifteen-hour block of combined environmental studies and a review of the disciplines as modes of inquiry took departmental freshmen of the past year to other states and major cities of the East. As the department experimented and shared results of its experiences in curricular meetings, staff members were encouraged to continue changes that broke from former patterns of instruction.

The third, the most ambitious program objective, was to prepare beginning school library media specialists as teachers who function as instructional leaders in their schools. This implied a need for well-grounded preparation in education and for opportunities to apply such preparation in instructional situations before graduation. This objective will be supported as the Division of Education moves toward further definition and implementation of off-campus experiences. The emphasis of the division is on interaction in the school and community. This interaction includes involvement with the learner; interpretation of educational goals to others; effective communication in attacking instructional problems; planning with teachers, administrators, board members, and lay persons; self-assessment of one's performance; and personal and cooperative study. These experiences point to the performance-orientation dimension of both the Department of Educational Media and the Division of Education. A possible approach toward realization of this dimension may lie in the development of long-term opportunities for collective study of contemporary educational problems, problems that are unique to particular schools and in urgent need of resolution. Topics to be studied might vary from school to school and change from year to year.

The initial step of the Department of Educational Media was to place students during student teaching in classrooms and media centers at three school levels. Students reported that they were able to view school programs in their entirety and obtained viewpoints from a greater number of professional educators than if assigned to one person. It is expected that school library media specialists graduated from the Millersville program will be in a better position to develop comprehensive programs in their own schools that are related to all subject areas and departments. While it is recognized that this was a long-range objective, it is believed that potential for achievement in this direction exists in a college that has established strong ties between its Department of Educational Media and other departments of the Division of Education.

## MODIFICATIONS

With staff participation in policy making and implementation of policies, it was inevitable that a new program would be modified at many points. Several modifications, such as staff response to recommendations by graduates that student teachers spend part of their time in classrooms, were covered earlier in this report. Another modification was in response to recommendations by student teachers that their time be divided principally between two school levels to provide greater involvement in school programs.

A major modification in the original approach to competencies was the staff position that only a percentage of competencies needed for administration of school media centers and programs could be identified with specificity and assessed objectively. During the second year, the staff adopted the performance-oriented dimension of the program, one which recognized that certain professional activities and responsibilities must still be assessed by means of professional judgments made by staff members and co-workers in the field.

The curricular outline of the department was

continually modified, largely as a result of the modules that were produced. Certain areas need more detail, e.g., the evaluation and selection of media for each of three school levels. More attention is needed for the contexts of Human Behavior and Learning Environment to relate selection and evaluation of media to characteristics of learners and conditions and settings in which learning occurs.

Two considerations were apparent at the completion of the experimental program for standardization in the writing of modules. A first consideration lay in the writing of expectations. A second was greater precision in assessment to assure that two or more staff members would arrive independently at nearly similar appraisals of student proficiency. As discussed earlier, several problems concerning grading remain unresolved. The original position that students should be evaluated on a "pass-fail" basis was inadequate for certain curricular areas. Whereas it could apply to competencies in psychomotor areas, such as equipment operation, it was unsatisfactory for areas where originality in problem-solving and decision making was sought as students worked with teachers and young people.

The program was modified in the second year by extending newer methodologies to all students in the department. More classes met for "blocks" of time, often doing so on an inter-departmental basis. Modules and experiences represented in the modules were constantly revised by individual writers and by the staff as a whole at meetings of the Program Development Committee.

The program drew more often upon contributions of teachers in other departments and in neighboring schools. In turn, the departmental staff worked more closely with other departments, principally those in the Division of Education. As experience is gained, more emphasis will be given to opportunities for students to work off-campus, an emphasis that will be reinforced by the recent commitment of the Division of Education to compentency-based performance-oriented programs for all teacher preparation. It is expected that the Department of Educational Media will soon extend its offerings to in-service training of teachers in the field, doing so with increasing frequency in the schools themselves by planning custom-designed sessions that apply to problems unique to individual schools.

Staffing patterns will continue to be modified as program staff spends more time outside classrooms and work more often with individuals and small groups of students. Staff members rotate more often than before in responsibilities for course offerings.

Few, if any, departmental offerings were considered to be the responsibility of any one staff member.

Three new members were added to the staff with funds from the School Library Manpower Project. As the funding period ended, this number was reduced to one. Efforts will be made to have one member of the staff released from teaching for half-time to continue coordination of the program. This half-time position will be increased in effect by joint participation of the department chairman, as time permits.

The Millersville occupational task analysis conducted with the 1970 and 1971 graduates will need up-dating. The analysis must be continued with graduates of the experimental program. Under present budgetary constraints, the department may not find ways to conduct on-site interviews as before. The analysis might be accomplished through correspondence, with instruments designed and coordinated by a staff or alumni committee.

At the time of this report the department was concerned that an original feature of the program, the Professional Awareness Team, was becoming increasingly difficult to sustain. Although the department wished to continue small group activities, it was confronted by an increasing number of students as the program expanded. The problem of numbers was compounded by the dual responsibility of the department for both educational media and education majors. In certain classes, both where selection of media and audio-visual production skills were covered, both types of students were found. Modularized instruction and flexible scheduling were features of these classes. Small group discussion was augmented by dividing standard size classes, on occasion, into three or four groups. Some of these groups met simultaneously, others met on alternate days.

The uniqueness of the original Professional Awareness Team, however, suggested that groups of educational media majors should continue to meet on a regular basis apart from other majors. This approach provided an added core of professionally-related experiences appropriate to the departmental major. It is anticipated that student guidance and counseling will be developed by this mode to a greater extent than achieved in the first two years of the program.

The conventional classroom setting was modified also by the development of blocks of instruction that combined course offerings of three or four classes. Meeting for longer periods of time than that of the average class, students and teachers found possibilities for activities that involved any desired number of persons. These blocks were offered interdepartmentally with the Departments of Elementary and Secondary Education. In these blocks, core professional experiences were provided for all preservice teacher candidates in both sophomore and junior years. Student feedback to instructors was easier to obtain than in former structures.

In summary, the modifications given above indicate that the program will be continued and revised at appropriate times. Most of the present changes resulted from refinements of elements in the program, increased cooperation with other departments, and expansion of activities that occurred off campus.

## OTHER RESULTS OF THE PROGRAM

The experimental program obtained a variety of impressions and reactions from students, staff and others who participated in the two years of the program. Several topics already covered will be highlighted. Additional results reflected the spirit through which many persons worked together toward the growth and status of an undergraduate program designed for the beginning school library media specialist.

The major highlight was the award made to the department by the School Library Manpower Project in 1971. Although the department began program changes in 1968, the award brought national attention and support to a local effort, accelerating its progress to an extent that could not have been accomplished by the department alone. The fact that Millersville was the only totally undergraduate school of the six in the nationwide project resulted in commitment and responsibility on the part of the staff to share experiences with outsiders. It is a staff hope that its efforts will encourage the American Library Association to study what is now occurring around the country in undergraduate media programs.

From the beginning of the program, the entire staff participated in program development. Every staff member wrote modules that are now a part of the program. Each was willing to display his instruction for review by others and to work with others on improving experiences offered students.

The staff was impressed by the fact that the Millersville occupational task analysis was conducted by the senior member of the department in the year before her retirement. On-site interviews of 1970 and 1971 graduates in fifty-two schools, a sabbatical project, gave the department first-hand information on tasks being performed by beginning school library media specialists. A scholarship fund in honor of Beatrice U. Datesman, the senior member who conducted the analysis, reached $5,000 in the first year, representing contributions from more than 300 people.

The new approach to student teaching provided experiences in classrooms and media centers at three school levels and helped students make decisions on careers. In a summary report after a semester of student teaching, one student wrote: "I feel that one of the more important aspects of this pilot program was the inclusion of all three school levels. This afforded the opportunity of comparison and experience that would not have been possible under the old student plan. For me this had great value because I saw a complete reversal as to the school level I would have preferred before student teaching."

By participating in classrooms as teachers, preservice media specialists saw results of their contributions in the responses of children. The department's field supervisor wrote these comments for a record of the program: "I am confident this new approach to student teaching will better prepare our graduates to assume the duties of a beginning school media specialist at any grade level, K through 12."

In one instance, the planning of student teaching experiences for three school levels strengthened relationships among media centers in a school district. An excerpt from the annual library report of the senior high media specialist to the superintendent of the pilot district was of special interest to the department: "It was and is exciting to be a part of the Millersville State College experimental program. . . . One of the many fringe benefits was that while the three librarians in our district have always worked closely together, this project served to weld us even closer."

An important force in program growth was the participation and support by others outside the department. Following a visit to the campus, the national director of the School Library Manpower Project gave his reaction in a report to the department: "The initial and expanding support of the institution has continued to be beneficial to the program's success. The financial support from the institution itself is significant, but even more important is the evidence of the personal involvement of the key college personnel and their professional commitment to the program. The philosophy, methodology and structure of the experimental program is bringing about a variety of changes in many areas of the total institution. This could not have happened so quickly without the initial leadership and involvement of key administrators."

From the beginning of the program, the commonwealth was strong and generous in its support of the Millersville program. Officials in the Pennsylvania Department of Education approved the original proposal and on February 17, 1971, wrote the president of the college: "You and your faculty are to be commended for the innovative nature of this program and for the keen and far-sighted plan to make School Library Media the very center of all teacher education programs."

In February of 1972, the Pennsylvania Bureau of Academic Services appointed an on-site visiting team to observe and report the progress of the program and to make recommendations. This team wrote in their report:

> There was no concern that students completing this program would have preparation of lesser quality than those enrolled in the regular program. In fact, there is much evidence to indicate that they will be more effective in the emerging school role for librarians.
>
> The program is competency-based and serves as a pilot study for the Pennsylvania endeavor to move all certification programs to competency bases. On February 8, 1972, it was noted that comprehensive competency charts have been made for the majority of the scheduled activities and experiences which constitute the total program.
>
> It was evident that the faculty has responded positively to the intellectual challenge and the resultant work load. Good morale was reported and the enthusiasm for the program was manifest by the fact that the regular program was "beginning" much of the experimental program.
>
> The program warrants special attention from teacher preparation institutions seeking help in moving to competency-based programs. It also merits the financial support of the Commonwealth in order to complete the excellent project started with the Knapp Foundation Funds.
>
> The visitors were impressed by the potential of the program to bring about improvements in the education of children in all areas. . . . The Committee recommends that initial appproval be extended to this alternate means of preparation. This new approach is focused on the future and has developed elements which may become part of the "regular" program. . . .

In the second year of the program, the Citizens Commission on Basic Education for the Commonwealth of Pennsylvania visited the Department of Educational Media. The Commission's purpose was to review elementary and secondary school offerings and visit institutions of teacher preparation in order to make recommendations for the improvement of education throughout the state. In their letter of October 5, 1972, the Staff Associate for the Commission wrote the department:

> The members of the Supportive Services Committee who were able to be at Millersville were intrigued and excited by their visit. They are anxious to explore the implications of your library media specialist program for the whole range of supportive services. I think they were especially impressed by your commitment to the idea that certain supportive services are and must be integral to the whole instructional process.

# Program Conclusions

## KEY SUCCESSES AND PROBLEMS

The key success in the experimental program was cooperative planning by members of the department, colleagues of other departments, and teachers in the field. Staff cooperation furnished a means by which the program was brought into public view for study by others. Through this visible display of what is currently offered, the department enlisted assistance of others in relating the fields of media and education more effectively. Because it identified the process by which the program evolved, it was able to lend assistance, in turn, to similar efforts by other campus departments as the Division of Education adopts a competency-based, field-centered, and performance-oriented approach to instruction for all teacher preparation. In its curricular planning, the department is demonstrating the nature and principles of cooperative planning it believes should be employed by school library media specialists as they work with teachers in their schools.

The short period of funding received from the School Library Manpower Project poses some problems for future planning. Although the Project support accelerated development of the Millersville program, more time is needed to achieve program maturity. The program has been extended to all students in the department however and will continue under local support with some adjustment.

The directions adopted by the department call for strong ties between the Department of Educational Media and other departments of education. A basic position of the Department of Educational Media is that beginning school library media specialists should relate media services to teaching and learning requirements of all school personnel. Needed in schools are media specialists who are concerned with education first and media second. Also needed are classroom teachers who are proficient in basic media competencies vital to instruction. Common loyalties help both groups to plan and develop programs together. Departments of educational media subscribing to this position carry a dual responsibility in the preparation of media specialists and teacher candidates.

## RECOMMENDATIONS

Following a two year experimental process in developing an undergraduate education program for school library media specialists the Department of Educational Media at Millersville State College recommends that:

1. Educational programs for school library media specialists should be coordinated with other departments of education.

On the basis of the philosophy and assumptions given for the experimental undergraduate program, it is believed that students of educational media should be encouraged to establish professional identity with educational goals and responsibilities that are shared by teachers in other fields.

2. Educational programs for school library media specialists should employ occupational task analysis in curriculum and instructional planning.

In order to implement a competency-based, field-centered and performance-oriented program that meets the needs of contemporary schools, the department studied occupational definitions from outside sources and conducted a local analysis involving its graduates of the two years prior to the experimental program. Whenever feasible, local task analysis should be conducted with graduates in the field. Acknowledging the immediate value of task analysis to programs of

school library media education, it is evident that local task analysis must be periodically up-dated and provide experiences for students that remain current with duties performed on the job.

3. Educational programs of media education should encourage student evaluation of prescribed activities and provide opportunities for students to design alternative avenues in learning that will result equally well in the attainment of basic competencies and professional responsibilities.

Millersville students entered the program at various stages of undergraduate preparation and represented diversity in motivation, interests and abilities. The policy of admissions followed in this respect is compatible with an essential feature of competency-based programs, i.e., emphasis on terminal rather than entry requirements. This emphasis calls for a high degree of flexibility and a considerable amount of faculty attention to the personal development of the individual student. Accommodations of this nature can serve as a major base in program design for flexibility, one from which students can progress on an individualized pattern toward successful achievement of terminal requirements.

4. Staff participation should be encouraged during early stages of conceptualization and implementation of a new program.

Program development may be equated with staff development in program planning. This principle is fundamental to completing the basic program as instruction is brought into view for study by others.

5. One faculty member should be released from teaching duties and devote full time to working with the staff and other departments on program development.

Coordinated procedures should be employed to capitalize on and support distinctive contributions of each individual. This kind of coordination by a full-time non-teaching staff member is crucial not only for a new program, but is essention as well to its continuation.

6. Outside assistance should be obtained and coordinated for both new and established media programs to help identify necessary competencies, extend learning activities to off-campus settings, and assess program objectives and accomplishments.

Assistance in program development may be obtained from outside sources through a variety of systematic strategies, one of which is an advisory board. An advisory board was utilized to obtain assistance for experimental program development and services from representatives of the college, school systems, professional organizations, the Commonwealth's Department of Education and the student body.

7. Primary emphasis should be given to staff development during a gradual process of program change.

A systematic process of curricular change can establish local guidelines for members of a department. At present, competency-based school library media education programs are in early stages of development with few guidelines available. Changes from traditional programs to those that seek to specify competencies and performance responsibilities with greater precision and to establish identity with school programs must draw upon the unique contribution of each staff member. Departmental study is needed to establish primary goals, to plan curricular components, to develop instructional media, to provide learning activities on and off campus and to apply adequate assessment procedures. The development of instructional products is an additional outcome of the process and is an integral element in program review and revision. The multidimension of such a department study would require time for development and maturation over a long period of time.

8. Departments of educational media should undertake identification and specification of competencies for school library media specialists as a total faculty effort—giving serious consideration to a performance-oriented dimension for those activities that are likely to remain subject to professional judgment rather than objective assessment.

On the basis of its experience in competency-based education, the Department of Educational Media endorses the principles involved in this approach to instruction. At present, the theory underlying the identification and specification of competencies for teacher education programs is far in advance of the state of the art. Initial attempts to specify competencies, design appropriate instructional activities and plan assessment techniques will likely prove unsatisfactory to the initiator, as revealed to him in products such as the instructional module. Nevertheless, the potential of competency-based programs is promising enough to suggest that precision in instructional design is not a temporary educational fad but a beginning in academic effort to make campus programs compatible with present and future requirements of schools.

9. The American Library Association should conduct a national study of undergraduate preparation for the school library media specialist with a view toward articulating these programs with those at the graduate level to encourage continuing educational alternatives leading to the master's degree.

The Millersville Department of Educational Media considers the award of the School Library Manpower Project to its program to be evidence of recognition by members of the school library profession of the importance of the role undergraduate programs play in the preparation of beginning school library media specialists. Further recognition of this belief is evident by the support that is currently being extended to such programs by local institutions and state departments of education.

Appendix A

MODULE DEVELOPMENT FORM
MILLERSVILLE PROGRAM-SLMP

| NAME OF WRITER: | DATE: | CONTEXT & SUB-CONTEXT: | NUMBER |
|---|---|---|---|
| COMPONENT: | | STUDENTS: | |

EXPECTATIONS:

PRE-REQUISITES:

ACTIVITIES:

MATERIALS:

EVALUATION:

Appendix B

REPRESENTATIVE MODULE

| | |
|---|---|
| Module Number: | 301.02.01 |
| Context: | MEDIA    Sub-Context:  Selection of Media |
| Component: | 301.02:  Apply appropriate selection criteria |
| Students: | All program participants |
| Expectations: | Following completion of assigned readings and listening to a taped discussion you will identify general guidelines for the selection of education materials and equipment by participating in discussions and summarizing the concepts treated in a written or spoken presentation. |
| Prerequisite: | None |

Activities:

1. Read the attached information sheets and other materials,* and

2. Dale, Edgar, Audiovisual Methods in Teaching. 3rd edition, pp. 162-185 (Reserve 371.335/D152), and/or

3. Erickson, Carlton, W. H. Administering Instructional Media Programs, pp. 65-91.  (Reserve 371.33/E68).  Begin on page 65 at "Evaluation of Audiovisual Media for Selection."

4. Listen to a discussion by Edward Bernard and Morris Freedman on some problems faced by those responsible for selecting materials in New York City Schools, Dial Access #10.  A study guide for this tape is attached.*

5. Participate in a small group discussion to be scheduled by instructor.

6. Upon completion of the above you will write a brief (200-300 word) summary of the most important points that constitute the general guidelines for the selection of appropriate educational materials and equipment, or

   Prepare a taped five minute discussion of these points. Recording equipment is available in the department.

   OR - Design your own instruction in lieu of the above. (You may have staff assistance in this if desired).

Evaluation: The written or spoken summary will be checked against an instructor prepared list of important points.  Your document or tape will be considered incomplete until all major points are included.


*Handouts for this module are not included in this report.

Appendix C

STUDENT MODULE EVALUATION

We are interested in knowing how you feel about the modules you have completed. Your "feedback" is an important part of our instructional process. Please respond to the following questions by indicating your opinions.

Module Nos._____Name (Optional)_____

|  | Agree | Neutral | Disagree |
|---|---|---|---|
| 1. I liked these modules |  |  |  |
| 2. Modules were profitable |  |  |  |
| 3. Textual materials were effective |  |  |  |
| 4. Objectives were easy to understand |  |  |  |
| 5. Evaluation sampled my learning |  |  |  |
| 6. Staff help was important |  |  |  |
| 7. Student help was important |  |  |  |
| 8. Modules were well organized |  |  |  |
| 9. Modules should be changed | * |  |  |
| 10. Materials were accessible |  |  |  |
| 11. More materials should be made available |  |  |  |
| 12. Module was easy |  |  |  |
| 13. (Where applicable) Lecture was helpful |  |  |  |
| 14. (Where applicable) Group discussion was helpful |  |  |  |

Average time required to complete one module_____

COMPLETION OF THIS EVALUATION FORM IS REQUIREMENT OF EACH MODULE
* * * * * * * * * * * * * * * * * * * * * * * * * * * * * * * * * * * * * * * *

*Please list any suggestions on how these modules should be changed; list module number to which your suggestion applies.

Comments (Optional)

# UNIVERSITY OF DENVER

GRADUATE SCHOOL OF LIBRARIANSHIP
Dr. Margaret Knox Goggin, Dean

## AN EXPERIMENTAL PROGRAM IN
# SCHOOL LIBRARY MEDIA EDUCATION
### 1971–1973

*Final Report by*

Lucile Hatch and Chow Loy Tom

## Contents

# GRADUATE SCHOOL OF LIBRARIANSHIP

## Dr. Margaret Knox Goggin, Dean

*Experimental Program Staff, 1971-1973*

Miss Lucile Hatch, Director, 1971-72
Dr. Chow Loy Tom, Director, 1972-73
Mr. Bruce L. Papier

*Cooperating Faculty*

Mr. John T. Eastlick, Director of Advanced Studies
Graduate School of Librarianship

Dr. Ralph A. Forsythe
Professor, School of Education

Mr. James H. May, 1972-73
Director, Center for Communication and Information
   Research
Graduate School of Librarianship

Dr. M. Chester Nolte
Professor, School of Education

Dr. Elaine F. Svenonius, 1971-72
Director, Center for Communication and Information
   Research

*Advisory Board*
1971-1973

Mrs. Patricia Baron, 1972-73
Student Member
University of Denver

Mrs. Christa Coon
Coordinator of Library Media Services
Jefferson County Schools

Mr. John T. Eastlick
Director of Advanced Studies Program
Graduate School of Librarianship
University of Denver

Dr. Nathaniel H. Evers
Dean, Graduate School of Arts and Sciences
University of Denver

Mrs. Philip Frieder, 1971-72
Colorado Board of Education

Dr. Margaret Knox Goggin
Dean, Graduate School of Librarianship
University of Denver

Dr. Peter Hiatt
Director, Continuing Education Program
   for Library Personnel on Higher Education
Western Interstate Commission

Dr. William H. Key
Chairman, Department of Sociology
University of Denver

Dr. James Lawson
Coordinator of Graduate Education
School of Education
University of Denver

Mr. James H. May, 1972-73
Director, Center for Communications and Information
   Research
Graduate School of Librarianship
University of Denver

Mr. James Meeks
Director
Colorado State Library

Miss Jean Nolan, 1971-72
Student Member
University of Denver

Mr. Bruce L. Papier
Director, Technology Laboratory
Graduate School of Librarianship
University of Denver

Miss Miriam G. Ricks, 1972-73
Student Member
University of Denver

Mr. Daniel B. Stukey, 1971-72
Superintendent of Schools
School District No. 12, Denver

Dr. Elaine Svenonius, 1971-72
Director, Center for Communication and Information
   Research
Graduate School of Librarianship
University of Denver

Mrs. Joan Wilkerson Stewart, 1971-72
Student Member
University of Denver

# Overview

## DESCRIPTION OF THE INSTITUTION

The University of Denver is the largest private independent university in the Rocky Mountain region. Located in Denver, the capital of Colorado, the University combines the educational advantages of a metropolitan cultural center with the employment opportunities offered by business, industry and government.

The University of Denver consists of three undergraduate colleges; the College of Arts and Sciences, the College of Business Administration and the College of Engineering. Within the College of Arts and Sciences are the School of Art, the School of Education and the Lamont School of Music. Within the College of Business Administration is the School of Hotel and Restaurant Management. Graduate programs are available through the Colleges of Business Administration, Engineering and Law as well as the Graduate Schools of Arts and Sciences, International Studies, Social Work and Librarianship.

The University of Denver is accredited by the North Central Association and other national and regional agencies. Its courses are accepted for credit by colleges and universities throughout the United States and abroad. The University's enrollment, originally provincial, is today drawn from all fifty of the United States and numerous other countries. Since its founding in 1864, the University has sought the life of the mind for all people and has never denied admission to any student because of race, religion or color.

The University has an enrollment of approximately 8,500 students, thirty percent of whom are engaged in graduate study. The total full-time faculty totals 550, sixty percent of whom hold doctoral degrees. The ratio of full-time students to full-time faculty is approximately nineteen to one. The University emphasizes individual attention in the classroom, through small classes and seminars, as well as in all other phases of student life. Moreover, as a private institution, the University of Denver has a unique opportunity, indeed it is a felt responsibility, to be experimentally oriented in developing curricula to meet current needs.

The Graduate School of Librarianship is the *administrative unit* within the University of Denver which implements curricula and directs activities for the education of professional librarians. The School was established at the University of Denver in 1931 and was accredited by the American Library Association three years later. In 1947 a nationwide trend was begun when the School started the first program leading to a Master's degree in librarianship. In June 1957, the School was reaccredited under the new standards adopted in 1951 by ALA. In 1970, beginning with the fall quarter, the Graduate School of Librarianship initiated a post-master's or Sixth Year Advanced Studies Program, a program in continuing education for librarians in positions requiring additional understanding of administrative principles or subject specialization.

The curriculum at the Graduate School of Librarianship, while solidly based on traditional aspects of librarianship such as book selection, cataloging, bibliographic searching and reference service to patrons, gives equal emphasis to the new fields of professional services such as documentation, data processing, systems analysis and theory, and media specialization. In addition to its instructional concerns, the Graduate School of Librarianship is interested in the service and research dimensions of education for librarianship. Opportunity for activities in this area are provided for by two adjuncts to the curriculum: a Center for Communication and Information Research and a Technology Laboratory.

The School Library Academic Committee is the *organizational unit* within the Graduate School of Librarianship that has the responsibility for designing programs for the education of media specialists at different levels of professional competency. This division is normally composed of two full-time and three part-time faculty members. Curricula are designed primarily for students at the master's and post-master's levels; however, the School works cooperatively with several graduate departments on campus in developing programs for those interested in pursuing a joint doctoral program.

## DESCRIPTION OF THE EXPERIMENTAL PROGRAM

Although the "knowledges" and "abilities" of a district school library media director were deemed important, it was believed that the emphasis in his education should be on developing the frame of mind to understand and cope with a variety of problems. The philosophy of the program, therefore, stemmed from the conviction that most crucial to the success of a district school library media director was his ability to perform effectively in an environment that is continually problematic. In the service of this need, a director of a district media program must be able and willing to cut through rigidities imposed by lack of money, tight politics, the conservative side of the generation gap, and most importantly, perhaps, simple disinterest. Such a person must be an opinion leader, a person not only responsible and imaginative, but one unafraid to cope with the unexpected, with discouragements and delay.

For this reason the educational program proposed used the methodology of directed field case study. Each student in the program was to design and plan the implementation of a balanced district-wide media program in a selected school district. The major content of the educational curriculum then was structured by the questions that would arise as the students attempted to formulate their designs and plans for implementation; it was to be a structure by learning, for the sake of trying to solve a problem, rather than a structure by subject *per se*.

The post-master's program which was developed at the Graduate School of Librarianship was designed therefore to assist current and potential district school library media directors to develop district-wide school library media programs. Central to the program of each student was the cooperation of the administrative and instructional personnel of a school district. Interdisciplinary study and attention to individual student needs and objectives were encouraged in the program through the methodology of directed field case study.

The program was planned for full-time study during the academic year of three consecutive quarters. A minimum of forty-five quarter hours of study was required for the Certificate of Advanced Studies which was awarded to students completing the program.

The major student objective during the fall quarter was designing the case study of his school district. Emphasis was given to the development of instruments for the collection of data during the on-site survey of the winter quarter. Also included in the fall quarter course of study were general orientation to the factors which affect the learning environment, a review of research methods, audiovisual communication and electives.

The curriculum of the winter quarter was divided into two five-week periods. The student spent the first period of the quarter in his school district conducting his field survey. During the field survey a member of the experimental program faculty coordinated the work of each student through student reports, telephone conversations and a three-to-four day visit with the student in his school district. The data obtained from questionnaires, interviews, observation and district records were analyzed by the student during the second period of the quarter when he returned to campus. In addition, the student attended three mini or short-term courses in the financial, architectural and legal aspects of district school library media programs.

During the spring quarter the student concentrated on two aspects of the case study—the final report and a multimedia presentation of the highlights of the case study. Electives were also a part of the student's spring quarter program.

Lecturers and consultants from several departments of the University—such as Speech Communication, Mass Communications and Sociology—contributed to the program through their emphasis on developments, research, and issues in their discipline which affect school library media programs. Independent study, often interdisciplinary, was another feature of the program which enabled a student to strengthen his background as he became increasingly involved in some of the major processes characteristic of the responsibilities of a district school library media director.

## PHILOSOPHY AND ASSUMPTIONS FOR CHANGE

The broad justification for new programs lies in the current and pressing needs of education. Interrelated developments during the sixties in the field of education and the resultant response of school library media personnel to these developments played an influential role in the formation of this post-master's program. A sharper focus on the teaching-learning process through educational research and psychological theory increased the recognition of the diverse learning styles of students and of the effects of peer and interage grouping and teaching. This knowledge, in turn, created new trends in organization, such as the open space concept school, flexible or modular scheduling, and a growing demand for the multimedia approach to learning.

The concept of school librarianship evolved from the traditional service orientation to a broader and more dynamic emphasis of school library media center programs. The Elementary and Secondary Education Act of 1965 gave much impetus to the development of school libraries, while the Knapp Foundation of North Carolina, Inc. funded the Knapp School Libraries Project in 1963 and the School Library Manpower Project in 1968. School librarians began to recognize their responsibilities as members of the instructional team and the importance of working toward a better media program in their schools and centers. In order to do this with optimum effectiveness they often needed the guidance of a district school library media director.

The position of district school library media director was set forth in *Occupational Definitions for School Library Media Personnel*[1] published by the American Library Association in 1971. Aside from short summer workshops, however, little attention had been given to this role in any of the library education institutions. Not only was there a need, but a challenge to orient individuals to the specific position as enumerated in the redefinition.

It was believed, therefore, that a program for the preparation of individuals for the specific position of district school library media director was called for, a program designed to promote in the student:

1. A broad understanding of the social forces and economic factors that affect schools.
2. A practical knowledge of learning theory, educational trends and goals, and the role of technology in the learning process.
3. A philosophy of service that would make the library media center in the school, complemented by the library media center at the district level, a resource center that adequately meets educational and recreational needs of both students and faculty.

Without directors who could help with the development of balanced district-wide school library media programs, neither *The Standards for School Media Programs*[2] nor the goals of the federal programs could be properly implemented. It was deemed in-

sufficient that only the concept of school librarianship be redefined; personnel too must be educated to fit the redefinition. This then was the particular justification for the University of Denver's proposed program to educate district school library media directors.

## IMPLEMENTATION REQUIREMENTS

The present University of Denver school library media education program for Sixth Year Advanced Studies students is a forty-five quarter hour program. Before admission to the program, the prospective student must state the objectives and goals he wishes to achieve in his study. When admitted, he then plans his own curriculum in consultation with his Faculty Advisory Committee, consisting of faculty from both the Graduate School of Librarianship and the School of Education. Although the student is free to take courses according to his interests and needs in any department of the University, he must take at least twenty hours of the required forty-five in the field of librarianship.

The proposed experimental program was built within the framework of the present program; it too was a forty-five quarter hour program. It differed, however, from the present program in several significant respects:

1. The experimental program incorporated more interdisciplinary cooperation and more influence from "outside the University" than did the present program. For instance, the Directed Field Case Study required the participation not only of faculty members from at least three other departments in the University but also the services of a media consultant. Further, to insure the success of the Directed Field Case Study approach, the cooperation of school district supervisors and staff, as well as of community leaders, was mandatory throughout the entire program.
2. Throughout the program the importance of research was stressed. Research methods in the social sciences were taught early in the program and an opportunity to use this knowledge occurred immediately when the student was engaged in an on-site survey of a particular community. This perhaps represented the most radical

1. School Library Manpower Project, *Occupational Definitions for School Library Media Personnel* (Chicago: American Library Association, 1971).

2. American Association of School Librarians, American Library Association, and the Department of Audiovisual Instruction, National Education Association, *Standards for*

*School Media Programs* (Chicago: American Library Association, and Washington, D.C.: National Education Association, 1969).

departure from the present program of Sixth Year Advanced Study.

3. The experimental program was specifically designed to educate district school library media directors. The impetus of the program change represented a concentration of interest through experimentation and innovative teaching for a specific purpose for a specifically defined target group.

The mechanics of getting the proposed program underway involved petitioning the Graduate School of Librarianship to allow the necessary modifications in admission and course requirements at the sixth year level. It also involved negotiating with other departments in the University to arrange for the release of their faculty to teach intensive one-to-three week mini courses where needed in the program sequence. Finally, it involved obtaining the assurances of school district superintendents that they would cooperate with the student in the experimental program.

# Program Goals and Objectives

As stated in the proposal to the School Library Manpower Project, there were two general behavioral objectives for the experimental program at the University of Denver.

1. To provide the student with the knowledges and abilities he must have to deal effectively with problems that arise in administering district school library media programs.
2. To inculcate or reinforce in the student attitudes a district school library media director should be expected to have—attitudes relating to professional relationships, such as enthusiasm for working "with district, county, regional, state and national level organizations, officials, academic authorities, mass media executives, contractors and other allied individuals and groups;" attitudes relating to assuming supervisory duties, such as interest in determining personnel needs and assignments, justifying budget requests and resolving fiscal problems, and developing, interpreting and implementing policy; and attitudes relating to the use of media technology in school libraries.

Determining course objectives involved both the outlining of general program and course structure and the detailing of specific student related objectives within this structure. The general outline was prepared by the experimental program faculty while details were supplied by the students, with respect to their needs and abilities, and by individual professors, who were responsible for the approach to, and ordering of subject matter. In both stages of development, program objectives and standards expected of all sixth year students at the University of Denver were observed.

The experimental curriculum designed to achieve these broad behavioral objectives was centered around a year-long case study of a specific school district. The rationale behind this approach was the belief that a district school library media director can function only if he understands (1) the strengths and weaknesses of the district, (2) the goals and purposes of its educational program, and (3) the role of the school library media center in assisting in the achievement of these educational goals.

The over-arching goal of the Denver experimental program was to prepare individuals for the position of district school library media director as defined in the *Occupational Definitions for School Library Media Personnel* through a program which emphasized the concept of district-wide coordination of media programs in accord with the educational philosophy and objectives of a specific district. To this end, the program sought to:

1. Provide students with a sensitivity to social problems affecting school media programs.
2. Examine the role of media center programs within the framework of developments in education.
3. Formulate a philosophy for a district school media program in a specific district.
4. Evaluate methods of establishing, developing, maintaining and evaluating a media center program.
5. Develop criteria for the evaluation of district school library media programs.
6. Consider the cooperative role of the district school library media program with other agencies in the community.
7. Use research methods in the design of a district-wide media program.

8. Become aware of the rights of pupils and school personnel in school law.
9. Provide an introduction to the principles of PPBS for more efficient achievement of district media program objectives.
10. Develop an understanding of the relationships between physical facilities and media programs through design or renovation.
11. Refine skills in the design and use of appropriate media and related technology.
12. Provide for professional growth through inter-departmental electives.
13. Enable students to work toward state certification for the position of district school library media director.

The program included three quarters of study with objectives specified for each quarter. The fall quarter focused on social problems, educational trends, school library media philosophy, standards for school media programs and the occupational definitions as defined by the School Library Manpower Project. Additional emphasis was placed on viable research approaches for the analysis of problems and human relations. This content coverage was intended to orient the students to conceptual problems they would have to consider in preparing a year-long case study.

The primary objectives for the fall quarter were, therefore:

1. To identify strengths and weaknesses of the current library media program in relation to the educational goals and social problems of the district.
2. To prepare research instruments to gather additional data for analysis and determining for future needs.
3. To develop effective human relations techniques to insure obtaining the data required as a basis for a viable district-wide program.
4. To provide for personal needs through five hours of electives.

The winter quarter focused on the design and modification of research instruments and the implementation of these instruments during the on-site study of a selected school district. To assist the students in designing their school library media programs and refining their recommendations, three mini courses in school finance, library architecture and legal aspects of education were provided. The primary objectives for the winter quarter were, therefore:

1. To conduct an in-depth study of a school district to obtain data on which to plan a district-wide school library media program.
2. To write a preliminary report of the proposed program with recommendations for changes and improvements.
3. To provide needed techniques and knowledges through three mini courses in school finance, library architecture, and legal aspects of education.

The spring quarter was divided into two broad segments. The major portion of time (ten hours) was assigned to electives which were chosen by students from graduate offerings in any school on the campus to meet personal needs or certification requirements that they had identified. The remaining five hours of the quarter were devoted to the completion of the Case Study Report and the preparation of the multimedia presentation. The specific outcomes agreed upon for the spring quarter were the final Case Study Report and a multimedia presentation of the total study. The rationale for the multimedia presentation was to provide students with a practical project for the effective use of media and to prepare a brief, to the point, professional presentation which would sell the recommendations in the Case Study Report to the district.

The Case Study Report and the multimedia presentation were then the culminating activities for a year-long program designed to prepare potential district school library media directors:

1. To analyze the needs of the district and an educational program.
2. To design an effective school library media program to undergird the educational program in all its facets.
3. To present the program so effectively that the school district would implement the proposed recommendations.
4. To learn effective human relations techniques which would facilitate open communication with administrators, librarians, teachers and students.

The behavioral objectives were based on those suggested by the School Library Manpower Project guidelines and course objectives prepared by individual professors. Student modifications of specific course objectives and their effect on total program structure were obtained from data collected through faculty and student taped interviews. The development of specifically stated, job-relevant objectives was a two-stage process, which of necessity varied depending upon the background of students involved in the program, the nature of the districts they examined, and the professional attitudes of the individual professors. The behavioral objectives established in Phase I of the School Library Manpower Project might require modifications or at least a weighting of priorities, but this can be decided only after program experimentation. Program objectives must be understood by the students and student objectives must be successfully communicated to faculty before a mutual input functions effectively.

## COMMUNICATION OF PROGRAM GOALS

Communication of the experimental program goals to both districts outside the program and to students and faculty within the program constituted a challenging yet demanding aspect of the entire program. Time and energy expended in this area were perhaps inordinately great in proportion to other concerns during the first year. Still, the translation of broad, general objectives into specific, detailed procedures required much definition and explanation. To remain flexible and responsive to students' needs, program format was of necessity skeletal in nature. Effective communication in the day to day working out of program details could only be achieved by constant effort on the part of both faculty and students to effectively express needs, aspirations, and problems.

Communication with districts took different forms before the program started and after it had actually begun. During the initial stages of soliciting interest, communication to districts entailed contacting district heads or school supervisors through community meetings, formal correspondence and personal exchanges. The second year this communication effort focused on the district administration. This was complemented by the distribution of program brochures to others involved in school libraries and media programs who might be interested in participating as students in the experimental program.

Response was particularly optimistic and enthusiastic in areas surrounding the University of Denver. Interest from districts outside Colorado was extremely promising but frequently other circumstances prevailed which prohibited participation. Occasionally concerns were voiced by district heads over personal job security, but as program goals were further explained many of these fears were alleviated.

District participation entailed the "lending" of its facilities for examination by a given student who might or might not already be employed by that district. Once permission was granted and the program initiated, responsibility for communication with districts was assumed by the students. Relationships with community members were established at the students' discretion, each approach and interpretation of commitment varying as individual personalities and situations differed. Familiarity with community problems, needs and goals prior to entrance in the program afforded a definite advantage to students who possessed this background.

Proximity and district encouragement facilitated communication as well as the acquisition of relevant data for the students' case studies. Distance, although an influential factor during the first year, was not as significant during the second year when students were informed before leaving their districts of the data they would be needing throughout the study.

Communication between the Graduate School of Librarianship and the University administration was minimal throughout the planning and implementation stages of the program. The coordination aspect of the program was the responsibility of the Dean, and because of the semi-autonomous nature of the Library School in the University organization, all decisions could be made within the School. Any discussions with the University officials were held primarily to inform them of what the School was doing.

Frequent and multi-directional communication with program faculty was imperative when program implementation was undergoing its first test of relevancy. During the initial stages of the program the program faculty met daily with each other to discuss plans, procedures, and problems, each consulted individually and in groups with participating faculty from the Library School and other departments as well as with students. Opinions concerning course structure, program development, student affairs and evaluation procedures were openly voiced and debated during staff meetings of the Library School faculty. Discussion of program development and individual concerns was imperative to achieve unification and group consensus.

Cooperation from specialists in other departments was arranged early in the planning stages when general program format and goals were explained to them. Although each professor's role in the program was outlined at this time, prescription of specific course structure or content was impossible without further knowledge of the students and their specific needs. When students were able to identify their needs, particularly those related to the case studies, more pointed communication ensued. At this time students and full-time faculty discussed problems, goals and needs with the interdisciplinary professors and resolved conflicts so that needs would be satisfied.

Faculty-student communication of program goals and requirements began with the first contact with prospective students and continued throughout the program year. This advance correspondence and the special meetings, individual counseling sessions, and group evaluation sessions after students arrived were used in conjunction with written tests and assignments to correlate goal compatibility, identify students' strengths and weaknesses, and verify understanding of program goals and means for their implementation. However, a clear understanding of what the program was designed to accomplish was not achieved by the students until they had actually begun to collect data for their case studies. In addition, differences in personality, educational and cultural background, and understanding of personal and program goals could not be ignored in the attempt to develop communication channels between faculty and students.

# Program Participants

## RECRUITMENT

A unique aspect of the experimental program was the need to recruit both students and school districts that were willing to cooperate. Several means were used to recruit students. For the first year, publicity brochures and letters were sent to individuals identified as school library directors or supervisors and extensive telephoning was done. The response was small, primarily because the notification date of the grant on March 5, 1971, did not allow sufficient lead time for interested media specialists to arrange for leaves and sabbaticals.

Concern about the timing and contract problems faced by students in the first year led to a decision to focus the recruitment campaign on the school districts the following year. For the second year, administrators of school districts were mailed recruitment material on the program early in September, about a year before the beginning of the second year of the experimental program. Interested school district personnel had time to identify prospective candidates and to explore sabbatical and professional leave possibilities. For example, the board of education of a school district granted the first sabbatical leave in the district so that the individual they had identified as a candidate could participate in the program. Professional friends of the faculty members of the program were invited to suggest the names of school district officials who might be interested in participating in the program.

Recruitment through library, audiovisual and educational professional associates and associations was also an important part of the process. University faculty members took program brochures for distribution at national, regional and state meetings which they attended. The Project directors, as well as the executive secretary of the American Association of School Librarians, aided in recruitment efforts.

## STUDENTS

Ten students completed the experimental program during the two-year period, three the first year and seven the second year. There were four students at the beginning of the first year, but one withdrew at the end of the first quarter because the individual's educational objectives were not consonant with the objectives of the program.

Students with Master's degrees in librarianship or education were admitted to this experimental post-master's program. Six were graduates of institutions with library programs approved by the ALA Committee on Accreditation and four were from institutions with a strong area in librarianship. Only one had less than eighteen hours of librarianship courses but presented a strong background in curriculum, graphics, photography and audiovisual methods supplemented by experience. All had had experience as classroom teachers. The teaching experience range was from the elementary school level to part-time appointments in library education programs in colleges and universities. The average age was thirty-nine.

Student financial aid was an essential part of this mid-career program. Six students received full tuition scholarships from the University of Denver and one accepted a one-half tuition scholarship. In addition to a sabbatical leave with one-half salary, one school district reimbursed its participant for tuition, meals, lodging, travel, educational and secretarial expenses. Another student who was on full tuition scholarship was granted an interest free loan of $2,000 from one of the established funds of the Graduate School of Librarianship. The scholarship of a third student was supplemented with a National Defense Student Loan. Two of the four students who were members of an ethnic minority group received United States Department of Health, Education and

Welfare stipends when such funding became available during the second year. One student who was on sabbatical leave with full salary also received a scholarship from the Delta Kappa Gamma Society. Two school districts contributed $200 and $500 respectively toward the field survey of students studying the given district. In addition, most of the students used personal loans and savings to cover some of the expenses of the program.

Expenses, exclusive of tuition, varied widely due to differences in living habits, personal circumstances (a few had to maintain two residences), and district support. The average cost per student was $3,500 and included lodging, meals, travel to and within the school district and survey expenses.

## SCHOOL DISTRICTS

Ten school districts in six states with a geographical spread from the mid-Atlantic seaboard to the Pacific Northwest were participants in the program. Colleges or universities were in proximity to most of the school districts. Counties, semirural urban centers, suburban and city districts were represented. Some communities were in older sections of the country, while others were in newly developing areas. Some of the districts had a tendency toward a traditional curriculum while others were developing open spaces and more progressive curricula. Of these ten districts, six had district library media directors.

The school district-university student relationship was one of the most unique features of the program. The successful participation of one depended on the interest of the other. The commitment and support of the school district affected the morale and satisfactory progress of the student. Commitment was evidenced in recommending candidates for the program, continuing interest in the progress of the student, cooperation during the on-site survey conducted by the student through encouraging participation of school personnel, supplying needed secretarial assistance, and in some cases, financial support to the student. This support took the form of sabbatical leaves with full or part-salary and small grants to nondistrict personnel to conduct the survey in a given district.

The interest and professional attitude of the director of curriculum or instructional materials of a school district varied from full cooperation and help in identifying an applicant for the program and continued support of the student throughout the program, to partial commitment and nominal support of the student's field case study. Four school districts granted sabbatical leaves with full, two-thirds or one-half salary. Two districts provided grants to non-

district personnel to conduct the survey in their specific districts. Such support ranged from $200 paid directly to the student to the sum of $500 deposited with the library school for use of the student for such needs as gasoline and other expenses for on-site visits, some secretarial help, fees for school district related workshops, etc. The financial aid given by the school district through sabbatical leaves was only one aspect of commitment. In some districts the students conducting the case study were provided with secretarial assistance in preparing questionnaires and other survey instruments for distribution to school personnel, and arrangements for the student to interview pupils, teachers, library media specialists, and administrators were facilited. A few school districts provided students with adequate work and office space during the fieldwork period. Some students were in touch with school district personnel by letter and telephone. The cost for these calls was borne by the student in most cases.

## STAFF

The original administrative pattern for the experimental program called for two co-directors. Although it was thought that this administrative structure would provide maximum guidance for students, it posed problems of communication and resulted in a lack of clarity in decision making. The problem of co-directors was resolved early in the first year of the program by a changeover from a dual directorship to a single directorship. Thus regular faculty for the experimental program consisted of a full-time director and a half-time faculty member for each of the two years and a full-time media consultant who was appointed as the director of the Technology Laboratory of the Graduate School of Librarianship. The director of the first year became the half-time faculty member in the program the second year, while the director of the second year was the half-time faculty member of the first year. These two faculty members were assigned cooperative responsibility during the two years of the experimental program. During the first year the half-time faculty member guided the case study of one student in the program and was in charge of recruitment for the second year; during the second year the number of students had increased so that the half-time faculty member guided the case studies of three students.

The planning faculty believed that a variety of experiences, both in depth and breadth, were necessary for the optimal guidance and direction of students in so particularized a program. Therefore, it was felt that versatile use of the interdisciplinary expertise of the University rather than heavy reliance on only three full-time school library and media personnel, would best serve the needs of the proposed experimental program.

Three professors, two from the School of Education and one from the Graduate School of Librarianship taught the three mini-courses. These two-week concentrated courses in library architecture, school law and school finance were specifically designed to meet the needs of each student in the program.

Other consultants and lecturers were drawn from professors in the Departments of Speech Communication, Sociology, Mass Communications and the School of Education to discuss early childhood education, elementary education, secondary education and accountability. The research component of the program was taught by the director of the Center for Communication and Information Research of the library school. There were also resource people from the Colorado State Department of Education, the National Assessment of Educational Progress, and the University of Denver Office of Grants.

Each part-time professor, consultant or lecturer and each faculty member of the library school was available as consultant for the student's case study. The administrative assistant to the Dean and selected graduate and student assistants were also involved in the development of the program.

Staff development was carried out on an informal basis rather than a formal basis. The districts themselves served as primary resources in the study of the respective districts and administrators and library media staff functioned as mentors in faculty understanding of the current program and the district needs and problems that had led to the formulation of current policies. In addition to the districts involved in the program, other districts with outstanding programs were visited as time and funds permitted. On campus the faculty grew in special subject areas as they participated in the mini-courses taught by professors brought in as specialist-consultants from other departments and colleges in the University. To these personal experiences were added formal planned programs of readings in areas of concern to the students and faculty.

As with any experimental program, the professional commitment of the faculty directly involved and the support of the Dean of the School and University administrations were *sine qua non*.

## ADVISORY BOARD

The Advisory Board for the program was composed of individuals from five groups who were invited to help in the development of the program: (1) The Graduate School of Librarianship—the Dean; Director of the Center for Communication and Information Research; Director of the Advanced Studies Program; and Director of the Technology Laboratory; (2) Student representatives from the Graduate School of Librarianship—a student-director liaison from the program and a student from the fifth year curriculum; (3) The University of Denver—the Dean of the Graduate School of Arts and Sciences; Acting Director of Audio-Visual Services; Coordinator for Graduate Education, School of Education; and Chairman of the Department of Sociology; (4) School district personnel—a coordinator of library media services and a superintendent of schools; (5) Community representatives—the Director, Colorado State Library; Colorado Board of Education; and the Director, Continuing Education Program of Library Personnel, Western Interstate Commission on Higher Education.

Advisory Board meetings were formal sessions during the first year and less formal during the second year. The presentation and critique of the proposed curriculum, suggestions for the recruitment of school districts, curriculum suggestions and critique of multi-media presentations were some of the agenda items for formal sessions.

Since a number of suggestions of the Advisory Board members were incorporated into the second year program, informal sessions were held with student representatives and faculty on campus. The Board had observed that the program was too comprehensive and that careful consideration would need to be given to the research component since some students might have had limited research experience. All Advisory Board members were invited to critique the multimedia presentations of the second program year.

Throughout the program, the school academic division members of the Graduate School of Librarianship served in an advisory capacity. Since this was a post-master's program, the Advanced Studies Program Committee members participated in approval of a number of experimental measures for specific students. These included the waiver of library degrees from schools with programs approved by the ALA Committee on Accreditation, three years work experience in a school library media center, and the three-quarter seminar in advanced studies for sixth year or post-master's students. Program staff members worked with this committee in refining the program and offering it as a part of the post-master's program at the conclusion of program funding.

# Program Components

The case study method—whereby each student would design a proposal for a media program in a particular school district—provided the focal point around which curriculum development was centered. The predetermined knowledges and abilities supplied the skeleton on which specific educational units were based and a course sequence was established which was expected would enable students to gradually realize the goals of their proposals. Professors from other schools and departments, such as Education and Sociology, were consulted and arrangements were made for their cooperation in the program.

The Directed Field Case Study method was developed in the belief that organization of the program around a single global problem area—the planning and designing of a district-wide school library media program—would inculcate the basic knowledges and develop the abilities deemed necessary for a district school library media director. Therefore, according to the original proposal,

> Each student in the program will himself design and plan the implementation of a balanced district-wide media program in a selected school district. The major content of the educational curriculum then is structured by the questions that arise as the students attempt to formulate their designs and plans for implementation; it is a structure by learning, for the sake of trying to solve a problem, rather than a structure by subject *per se*.

It was felt that such an approach, focusing on a problematic situation would provide unity and cohesiveness, motivate students to learn, promote independent thinking and develop leadership qualities in an impirical situation.

The experimental program was designed for a full-time study during an academic year of three consecutive quarters. Six components were developed to meet the program goals mentioned earlier: (1) orientation, (2) tutorials, (3) research-consultation, (4) media production, (5) field survey and (6) mini or concentrated two-week courses. Electives were also a part of the experimental program during the fall and spring quarters.

As shown in Appendix A, the three main elements of this 45 quarter hour program included (1) the field case study which was assigned a block of 24 quarter hours, (2) mini or concentrated two-week courses which totalled 6 hours and (3) 15 hours of electives. Individualized instruction, except for the electives, was the norm rather than the exception throughout the year at the University of Denver. Because the educational backgrounds and professional experiences of the students selected varied considerably it was imperative that specific course content be tailored to student needs. The field case study of 24 quarter hours was divided into 10, 9, and 5 quarter hour blocks for the fall, winter and spring, respectively. The quarter hours assigned to the several components within these blocks were informal and are shown in Appendix A. An examination of Appendix A indicates that continuity in three of the four components of the fall field case study block (tutorial, research consultation and media production) was provided in the two remaining quarters of the program.

The winter quarter on-site or field survey consisted of 9 quarter hours. Further study of Appendix A shows these were informally divided into four parts: (1) six hours for the field survey, (2) two hours of tutorials for the preparation of the formal or technical report of the study and seminars where students shared their field experiences in group sessions, (3) one-half quarter hour for consultation with the research methods instructor and other professors in the program, and (4) one-half quarter hour for planning the multi-media presentation in consultation with the media consultant.

The spring quarter case study of 5 quarter hours was informally divided into three parts: (1) two and one-half quarter hours for tutorials to prepare the formal report, (2) one-half quarter hour for consultation with the research methods instructor and other professors in the program, and (3) two quarter hours for the production of materials and preparation of the multimedia presentation. Concentrated mini courses of about two-weeks duration received major emphasis during the winter quarter.

In general, each student carried 15 hours of course work for each of the three quarters. Students who completed the 45 quarter hours were awarded a Certificate of Advanced Studies (C.A.S.).

The program elements described here represent, in the main, the program as revised after the first year and implemented during the second year. Students, faculty and Advisory Board members were involved in the evaluation of the program for the first year. Reference will be made to major changes made in the program during the second year.

## FALL QUARTER

During the fall, or first quarter of study, the objectives, in terms of the student, were reviewing or studying research methodology, designing the study of his school district and developing instruments for his field survey. One of two faculty members was assigned to guide each student in conducting the case study of a given school district; thus each student was assigned an advisor at the beginning of his program of studies.

*Orientation.* This component was developed in three phases: (1) the student—the program—the learning environment, (2) student identification of self and group goals, and (3) student consideration of district school library media programs in relation to the educational milieu and socictal problems and progress.

Informal orientation sessions were used to welcome the students to the University and to the experimental program. Students met other participants and regular faculty and were involved in preprogram inventory sessions. Skits, interviews, or panels were used to introduce both students and faculty as part of these orientation sessions. An overview of the program objectives and the curriculum was given; learning facilities of the campus and the metropolitan area were highlighted. The Technology Laboratory of the library school was visited and its facilities for the production of audiovisual materials were explained. Tours of the University library, the city library, and suburban school and public libraries were included in this phase of orientation.

There were three parts to the informal preprogram inventory: (1) an assessment of the understanding each student had of the four occupational definitions presented in *Occupational Definitions for School Library Media Personnel* (2) student self-evaluation of competencies and needs as district school library media directors, and (3) student listing of three-to-five personal program goals. Student-written replies in these areas were used by faculty to guide them in counseling sessions where course electives were discussed to understand the student's objectives, and to gauge the understanding the group had of broad program goals. During the first year the students who found it difficult to see the relationships of the experimental program components had difficulty orient-

ing to the program. Therefore, emphasis was placed during the second year on the development of group understanding of the program goals. Consequently, there was less confusion in this area, the program got underway more quickly, and morale was higher. This might have been due, in part, to the strong self-image of the members of the second year group and the experience the faculty had during the first year.

For the formal phase of the preprogram inventory the students took two tests developed by the Institute for Personnel and Ability Testing (IPAT); these were the Motivational Analysis Test or MAT and the Sixteen Personality Factors Test or 16PF. These diagnostic tests were selected after the Director of the Center for Communication and Information Research, who was involved in the evaluation of the program from its inception, had consulted professors in the Psychology Department of the University. These tests were used on an experimental basis and their limitations in this program were recognized by the faculty. However, it was felt that these tests might be relevant as internal checks of the program, such as indicating some measure of student attainment of such specific program objectives as developing leadership and creativity as well as possible prediction of achievement. An analysis of pre- and post-test results are shown in Appendix B.

As part of the orientation component, each student introduced his school district to the other participants and faculty. Students, informed that this would be part of the orientation, brought slides of their community, transparencies, and other materials to present information on the past, present and future of each district and of the school library media program. These presentations gave the faculty, and in particular the media consultant, a general idea of the level of sophistication of the group in the use and production of audiovisual materials, knowledge which was utilized in planning and presenting the media production component. In discussions which followed each presentation, students identified their own goals within the framework of the philosophy of education of their school district. Both the students and faculty also found some common group goals. This provided the background which enabled students and faculty to identify the interests and problems of each school district in meaningful ways. Both faculty and students were then able to recommend references which might be of interest to a particular student, to share experiences or reactions to certain innovations of the school district of a student, or to involve a particular student as a resource when studying a topic.

Interpersonal communication was a topic which

was explored early in the fall quarter sessions. One of the speech communication lecturers helped the group review the role of human relations in communication and gave each an opportunity to become more aware of his own reactions in the communication process. These sessions also stressed human relations at all levels in a district media program. This involvement in group sessions and understanding of personal program objectives in relation to those of others contributed much to the *esprit de corps* which was lacking during the first year of the program when the human relations component was scheduled at the end of the quarter.

The lecturer on sociology helped the students to see their school library media programs in relation to the education milieu by examining the industrial developments in society which have shaped progress on one hand and created problems on the other. Such problems as the breakdown of the family, the dropout, poverty, drugs, and crime challenge education and by extension, the school library media programs of a school district. Lecturers in education stressed research, issues and trends in educational sociology, early and middle childhood education, secondary education and accountability.

Concomitant with efforts to help the students refine their thinking about the role of the school library media program in the teaching-learning process, the media consultant, the faculty and the specialist in research worked with the students in the areas of media production, the research component and tutorials.

*Tutorials.* These group and individual sessions enabled the student to meet with his advisor for general guidance and to relate the content of the orientation, research, and media production components to the student's study. For example, students discussed possibilities of their study and received direction from their advisors in developing the research proposal, preparing instruments to collect data, and developing report procedures and schedules for conducting and evaluating the field survey experiences of the winter quarter. The tutorial approach assisted in providing program development on an individual basis. This enabled each student to progress at his own rate in the direction most suited to an individual's needs and capabilities.

Group tutorials were an important component of the program during the second year. During the fall quarter of the first year, students requested that group tutorials be discontinued, but program evaluation at the end of the year indicated that synthesis had been lost through omission of these sessions.

*Research-Consultation.* There were three interrelated parts to the research-consultation component: (1) a review of research methodology which included: (a) principles and techniques used in a case study, (b) guidelines for writing a case study proposal and (c) development of instruments for the collection of data; (2) tutorials as described earlier; and (3) optional consultation of students with professors from librarianship and related disciplines who participated in the orientation component on the designing of the research proposal and in the development of instruments.

The research component was specifically designed to help the student analyze his school district and community in relation to the philosophy of education, long-range plans, financial support, legal boundaries, factors affecting growth and development, and the state of school media programs in the school district. The student formulated questions or objectives for his study, determined the research techniques to be used for gathering information, considered ways of analyzing data, and presented a draft of his proposal for the case study. Working proposals were used by the students to develop instruments for the collection of information to answer some of the problems or questions posed in the design of the study and to evaluate the possible approaches to the analysis of the data collected. Students relied on tutorials and consultations with the research specialist and other professors to develop this phase of their case study during the second half of the fall quarter.

Toward the end of the quarter students reviewed, in class sessions and in tutorials, techniques for the preparation and scheduling of interviews, administration of instruments, on-site observations and other tasks related to the methodology of a field case study. Accordingly, students developed tentative schedules for the interviewing of school district administrators, teachers, and school library media personnel, the administration of instruments, the examination of documents and other material in the school district, on-site visits to schools included in the study and the tabulation of information.

Each student made tentative arrangements with his advisor, who would visit during the on-site study, concerning the dates of the advisor's visit and schedule for reporting his progress during the field study.

Students were also prepared, through the media production component, to record some of their field observations and interviews on film or on tape.

The design of each case study was tailored to the specific school district designated for study by a particular student. In general, the studies were limited in scope and design. In school districts with a smaller number of schools, practically all of the schools in the district were included in the survey; in large districts, schools in certain geographical areas were identified for study; some studies concentrated on elementary school programs while others included selected schools with grades in the general range of kindergarten through grade twelve.

School documents from the case study district which were identified for examination by the student consisted of the written philosophy of education, school media selection policy and procedures, district school media standards, long range building or remodeling plans, and instructional and school library media programs.

Students developed questionnaires, interview questions and observation check lists and examined district documents in their collection of information for the on-site survey. Questionnaires were developed for a sampling of pupils, teachers, media personnel, administrators, and in some cases, parents and opinion leaders in the community. A number of the studies included interviews of a sampling of pupils, teachers, media personnel, and administrative personnel. Some on-site observation instruments were detailed checklists of physical facilities, the degree of media personnel involvement with pupils, and the ways in which pupils were using the school media center facilities.

During the first year when there were fewer students, the research specialist worked very closely with the students in their development of survey instruments. This helped to lower the frustration level of students involved in meeting deadlines imposed by time and limited background.

As a further aid to the student's preparation for his field or on-site survey, professors of library architecture and financial aspects of district school library media programs presented the introductory phases of their courses during the first quarter. These mini course introductory and planning sessions were not included in the fall quarter the first year. Program evaluation from the first year pointed up the advisability of including such sessions, along with a general orientation component, during the first quarter of study.

The mini-course professor for library architecture stressed principles of building programs and guided each student in the selection of areas in his school district building program to explore during the field survey. Each student was thus prepared to look for specific information bearing on the physical problems of building or remodeling a specific media center or the possibilities of new district-wide school library media facilities.

The professor for school finance discussed principles of a systems approach to education and stressed the ways in which careful program planning involved wise use of the time and effort of media personnel. Students were alerted to the areas where directors of school library media programs and librarians might become involved in the trend toward accountability. Students identified areas in which they could collect data for their school finance project during their field survey. For example, one student obtained the cooperation of one librarian in keeping track of how much time was devoted to specific tasks over a given period of time. Another student conducted an in-depth interview with a librarian in a school selected for study in relation to developing a program planning budgeting system for the particular library program.

As part of the orientation component, the students were also provided an opportunity to explore the concept of leadership with a professor in the department of speech communication. In addition, they had occasion to discuss some of the principles of library administration in a clinic conducted by one of the professors of administration in the library school. Standards for school library media programs and the certification of librarians and district school library media directors on the local, regional and national levels were studied with one of the professors in the program. A professor in the department of mass communications presented research and trends and issues of the field. Students were also urged to think through the implications for dynamic school library media programs.

Early in the quarter, while identifying their program objectives, several students expressed a desire to explore proposal writing. Accordingly, a session was held with the University Director of Grants. While the students did not have time to write proposals for submission to their school districts, they became aware of some of the principles involved in proposal writing.

*Media Production.* The media production component, one of the year-long components of the program, was designed to prepare the student for the multi-media presentation of the highlights of his study during the spring or final quarter of the program. In the fall quarter an assessment was made of the students' backgrounds in the reproduction and use of audiovisual material and equipment before specific plans were developed to help the students gain competencies and skills useful in gathering material during the field survey of the winter quarter. In the field survey, for example, students were prepared to use cassette recorders for interviews and to take slides or pictures of various methods used in storing audiovisual equipment and of pupils using school media centers. Instruction during the second quarter consisted of media consultant-student critique of slides or recordings taken during the field survey. During the third quarter the student concentrated on refining some of his techniques in presenting data through transparencies and preparing a multimedia presentation of his case study. The program provided each student with $150 to use for audiovisual materials while on campus and during the field survey.

The media consultant used formal and informal class sessions and tutorials to present such areas as communication theory, photography, overhead transparencies, audio systems and video taping. A wide range of media was used in presenting the content of the course to the students. Demonstrations were built into class sessions, i.e., various techniques of using transparencies with overhead projectors were used in presenting projection techniques. Students were encouraged to utilize information pertaining to their school districts in the preparation of transparencies. The facilities of the Technology Laboratory were available for student use throughout the school year during regular class hours and by appointment.

Photography assignments included work in and out of the Technology Laboratory. Students identified events which would be effective when photographed as a series. Basic instruction in photography was given for students who needed to become more competent in their use of the camera. They took pictures of class sessions, the campus and in the community. Pictures and slides were then critiqued by the instructor and by their classmates. A similar process was followed with cassette recordings of class sessions. Along with developing basic video tape recording techniques, video tape recording sessions gave students an opportunity to present what they had learned regarding the preparation and use of transparencies and recording equipment and the preparation of visuals for video tape recording sessions.

The media production component also provided for the growth of a few students who were rather sophisticated already in their production of materials and use of audiovisual equipment. One student took time to develop an interest in polarization and in the use of two cameras in video taping.

Program evaluation of this component during the first year indicated a strong desire for media production instruction to begin during the first quarter rather than in the second quarter. In the second year,

students received instruction and practice during the first or fall quarter and were much more confident in their use of the camera and recording equipment while in the field or during the on-site surveys.

## WINTER QUARTER

The program during the second or winter quarter was divided into two five-week sessions. The student spent the first session in his school district conducting his field survey. After his return to campus for the second session, he shared his field experiences with others, completed mini courses, analyzed data collected, drew tentative recommendations for his study and formulated plans for his multi-media presentation. Student objectives for this quarter were related to these activities.

*Field Survey.* The field or on-site survey was one of the unique features of the program. At the conclusion of the fall quarter (early in December) students spent from one to two weeks preparing for the five weeks set aside for field activities of the winter quarter; thus, the students actually spent from six to seven weeks conducting the field surveys. This preparation for the January activities consisted of confirming interview schedules, checking questionnaire items with district personnel before duplicating questionnaires, revising procedures for the administration of instruments, and studying school district documents and policies relating to the study.

District personnel in the school districts most keenly interested in the study were cooperative and their support expedited the study and did much for the morale of the student during this important interim period. In every district either the superintendent, the administrator in charge of curriculum, or the library coordinator introduced the student and explained the purposes of the study in a letter or memorandum that requested the cooperation of school personnel. Some school district officials included such specific information as how long the student would spend in the elementary and secondary schools, identification of groups selected for interviews, and estimates of the time interviews with different groups would take.

During the first three weeks of the winter quarter in January, students administered questionnaires to pupils, teachers, media personnel, administrators, parents and community leaders. The procedure for the administration of questionnaires varied in the school districts with the different groups. In some cases the student went directly into the classrooms and administered the questionnaires to pupils; in others, teachers were asked to administer the questionnaires. Cover letters accompanied the questionnaires in situations where it was difficult for the student to meet with the teachers administering the questionnaires to pupils.

Media personnel received their questionnaires either at a regular or special meeting or the questionnaires were sent through school district channels. In a few instances, when an appointment could not be made, questionnaires were sent through school district mail to principals and other district personnel. Teacher and pupil questionnaires were returned either through district mail channels or left with a member of the office staff for pick up by the student. Questionnaires intended for parents were usually given by teachers to pupils to be taken home and returned to the teachers for forwarding to the student. When community leaders or school board members were surveyed, questionnaires were mailed directly to individuals with a self-addressed stamped envelope enclosed for the reply.

Follow-up procedures varied with the individual student and the school district. Since anonymity of respondents to questionnaires was preserved in practically all of the studies, students either telephoned or sent general reminders through principals or media personnel requesting cooperation in the completion and return of the questionnaires.

Questionnaire items varied with the objectives of each study. Questions for pupils, teachers, media personnel, and administrators were concerned with accessibility or the hours the media center was open, reasons for using the facility, personnel available to assist pupils and faculty, the services available, physical facilities, book and non-book materials, equipment, and faculty or pupil involvement in building the collection. Adequacy of funding, long-range plans, and the public relations program of the media personnel were included when appropriate. Questionnaires designed for parents usually concerned pupil use of school and public libraries, types of library materials pupils borrow for home use, and the parent's awareness of a library in a given school.

Several methods for recording interview information were used. Some students depended upon cassette recordings; others took notes and used the tape or cassette recorder, while others made notations immediately after each interview. Some interview questions concentrated on broader aspects of questionnaire items, for example: how the library program might contribute to the teaching-learning processes in the classroom, the responsibility of teachers and media personnel in developing library and study skills, the availability of written job de-

scriptions for media personnel, the material selection policy, groups involved in formulating media center policies, how additional personnel would be utilized, strengths and limitations of media center programs, media center programs in relation to the curriculum, in-service plans, long-range plans, and when appropriate, budget allocations.

Observation checklists emphasized the following factors: areas for quiet, independent and group work, seating capacity of specific areas, availability of specific equipment for pupil use, materials for home use, areas for the production of materials by pupils and faculty, equipment storage, circulation areas, special facilities and public relations materials about the library program, such as handouts and student handbooks.

Program student and university faculty contact was maintained throughout the five-week period of the student's field survey. Students kept diaries of their activities which aided them in writing up weekly reports of their activities for their faculty advisor. These reports included such topics as the methods or processes used in setting up and conducting the field survey, a summary of activities for each day, reactions of personnel in the district, evaluation of the work completed and any questions and/or problems. Two examples of the Progress Report maintained during the on-site survey are found in Appendices C and D. Each report was studied by the student's faculty advisor and discussed with the student by telephone at least once a week. Problems, questions, and unusual situational factors were analyzed and ways in which the student might meet problems or situations were explored. Both student and faculty found these weekly conferences worthwhile and reassuring.

During either the third or fourth week of the student's field survey, the faculty advisor visited the student. The on-site visits of the faculty advisors were carefully planned. Tentative plans made before the end of the fall quarter were revised before the faculty advisor arrived on-site. A typical day usually included arrival at a school before classes began in order to meet administrative personnel; visits with school media personnel in the media center(s); luncheon with media personnel or other school personnel; an after school meeting with the public librarian or a visit to some district facility; dinner with individuals interested in the study and a conference with the student on the activities of the day.

These three to four day on-site visits were invaluable for both the student and faculty member in four general ways: (1) they provided the student and advisor an opportunity for on-the-spot in-depth discussion and analysis of the student's field experiences. The student usually arranged a schedule of school visitations in order that the faculty advisor might visit representative schools in the district. The faculty member often observed the student as he conducted an interview or administered a survey instrument; (2) school district administrators, teachers, media center personnel, community leaders, and school board members could meet both student and advisor to ask questions about the study, the field survey and the program in general when they attended meetings of library media personnel, school boards, and faculty; (3) the faculty advisor also had occasion to become aware of the concerns of school district administrators, teachers, and media personnel for the media program of the district; (4) visits to the central instructional media center and selected libraries of a district provided background for the faculty advisor in the analysis of data collected.

In addition to the weekly progress reports, a broad Summary of Activities for the entire on-site survey was submitted to the advisor. (See Appendix E.) The student also prepared a self-evaluation report of the time and effort expended during the on-site survey in the selected school district. A sample student evaluation is included in Appendix F. Program evaluation by students and faculty indicated an overwhelming recommendation that on-site visits be continued as a part of the program.

Students returned to campus for the second half of the ten-week winter quarter. The field experience seminar enabled students to report, compare, and evaluate the processes they were involved in during their field surveys. Students were enthusiastic about their experiences and found much to discuss and share for the duration of the experimental program. This was done in both formal and informal sessions.

Tutorials during this period were designed to help the student analyze the data collected and draw tentative conclusions and recommendations. Students tabulated the data collected and consulted with the research professor and other faculty as well as their advisors in the analysis of data collected and in reporting findings, reaching conclusions and making recommendations. Individuals varied in their adjustment to this phase of their study with the frustration level during the second year of the program appearing higher than during the first year. This may have been due, in part, to the comprehensive nature of the studies, the uneven preparation for the analysis of data, and the time element. The size of the group and the variance of research backgrounds were also factors which added to the usual "research blues" of this period.

On the basis of tentative conclusions and recommendations, students identified highlights of their study for the multimedia report of the spring quarter. They consulted with the media consultant and considered ways in which they would present some of their findings, whether by slides, transparencies, 8mm film or cassette recordings.

*Mini Courses.* The three concentrated two-week courses in architecture, finance, and legal aspects of district school library media programs were also conducted during this period. The professor of the architecture course built upon the orientation sessions of the fall quarter and guided each student in the preparation of a library building program for either a new or remodeled facility on a building or district level. These library building plans considered long-range plans of the district and the district's philosophy of education, in addition to general conditions of the physical facility, such as location, area, lighting, sound; organization of resources and equipment; relationships of the different areas in the facility (study and reference, reading and viewing, card catalog, work room, and production of materials); and a suggested schematic presentation, drawn to scale.

As a background to an understanding of accountability and the planning programming budgeting system, the course in finance provided an overview of school finance—federal, state and local; sources of local funds, how total funds for a local school district are determined; local school budgets; and the allocation of funds to programs. The professor drew upon orientation sessions conducted during the fall quarter in assisting each student to complete a finance project based on data collected for proposed projects during the field survey. Projects ranged from budgets for specific buildings to ones considering the financial needs of the entire district. Whatever the topic, the general focus was on the planning programming budgeting system and students wrote performance objectives and projected costs for specific phases of the media programs. The professor of this course involved several of his doctoral candidates as consultants in helping students develop their projects.

The University of Denver computer was available for student use, but time limitations did not permit students to prepare and code data for the computer program. This unfulfilled phase of the course was a cause for concern by several of the students.

As part of their work in the legal aspects mini course, students studied educational landmark cases and prepared briefs on cases involving such topics as the legal status of the librarian or teacher, negligence or tort liability, personal administration—tenure rights, due process, equal educational opportunity, public records, and financing education. The School of Education professor of this class discussed the briefs written by the students. The Westminster Law Library of the University of Denver's College of Law was essential to this phase of the program.

## SPRING QUARTER

The student concentrated on three objectives during the spring or the third and final quarter of the program: (1) completion of the written report of the study, (2) presentation of a multimedia report of the highlights of the study, and (3) electives.

An examination of Appendix A shows that the program for this quarter included ten quarter hours of electives and five quarter hours for the case study. The case study was informally divided into two and a half quarter hours for the tutorial which concentrated on the preparation and completion of the formal report of the study, two quarter hours in media production for the preparation of the multi-media report of the study, and one-half quarter hour for research consultation.

During the second year a majority of the students submitted proposals for credit beyond the two and one-half quarter hours designated for tutorials. Two reasons for such requests were the need for more time to refine the overall case study and a desire to work on separate reports for given schools in the district. Approval was granted to students submitting acceptable proposals for additional credit, ranging from two to four quarter hours; thus, the number of quarter hours students used for the case study during the spring quarter varied from five to nine, depending upon the student.

Several students also submitted proposals for interdepartmental independent study in order to concentrate on specific phases or related areas of their study. For example, one student worked with the professor of the mini course in school finance in developing a line item budget, with justification for a three year period for a projected media center. Another student from a state which is emphasizing certification for early childhood education studied with the major professor of early childhood education in the School of Education; one student, guided by a professor in the Department of Speech Communication, read intensively in the area of interpersonal communications in preparation for leadership in directing workshops in communications in her school district.

*The Case Study Report.* Students consulted with their faculty advisor, the research professor, and other faculty in presenting their findings, drawing conclusions, formulating recommendations, and working on the formal or written report of their study. Some of the students, probably because of a lack of experience in research reporting, found this phase of the program extremely difficult and very frustrating. A few consulted so many individuals that they were in a quandary over the best approach to take regarding the presentation of data or the emphasis to be given to different aspects of the study. This situation was further complicated by the fact that the data was often extensive and students found it difficult to delete irrelevant data from their reports.

During the first year, partly because there were only three students and the studies were less extensive, all formal reports were completed in time for students to meet graduation requirements during the spring quarter. The second year, because of illness, heavy elective course loads and a concern to present "the best study I can," only two of the seven students completed their formal reports in time for the spring commencement. The rest of the students, who completed program requirements to receive their Certificates of Advanced Studies at the end of the summer quarter, differed considerably in the time required to complete their studies.

The student attitude toward the ownership of their case studies differed, too. The first year all three students accepted the plan identified in the program proposal that the district would receive a copy of the report. During the second year, particularly since several of the students did not receive any direct financial help from the school districts they were studying, there was some question at first as to whether the reports belonged to the school district or to the student conducting the study. This question was resolved through general agreement that the reports were the property of the students and that each student would provide one written copy of the Case Study Report to the school district.

*The Multimedia Presentation.* Students presented multimedia reports of the highlights of their study in May of each year. The two objectives for this activity were: (1) to give each student an opportunity to become involved in the process of reporting selected aspects of his study to specific audiences within his school district, and (2) to give each student an opportunity to demonstrate his understanding, preparation and use of appropriate audiovisual resources in communication. Students were prepared for this activity of the program during the two preceding quarters. During the first quarter they received instruction in photography and recording interviews before their field survey. Following the on-site surveys, students evaluated, with the help of the media consultant, the slides, tapes or cassettes made of activities within the school districts. Toward the end of the winter quarter when the students had progressed sufficiently to draw preliminary conclusions and to begin to formulate the final recommendations, they made tentative plans for multimedia presentations.

During the first part of the spring quarter each student developed a multimedia report. A time schedule and outline were prepared for the presentation, including proposed audiovisual resources to support the report. The media consultant then used these outlines to coordinate the presentations. Students worked in the Technology Laboratory of the library school on such activities as preparing appropriate transparencies, converting transparencies into slides, editing tapes or cassettes, and developing techniques in the etiquette of multimedia presentations. Students also were critiqued at the final rehearsal in the auditorium where the presentations were given.

The multimedia presentations were given each year during the third week in May. Invitations for these presentations were sent to individuals identified by students and program faculty. In addition to members of the Advisory Board of the program, the Directors of the School Library Manpower Project, faculty of the University, and students in the library school, invitations were sent to selected administrators and faculty in the school districts studied and to members of the immediate family and special friends of the students.

These presentations were attended by members from the Advisory Board, cooperating faculty of the University, faculty and students of the library school, the Directors of the School Library Manpower Project, superintendents and coordinators of instructional materials centers, and faculty from school districts in the metropolitan Denver area included in the studies. One out-of-state library supervisor came over 1,200 miles to attend these presentations during the second year of the program.

To give focus to the presentation, each student identified his district audience and invited those present to listen as individuals would in such groups. Some expected to report to media specialists, teachers and PTA parent volunteers, while others selected combinations of the school board, supervisory staff, principals and teachers. Whatever the group, both the text of the report and the audiovisual materials were addressed to their interests and concerns. The first year, the formal part of each report took about

forty-five minutes followed by a thirty minute question and answer period. Since there were more students participating the second year, this time was shortened to twenty minutes for the report and ten minutes for questions.

As a means of an internal check of the effectiveness of the program, individuals attending these presentations were invited to check items on a short checklist as shown in Appendix G. The results of these ratings are reported in Appendix H. Although these ratings were not used to evaluate the work of each student, they served as feedback to the student and the program faculty.

The first year a luncheon for students and guests was given on the day of the presentations; the second year, a reception followed the day's activities. These occasions gave some of the guests further opportunity to discuss the presentations with the students.

*Electives.* Electives were an important aspect of the program. As indicated in Appendix A, the program provided for a minimum of five quarter hours of electives during the fall quarter and ten quarter hours during the spring quarter. Students were encouraged to consider electives to develop background in such areas as supervision, administration, library mechanization, and interpersonal communications and to qualify for administration and supervisory certification in a given school district. Interdepartmental courses included the areas of business administration, education, history, librarianship, mass communications, and speech communications.

ASSESSMENT

*Student.* Relative improvement was the primary consideration in assessing the proficiency of students whose educational and occupational backgrounds varied extensively and whose needs with respect to the development of their case studies differed. Individualized evaluation of student growth and development in an educational environment is an often sought-after, but rarely-attained ideal. Due to the nature and scope of this experimental program and the total commitment and involvement of the faculty concerned, it was possible (indeed necessary) to approximate this ideal as closely as could be achieved. The hazardous aspect of such evaluation, however, was over-involvement and hence over-subjectivity in assessing student proficiency. Clarification of procedures was necessary only once—at the beginning of the year. After this, student requirements and professors' considerations in evaluation were carefully spelled out and a professor delegated as consultant to avoid further confusion and to insure quality control. In this post-master's program where the objective, in terms of the student, was the completion of a study of a specific school district, assessment was divided into two major phases: (1) student self-assessment by written progress reports, tutorials, and faculty conferences as reflected in the progress of the formal case study reports, and (2) program testing as measured by attitude and personality tests and a review of the Presentation Checklist (see Appendix G) made by the audience during the multimedia presentations.

During the orientation component of the fall quarter, the philosophy of student assessment was discussed with the group. This involved student self-evaluation of progress toward specific goals identified for each quarter along with faculty assessment. Students were informed that their individual progress was of major concern and that individuals would not be compared with others in the group. In addition to student-written progress reports, assessment also included such factors as performance in tutorials and faculty observation of student progress in the case study. During the five-week period when the students were off-campus, the advisors visited the districts and talked to library media staff and administrators at both the building and the district level. These visits offered the advisor opportunity to evaluate the student's interaction with district staff and to assess his or her general effectiveness in obtaining support and cooperation.

At the end of each quarter students submitted written progress reports to the director of the program to justify the suggested grade. Growth in five areas was considered in measuring the progress of each student: (1) ability toward self-direction, (2) development and adjustment to work schedules related to the study, (3) objectivity in self-evaluation, (4) personal factors such as maturity and interaction in group sessions, and (5) professionalism.

Student-written progress reports were reviewed by the faculty before letter grades were assigned. This process of student assessment, developed from the experience of the first year, appeared to add a positive dimension to the general school policy of assigning letter grades at the end of each quarter. Study assessment in the mini courses of the winter quarter and electives during the year were the sole responsibility of the professors of the various courses.

*Program.* Formal group evaluation sessions were used during the first year, but the program was so highly individualized that most of the sessions lacked focus; consequently, formal group evaluation sessions were not scheduled during the second year.

Experience during the first year also led to the early establishment of avenues for student suggestions and the alleviating of grievances in the second year. The group elected one student to serve as liaison between the students and the faculty. Students had the option of taking their suggestions or grievances directly to the faculty member concerned or, when anonymity was desired, to the student-faculty liaison who then transmitted the matter, in writing, directly to the program director for action.

Without sacrificing the overall experimental program goals, individual program objectives were frequently modified to meet students' needs. This modification was based essentially on the respective district environments and particularly on the individual's ability in, and sophistication of, coping with a particular district's needs. Input from the case study district for program evaluation was minimal. Rarely did the district initiate any conversation about the program with the advisors. The primary feedback occurred only when the advisors visited schools and administrators in the district and solicited their expression of needs, hopes and expectations. Evaluation of program flexibility relied heavily on the written comments of faculty, student evaluation sessions, and interviews with students and professors. Because the experimental program at the University of Denver could not be overly structured and still meet the needs of its participants, program responsiveness was implemented primarily through informal procedures. Time limitations were another factor affecting program flexibility. It was frequently necessary to establish priority considerations for the case study—based on the weighing of needs for the respective districts. This setting of priorities was considered a learning experience in itself. However, it could also be argued that original program and student objectives were disproportionate with the amount of time available for their accomplishment. The small number of students who participated in the program and the highly individualized nature of their instruction and work permitted interaction—and hence daily evaluation—to be conducted almost exclusively on a personal basis. Because each student's abilities and needs differed considerably, it was primarily on this one-to-one level of interaction that program evaluation operated most effectively.

*Program Diagnostic Tests.* As noted in the discussion of the orientation component of the fall quarter program, the formal phase of the preprogram inventory included the administration of two diagnostic tests to the students during both years of the program. Post-program inventory testing was conducted in May of each year. The tests developed by the Institute for Personnel and Ability Testing (IPAT) were given to students so that some indication of their relative knowledge and abilities might be obtained and a starting point established from which to review their growth and, by projection, serve as a measure of the program. The Sixteen Personality Factors Test (16PF) is an all purpose test known for its wide applicability. Further, the reliabilities and validities of the 16PF have been subject to constant experimentation over a period of two decades. Although the test is comprehensive, two personality traits, motivation and interest, require an additional instrument for measurment. For this, the IPAT Motivation Analysis Test was used. From these tests on motivational analysis (MAT) and sixteen personality factors (16PF) student profiles were constructed which summarized personality characteristics to be used to determine program effects on students at the end of the year. The results of the MAT profiles were inconclusive and, consequently, are not included in this report. This is not to imply that they were negative.

The IPAT 16 PF tests, Forms A and B, were analyzed to obtain predictions of school achievement, criteria of leadership, creativity, and stability. The analysis of predictions of school achievement was limited to the fall quarter. The results are shown in Appendix B. A high score indicates possession in high degree of the given trait. It can be stated that in general the scores which were predicters of school achievement fairly well represented what turned out to be the case during both years of the program.

In the interest of judging whether the program met the stated goal of reinforcing qualities which a District School Library Media Director might be expected to have, the immediate question was whether the students showed significant change in becoming more creative and better leaders as a result of the program. The results were a little confusing. As can be seen in Appendix B, there were changes in the scores on leadership and creativity for all the students. The cumulative results of the two years showed two of the ten students increasing in leadership scores, with eight evidencing a decrease. Five students showed an increase in creativity. The results of the first year students appeared more positive than those of the second, since all first year students showed an increase in creativity. One first year student also increased in leadership.

Several considerations arose in interpreting the results of these tests. First, due to the complexity and the nature of the tests themselves, was the ques-

tion of whether these changes were statistically significant. Another concern was the apparent negative correlation between leadership and creativity. This was especially evidenced in the first year of the program. The first year results showed that the two students who increased considerably in creativity also dropped slightly over a point on their leadership scores. The third student increased considerably in leadership ability, but only slightly in creativity. The relationship, if any, between leadership and creativity appears to be in question. Possibly the two are negatively correlated—either in reality or in the tests—in which case, the program could not hope to bring about improvement in both these abilities.

The majority of the second year results seemed to coincide with those of the first. An increase in either creativity or leadership corresponded with a decrease in the other. A review of the literature to see if the program was really trying to achieve incompatibilities is called for.

The program seems to have been fairly successful in developing creativity, and in this respect achieved one of its major objectives. The failure to develop leadership in more students must be recognized as an area of concern. Possibly advisors worked so closely with students throughout the year that the students had less opportunity to develop leadership than would have occurred otherwise. Another alternative might be the attitude of the students themselves during the final quarter. The extreme pressure and concern regarding the final report may have made the tests an insignificant and indifferent aspect of the program to which their full attention was not given.

*Presentation Checklist.* The multimedia presentations of the students were reviewed by means of a Presentation Checklist (Appendix G). Members of the audience at these sessions assessed the elements in each presentation according to a scale of A, B, C, or D the first year, and a corresponding scale of Excellent, Good, Average, or Poor the second year. An average numerical grade where A=Excellent=4, B=Good=3, C=Average=2, and D=Poor=1 was calculated for each participant on specified elements of the presentations. Respondents were also asked to indicate whether they were faculty, library school student, Advisory Board member, professional librarian or a member of the case study district. No tendencies according to the occupation checked could be observed in the data. In general, ratings by faculty and professional librarians were in close agreement.

Averaging the numerical scores of the students

for each element gave a rough ranking of the strengths and limitations of the program in terms of the elements reviewed. Appendix H shows this ranking for the combined two years. The scores indicate a fairly even distribution, ranging from a low of 3.1 to a high of 3.7. The low scores were obtained in the categories of consideration of legal requirements, economic feasibility of the program, and awareness of related special programs in the community. Since the area of general knowledge of school and community characteristics was basic to the studies, the high score of 3.7 in this area was not unusual. The abnormally high number of no opinions and the low score of 3.1 in the categories of consideration of legal requirements, awareness of related special programs in the community, and awareness of peripheral organizations reflected the fact that these elements were not stressed in the time allowed for the presentations.

Averaging overall elements for all students in the program, a rating of 3.3, corresponding to a B+ was obtained for both years of the program. It might be said that this was the degree to which the program achieved success in developing knowledges and abilities essential for the district school library media director.

The results of the checklist data, however, must be viewed with circumspection. The preceding review was limited in two ways: by the limited number of students involved which makes averaging questionable; and by the fact that the presentation did not represent the total program content. Individuals in attendance at the presentations saw only what was a *fait accompli*. They had no way of judging how far the students had come, how far they had progressed as a result of the program, nor how much the final or technical report included. With this in mind, these presentations could be seen as an overview of the study as well as a learning experience for students in presenting selected highlights to their school districts.

# Program Results

## ATTAINMENT OF PROGRAM GOALS

The experimental goals and objectives were met in varying degrees throughout the two-year period. In general, the objectives were met through interdepartmental seminars, tutorials, mini courses, the field survey and the development of the study for specific districts.

Specifically, the students became more sensitive to the social problems and educational developments which affect school media programs through seminars conducted by lecturers and consultants. Students used research methods in designing the study and evaluation of the school media programs for a specific district. Various media center programs were evaluated by the students through consideration of programs and standards during their field survey and in other school districts. Although not reflected in final recommendations, students considered community agencies in their case studies; perhaps more attention might be given to this aspect in other studies.

Through the mini courses, students became aware of school law, principles of PPBS and planning library facilities. Students formulated a philosophy for district-wide school library media programs for specific districts throughout the program in the development of their case studies, tutorials, interdepartmental studies, mini-courses and electives. The philosophy which was evolved was reflected in the final or technical report.

The media production component, the multimedia report and the preparation of graphics for the technical report of the study helped students to refine skills in the design and use of appropriate audiovisual material and related technology.

Students elected courses which provided for aspects of their professional growth and worked toward varying state certification requirements for the position of district school library media director. Courses often were not scheduled during the times students were able to take them, but interdepartmental independent study met some of their needs. The Certificate of Advanced Studies which was granted at the completion of the program made a difference in the compensation some students received when they returned to the field.

In addition to meeting the program objectives mentioned above, two related developments may be cited. The concerted effort to recruit members of ethnic minorities for the program resulted in four representatives of a minority group completing the program. Several participants in the program had had limited contact with members of ethnic minority groups and the structure of the program enabled the participants to learn in a climate of trust and respect. The program as described was modified in some degree and offered as part of the advanced studies or post-master's program of the Graduate School of Librarianship, effective September 1973.

## PROGRAM IMPACT

The impact of the experimental program will undoubtedly continue for sometime for each participant, whether student or school district. Preliminary field reports by participants and school district personnel of the first year program and school district plans reported by several participants in the second year program appear encouraging. The following are some of the program results:

1. The position of district school library media director was established in two school districts which did not have designated directors at the time of the studies.

2. In one school district where there was an established director, the program participant developed models of personnel, materials, and facilities for the elementary schools in the district. As a direct result of the study, each of the eleven new elementary schools in the district benefited over a two year period in the following manner: (a) a professional school library media specialist was employed; (b) $15,000 was budgeted for library materials the first year of operation; (c) building specifications, including furniture, were adapted for these media centers from the model plan; and (d) full or half-time aides were provided for all new elementary media specialists.

3. Curriculum planning has been implemented in one school district on a K-12 grade level. Prior to the study, principals in the elementary and secondary schools did not meet together to discuss curriculum matters. During the study administrators and teachers began meeting to consider the total educational program. One apparent outcome was the establishment of the position of director of school library media programs for grades K-12.

4. One participant was able to implement some of the recommendations of the study in the development of a model center in a new open space concept school in the district. This individual also used data gathered on staff, materials, facilities, and programs during the case study to submit a proposal to the state library for a special purpose grant, funded by ESEA, Title II. This model elementary media center was designated as an exemplary school library media program by the ESEA, Title II board and was granted $18,000 for further expansion and development as a demonstration center for the state. This grant was one of twenty-four selected from 127 proposals submitted.

5. Remodeling plans developed during the program were considered in the remodeling of a specific library in another district.

6. One district planned a workshop on communication for library media personnel and is moving toward PPBS in developing library media programs.

7. As a direct result of questions asked in interviews of school library media personnel during the field survey, several media specialists in one district indicated that they have implemented some of the ideas brought out in the interviews.

These program results reflect a statement by a participant, that "the district sent me to get ideas and new ways to approach school library media programs."

As participants developed their studies and realized that effective district-wide library media programs involved curriculum considerations on the K-12 grade range, some began to evaluate their lack of library experiences. As a result, several students elected to round out their experiences. Several who were oriented toward high school media centers accepted assignments in elementary schools, while several with junior high school experience accepted positions in high schools. One participant with extensive library experience in the K-12 grade range accepted an assignment as director of an early childhood specialist program in a library school.

Several developments in the library school and the University were the direct result of the experimental program. Funds from the grant were used to employ a media consultant for the program who also served as director of the Technology Laboratory of the school. This laboratory was established in 1969 as an adjunct to the academic program of the library school. This first full-time director was able to give attention to the development of three major objectives of the facility concerning library collections and programs: (1) the educational concept of using print and audiovisual materials, (2) a demonstration center where related technology and materials might be used, compared, and evaluated, and (3) a production center for audiovisual materials.

The facilities and staff of the Technology Laboratory were important in the development of the multimedia presentations of the students in the program as well as in the preparation of graphics for the technical report.

It would appear that the consultants and lecturers of the experimental program, drawn from the University and the metropolitan area, developed deeper understanding of and insight into school librarianship from their discussions with students and faculty of the program. Similarly, program faculty learned much from these individuals to apply in their teaching.

The contacts of program faculty with professors in the interdisciplinary phase of the program facilitated the development of a workshop for the continuing education of school media personnel. The professor of the finance course conducted a workshop on accountability and PPBS with computer application of data. Several of the participants in the workshop were district directors and school media specialists from widely scattered geographical regions.

The effect of the experimental program on librarianship and library education may be seen in several other areas. The master's program was strengthened through discussion with personnel in the field, on-site visits of the faculty to the districts involved, and suggestions from students in the program. Contacts in the districts, representation of different agencies by members of the Advisory Board, the multimedia presentations and the recruitment activities, both of the Graduate School of Librarianship and the School Library Manpower Project office, furthered this impact.

# Program Conclusions

In achieving program objectives, the strength of the case study methodology, field survey, and the interdisciplinary aspects of the program outweighed the limitations. A discussion of problems or limitations would include the following considerations.

Evaluation by students and faculty supported the observation of the Advisory Board that the program was too demanding or comprehensive for the time allowed. One indication of this was the fact that five of the seven students in the second year were not able to complete their formal reports in three quarters. This may be attributed, in part, to the varied and limited research background of the students and the limitations of the research component. Three conditions contributed to the latter: (1) one of the professors, new to the program the second year, did not have the experience of the first year for guidance, (2) even with independent study and tutorials, students lacked the research background and experience needed to complete the program in the time alloted, and (3) unwillingness of some students to limit the scope of their study.

The quality of some of the research instruments developed for the case studies was affected by the time element, especially the lack of time for adequate field testing to achieve the quality of case studies desired. The time element also hindered second year plans for the presentation of the case studies in three forms: a formal or technical report, a popular report, and a multimedia report. Students were only able to complete the technical and multimedia reports.

The fall quarter interdisciplinary component was comprehensive in the variety and depth of material and concepts presented. Some students were unable to effectively synthesize the many sources of information, although the bibliographies prepared by some of the lecturers were useful. Time was of an essence and did not permit follow-up group tutorials for some of the interdisciplinary lectures and discussion.

Communication on several levels affected the morale and progress of the program, the participants, and the faculty. University student-school district and school district-university student relationships were unique features of the program. In cases where students received school district support, either in the form of financial assistance or cooperation of the district personnel, morale was high. The progress of such students during the field survey was only limited to preparation and self-perception. But in cases where cooperation and financial support was minimal, student morale was often low, however well prepared and perceptive the student was of his work. The support of school district personnel appeared to be limited when they felt threatened by the program. This factor made recruitment difficult whether through supervisors or school district administrators. Because of the nature of this program, there was no one in the district who could be appointed as supervisor or evaluator as is typical of the average fieldwork experience. Rather, the directors had to rely on what the student reported, the feedback they obtained when visiting in the district, and the final report. Monitoring was complicated by the faculty's inability to follow everything that was happening, and to assist in the reaching of decisions when students were in the district.

Student-faculty and faculty-student communication patterns were often sensitive areas. The adjustment of some of the students to new learning styles was sometimes complicated by the self-image of the student and the faculty member. Student adjustment to the world of academia during the post-master's level is often difficult due to personal and professional responsibilities. Conversely faculty had adjustments to make to students with considerable professional experience and responsibility. The major difficulty here was providing for the needs of the students without compromising the integrity of the Case Study Method or failing to provide for the district the plan that had been promised.

This innovative program was developed by faculty who had had little prior experience in working as a team in the school and with professors in other departments of the University. Program coordination with the latter improved during the second year. The decision to have dual directors was changed within a month after the program was underway. One individual was designated as the director with the other assisting as a faculty member in the program; these positions were reversed during the second year.

Despite the problems described above and elsewhere in this document, neither faculty nor students challenged the validity of the method. The students found their surveys of the district and the resulting development of a plan challenging and rewarding. The faculty saw growth not only in the students but also in their own thinking. Finally, each student produced a plan which was believed to be a contribution to the development of a sound school library media program. The faculty concurred in this belief and looked forward to seeing the plans implemented in the districts.

As the Case Study Report took shape, the advisor could assess the quality of data reporting by skillful questions. The individualized nature of the program and the limited number of students allowed the advisor to meet frequently with each student. These planning and counseling sessions revealed the current success of the student in working with personnel in the school district and the general level of support the district was providing for the case study. Visits to the district and interviews with administrative and media personnel corroborated impressions of the advisor and provided further insight. The final measure, however, was the Case Study Report itself and the quality and feasibility of the recommendations it contained. Although it is conceded that no valid appraisal can be reached until the school district has had an opportunity to implement the recommendations, the sum of the above factors provided a sound basis for evaluation.

Although neither advisor would consider the methods enumerated above as wholly adequate, it was amazing how much each knew about the activities of the assigned advisee. It is safe to say that rarely has a teacher had a better picture of her students' activities than was true of these field surveys.

TRANSPORTABILITY

One of the general benefits derived from an experimental program is the identification of certain components of that program which may be transported to other institutions. The following observations for transportability are based on the two year experimentation and should be studied carefully before initiating a program of this type.

1. The case method, the field survey, on-site visits by faculty, tutorials and the number of consultants require a significant investment of institutional finance and faculty time. Especially needed are additional funds for the Technology Laboratory, supplies, secretarial and student help, and travel.

2. The individualized nature of the program necessitates a low student-faculty ratio. Over the two-year period, the ratio of student to faculty was five to one. More conference time was given to the students in the program than to the usual post-master's student; for this reason, a desirable student-faculty ratio should be low.

3. Some students may need more than one academic year of study for the program since the research component requires special consideration to meet individual needs and to provide sufficient time for the completion of the study.

4. The relationship between the student and school district contributes to the success of the study and the morale of the student.

5. The interdisciplinary nature of the program necessitates the coordination, commitment and time of the faculty.

6. The flexibility of the program requires the exclusive use of a classroom to permit scheduling of consultants and lecturers when most convenient. As

there is also much need for informal discussion among the students, an area should be available for such use.

7. The field survey necessitates added financial outlay by the student for the cost of transportation to and from and within the district, and, for some, the maintenance of two residences during the period of the field survey.

8. Both a media consultant and a technical laboratory are requisites for the multimedia presentation.

9. Recruitment is dependent upon the cooperation, commitment and financial support of school district personal and the economic restraints of the period.

## RECOMMENDATIONS

The experience gained from this two-year experimental program for the preparation of district school library media directors leads to the following recommendations that:

1. The case study method with its tutorials and interdisciplinary aspects should be employed as vital to this type of program.

2. The field survey, including faculty on-site visits should be retained in a similar program.

3. A close liaison should be established with each school district by the advisors to facilitate communication and insure continuous feedback from school district to university and university to school district.

4. Any insecurities apparently created by the flexibility of the program and the interdepartmentalization of staff should be assuaged by a firm structure of tutorials throughout the program.

5. The research component of the case study should be introduced very early in the program so students will comprehend the steps that must be taken to develop a district-wide school media program.

6. The program should continue to modify its requirements to meet the needs of the school districts involved, so long as the modifications do not prevent the meeting of sixth year standards.

7. The case study requirements should be given to students prior to the start of the academic program to facilitate the collection of necessary school district data.

8. No less than one academic year of study should be considered for the completion of the program.

9. The optimum size of a school district in this type of program should be considered carefully. When the size of a school district is too large, the student should be counseled to establish feasible priorities for the case study.

10. Prior to the start of the program, there should be agreement among the program, students, and participating school districts which identifies the ownership of the case study and the rights and responsibilities of those involved.

Participation in the School Library Manpower Project as one of six experimental programs in school library media education has convinced the University of Denver that the program designed for the education of a district school library media director is viable. As evidence of this, the program, with modifications, has become a part of the post-master's program of the Graduate School of Librarianship.

Appendix A

UNIVERSITY OF DENVER
GRADUATE SCHOOL OF LIBRARIANSHIP

SCHOOL LIBRARY PROGRAM*
1972-73

| | FALL Quarter Hours | WINTER Quarter Hours | SPRING Quarter Hours | TOTAL |
|---|---|---|---|---|
| FIELD CASE STUDY** | 10 | 9 | 5 | 24 |
| Orientation | (3) | | | |
| Research - Consultation | (3) | (.5) | (.5) | |
| Media Production | (2) | (.5) | (2) | |
| Tutorial | (2) | (2) | (2.5) | |
| Field Survey | | (6) | | |
| MINI COURSES*** | | 6 | | 6 |
| ELECTIVES | 5 | | 10 | 15 |
| TOTAL | 15 | 15 | 15 | 45 |

*A post-master's program designed for current and potential district school library media directors using the methodology of directed field case study. Students completing the 45 quarter hour program will be awarded a Certificate of Advanced Studies.

**The field case study of 24 quarter hours is divided into 10, 9 and 5 quarter hour blocks. The quarter hours assigned to the several components within these blocks are informal and are shown in parentheses.

***Three mini or concentrated courses of 2 quarter hours each are of architectural, financial and legal aspects of district school library media programs.

Appendix B

PERSONALITY PROFILE CHANGES

| Students | Prediction of School Achievement | Leadership | | Creativity | | Stability | |
|---|---|---|---|---|---|---|---|
| | Oct. | Oct. | May | Oct. | May | Oct. | May |
| KX | 5.80 | 6.60 | 8.42 | 5.42 | 5.89 | 4.26 | 2.90 |
| NX | 3.09 | 6.14 | 5.11 | 2.97 | 4.13 | 5.59 | 5.36 |
| NM | 7.84 | 4.46 | | 8.04 | | 4.64 | |
| KD | 9.65 | 9.43 | 8.30 | 6.38 | 8.18 | 2.29 | 2.65 |
| XI | 7.30 | 5.59 | 3.62 | 9.52 | 6.08 | 6.45 | 7.97 |
| XJ | 8.42 | 8.25 | 7.34 | 7.20 | 6.55 | 1.79 | 2.60 |
| ZK | 8.73 | 8.78 | 9.05 | 5.90 | 5.45 | 3.62 | 2.59 |
| ZB | 5.30 | 6.14 | 5.01 | 4.25 | 4.76 | 3.60 | 6.23 |
| ZC | 6.77 | 5.82 | 4.24 | 6.53 | 6.40 | 4.06 | 5.70 |
| YK | 7.77 | 5.49 | 3.88 | 5.77 | 6.09 | 7.93 | 7.59 |
| YG | 4.12 | 5.56 | 3.91 | 3.98 | 2.32 | 8.30 | 8.24 |

Appendix C


PROGRESS REPORT
OF
ON-SITE SURVEY


PROGRESS REPORT   December 15, 1972 through January 4, 1973


Methodology or processes

   With the assistance of the district's Director of Research, I decided
on the method to use in selecting a representative sample of teachers and
a sample of students for the questionnaires.  I am sending the teacher
questionnare to approximately 200 teachers and the student questionnaire
to approximately 300 students.

   I learned the district's policy and procedures for including students
in a study and I made the necessary contacts with principals and teachers
for the administration of the student questionnaire.

   After talking with the Director of Research, I revised my questionnaires
to include some of the technical suggestions made by him.  He wants all
questionnaires which involve the time of district personnel to be as
refined as possible.

   I gained experience in conducting interviews, as I interviewed most
of the twelve curriculum coordinators, a principal, several teachers, and
a librarian.  I enjoy the interviews and I feel I am getting valid information.  I have, also, gone through the process of conducting one on-site
visit to a school.

Summary of activities

December 15

   1.  Field tested teacher questionnaire at a high school in another
       district.  As a result, some minor changes were made in the question-
       naire.

December 18

   1.  Met with the Director of Instructional Materials, and discussed
       my case study.

   2.  Met with the Director of Curriculum and obtained clearance for
       my interviews with the curriculum coordinators.

   Appendixes C, D, E, and F are included with permission of Iris Fye,
Student, University of Denver, Experimental Program, 1972-73.

3.  Scheduled the interviews with the curriculum coordinators.

4.  Wrote a letter concerning my case study to be signed and sent by the Zone Superintendents to the principals.

5.  Typed and made copies of the questionnaire for the curriculum coordinators.  It was necessary for me to do this so that it could be distributed the following day.

December 19

1.  Met with the Director of Research and discussed my study.

2.  Made some minor technical changes in my questionnaires as a result of the above discussion.

3.  Interviewed one curriculum coordinator.

4.  Worked on details of case-study.

December 20

1.  Wrote information for the letter which will go to the parents of the students in my study.

2.  Revised cover letters to the principals, teachers, and librarians so that the Director of Instructional Materials will not have to send out letters.

3.  Interviewed three curriculum coordinators; read job description for each coordinator prior to the interview.

4.  Gave the Director of Research copies of my four questionnaires.

December 21

1.  Interviewed four curriculum coordinators.

2.  Talked with the Audiovisual Coordinator about the media presentation for my study.

3.  Met with the Assistant Superintendent for Planning.

4.  Worked on method of picking a sample of teachers and students for the questionnaires.

December 22

1.  Met with the Director of Research.  He gave me various specific recommendations for how my questionnaires could be  technically refined.

2.  Worked on the librarians' questionnaire and incorporated some of the suggestions made by the Director of Research.

3.  Worked out schedule for school visits.

Weekend

1. Revised all questionnaires.  This was suggested by the Director of Research.

2. Started retyping all questionnaires.

December 26

1. Finished typing questionnaires at home; office closed at school district.

December 27

1. Met with the Director of Research.  He approved my revised questionnaires and my methods of sampling.

2. Talked with the Chief Accountant about budgeting procedures used in the district.

3. Selected schools and classes for the student questionnaire through a random process.

4. Scheduled two on-site visits in telephone conversations with the principals of the schools.

December 28

1. Met with the secretary of the Director of Research to learn how the student questionnares would be set up for the computer tabulation.

2. Called principals and scheduled as many on-site visits to the schools as possible.  Some of the principals were not available, and thus did not complete scheduling as planned.

3. Wrote draft of a letter to send to the teachers of the classes in the student sample.

4. Worked on a form for comparing district with the State and National Standards.

5. Proofread typing of questionnaires and cover letters.

December 29

1. Went to two schools to obtain addresses of parents of the students in the student sample.  This was required so that letters could be sent in keeping with the district's policy.

2. Proofread the typing of questionnaires.  Materials sent to the machine room for duplication.

3. Started grouping teachers by subjects taught in order to select random sample of teachers.

Weekend

1. Drew random sample of teachers; addressed over 220 envelopes.

2. Read part of a book on photography.

3. Reworked interview questions for principals. After talking with the Director of Research, I decided to drop the principal questionnaire and incorporate the questions into the interview.

4. Met with the librarians' representative to the district's professional organization. Discussed the proposals made this year for increased library staffing and the procedures to use in presenting the findings from my study.

5. Typed some material for case study.

January 2

1. Continued scheduling on-site visits to the schools. This took a great deal of time as it was necessary to call each principal.

2. Called teachers to obtain their cooperation in administering the student questionnaire.

3. Interviewed two curriculum coordinators.

4. Made arrangements to get the addresses of the parents of the students in the student sample.

January 3

1. Wrote letter to principals in the schools in which the student questionnaire will be administered.

2. Scheduled on-site vists.

3. Worked on details of case study.

January 4

1. On-site visit to a junior high school.


## Reactions of officials and personnel in district

The Director of Instructional Materials, the Director of Research, and the other people with whom I have had contact have been most helpful and supportive. The principals have all been very cordial and willing to participate in the study.

The Director of Research has had a great deal of experience and has given me some helpful advice. Although he wanted me to further refine my questionnaires, he said my original ones were much better than most of the ones he sees. He seemed to be quite impressed with the scope of the study. Having an expert in the field of research within the district is a definite asset.

Appendix D

PROGRESS REPORT
OF
ON-SITE SURVEY

PROGRESS REPORT for January 19 through January 26

## Methodology or processes

This week I continued making school visits and collecting factual
data about the local school district. The information about enrollments,
funding, and remodeling projects is in different offices and sometimes
it was difficult to know where to go for a particular piece of information.
I also obtained the information I will need for the architectural mini
course this week. In addition, I have been busy in the evenings attending
meetings related to my case study.

## Summary of activities

January 19

1. On-site visit to an elementary school.

2. Met with the audiovisual specialist at a high school, as I was
   not able to interview him during my previous visit. I also went
   through his slides and selected some to have copied for possible
   use in my media presentation.

3. Called miscellaneous people for information needed in my case study.

4. Had dinner with friends who work at an adjacent metropolitan
   public library; they filled me in on a proposal for state funding
   of public library services.

Weekend

1. Went to the university book store and bought books on librarianship
   and education.

2. Went to an adjacent metropolitan public library and looked for
   information on school budgeting and communication.

3. Bought a wide-angle lens for my camera.

4. Went over some of the material gathered the previous week on my
   visits to the schools.

5.  Made a detailed list of questions to ask the Director of Instructional Materials as I have an appointment to meet with her next week.

6.  Finished reading a study put out by the local city government.

7.  Clipped articles relating to education from the December and January issues of the metropolitan newspaper.

8.  Did some reading on budgeting in Garvue, <u>Modern Public School Finance</u>, and on other sources.

January 22

1.  On-site visits to two elementary schools.

2.  Brief meeting with the Director of Instructional Materials; discussed procedures related to my assignment next year.

3.  Worked on some details connected with the case study at home in the evening.

January 23

1.  On-site visit to an elementary school.

2.  Long conference with the Director of Instructional Materials; obtained information needed for my study.

3.  Turned in "bubble cards" for the student questionnaire and talked with a programmer about how I wanted the data tabulated.

4.  After work had cocktails with my former principal and some of the people with whom I had worked the previous year.

5.  Attended the school board meeting.

January 24

1.  Called and saw various people about information I need for my case study.

2.  Took pictures at a junior high school.

3.  Had a lengthy conference with the principal of the building which I will be using for my remodeling project.  Took additional slides of the library.

4.  Saw the chairman of the League of Women Voters and obtained information about the methods of financing education in the state.

5.  Attended an evening meeting on the special levy election.  Approximately 40% of the district's operating budget for 1973-74 depends upon this election.  Talked with a vice-principal about Denver's experimental program and my work this year.  He invited me to attend a class he teaches as a guest on Thursday as it is related to communication within schools.

January 25

1.  Gathered data about the library programs in the district.  The Director of Instructional Material's secretary has been absent for over a week and her substitute had a difficult time locating the information.  (Past inventory figures, etc.)

2.  Interviewed a curriculum coordinator.

3.  Went to various offices to obtain such data as the dropout rate and the district's statement on student rights and responsiblities.

4.  Met with the secretary to the Assistant Superintendent for Planning.  She explained how I could make an enrollment projection that would be fairly accurate.  The district's projection for next year will not be available until this Spring.

5.  Wrote rough drafts of "thank you" letters to the principals and assistant superintendents who were involved with my study.

6.  Wrote rough draft of my proposal for independent study.

7.  Attended an evening class on current issues in education.

January 26

1.  On-site visit to a junior high school.

2.  Gathered information about the age of the libraries in my study and the district's remodeling schedule.

3.  Attended a staff meeting of the certificated people in the Instructional Materials Department.

4.  Compiled information on the 1970 inventory reports for the building libraries.

5.  In the evening, wrote and typed my Progress Report.

### Reactions of officials and personnel in the district

The district continues to cooperate in every way possible and everyone expresses great interest in seeing the results of my study.  I was not able to see the director of Finance because his secretary indicated that he was extremely busy this month.

Evaluation, concerns, and questions

My only concern right now is whether or not I have sufficient background information about the district and community and whether or not I fully understand questions related to the district's total budget.

It is difficult right now to make economic projections for the future because the area has just come through an unstable economic period and (by law) a large portion of the operating budget is funded on a yearly basis and must be voted on by the public.

I am looking forward to meeting with you and discussing the results from my surveys and interviews and types of recommendations which I will make.

Appendix E

SUMMARY OF ACTIVITIES
OF
ON-SITE SURVEY

<u>Summary of on-site activities for the case study while in the selected
school district.</u>

1.  Selected a representative sample of students and teachers for the
    questionnaires.  Consulted with the Director of Research about
    the validity of my sampling.

2.  Informed myself of district procedures and policies related to my
    study, and made a special effort to follow these.

3.  Obtained approval for my study from the Director of Instructional
    Materials, the Director of Research, and the two Assistant Super-
    intendents whose zones were involved.

4.  Wrote or revised the necessary letters connected with the study -
    approximately 14 different letters.

5.  Scheduled visits to seventeen schools.

6.  Visited seventeen schools.  At each school I observed the library;
    interviewed the principal, the certificated members of the library
    staff, and two teachers; and took photographs.  In a few cases I
    briefly visited classrooms to give me a better understanding of the
    school.  No record was made of these observations.

7.  Interviewed twelve curriculum coordinators.

8.  Sent questionnaires to the curriculum coordinators, teachers,
    building librarians, audiovisual specialists, and students.

9.  Consulted with the Director of Instructional Materials, the district
    Audiovisual Coordinator, a district Audiovisual Specialist, the Profes-
    sional Librarian, the Assistant Superintendent for Planning, the
    Assistant Superintendent for Business/Operations, the Director of
    Research, and the Chief Accountant.

10. Met with the president of the local education association - the
    negotiating body of the professional employees.

11. Met with the librarians' representative to the local education asso-
    ciation.

12. Met with the children's librarian at the local public library.

13. Attended the following meetings:  a meeting of the Library Advisory Council, a meeting of the Junior High School Librarians, a School Board Meeting, and a community levy meeting.  I also attended a class session on education conducted by an assistant principal, and talked to him about in-service and credit courses offered in the district.

14. Obtained other relevant studies and background information for my case study.

15. Obtained information for my finance and architecture courses.

16. Viewed my slides and sorted out some of the better ones.

17. Did some reading on school finance and on photography.

18. Wrote a proposal for independent study.

19. Did other activities as listed in my weekly progress reports.

Appendix F

STUDENT EVALUATION OF ON-SITE SURVEY

The on-site survey was an extremely valuable experience for me.
It broadened my understanding of the role of the school library in the
educational process and gave me further insights into the functions of
a district director.

The survey permitted me to see education from the perspective of
an administrator.  Since I have always worked as a building teacher or
librarian, I consider this an important gain.  I feel especially fortunate
to have had the opportunity to conduct the case study, for I do not think
this perspective could have been obtained from just reading about administration.

The local school district cooperated with me completely in the study,
and thus it was both a productive and enjoyable learning experience.

Since returning to Denver, I feel I am progressing very well with
my study.  I plan to do some further work on it during vacation and I
hope to make out a time schedule for myself so that I will not become
rushed at the end.

While I was studying my data and writing recommendations, I thought
of ways to improve my questionnaires and interviews.  I'm sure this is
part of the learning process and the knowledge I have gained about
research will aid me in a director's position.  (I would have been dis-
appointed in my own critical thinking if I had not seen ways to improve
my study.)  Basically, however, I feel my study was well planned and
carefully carried out in the district.

Besides learning how to gather data, I also learned how to arrive
at recommendations for the development of library programs.  In my opinion,
this ability is very important for a director.

I appreciated the assistance and advice which you gave me during
the year.  I want to learn as much as possible this year, and it is good
to have an objective person whom I can consult about my work.

In summary, I feel the case study has been one of the most beneficial
learning experiences which I have had.  I feel that I am accomplishing my
objectives and I am confident that I will have a worthwhile final report
and media presentation.  I am looking forward to sharing the results of
my work with the educators in my case-study district.

Appendix G

PRESENTATION CHECKLIST

The experimental program at the University of Denver was designed to prepare School Library Media Directors by using the Case Study Method. Each student studied the needs of a school district (or a group of schools within a district) and, on the basis of this study, designed a media program for the area. The presentations you will see capsulize these case study reports.

To achieve objectivity in reviewing the Denver program we would like the assessment of certain elements in the presentations by a panel of outside observers. Would you be willing to serve as one of these observers? If you find it impossible to adequately judge a given characteristic, you may enter "no opinion" or request more information in the discussion period following each presentation.

Which student are you reviewing? (check one) //AB, //CD, //EF, //GH, //IJ, //KL, //MN.

Are you? (please check all that apply) //Faculty, //Student, //Advisory Board Member, //Professional Librarian, //Member of District Reviewed.

Please check the following:

| | No Opinion | Excel-lent | Good | Average | Poor |
|---|---|---|---|---|---|
| **I.  Quality of Presentation** | | | | | |
| A.  Use of Media | | | | | |
| B.  Effectiveness of Expression | | | | | |
| C.  Degree of Commitment, Enthusiasm, and Self-Confidence | | | | | |
| | | | | | |
| **II.  Knowledge of District Studied** | | | | | |
| A.  General Knowledge of School and Community Characteristics | | | | | |
| B.  Awareness of Peripheral Organizations (i.e., Governmental educational agencies) | | | | | |
| C.  Awareness of Community Related Programs (i.e., for exceptional children, minorities) | | | | | |
| D.  Consideration of Legal Requirements | | | | | |
| E.  Assessment of Existing School Library Programs | | | | | |
| F.  Identification of Needs for a Balanced Program | | | | | |
| | | | | | |
| **III.  Plan Designed for District Media Development** | | | | | |
| A.  Degree to which the Plan Answers the Needs Identified | | | | | |
| B.  Degree of Feasibility of the Plan with Respect to: | | | | | |
| 1.  economic constraints | | | | | |
| 2.  administrative considerations | | | | | |
| 3.  facility design and construction | | | | | |
| 4.  personnel requirements and needs | | | | | |
| 5.  equipment and media resources | | | | | |
| 6.  school library standards | | | | | |
| | | | | | |
| **IV.  Synthesis of the Above Elements in the Presentation** | | | | | |

Appendix H

SUMMARY RESULTS OF PRESENTATION CHECKLISTS

| Element Judged | Average of Student Scores* | Total No Opinion | Total Not Answered |
|---|---|---|---|
| I. Quality of presentation | | | |
| Media | **3.4** | 0 | 6 |
| Expression | 3.3 | 0 | 9 |
| Commitment | 3.4 | 0 | 7 |
| II. Knowledge of district | | | |
| General knowledge | 3.7 | 2 | 2 |
| Peripheral organizations | 3.3 | 46 | 4 |
| Related programs | 3.1 | 47 | 6 |
| Legal requirements | 3.1 | 57 | 7 |
| Existing programs | 3.5 | 3 | 4 |
| Identified needs | 3.5 | 7 | 5 |
| III. Development plan | | | |
| Plans | 3.2 | 5 | 12 |
| Economic constraints | 3.1 | 8 | 12 |
| Administrative consider-ations | 3.2 | 6 | 9 |
| Facility design | 3.4 | 12 | 10 |
| Personnel needs | 3.4 | 7 | 8 |
| Equipment | 3.4 | 4 | 10 |
| Standards | 3.3 | 16 | 14 |
| Synthesis | 3.4 | 0 | 22 |
| Average | 3.3 | | |

* A=4, B=3, C=2, D=1

# UNIVERSITY OF MICHIGAN

SCHOOL OF LIBRARY SCIENCE
Dr. Russell E. Bidlack, Dean

## AN EXPERIMENTAL PROGRAM IN
# SCHOOL LIBRARY MEDIA EDUCATION
### 1971–1973

*Final Report by*
HELEN D. LLOYD

## Contents

# SCHOOL OF LIBRARY SCIENCE

## Dr. Russell E. Bidlack, Dean

*Experimental Program Staff, 1971-1973*

Dr. Helen D. Lloyd, Director
Dr. Warren G. Palmer, Associate Director
Dr. Thomas W. Downen

Mr. Edward F. Newren
Dr. Kenneth E. Vance
Miss Rowan Murphy, Media Technician

*Advisory Board*
1971-1973

Dr. Lowell Beach
Assistant Dean for Instruction
School of Education
University of Michigan

Miss Arlene Berman, 1971
Student Member
University of Michigan

Dr. Frederick W. Bertolaet, 1972-73
Assistant Dean for Instruction
School of Education
University of Michigan

Dr. Russell E. Bidlack
Dean, School of Library Science
University of Michigan

Mr. Rolland G. Billings
Director of Instructional Media
Ann Arbor Public Schools

Dr. John Boeve
Principal, Rosedale Elementary School
Livonia Public Schools

Mrs. Frances Cook
Assistant Professor of Library Science
Eastern Michigan University

Mrs. Martha Cornish, 1972
Student Member
University of Michigan

Mrs. Christine Getty, 1973
Student Member
University of Michigan

Dr. Robert J. Graham, 1971-72
School Library Consultant
Bureau of School Libraries
University of Michigan

Mrs. Bertha Green
Director of Libraries
Plymouth Community School District

Dr. George Grimes
Supervisor, Curriculum Laboratories
Detroit Public Schools

Mrs. Mary Ann Hanna
Head Library Consultant
Michigan Department of Education

Dr. G. Sutherland Hayden
Assistant Director, Bureau of School Services
University of Michigan

Dr. Irene Heller
Associate Professor, School of Education
University of Michigan

Mrs. Maxine Larson Hough, 1972-73
School Library Consultant
Bureau of School Services
University of Michigan

Miss Babetta Jimpie, 1973
Student Member
University of Michigan

Miss Penny Jones, 1972
Student Member
University of Michigan

Dr. Charles F. Keen
Assistant Professor of Education
University of Michigan

Mrs. Kristin Kerr, 1971
Student Member
University of Michigan

Mr. Burton M. Lamkin
Supervisor, Curriculum Laboratories
Detroit Pblic Schools

Dr. Helen D. Lloyd
Associate Professor, Library Science, Education
School of Library Science
University of Michigan

Miss Carolyn Mathis, 1971
Student Member
University of Michigan

Mrs. Faith Murdock, 1971-72
Director of School Libraries
Detroit Public Schools

Dr. Warren G. Palmer
Associate Professor, Education, Library Science
School of Education
University of Michigan

Dr. Rudolf B. Schmerl
Assistant Dean of Research
School of Education
University of Michigan

Dr. David D. Starks
Associate Professor, Dentistry, Education
Center for Research on Learning and Teaching
University of Michigan

Dr. Kenneth E. Vance
Assistant Dean, School of Library Science
University of Michigan

Dr. Ella Willson, 1972-73
Director of School Libraries
Detroit Public Schools

# Overview

The University of Michigan, founded in 1817, includes sixteen schools and colleges, a complex array of research and service organizations, and the University Libraries with a collection of four and one-half million volumes. The Michigan tradition of administration is one of flexibility and decentralization. Cooperation between units within the schools and colleges is encouraged, making possible the development of interdisciplinary programs including the experimental program for the school library media specialists, funded by the School Library Manpower Project.

In addition to the two schools most closely involved in the planning and operation of the experimental program, Library Science and Education, the College of Literature, Science, and the Arts, and the School of Business Administration provided courses which could be elected by students in such fields as speech, psychology, and management. Faculty members in some of these fields served as consultants during the planning and implementation of the experimental program. Since the program leads to a graduate degree, it was also influenced by the Horace H. Rackham School of Graduate Studies. The Center for Research on Learning and Teaching was involved in planning for the evaluation of the program and both the Audiovisual Center and the Computing Center provided supportive services.

Historically, the University of Michigan has been a leader in the field of education, having been the first institution of higher learning in the United States to create, in 1879, a full-time chair in the science and art of teaching. The School of Education celebrated its fiftieth anniversary in 1971. The University has also had a long involvement with elementary and secondary schools operating a consultant and accrediting agency, the Bureau of School Services, which helps schools throughout the state with planning and evaluation.

The School of Library Science was created in July, 1969, giving the former Department of Library Science full status as a professional school within the University. The School offers a program leading to the Master of Arts in Library Science, which is accredited by the American Library Association. An advanced program leading to the Doctor of Philosophy is also offered. Graduates of the University of Michigan now serve in many types of libraries throughout the country.

Early in August, 1970, a joint Committee on Educational Media Programs was established representing the Schools of Education and Library Science and reporting to the two deans. The committee's purpose was to plan a cooperative program for educating professional media personnel. Its responsibilities included planning and implementing the School Library Media Program. Representing the School of Education on the committee were the newly-appointed Director of the Educational Media Center and the chairman of Teacher Education, one of the four divisions within the school. Representing the School of Library Science were the Assistant Dean and another faculty member, both of whom were experienced in the school library field. Education's Assistant Dean for Research and a representative from the Center for Research on Learning and Teaching also participated on an advisory basis. All members of the joint committee have had continuing involvement with the program, either as instructors or members of the Advisory Board.

## DESCRIPTION OF THE PROGRAM

While cooperatively planned and implemented, the experimental program was administered through the School of Library Science and led to the degree of Master of Arts in Library Science. Students were expected to have acquired as undergraduates a strong liberal arts background (a minimum of ninety semester hours) and a teaching certificate. In some cases, however, students could earn the teaching certificate while pursuing the graduate program in library media by taking the additional educational courses required, including a semester of student teaching.

Though all were expected to develop competencies in the areas of media, management, curriculum and learning, human relations, and research, each student was counseled individually and helped to choose courses and independent studies that were best suited to personal background, interests, and goals. In credit hours, the program varied from thirty to thirty-six semester hours, dependent upon a student's previous education and experience.

The program had a close relationship with area schools. Field trips and other experiences in a school setting were included each term, and an internship of at least ninety hours was arranged during the student's final term so that principles and skills learned could be demonstrated, refined and extended.

## PHILOSOPHY AND ASSUMPTIONS FOR CHANGE

In 1969, *Standards for School Media Programs*[1] mandated unified media programs staffed by professionals with multimedia competencies, knowledge of curriculum and learning, and skills in leadership. Indeed, many schools had already taken steps in this direction following the publication of the 1960 *Standards for School Library Programs*.[2] Most institutions of higher education, however, were offering separate traditional programs for preparing librarians and audiovisual specialists.

In 1970, when the experimental program proposal was written, the University of Michigan, like most similar institutions, had not offered a Master's degree program specifically designed to provide the combination of competencies needed for the role of the school library media specialist. Yet schools in Michigan and adjoining states were and are seeking, even in these somewhat austere times, library media

specialists. Phase I of the School Library Manpower Project gave educators a blueprint on which to build a viable program for the professional education of school library media personnel and grants offered during Phase II of the Project promised funding for program development and purchase of additional resources needed to implement an experimental program. This fortuitous combination of demand from school administrators, guidelines and money from the School Library Manpower Project, and a climate of cooperation and interest within the University, exemplified by the joint Committee on Educational Media Programs, provided the rationale and means for change. Philosophically, it was the belief of the planners of the University of Michigan program that the ultimate beneficiaries would be the school children and young adults served by the University's graduates.

In assessing the program for school librarians provided prior to the experimental program, the following changes seemed essential: (1) better integration of, and more emphasis on nonprint media and its technology, (2) greater depth in knowledge of all media at the elementary and secondary school levels, (3) the addition of curriculum development, learning theory, and human behavior components beyond the basic teacher education program, and (4) supervised field experiences for all students beyond the student teaching level. To allow time for these new emphases, some of the traditional requirements for the Master's degree in library science had to be eliminated, remaining courses had to be restructured, and new courses had to be added. Further, an increase in flexibility for individual students had to be incorporated, especially for those with an undergraduate concentration in library science.

---

1. American Association of School Librarians, American Library Association, and the Department of Audiovisual Instruction, National Education Association, *Standards for School Media Programs* (Chicago: American Library Association, and Washington, D.C.: National Education Association, 1969).

2. American Association of School Librarians, American Library Association, *Standards for School Library Programs* (Chicago: American Library Association, 1960).

# Program Goals and Objectives

The broad goal of the experimental program was to prepare library media specialists who were competent to function effectively in schools of today and tomorrow. To define goals and objectives, then, the role of the school library media specialist had to be carefully examined. Phase I of the School Library Manpower Project was very helpful in this respect. The joint planning committee utilized the occupational definition for the school library media specialist developed during Phase I of the Project and the

*Standards for School Media Programs* to define twelve role-related program objectives.

## OBJECTIVES FOR THE SCHOOL LIBRARY MEDIA SPECIALIST

1. To communicate to faculty and students a knowledge of materials and equipment available and their appropriate use.
2. To contribute regularly to curriculum development through one's knowledge of available ma-

terials and the ability to analyze and use results of past institutional experiences and research data.

3. To communicate regularly with media staff, faculty, parents, public library, and other community agencies in planning and interpreting programs and activities.
4. To interpret the content of any print or non-print materials selected at random from the media collection.
5. To provide and use suitable criteria for evaluation and selection of materials and equipment.
6. To organize the media collection for easy accessibility.
7. To instruct students in the use of materials.
8. To locate information needed by students and teachers whether or not the information is available within the school library media center.
9. To recommend to students a wide range of materials suitable for their developmental level.
10. To design and produce media using available resources.
11. To arrange media facilities in a functional manner.
12. To demonstrate the ability to develop, promote, and evaluate the media program and resources.

Since the program also had implications for the University's performance, the committee identified several additional objectives.

## OBJECTIVES FOR THE UNIVERSITY

1. To demonstrate an increase in interdisciplinary cooperation through the proposed program.
2. To hold seminars on the use of media to increase productivity in teaching within the Schools of Library Science and Education.
3. To provide opportunity for individualized learning within the Schools of Library Science and Education.
4. To increase the use of its media facilities and collections.
5. To make appropriate resources available for the evaluation of the proposed program.

Both the primary objectives relating to the content of education for school library media specialists and the secondary objectives relating to the role of the University in this educational process can now be observed and, in a sense, evaluated, although not quantitatively measured. A real evaluation of the school library media specialist's education must take place later on the job. Ultimately, the program should also improve the effectiveness of teachers and learners within the elementary and secondary schools. While

an evaluation of the total impact of an adequate number of fully competent library media specialists upon the school would require a complex research project not now specifically planned, recognition of its importance is shown through the long range goals for elementary and secondary school teachers and students.

## LONG RANGE GOALS FOR ELEMENTARY AND SECONDARY SCHOOL TEACHERS AND STUDENTS

In a school which has a well-staffed library media center, the teacher should be able to locate, with the help of a library media specialist, all available materials needed for teaching or information; to design and produce, with the assistance of media personnel, needed materials for instruction (this is not meant to imply that all locally-produced materials should be teacher-made); to evaluate materials at the level of specialization and in the field of the teacher, making recommendations for acquisitions or removal; to use any appropriate combination of media for instruction; to identify all available media in the particular school; and to use properly any media equipment available in the school intended for individual use.

In a school which has a well-staffed library media center, the student should be able to locate, interpret, and use needed learning materials appropriate to his or her developmental level; to read and evaluate books; to view and evaluate films, pictures, etc.; to listen to and evaluate recordings; to produce, with adult help when necessary, learning materials at the appropriate developmental level; to identify all types of media for learning and available equipment intended for individual use; and to show respect for the rights of others by using resources carefully.

## DEVELOPMENT OF OBJECTIVES

During the summer and fall of 1971, the primary program objectives became the framework for more comprehensive objectives beginning with the selection and modification of statements from the Phase I Regional Conferences of the School Library Manpower Project. These objectives went through several stages of refinement as faculty members attempted to make them more specific and to eliminate duplication or overlap. A Q-Sort technique was used to involve the program's Advisory Board in the refinement process. Sets of objectives, each item on a separate sheet, were distributed to all members of the Advisory Board who were requested to sort them into priority order, modifying any statements for clarity or to improve job-relatedness. Items a Board member viewed as unimportant or a duplication of another objective were to be so marked. These suggestions were incorporated as revised objectives were developed.

Finally, performance objectives were fitted into the course structure in one of the following ways: (1) some were designated as appropriate for existing courses, (2) some were used as a guide to restructure certain existing courses, and (3) some were used as a basis for three new courses. The latter included a seminar in selection of media for children and young adults, a laboratory course in design and production of media, and a seminar in media design and production. Details of course revision and development can be found later in this report. Objectives and courses continued to be revised based on student and faculty feedback.

Performance objectives assigned to specific courses were closely related to the broader program objectives for the school library media specialist. Course objectives are listed under the appropriate program objective. The two should not be viewed as a syllabus, but rather the more specific statements should be seen as illustrations of the way particular program objectives were actually encountered by the student. In the sections that follow, statements of condition and of criteria for measurement have not been included although such statements are to be expected in a complete performance objective. Within the program these statements varied for different students because of the school level the student would be seeking for employment and the degree of proficiency previously attained by the student.

## OBJECTIVES—GENERAL AND SPECIFIC FOR THE SCHOOL LIBRARY MEDIA SPECIALIST

I. To communicate to faculty and students a knowledge of material and equipment available and their appropriate use.
   1. Identify two research findings related to media and/or management and their implications for school media program improvements.
   2. Plan an in-service education session for teachers on the effective use of media.
   3. Guide children and teachers in reading, viewing, and listening activities by encouraging them to use media available and respond to it through written reviews, group discussions, evaluation forms, stories told, book talks.
   4. Identify sources from whom information could be gained about the student, contact, these sources, obtain the desired information, and locate media which will meet an identified need of the student.
   5. Demonstrate competency to set up, operate, and put away projection and audio equipment.
   6. Demonstrate ability to perform simple maintenance tasks on projection and audio equipment.
   7. Demonstrate efficient utilization of various audiovisual materials.

II. To contribute regularly to curriculum development through one's knowledge of available materials and the ability to analyze and use results of past institutional experiences and research data.
   1. Provide information on curriculum trends in a specified subject field and relate the library media center's role to the curriculum trends cited.
   2. Function as a part of a committee to develop a research unit including instructional objectives and media.
   3. Identify three research needs within the school media field, based on observations and/or the literature of the field.
   4. Identify current research methods and describe their appropriateness in studying school library media center problems.
   5. Participate in research activities that diagnose, assess, and evaluate learning environments and media support systems.
   6. Demonstrate systematic application of learning principles to achievement of learning objectives.

III. To communicate regularly with media staff, faculty, parents, public library, and other community agencies in planning and interpreting programs and activities.
   1. Create a climate of freedom to learn by listening to and observing individuals within a given school environment and helping each to assess and fulfill his own informational and affective needs.
   2. Describe ways in which the media specialist might work with the sponsoring group of a specific co-curricular activity to attain its goals or promote its program.
   3. Assist a specific teacher in providing instruction by identifying media needs for specific instructional objectives, locating appropriate resources, and helping to imple-

ment the instruction in the media center or classroom.

4. Demonstrate cognizance of specific professional organizations by describing the purpose of each in paragraph form and listing the journal publications of each.

5. Formulate policies and procedures for selection and acquisition of media.

6. Interpret through printed, oral, and/or visual media, the goals and functions of the total media program as they relate to a variety of audiences who support education, e.g., school boards, P.T.A., civic organizations, and industry.

IV. To interpret the content of any print or nonprint materials selected at random from the media collection.

1. Interpret by written or oral resume the contents of ten print and/or nonprint materials selected at random from a given media collection.

2. Tell stories and/or give book talks to interpret specific materials in a collection.

V. To provide and use suitable criteria and tools for evaluation and/or selection of materials and equipment.

1. Utilize a class-developed list of general and specific criteria for evaluating media and write reviews of three items of media, each representing a different format.

2. Cite the purpose, level, strengths, and limitations of each of thirty given selection aids.

3. Establish a priority list of thirty bibliographic and professional tools to be used in a specific school for selecting and acquiring media and for guiding users to appropriate media.

4. Demonstrate knowledge of functions, elements, and arrangement principles of good design by describing, in written form, the way in which a specific illustration serves as either a good or a poor example of each of the above.

VI. To organize the media collection for easy accessibility.

1. Apply principles of cataloging and classification to the media collection to provide accessibility to these resources.

2. Define educational specifications and write them for media facilities in a specific school.

3. Apply principles of systems analysis to one or more procedures in the operation of the media program, e.g., acquisition of media, circulation of media.

4. List and justify five policies relating to utilization of the media center and describe the procedure for establishing or changing the policies.

VII. To instruct students in the use of materials. Write specific instructional objectives for teaching appropriate library skills for a given resource unit.

VIII. To locate information needed by students and teachers whether or not the information is available within the school library media center.

1. Answer inquiries through the use of the reference collection or cite tools which could best answer the question.

2. Process a user's information need through question negotiation to learn what specific information is sought, and through knowledge of the reference collection and of valid outside sources, to provide the best possible answer within time contraints.

IX. To recommend to students a wide range of materials suitable for their developmental levels.

1. Provide two specific children and young adults each with a briefly annotated list of ten media titles chosen because of their possible interest and suitable level of difficulty.

2. Give book and media talks on topics of interest to specific groups of children and young adults.

X. To design and produce media using available resources.

1. Enlarge and/or reduce a given illustration by projection, pantograph, or grid method.

2. Demonstrate knowledge of the seven laws of perspective and skill in using these laws by visually illustrating the object and identifying laws used.

3. Reproduce language symbols with a variety of lettering techniques including use of mechanical pen and template, stencil guide, dry transfer lettering, die-cut adhesive-back letters, and optional technique preferred by the student.

4. Demonstrate knowledge and skill in the dry mounting process.

5. Demonstrate knowledge and skill in magnetic tape recording by producing a tape incorporating specified techniques.

6. Produce a mounted, hand-made transpar-

ency selecting type of acetate and method best suited for successfully presenting content.

7. Produce a color lift transparency.
8. Prepare two masters, one for a thermal-type transparency and one for a diazo-type transparency, selecting best suited methods and materials for successfully presenting the specific content.
9. Demonstrate knowledge and skill in photography by producing a sequence of slides and of motion picture footage.

XI. To arrange media facilities in a functional manner.
1. Write educational specifications which include spatial relationships and basic locations of essential furniture and equipment.
2. Identify components of an atmosphere in which media staff, faculty, and students can work harmoniously at optimum levels.

XII. To demonstrate the ability to develop, promote and evaluate the media program and resources.
1. Specify qualifications for each given position classification in a school media center.
2. Supervise and evaluate personnel in relation to the effective use of their time and abilities.
3. Identify sources of funds available, the basic needs of the media center for which funds should be budgeted, and the recommended procedures for expenditure of funds.
4. Identify appropriate guidelines, criteria, instruments, and persons for evaluating the existing media program.
5. Develop a plan for utilizing these feedback measures.
6. Establish long-range and short-term goals for the media program and means for incorporating them into the media program.
7. Specify procedures for continuous evaluation of the media program.

## SUMMARY

Program objectives stated areas of competency which were deemed necessary to the role of the school library media specialist at the building level and for which the University of Michigan experimental program prepared its students. Specific objectives for courses were related to these broader program objectives and the relationship was illustrated in the preceding section. A number of school administrators, practicing library media specialists and supervisors, and University faculty members contributed to the development of these objectives which con-

tinue to be revised based on feedback from students, faculty, and practitioners in the field.

As an example of the way specific objectives were used within a course structure, the following objectives from "Teaching with Media" are cited.

*Objective I.* Given access to the ERIC Center for Guidance and Counseling, the University Libraries, and the Educational Media Center, the media specialist should provide information in writing on one or more curriculum trends in a subject field and at a school level to be specified by the student.

The completed paper should not exceed five typewritten pages and should include the following:

1. A selected, annotated bibliography of five reports of research or descriptions of current practices with an indication of index used to locate each.
2. A list of two to five professional journals which are most useful for keeping up with the subject field chosen above.
3. A discussion of the library media center's role in relation to the field chosen and, specifically, the trends reported.

Tools to be used in completing this objective:
*Current Index to Journals in Education*
*Education Index*
*Research in Education*
"Selected Bibliography" for this class.

Instructor's evaluation of student performance will consider:
1. Extent of use of tools
2. Selectivity, judgment, and accuracy in preparing the annotated bibliography
3. Extent and appropriateness of description of the media center's potential role in subject field chosen
4. Creativity and clarity of expression.

*Objective II.* Given a broad curricular area (e.g., Humanities, Science and Mathematics, and Social Studies) and a group of fellow students, the student and his/her colleagues will function as a committee to develop (in part) a resource unit. This objective will include three steps to be done in groups and the remaining four steps to be done individually.

Each committee should:
1. Determine a topic and a general instructional level (primary, intermediate, junior high, high school)
2. Define broad unit goals
3. Describe student characteristics (group, not individual).

Individually, committee members should:
1. Write at least one specific learning objective for this unit
2. Identify specific items of media and activities to be used by students as they complete that learning objective
3. Determine an appropriate means of evaluation for the objective
4. List all tools in which media for this unit might logically be found, evaluating each tool in terms of its actual usefulness in this project (e.g., *Children's Catalog* had five books on this topic which might be appropriate for unit goals and student level).

Instructor's evaluation of student performance will consider:
1. Appropriateness of topic chosen for instructional level, including interest to students at that level
2. Success with which broad unit goals define the scope of the unit
3. Completeness and clarity of specific learning (behavioral) objective selected
4. Appropriateness of media, activities, and evaluation procedure identified

5. Completeness of tool exploration
6. Creativity and judgment demonstrated in this assignment.

*Objective III.* Given a list of bibliographic and professional tools and the opportunity to examine them, the media specialist will establish a priority list of tools to be used in a new media center in a school of specified size and level.

The list should not exceed twenty-five titles, which are appropriate for building level purchase. Availability of a district or regional center should be assumed. Each title should be justified on the basis of its importance for one or both of the following:
1. Selecting and acquiring materials
2. Guiding users to appropriate materials.

Instructor's evaluation of student performance will consider:
1. Appropriateness of tool for school chosen
2. Clarity and completeness of statement justifying inclusion
3. Ability of total list to meet anticipated needs of collection building and guidance of users (students and teachers).

# Program Participants

## STUDENTS

The recruitment of interested and capable students is essential to the success of any graduate program, but it is especially vital to a new program that information concerning it reach those most qualified to participate. To introduce the experimental program, a brochure was developed and mailed to school systems and individuals within the state and region. An effort was made to inform graduating teacher-education students from The University of Michigan, Eastern Michigan, and other state colleges and universities. To complement publicity from the Project Office at the national level, information about Michigan's program was sent to state library agencies for further distribution. The 1971-73 School of Library Science Catalog, containing a section devoted to the program, was distributed to all persons requesting information about the School. As applicants who held teaching certificates were identified, a letter informing them of the experimental program and a questionnaire to ascertain their interest were mailed to these prospective students.

Probably the most effective recruitment procedure was "spreading the word" from person to person. Library science alumni, public school personnel interested in a more dynamic media program and members of the Advisory Board for the program identified prospective students and informed them of the unique opportunities of library media service. As staff members talked with persons inquiring about professional opportunities, they were able to recruit some of them. Students in the program also reached other prospective students with the library media specialist message.

Financial awards were made available to students through several sources including the School of Library Science Alumni Association, the University's Opportunity Awards Program, and regular University of Michigan grants-in-aid. Eleven of the 25 full-time students during the two years of the program received financial awards which totaled $27,-740. Seven of the awards were tuition grants only. Four given to minority students included tuition and a stipend for personal expenses.

Eight full-time students were admitted to the experimental program in January, 1972, and by the end of the 1973 summer term, 25 full-time students completed the program and received their AMLS degrees. Only one person requested to withdraw from the experimental program in order to specialize in public library services. Of the 25 enrolled, there were two males.

The students came with varying backgrounds in both education and work experience. For example, 14 of the 25 received degrees from institutions outside Michigan and of the 11 "in-staters," 7 attended the University of Michigan. All but one had been granted a teaching certificate prior to admission and were able to complete the requirements while pursuing the library degree program. Of the total group, 18 held secondary and 6 held elementary certificates. Nine of the 25 had actual teaching experience prior to admittance. Four had either a major or a minor in library science as undergraduates.

Because of the diversified backgrounds and interests not all enrolled in identical programs. Flexibility was a key word in the counseling process. Undergraduate work in such courses as audiovisual education, children's and young adult literature was not repeated, nor was graduate level work in curriculum, psychology and learning, etc. Therefore, the number of semester hours needed to complete the program varied from 30 (only 4 students took the minimum) to 44 hours (an unusual case of an excellent student wishing to take additional work). Eleven students elected 34 or more semester hours.

Because the program was developed in cooperation with the School of Education, it is interesting to note that the 25 students made 83 elections in that school in order to meet program requirements for competencies in curriculum and learning, human relations, and basic audiovisual methods. Among those which were elected most frequently were: Curriculum development (23); audiovisual (16); mental hygiene (8); child development (7); and psychology of learning (7). Several students elected courses in reading problems, language development and instructional gaming.

In regard to the choice of internship experience, an essential part of the program, the 25 students were divided as follows: 3 chose to work in a middle school, 11 at the high school level and 11 at the elementary level.

In addition to these 25 degree candidates, there were approximately 40 more students enrolled in the program, some on a full-time and others on a part-time basis. These students did not complete the program before August of 1973.

Students are admitted to the School of Library Science in September, January, and July of each year. This means that there were always students at different states in the program, making it difficult to speak in terms of "first year students" and "second year students." The frequent influx of new students, however, made possible a valuable communications link among students as they were at various stages in the program. To be admitted to the AMLS degree program, which includes those preparing to enter the school media field, a student must have earned a bachelor's degree from an accredited college or university, with a grade point average of 3.0 (A=4 points, B=3, etc.). Previous academic work must include at least ninety semester hours of liberal arts courses. Students must show a personal aptitude and general interest in a career in school librarianship. Admission requirements for the program also emphasized the need for a teaching certificate.

Retention criteria for the experimental program stressed the continued interest in becoming a media specialist and maintaining a grade point average of 3.0 or better.

During counseling and registration periods, all students were scheduled in such a way that at least two faculty members, and often three, met simultaneously with each student. In addition, formal and informal meetings were held with students in a group.

All faculty members had regular office hours and were available by appointment at other times to discuss academic and nonacademic concerns of individual students. One area of major interest to all students was placement. Students in the program had access to the placement office in the School of Library Science and also to the University of Michigan Career Planning and Placement office. Both these services were used extensively by school library media students enrolled in the experimental program.

STAFF

Because the term "staff" is more often used in university parlance to refer to non-teaching or non-faculty personnel, planners and implementors of the experimental program were generally known as "core faculty" to distinguish them from other faculty members who might also be instructing students in this program but were not involved primarily with it. The core faculty was really an extension of the interdisciplinary Committee on Educational Media Programs mentioned earlier. It included the program director, the associate director, who was also director of the Educational Media Center, and the Assistant Dean of the School of Library Science, all of whom were members of the original committee and had school library media backgrounds. Other members of the committee continued to be involved with the program but not on a full-time basis. Finally, the core faculty included two new faculty members recruited and employed through the Project grant funds to complement existing faculty and provide expertise for the new components in the program. Both of these persons also had school library media experience and represented expertise in media design and production and in media for children and young adults.

When the joint committee was considering the feasibility of initiating the program, the variety of faculty expertise available in both the Schools of Library Science and of Education, as well as in other schools and colleges within the University of Michigan, was noted as a strength. Faculty specialities significant for the new program included elementary and secondary curriculum development, educational psychology—both behavioral and interpersonal, media management, documentation and information science, cataloging and classification, reference and subject bibliography, selection of media, literature for children and young adults, library cooperation, administration of school library media programs and of all other major types of libraries. The planners felt that students in the program should not be isolated, but instead should have access to the full range of university resources and be encouraged to participate in classes with students whose goals were different from their own. Similarly, the supportive staff and resources of the University Libraries and the Educational Media Center were viewed as strengths.

The University's faculty needed greater depth in two major areas affecting the proposed program; (1) media design and production, and (2) media selection and utilization for children and young adults. Several prospective faculty members were screened and interviewed during the spring of 1971 and two persons were selected by the faculty of the School of Library Science, with advice from a student committee.

The Project grant made it possible to employ an additional staff member to serve as media technician for the program. Since this was an entirely new position within the university, (there were graphic artists, photographers, TV camera men, etc., but no composite of these skills) a job description was written and a person competent in graphic design, photography, and the use of audiovisual equipment was sought. The person employed was well-qualified in

the first two categories listed above and showed a willingness to learn more about equipment operation. The technician proved very helpful to students in the production laboratory and to faculty members in the interpretation of their instructional ideas.

In the early planning stages it was recognized that the new faculty members must be involved in a significant way in program development. The fall term of 1971 was designated as a time for planning and trying out some of the proposed changes. The Dean of the School of Library Science assigned core faculty members two rather than the usual three courses. This reduced class load allowed them to spend time together in multi-weekly planning meetings and enabled them to select media and equipment needed for program implementation. These planning meetings continued, with slightly reduced frequency, throughout the program and represented the major staff development activity. The meetings helped to develop a team spirit and also provided the means for writing more specific objectives for the program, examining courses taught, planning student counseling and informal activities, refining evaluation plans, and developing public relations programs. Feedback from students, persons in the field, and other faculty members was useful in all these undertakings. This feedback came about through informal remarks, responses to questionnaires, and observations made by core faculty members.

The core faculty also considered ways of involving other faculty members in program change. Meetings were held with education faculty members who taught in the area of curriculum and learning and with staff members in the Educational Media Center to gain their support for program plans and goals. A demonstration workshop was held to introduce faculty members to the media opportunities available, including the services of a technician and a faculty member whose expertise was media design. Following this, faculty members were encouraged to schedule conferences with the media design consultant and/or technician to discuss specific instructional media needs. Though laboratory facilities were located in the School of Education Building, the media technician maintained a weekly schedule in Winchell House, the location of the library science faculty offices, in order to promote faculty use of the technician's services.

A further-ranging form of staff development brought some faculty members in education and library science together with others from such varied disciplines as history, psychology, public health, dentistry, English, architecture, and engineering to explore effective uses of media on the university campus. CREE, Combined Resources for Educational Electronics, held several meetings since the fall of 1971. The associate director of the experimental program served as co-chairman of CREE, and the program's director spoke at one of the meetings.

Participation in several national meetings, i.e., the American Library Association, the Association for Educational Communications and Technology, and the Association for Supervision and Curriculum Development, afforded growth experiences for staff members, as did participation in state library and audiovisual meetings and in the two day "Plan-In" held by the experimental program in December 1972. The latter is described more fully later in this report.

## ADVISORY BOARD

Even before the Project grants were awarded in the spring of 1971, the interdisciplinary planning committee at the University had identified several persons who could give them guidance in developing the experimental program. These included the Assistant Dean for Research from the School of Education, a representative from the University's Center for Research on Learning and Teaching, library media supervisors from three cooperating school systems, consultants from the University's Bureau of School Services and the State Library, and a representative from Eastern Michigan University's Undergraduate Library Science Program. They reviewed the program proposal and agreed to advise and assist in its implementation. Joining these persons in the formation of the official Advisory Board of the program in April 1971, were two school administrators, the Dean of the School of Library Science, the Assistant Dean for Instruction, a representative of the Teacher Education Division of the School of Education, an additional media supervisor who was also president-elect of the Michigan Audiovisual Association, and two students. All these roles continued to be represented on the program's Advisory Board although personnel changed in some cases. In the early planning stage, the student representatives were selected by the core faculty to include one person who had done fieldwork at the elementary level and another who had recently completed a student teaching assignment at the high school level. Later, when the first group of students enrolled in the experimental program, student representatives were chosen by their peers. As these students completed the program, two others were elected to succeed them on the Advisory Board. Members of

the interdisciplinary planning committee, later the core faculty, also met regularly with the Advisory Board.

Present at the first meeting to orient the Board to the School Library Manpower Project was the Project's associate director. Three sub-committees were formed to advise in the specific areas of the field experience, evaluation and dissemination of information about the program, and campus courses. The sub-committees met several times during the summer of 1971, reported their activities at the Fall, 1971 meeting and met at intervals since that time during and/or between semi-annual Board meetings.

The Board and its sub-committees developed guidelines for the internship experience, helped to refine program objectives, advised the core faculty on evaluation plans, recommended audiences and distribution procedures for program brochures and other public relations activities, reviewed plans for changing several courses, talked with student representatives about their impressions of the program, recommended visitation sites for the field experience, and reviewed program progress regularly each fall and spring since 1971. In addition, help from individual Board members was requested and was freely given by them.

The Advisory Board members served as an important communications link between the experimental program and the various constituencies to which each belonged. Especially vital in this regard was the student representation on the Board. Two students, although not always the same two, held membership on the Board from its beginning. They brought their viewpoints to the Board and sub-committee discussions and they reported to the students who elected them. Other members of the Board helped to smooth the way for the program in the cooperating school districts, in the Schools of Education and Library Science, and in the State Department of Education.

The Advisory Board was asked to serve at least through the 1973-74 year as the U-M program continues the process of experimentation and change.

Another group from the field crucial to the program was the school-based team, the cooperating library media specialists and directors who made the internship experiences possible and made valuable suggestions for pre-internship instruction. They participated in campus seminars, attended convocations and special programs when guest speakers were present, and guided students, both individually and in groups, as these aspiring media specialists sought knowledge of the profession from those on the job.

# Program Components

## CURRICULUM DESIGN

The experimental program at the University of Michigan was carried out primarily through a series of courses fifteen weeks in length during fall and winter terms and six to eight weeks in length during spring and summer half-terms. Format for courses varied to include seminar, laboratory, discussion, lecture, independent study, and fieldwork. This was not new. Many universities, most in fact, have a similar organizational pattern, and the University of Michigan has long had this one. But curriculum and organization are not synonymous although they are closely interrelated. It is possible to have curriculum change, to have a curriculum design with content based on a series of competencies described in course objectives, without drastic change to the organizational pattern.

To develop a set of program objectives, core faculty members utilized *Standards for School Media Programs, Occupational Definitions for School Library Media Personnel,*[3] and professional advice from the field. This advice came from Advisory Board members and media specialists in the cooperating school systems. Another source was a questionnaire (see Appendix A) to library science alumni who had taken school library administration three to five years earlier. If they were employed in a school library media position, they were asked to rate the value to them of courses taken at the University in both library science and cognate fields. Further, they were asked to note areas of importance in their professional positions which were not covered in their educational preparation. Return of completed questionnaires was relatively low, 13 out of a total of 30 mailed. Several graduates could not be located; others responded that they had not been employed in the school library field although they had taken the course in school library administration while earning a Master's degree at the University of Michigan. Of those responding, 7 were in elementary school positions, 5 were in secondary schools and 1 worked at the district level. Most noted satisfaction with general library science and school-related courses, but expressed need for more skill in

working with nonprint media, with design and production of media, and with curriculum. Several noted the importance of communication and public relation skills, and those employed at the elementary school level noted that subject bibliography was not of much value to them in their jobs. In spite of the small number responding, these alumni gave thoughtful consideration to their educational preparation for their roles in school library media centers. This feedback supported program changes proposed and implemented.

In designing a curriculum for future school library media specialists, program objectives provided the basis for examining courses offered in library science and in other areas of study. Before new courses were developed, it seemed essential to ascertain that content was not already being offered in an acceptable form. It was deemed impractical and unnecessary to develop segments in curriculum, learning, and human relations when a number of such courses were already being offered within the University by the School of Education and other campus units. The opportunity for students to study outside the School of Library Science and gain an interdisciplinary experience was valued highly.

The traditional library science core came under careful scrutiny. If students were to develop competence in several new areas such as curriculum and learning, human relations, and design and production of media, they had to engage either in a much-lengthened program or be allowed to omit certain requirements in the traditional core—which then included cataloging, book selection, reference, a subject bibliography course, and a general introductory course to librarianship for a total of fifteen semester hours.

The first to go was the subject bibliography requirements. While the reference and retrieval function was considered essential to all libraries, including school media centers, highly specialized sources in a single broad subject field seemed of less importance to many school librarians than a course in storytelling or a seminar on media for children and young adults. A number of students elected to take a subject bibliography course if their employment goal was a large high school or a district media center role, but such a course was not required.

Organization of library media collections seemed an essential area of competency for all students. Pro-

---

3. School Library Manpower Project, *Occupational Definitions for School Library Media Personnel* (Chicago: American Library Association, 1971).

gram planners purposely did not choose to separate prospective media specialists from other library science students in this area but allowed the basic cataloging course to remain a requirement. This permitted students in the program the option of continuing study in this area if later they decided to change career goals and specialize in technical services, perhaps becoming head of a processing center. Students did not always agree with the faculty on this decision, although one could not really get student concensus for a separate course for prospective school library media specialists either. A basic concern to students, not exclusively those in the program, was that classification was a separate, elective area of study rather than a part of the required course. Some students solved this problem by electing classification, but core faculty members tended to discourage this for most school library media students as a poor investment for three hours of credit. A number of students used a programmed text and/or experience during the internship as an individualized way of solving the problem. A module for self-instruction was proposed but was never developed since a change, recommended by the Student-Faculty Curriculum Committee and approved by the general faculty, will make classification a component in the basic course beginning with the 1973-74 academic year. Also to be included in greater depth, is the organization of nonprint media.

How much skill in the area of cataloging and classification beyond a general understanding of them as means of organizing library collections is necessary for a school library media specialist? *Standards for School Media Programs,* and most leaders of the profession do not recommend that cataloging be done at the building level. However, many school library media specialists are doing their own cataloging and are expected by school administrators to be able to do this. It remains a problem area and a gap between principle and practice.

Retention of a general course in librarianship for the experimental program was justified by planners who wanted school library media specialists to perceive themselves as part of the total library profession. Rather than the three hour survey course generally required as part of the library science core, a two-hour course was chosen. The course selected emphasized the importance of cooperation among all library agencies and participation in information networks to meet the needs of persons at all age levels and degrees of specialization. In addition to exploring cooperative plans of service, this course exposed students in the program to many dimensions of librarianship today and to persons who will be choosing library roles in other than the school field.

All students taking a course in basic reference materials and services, including students in the program, had the option of taking it as independent, computer-assisted instruction in place of the regular lecture-discussion section. The CAI course was developed and tested at the University in 1969, by a library science faculty member and his research associates with the aid of a federal grant.[4] The course is updated regularly. Students participated in simulated reference interviews adapted from real situations in libraries of various types including school library media centers. To support student use of the computer, the University provided terminals in various campus locations, including two within the building which houses the School of Library Science offices. Cost of computer time for experimental program student use was also provided by the University. An average of approximately $80 per student was spent for the use of the computer by all Library Science Students who took the reference course during the 1972-73 year. Most of the students in the experimental program chose this independent study approach. They were encouraged to do so by core faculty advisers who considered the experience with CAI as well as the course content to be of importance for their future professional roles.

Selection of media in all formats was considered to be an essential competency for the prospective school library media specialist. Study of the objectives and outline of the book selection course, however, showed some duplication with those in children's and young adult literature, audio-visual methods, administration of school library media centers, and curriculum materials. In the general book selection course, content was largely, although not exclusively, adult and public library oriented. It was proposed that the various skills and knowledges essential to the experimental program in the area of selection be attained through a series of courses which were both multimedia and youth-oriented.

Objectives for the courses listed above were carefully developed and course content revised to make certain that there would be no gaps and only a minimum amount of overlap for students in the program. Some aspects of selection relating to policy-

4. Thomas P. Slavens, *The Development and Testing of Materials for Computer Assisted Instruction in the Education of Reference Librarians* (Washington, D.C.: Bureau of Research, U.S. Department of Health, Education and Welfare, April, 1970).

making were deemed most appropriate for the administration course and were included there. The new course sequence to provide competency in selection and utilization of media for students in the program included:

*Audiovisual Methods,* which provided a basic understanding of the uses and limitations of various nonprint media and skill in operating media equipment.

*Literature for Children,* considered criteria for evaluation and basic tools for selection of media appropriate for children pre-school through middle school. Students were expected to demonstrate knowledge of the content of selected examples of children's literature, in various formats, and skill in introducing media to children.

*Literature for Young Adults,* provided similar experiences geared to meeting the media needs and interests of youth at the high school age.

*Seminar in Media for Children and Young Adults,* a new course designed to consider problems in selection of media for children and young adults and in a planning program to meet user needs.

*Teaching with Media,* was a revision of a curriculum materials course. It provided students with opportunities to develop knowledge and skill in using a variety of selection tools to locate media for instruction. Aspects of systematic instructional design and greater emphasis on teacher-media specialist interaction were included.

Thus the fifteen hour core was shortened to eight hours for students in the experimental program. It included cataloging, reference and contemporary library development. Selection competencies were integrated into other courses.

One new course, Seminar in Media for Children and Young Adults, was mentioned earlier as a part of the multimedia selection and utilization sequence. Another segment entirely new to the School of Library Science was in the area of media design. A first course, Design and Production of Media, assumed a basic knowledge of media utilization and incorporated skills in lettering; dry mounting; transparency making; photography, both slides and 8mm motion pictures; audio and video production; and basic principles of design. A second course, now elective, offered students an opportunity to follow a program of instructional media from idea through design and production, to field testing. Some students combined projects for the internship experience with the design seminar and others worked with campus faculty members to develop instructional media to

be used in library science classes. One very successful example was the work done by a student for the course in documentation and information retrieval. This student, after consultation with the instructor, designed and produced a set of transparencies on Boolean Logic and Set Theory. The instructor found them to be more effective in clarifying these concepts than his former chalkboard illustrations. Other production electives in photography, television, graphics, and filmmaking were taught in other schools and colleges within the University and were open to program students who met basic requirements.

While modules were not really a part of the Michigan program, all courses had stated objectives which, in some cases, provided activities, materials of instruction, and criterion measurement for the student to use on an individual basis. In most courses, students had an opportunity for choice of independent or team projects allowing them to explore areas of interest in greater depth. Students could also elect to do one or two hours of directed research, which could be action research related to problems encountered in the internship experience. A proposal and the approval of both cooperating library media specialist and faculty member were required for the latter. While most of the program was, as has been noted, course-oriented, there were many opportunities for independent study and individual choice both within and without the course structure.

The key to individualization in the Michigan program was through extensive counseling involving conferences with several core faculty members for each student. The program, differing for students according to interests, goals, and educational background, was planned during the first term on campus and modified through subsequent conferences until graduation. Choices for the interdisciplinary components were varied. Language and Cognitive Development in Children, Instructional Gaming, Teaching of Reading, and Theory of Learning were some of the courses which were elected to meet the requirement for competency in learning. Growth of Self, Mental Hygiene, and Applied Group Dynamics were some of the choices for the human relations component. Different curriculum development courses were offered for those interested in elementary, middle school, or high school. Choice of level was expected to correspond to choice of internship experience, and it usually, but not necessarily, also corresponded to past experience and the level of student teaching done as an undergraduate. Feedback from interns and their cooperating media specialists could lead the core faculty to recommend that those wishing to make a change in the level of preparation should take extra work at the new level or pass a proficiency examination to show that sufficient background in materials, human development, and curriculum content had been attained.

Basic competencies in all other aspects of the experimental program were included in the following courses:

> Literature for Children
> Literature for Young Adults
> Audiovisual Methods
> Seminar in Media for Children and Young Adults
> Teaching with Media
> Design and Production of Media
> Administration of School Library Media Centers
> Seminar in Library Media Research
> Basic Reference Materials and Services
> Cataloging and Classification
> Contemporary Library Developments
> Library Media Internship

Students who had not previously attained these competencies usually were expected to take the courses listed above and to complete the required number of hours with electives. Considerable flexibility was allowed in interpreting whether a student had previously attained some of the required competencies. The core faculty members who served as the counseling team reviewed with the student his previous academic and practical experience to determine appropriate modifications for the individual's program. In some cases, students chose to prepare independently for examinations in basic reference and/or cataloging.

All students had some opportunity for electing courses to extend their competencies in one or more directions. Frequently elected courses in library science included:

> Introduction to Documentation and Information Retrieval
> Storytelling
> History of Children's Literature
> Humanities or Social Science Bibliography
> Seminar in Design and Production of Media

## CURRICULUM CONTROL

The concept of academic freedom is a strong force in most universities and is certainly no less important at the University of Michigan. Traditionally, each faculty member has had the right to plan and teach assigned courses without interference as long as content is consistent with the brief descriptions in the school's catalog. Members of the core faculty agreed to work together in developing course objectives that expanded the stated program objectives. Working as a team during the first term of the experimental program, fall, 1971, core faculty members shared planning responsibilities for all courses taught by any one of the group. These included courses dealing with media for children and young adults, with design and production of media, and with administration and fieldwork in a school library media center.

The director and other core faculty members worked with instructors of other courses taken by students in the experimental program to make certain they were aware of program goals. Students gave feedback on all courses through course evaluations (see Appendix B). Deans and assistant deans in library science and education encouraged cooperation of all faculty members with the program, and in a number of cases, non-core faculty members modified their courses to make them more consistent with experimental program goals. All faculty members expressed interest in extending the use of instructional media in their own teaching. A total of eighteen faculty members from library science and education took part in the December Plan-In mentioned earlier in this report.

As an example of the circuitous, but ultimately effective means of curriculum change, one might look at the content and hours change in the course in cataloging the fall, 1973, term. Student dissatisfaction with the omission of classification has already been mentioned. This led to a lengthy discussion during the December Plan-In, primarily in a small student-faculty work group which included the Dean of Library Science. That group recommended a change to incorporate both classification and work with non-print media. Following the Plan-In, the Dean drafted a memorandum requesting the school's Student-Faculty Curriculum Committee to consider the recommendation. Membership on this committee included the director and two students in the experimental program who gave strong verbal support to the proposal. The Curriculum Committee discussed the issue, held hearings with the cataloging instructors, surveyed the entire student body to learn the extent of student support for change, and finally voted to recommend to the faculty the suggested changes in content from three to four credit hours. The library science faculty discussed the issue and voted their approval of the changes. The Dean requested and received permission from the Rackham School of Graduate Studies to change the course description and credit hours. Approval of the graduate school is largely a formality, but is an essential step. The means of implementing the change was left to each of the several cataloging instructors.

In another session of the Curriculum Committee, student members presented a petition requesting an increase in the number of credit hours for Design and Production of Media. The program director asked that any action be deferred until the core faculty could consider the matter, since a change in credit hours for this course would affect the total length of the program. The director later reported, after consultation with the core faculty, that some reduction in required assignments for the course would, at present, be a more desirable solution than an increase in credit hours since students in the program already were quite limited in the number of hours they might elect beyond the required competencies. The Committee agreed to this solution.

Communication is one of the problems of an inter-disciplinary program. Simply finding out what courses will be offered outside one's own school and when, can be time-consuming and subject to errors or even to last minute changes which can affect the schedule of one or more students. Four joint-listed courses for library science and education were a mixed blessing because it was often difficult to learn exactly how many students had enrolled in these, and in some instances, class enrollment could exceed desirable numbers.

In short, there were few instances of curriculum control in the program. The director, however, maintained that cooperation usually did work in situations where control simply would not. It just takes longer than one would like sometimes.

## UTILIZATION OF EDUCATIONAL MEDIA

The Educational Media Center, located in the School of Education Building, served students and faculty members in education and library science with a multi-media collection for teaching and learning. Students could sample textbooks and trade books or use carrels equipped for individual previewing of filmstrips or recordings. Instructional games could be borrowed and classroom tested by the student teacher or intern. Reference books, periodicals, and curriculum guides were available for use in classrooms and laboratories. An exception would be the item assigned permanently to the Self-Instructional Laboratory and used there with teacher-selected programs, including some programs to mas-

ter the operation of audiovisual equipment. A graphics laboratory provided space and equipment for visual production, and a television studio was sound-proofed for audio and video recording.

Until the winter of 1972-73, nonprint media circulated only to members of the faculty. Responses to a Student Questionnaire (see Appendix C) distributed to those in the experimental program in October 1972, urged that all media be available for student use outside the Educational Media Center. Staff members agreed and were pleased with the results. None of the problems feared (loss, damage, and inaccessibility to faculty members) developed.

Elsewhere on campus, the Audio-Visual Center has a large collection of films and audio tapes for use in campus classes and by student interns in assigned schools. The Audio Room in the Undergraduate Library has an extensive collection of recordings for listening, and the Library Science Library has begun to build a nonprint collection in addition to its microforms. Tapes of library science convocation speakers are housed there for student and faculty review.

One of the program objectives for the University concerned the increased use of educational media for teaching and learning. In support of this, funds from the School of Library Science totaling $18,500 were spent for nonprint media for the Educational Media Center, equipment for individualized viewing and listening in the EMC Library and in its Self-Instructional Laboratory, and equipment for use in the production laboratory and in other library science classes. These funds for the EMC supplemented the regular budget from the School of Education for the Center.

One problem relating to the use of media which required equipment for library science classes was the absence of regularly assigned classroom and adjoining storage space for library science. Although classes for the experimental program were held in the School of Education Building and thus had ready access to equipment, other library science classes were scheduled in various campus buildings. The necessity for transporting equipment for each classtime was not likely to promote the use of media. An exception was the availability of 16mm projectors distributed through the Audio-Visual Center for classroom film presentation. The classroom problem has reached the consciousness level of University administrators, and long-range plans include well-equipped classrooms designated for library science. Still, most library science faculty members indicated an interest in developing and using instructional media. A Faculty Questionnaire (see Appendix D) distributed to all library science faculty in October 1972, showed that 41 percent felt they were using nonprint media as much as possible in their classes and another 25 per cent would use it if appropriate media were made available to them. Sixteen per cent felt they had increased their use of media since the beginning of the program in January 1972. One hundred per cent of the core faculty indicated on the Core Faculty Questionnaire (see Appendix E) that they were using nonprint media for instruction as much as possible.

Employment of the media technician as a part of the experimental program was a positive step toward increasing the use of media in instruction. The technician's time was divided between assisting students in the production laboratory and assisting program faculty members in both library science and education with their instructional media needs from graphic production to the operation of video taping equipment. Some of the projects developed by the media technician and/or students in the advanced production class included slides of selection tools for use in several classes, slides of library furniture and floor plans for administration class, slides of rare books for History of Books and Printing, slides for Government Documents, audio and video tapes of guest lecturers, transparencies for several classes including Introduction to Documentation, a slide-tape simulated visit to media centers, and a graphic presentation of dry mounting techniques. The two latter programs are now being used in the Self-Instructional Laboratory.

## TEACHING AND LEARNING METHODOLOGY

Teaching techniques involving use of media have already been discussed in general. Responses to the Student Questionnaire in October 1972, noted small group discussion and the use of individually selected projects as methods they favored. Use of the Student Questionnaire (see Appendix F) in June 1973, with a second group of students elicited a longer list of favored methods including: "hands on" experience in production techniques, use of film in presenting problems and solutions, computerized reference course, actual experience in the field, seminar term paper discussions, student-directed classes within a framework provided by the instructor, field trips including follow-up discussions and role playing. Faculty members tended to agree with students that these were good methods.

Students in June 1973, suggested the following

improvements: more student participation in selection of program and course objectives; greater use of outside resource people; more small group work and more extensive use of video tapes, problem solving and role playing; and more innovative teaching.

A method which deserves to be described was the use of trigger films. These were short, one to two minute 16mm films which could be used to initiate an open-ended discussion of a problem. The University of Michigan Television Center had produced a number of these brief films since 1967, primarily in the fields of health and safety education.[5]

Several of the drug and driver education films were used effectively in library science classes on literature for young adults and the seminar on media. Recently, the core faculty developed a series of library media problem situations and worked closely with the Television Center in the production of three of the situations. These three were filmed by the professional staff at the TV Center in one of the experimental program's cooperating library media centers. They were designed to be used to stimulate discussion in administration classes, and one was used also by interns and by library media specialists to develop student discussion of the "Rip Off" problem. Best use of a trigger film occurs when the film is shown once, discussed very briefly and then shown again before an in depth discussion is held. Students and cooperating library media specialists in the program responded favorably to this method. Students also showed an interest in producing trigger video tapes. One group of students made a trigger tape on limiting access of materials to children as part of the design and production class.

## FIELDWORK COMPONENT

The fieldwork component was very important in the experimental program and represented one of the major changes from earlier school library education programs at Michigan. Planners viewed fieldwork in three phases:

1. Field trips, both actual and simulated, to introduce students to several different school library media programs,
2. field-based projects to meet course objectives in several media courses,
3. an internship experience to provide at least ninety hours of work in a single school.

The field trips were intended to provide a frame of

5. Ellen J. Miller, "Trigger Filmmaking," *Audiovisual Instruction* (May, 1971), pp. 64-66.

reference for campus classwork, beginning with the student's first term in the program. The internship experience, on the other hand, was expected to take place during the student's last full term in order that all basic course work would have been taken.

All these phases were realized with some success in spite of a number of problems. The concept of curriculum control, difficult within the campus community, was even more complex for the development of a fieldwork component. Cooperating school systems were most helpful, and their participation in program planning and evaluation, as well as in work with individual students, was invaluable. Their primary obligation, however, was to the educational program at the elementary and secondary school level. Extensive time demands by University programs can become a serious problem to the public schools. The program involved a number of schools to minimize the time drain on any one of them.

Time demands on students and core faculty were also great and were highly diversified as well. Although program-wide field trips to selected schools were arranged and carried out during the spring and fall terms of 1972, it was easier to plan trips as a part of a particular course, e.g. administration of school library media centers. This was the practice during the winter, spring and summer terms of 1973. Actual trips were supplemented by simulated trips utilizing slides or filmstrips and audio tapes which included questions for student response. The trips were also supplemented by guest speakers from the field who participated in classroom discussions, convocations, and informal meetings with students.

Field-based projects were successful in some cases, but again, faculty members must be cognizant of the possibility of excessive infringement on the time of school personnel. In addition, any project which will involve students from an elementary or secondary school must be properly cleared with school authorities. Enthusiastic university students are not always aware of these necessary procedures and must be informed. Projects which proved most successful for program students as well as cooperating schools were those initiated during the internship. Following the internship orientation, the student had a better grasp of the school's purpose and procedures and could more freely develop projects which might well meet the objectives of some campus course. The student was expected to obtain approval from the cooperating school personnel as well as from the faculty member involved before beginning a project.

The internship experience was not entirely new to the Michigan program. For several years there were some students who did fieldwork in school library media centers, but participation was limited and voluntary. Students who did participate invariably found the experience to be rewarding.

One of the problems which faced the core faculty as they expanded the internship to its present required status was the need to accommodate a growing number of students. Cooperating school systems were very willing to extend their resources during the period of experimentation, but they did not wish to commit themselves to this degree on a permanent basis. Ultimately, it was the individual library media specialist whose time and skills were demanded. No student could be placed in a school unless the media specialist in charge was eager to accept the responsibility of professional guidance and was fully qualified to do so through experience and graduate library education. All cooperating school personnel expressed pleasure in participation and felt they were professionally enriched by it.

It was the position of the University that persons with teaching certificates who spent time in a school were themselves making a contribution to the school's educational program. In such a situation, the University was unwilling to provide any stipend for the cooperating educator or any financial reimbursement to the school, as was the case with the student teaching assignments. Some teacher organizations did not accept this premise and asked their members not to participate without receiving payment. A permanent solution has not yet been reached on this matter, which is crucial to the long range development of the program. The Assistant Dean of Library Science has recently been appointed to a teacher education committee which will consider this and similar problems related to cooperation with public schools.

A subcommittee of the Advisory Board worked with members of the core faculty to develop "Guidelines for the Internship Experience." These guidelines were used for planning the best possible experience for the individual student. Students were encouraged to take problem-solving approaches to the experiences available to them. Core faculty members served as liaison persons between the University and public schools. In this capacity they visited assigned schools to observe and to talk with both student and school personnel. Students, core faculty, and in some instances, the cooperating library media specialists explored internship experiences in several seminar sessions each term.

One could not take lightly the complex and time-consuming task of planning, initiating, and evaluating a fieldwork program. All steps and phases required coordination and called into use a wide range of communication skills. As has been noted, many persons were involved in the fieldwork program. In the schools, not only the principals and media specialists needed to be contacted, but also media program directors, personnel directors, and superintendents needed to be informed. The initial contact was always made with the district media director or supervisor, although the approval sequence was often different from one district to another. In one district, an early meeting of the core faculty with all principals and media specialists to be involved was scheduled through the help of the district media supervisor. This proved very useful in establishing a basis for lasting cooperation.

Meeting with Advisory Board members, with student interns, and with cooperating library media specialists required planning and scheduling, and often, follow-up activities. In addition, many visits were made to determine which centers and which persons could make the most effective contributions to the program.

The Assistant Dean of Library Science and the Program Director shared many of the coordinating tasks for the fieldwork component while continuing with the other teaching and administrative responsibilities. Supervision of students in the internship experience was divided among all of the core faculty members. Although there were problems related to this divided and shared approach to coordinating and supervising the fieldwork program, the faculty members involved felt that the communications link with students, cooperating library media specialists, and other educators, and the opportunity to make frequent visits to schools proved valuable in their classroom teaching assignments.

As one means of evaluating the internship and its relationship to the campus classwork, a questionnaire incorporating all the items from the Guidelines was designed and mailed to all those who had participated in the internship experience, either as a student or as a library media specialist. Participants were asked which of the twenty-nine activities from "Guidelines for the Internship Experience" were included in their programs and how highly they valued each experience. Two categories, media services experiences and orientation experiences, were considered. Twenty-six students and 18 cooperating library media specialists were sent questionnaires. Twenty-two students and 17 library media specialists responded. This was a return of 85 per cent for the student group and 94 per cent for the cooperating library media specialists. Tabulation of responses for the 2 groups is shown in Appendices G and H.

Initially, responses were tabulated separately for students by grade level and by term during which they served as interns. Reporting by grade level were 7 from elementary schools, 6 from middle schools, and 9 from high schools. Reporting by term were 6 from fall, 1972; 12 from winter, 1973; and 4 from spring, 1973.

There were few differences in grade level groups. The elementary school group had, however, the highest number of items not experienced by a majority of those reporting, 11 of 29 possible activities, in comparison to 6 for a majority from middle schools and 4 for a majority from high schools.

Responses by term showed fewer items omitted from the internship experiences of a majority of the winter, 1973, group than from a majority in fall or spring. Number of activities omitted by a majority:

> Fall, 1972—10 items
> Winter, 1973—4 items
> Spring, 1973—6 items.

This indicated some growth in the scope of the internship following the fall term and reflected formative evaluation of that first term by the Program Director, core faculty, students and cooperating library media specialists. The spring term was a shortened one which was used for an internship only when no other arrangement was possible for the student. Four students participated during this term.

Further evidence of growth in the scope of this internship experience is gained by a look at the following:

> Fall, 1972—5 items included by 80 per cent of the students
> Winter, 1973—16 items included by 80 per cent of the students
> Spring, 1972—18 items included by 75 per cent of the students
> Spring, 1972—8 items included by 100 per cent of the students.

Only one item, number 5, "Implemented utilization of community resources," was omitted from the experience of a majority of students each term. Although it was valued highly as a potential activity for the internship by a majority of students, only 29 per cent of the cooperating media specialists rated it "of great value." This activity might be unrealistic in some media programs while possible in others. Perhaps, however, some library media specialists did not perceive their roles to extend beyond the school building as frequently as students had been prepared by their classwork to expect.

Only one item, number 20, "Cooperated with the school media specialist in the application of systems analysis to a selected work procedure," was valued highly by less than 50 per cent of the students responding. A majority of cooperating library media specialists agreed with students in this evaluation. Core faculty members considered this a possible activity and a useful management technique in any media center. The item apparently needed to be restated or given a more effective explanation with both students and cooperating media specialists.

A majority of the library media specialist group did not value highly four other items. These were:

5. Implemented utilization of community resources
17. Studied the selection, arrangement, and utilization of media center furnishing and equipment.
21. Studied techniques of working effectively with sales representative in the media field.
Orientation Item 2. Observed and/or participated in area and/or district level meetings for media personnel.

Item 5 has already been discussed. Item 17 was possible in any media center and could have served as an extension of classroom discussions on this topic with a minimum of time and effort from the cooperating media specialist who might not have perceived the student's interest and need to know. Item 21 was not a possible activity in all media centers. It was, perhaps, more appropriately handled through discussion in the classroom. The Orientation Item 2 was appropriately valued by students. It, however, might be difficult to accomplish in some internship experiences due to problems of time and distance.

It is interesting to note that 7 media service activities and one orientation activity were highly valued by 80 per cent or more of each group, students and cooperating library media specialists. These items were:

1. Cooperated closely and planned with the school media specialist.
2. Consulted with and provided services and media to meet the needs of pupils, teachers, administrators, and the curriculum.
6. Maintained an atmosphere conducive to learning.
7. Provided reference service.
8. Contributed unique talents to special projects.
10. Worked intensely with groups of pupils, i.e., storytelling, book talks, developing media research skills, working with student media assistants.

22. Maintained and improved professional skills.
Orientation Activity 4. Received orientation at the building level, including introduction to administrators, teachers, and students; community characteristics; school regulations and policies; media program status and needs.

In addition, 80 per cent of the student group valued highly item 18, "Took inventory as a quality control factor—perhaps on one small part of the collection, analyzed the strengths, weaknesses, and relevance of items in the collection in light of needs of the pupils, teachers, and curricular offerings." Many cooperating library media specialists, 65 per cent, also valued this activity highly. Perhaps others viewed the activity as primarily routine, without considering the more positive analytical and evaluational skills involved.

Of the 8 items listed above as valued highly by 80 per cent of the students, 7 were included in the experiences of all spring, 1973, interns. All 8 items were included in the experiences of 80 per cent of the winter, 1973, interns. Only 4 of the items were included in the experiences of 80 per cent of the fall, 1972 interns. This indicated that internship experiences emphasized desired activity patterns in addition to showing an increase in scope.

Projects or activities cited as most important were of a similar type for many respondents in both groups. These concerned working with people and included:

> The chance to work with live rather than hypothetical situations.
> The opportunity to see how the theories we learned worked with kids—in a classroom AV presentation and in the library "on the floor."
> Coping with everyday tasks that occurred—reference, circulation, pulling materials for a classroom unit, problems with student help, discipline in the media center, etc.
> Working closely with the local public library.
> Working on a puppet play of "Nail Soup" with three fifth graders.
> Planning with teachers and as a result teaching library media skills to small groups of students.
> Storytelling and other group interaction with students.
> Working with a particular teacher in developing a unit and corresponding reserve media collection for a class.

Conducting a survey on the student's ability to use library materials.

Leadership experiences — especially directing non-professional staff members.

Other special projects completed during the winter term as independent study, a means of extending the internship and emphasizing a problem solving approach, were highly valued by the students and cooperating library media specialists involved. They included:

Preparation of a program budget in consultation with the media director.

Planning, teaching, and evaluating a unit on media production for elementary students.

Designing, using, and evaluating a program of individualized library instruction on the card catalog.

Several students and cooperating library media specialists made useful suggestions for improving the internship experience. One student proposed electing to do an internship at more than one school. It was interesting to note during the spring, 1973, term one of the students did do fieldwork at both elementary and high school levels. Most often suggested were greater time concentration, need for expansion of the experience for more hours and/or more credit, greater involvement with teachers.

Most of those responding felt that the pre-internship course work provided satisfactory preparation. Some were especially enthusiastic: "Definitely," "Yes, extremely," "All courses have been excellent in preparation as a professional," "Yes, I felt ready to begin." Some qualified their responses, mentioning areas of weakness they perceived in their competencies and in the course work before the internship. Dewey classification, AV equipment operation and knowledge of children's books were items mentioned more than once as areas of weakness by those responding to the questionnaire.

The responses to this survey provided evidence of growth in the internship experience since the first group of students in the experimental program participated in the fall, 1972, term. This was consistent with core faculty observations and judgments. The questionnaire also provided the program with valuable information on which to plan for further improvement.

## ASSESSMENT OF STUDENT COMPETENCIES

Students in the program were evaluated in a variety of ways. Tests and examinations over course work continued to play a part in assessing students' ability to handle information by analyzing, synthesizing, and evaluating it. Proficiency examinations covered basic cataloging and reference and were available as options. These were used primarily by students who had undergraduate courses or experience in these subjects. Credit was not given for these examinations but persons who passed them were excused from taking the otherwise required courses. In Design and Production of Media students were offered a "test out" option for each course objective.

In the Self-Instructional Laboratory of the EMC, testing was a part of the learning process. Students threaded the projector, mounted the picture, identified the appropriate response, and got immediate feedback on their performance. This was also true of the computer-assisted instructional program in reference services. Students could use computer terminals in any of several locations on campus, sign on with the proper code, and begin a simulated reference interview with a library patron.

Papers, projects and oral presentations were used to reveal student creativity, initiative, and ability to communicate. Topics were chosen by the students who then worked individually, or sometimes in teams to explore the subject and report on their study to instructor and classmates. The report might be in visual or verbal format or in a combination of the two. Students usually favored projects over examinations, according to their comments in classes and on the "Student Questionnaire" used in October 1972, and again in June 1973. All of the methods discussed could, however, be used to measure student competency as stated in the course objectives.

Most student-faculty discussion eventually came to the subject of grades. Some students preferred a pass-fail method to the use of letter grades. These persons believed that satisfactory completion of an objective or of a set of course objectives should be rated that way—as satisfactory. The School of Library Science and other graduate programs at the University used the "S" for satisfactory completion of work only in assessing the internship or an independent study. In all other courses, letter grades were used as a reflection of a student's performance level in a given area. All grades from "B" to "A+" were an indication of satisfactory performance, but there were differences in the degree of excellence which cannot be revealed by pass-fail.

In the internship experience, observation of a student's performance by a cooperating library media specialist and by the supervising core faculty member was the primary method of assessment. This experience in an actual school media center gave students an opportunity to demonstrate many of the skills and the kinds of knowledges which they studied in the classroom.

Students were encouraged to assess their own competencies and to plan towards strengthening their level of proficiency. Student-faculty conferences were scheduled each term for individual program planning. During these meetings and at other student-initiated conferences, students were helped to clarify goals and current learning needs. Pre- and post-testing of student interests and perception of competency was conducted and results can be found later in this section. The instrument utilized program objectives as items in a two part scale adapted from an EMIE Project Self-Appraisal Scale.[6] A second pre- and post-test, a Semantic Differential Scale,[7] examined attitude change among students in the program. Results of this evaluation can also be found in the section discussing program results.

Written evaluations were prepared by faculty members for the student's placement file at the request of the student. These evaluations, reflecting a faculty member's total perception of the student's competencies and potential for success, are valued by prospective employers and are, therefore, important to the student.

## SPECIAL PROGRAM FEATURES

Of great importance to the program were the informal aspects which brought students and faculty members together outside of the classroom. The University of Michigan School of Library Science and LSSO, the School's student organization, sponsor a number of informal social activities each year. These include coffee hours held at the beginning of each term to welcome new students and also at the close of several of the regular Thursday afternoon convocations. A notable school-wide event each spring is the Alumnus in Residence Program. One or more alumni who hold important positions in the library profession are invited to spend two days on campus meeting informally with students and faculty members. Traditionally, the guest alumnus has spoken at a banquet honoring students elected to Beta Phi Mu, a library science fraternity. During the past year, one

of the two guest alumni had extensive experience in the school library media field, making this speaker an especially valuable resource for students in the library media program.

Students in the experimental program participated in the schoolwide informal activities described, and in addition, they took part in a number of special program activities. Knapp-sack lunches were found to be a successful means of bringing students and faculty together on an informal basis. Several of these were held each term. On some occasions there was a brief program, e.g., reports from student representatives to a national conference or comments from a special guest. Sometimes, however, these lunches were just a chance for "rapping" and getting better acquainted.

Field trips held outside classtime and open to all students in the program gave them a clearer picture of inner city school problems and innovative media programs in both city and suburban settings. Guest speakers with special school library media expertise were invited to speak to students and to meet informally with them at afternoon or evening coffee hours.

A special program feature which was particularly well received by those who participated was the Plan-In, a two-day experience in group process held in December 1972. This time was chosen because the first group of students was completing the program at the end of December. For them it was an opportunity to reflect on the total program as they had experienced it. Students who entered in July and in September were also participants and brought their mid-program perceptions to the discussions. A total of thirty students participated in the Plan-In, including several who were enrolled part-time. The eighteen faculty and staff who participated included all members of the core faculty and representatives from both education and library science faculties who had contact with the program, but not on a full-time basis.

To design and facilitate the group process activities, a person was employed from outside the University of Michigan campus community who had special training and experience in working with groups and a knowledge of both library and educational programs. The consultant met with a small planning committee of students and faculty members before the event and provided guidance and training materials throughout the workshop.

For many students and faculty members it was a unique experience in group problem solving through the use of training laboratory methods. The

6. Educational Media Institute Evaluation Project, Department of Audiovisual Instruction, *Evaluations of Summer 1966 NDEA Institutes for Educational Media Specialists and School Library Personnel* (San Jose, Calif.: Educational Media Institute Evaluation Project, 1966).

7. Charles Osgood, *The Measurement of Meaning* (Urbana: University of Illinois, 1967).

design provided for some student group versus faculty group interaction and for some in-depth planning in small groups which were composed of both student and faculty members. At the close of the two-day workshop, participants were asked to respond to a Workshop Evaluation (see Appendix I) developed by the group trainer. Tabulation of the Workshop Evaluation (see Appendix J) showed a high degree of satisfaction by most of the participants in terms of methods used and work accomplished. Students were particularly pleased to have the opportunity to work so closely with faculty members. Recommendations made by the six work groups influenced program modification and continue to serve as guidelines for long term program development.

# Program Results

It must be kept clearly in mind that the essential program is still in the process of changing and developing. It was not a completed experiment as the designation "Final Report" might suggest, nor was it a controlled experiment with matched groups of participants and non-participants. An early attempt to compare students in the program with a sample of others enrolled in a degree program within the School of Library Science was abandoned because several required courses and electives were taken by all students, not just those participating in the experimental program. Furthermore, experimental purpose goals emphasized change in teaching methods and content in a wider range of courses than those required for the master's program, and as the experimental program changed, the regular master's degree program for library science students changed also. Therefore, a comparison of perceptions of the two groups of students would not reveal the degree of change for the experimental program.

In an effort to determine student competencies after completion of the program and also to learn the effect of the program on students' ability to perform role-related tasks, the idea of a comprehensive mastery test was considered but was rejected as not feasible with the time and resources available for the program. To develop appropriate measurement scales which would take into consideration all the individual differences in program choices would demand long-term commitment from persons outside the program staff.

An alternate plan was developed with the aid of a research assistant assigned to the program during the summer, 1971, term by the Dean of the School of Library Science. The plan, approved by the Advisory Board subcommittee on Evaluation and Dissemination provided for the use of two instruments, one to measure student perceptions of their interest and competency in role-related program objectives, and one to measure their change in attitude to words which would be given special emphasis during the program. The first of these instruments substituted student perception of mastery over competencies for the non-existent comprehensive tests. It also sought to learn whether the program had significantly modified the students' interests in the role-related objectives. The instrument, Inventory of Interest and Competency (see Appendix K), requested students to rate their own level of interest and competency on twenty-five items adapted from the statement of program objectives. A nine point scale (1 = low; 9 = high) was used to rate both interest and competency. The inventory was administered to twenty-five students in the program as they entered and again as they completed the degree requirements. Mean Scale values, pre and post, are shown in Table 1 for interest and Table 2 for competency. Table 1 reveals that few significant changes occurred in student interest. Only three items were found to be significantly more interesting to students following the program. Item 10, "Communicate regularly with the public library and other community agencies in planning media center programs and activities," showed the greatest amount of change, significant at the .01 level. The program attempted to show the interrelationships among community agencies and the importance of interlibrary cooperation in several courses, most specifically in Contemporary Library Developments. It was gratifying to learn that students had broadened their perspective of the school library media program and now recognized the importance of involvement with agencies beyond the school building.

At the .05 level of significance, student interests in Items 11 and 12 changed. These two objectives were concerned with interpreting content of specific print and nonprint materials. Courses in selection and utilization of media emphasized the need to write, view, and listen widely and to share knowledge of content of media creatively.

It was not surprising nor indeed disappointing,

TABLE 1. DIFFERENCES BETWEEN INTERESTS IN PROGRAM OBJECTIVES AS PERCEIVED BY STUDENTS PRE- AND POST-PARTICIPATION IN THE EXPERIMENTAL PRORGAM

| Objective† | Mean Scale Values | | t | P |
|---|---|---|---|---|
| | Pre Program (N = 25) | Post Program (N = 25) | | |
| 1 | 8.04 | 8.60 | —1.474 | |
| 2 | 7.60 | 8.24 | —1.535 | |
| 3 | 8.24 | 8.80 | —1.652 | |
| 4 | 7.96 | 8.48 | —1.307 | |
| 5 | 8.32 | 8.48 | — .579 | |
| 6 | 7.68 | 7.68 | .000 | |
| 7 | 8.40 | 8.72 | —1.509 | |
| 8 | 8.44 | 8.56 | — .553 | |
| 9 | 7.24 | 7.48 | — .544 | |
| 10 | 7.20 | 8.12 | —2.884 | ** |
| 11 | 7.00 | 8.04 | —2.374 | * |
| 12 | 7.28 | 8.24 | —2.546 | * |
| 13 | 8.20 | 8.40 | — .535 | |
| 14 | 7.72 | 8.16 | — .991 | |
| 15 | 8.40 | 8.60 | — .866 | |
| 16 | 8.40 | 8.44 | — .129 | |
| 17 | 8.04 | 8.48 | —1.379 | |
| 18 | 8.52 | 8.56 | — .163 | |
| 19 | 7.84 | 7.92 | — .165 | |
| 20 | 7.84 | 7.92 | — .164 | |
| 21 | 8.08 | 8.32 | — .698 | |
| 22 | 8.52 | 8.76 | — .879 | |
| 23 | 8.32 | 8.84 | —1.661 | |
| 24 | 8.36 | 8.76 | —1.408 | |
| 25 | 8.56 | 8.64 | — .336 | |

$df = 48$     **P $(2.681 \leq t \leq -2.68)$     $\leq .01$
*P $(2.010 \leq t \leq -2.010)$     $\leq .05$
†Objectives are listed in Inventory of Interest and Competency, Appendix K.

TABLE 2. DIFFERENCES BETWEEN COMPETENCIES IN PROGRAM ORJECTIVES AS PERCEIVED BY STUDENTS PRE- AND POST-PARTICIPATION IN THE EXPERIMENTAL PROGRAM

| Objective† | Mean Scale Values | | t | P |
|---|---|---|---|---|
| | Pre Program (N = 25) | Post Program (N = 25) | | |
| 1 | 4.48 | 7.08 | —5.068 | ** |
| 2 | 4.16 | 6.64 | —4.911 | ** |
| 3 | 4.68 | 7.48 | —6.222 | ** |
| 4 | 4.32 | 7.00 | —5.265 | ** |
| 5 | 4.08 | 7.32 | —6.599 | ** |
| 6 | 3.72 | 6.12 | —3.987 | ** |
| 7 | 4.76 | 7.52 | —5.054 | ** |
| 8 | 4.44 | 7.52 | —5.310 | ** |
| 9 | 3.92 | 6.48 | —4.391 | ** |
| 10 | 3.52 | 6.52 | —4.902 | ** |
| 11 | 5.40 | 7.44 | —3.901 | ** |
| 12 | 5.12 | 7.40 | —4.207 | ** |
| 13 | 5.56 | 7.60 | —3.446 | ** |
| 14 | 4.52 | 6.84 | —4.188 | ** |
| 15 | 4.80 | 7.32 | —4.131 | ** |
| 16 | 5.24 | 7.68 | —4.108 | ** |
| 17 | 4.88 | 7.24 | —4.140 | ** |
| 18 | 4.84 | 7.12 | —4.238 | ** |
| 19 | 4.88 | 7.00 | —4.206 | ** |
| 20 | 4.84 | 7.08 | —4.349 | ** |
| 21 | 4.64 | 7.40 | —4.402 | ** |
| 22 | 5.84 | 7.72 | —3.488 | ** |
| 23 | 5.36 | 7.48 | —3.772 | ** |
| 24 | 5.40 | 7.64 | —4.029 | ** |
| 25 | 5.16 | 7.36 | —3.963 | ** |

$df = 48$     **P $(2.681 \leq t \leq -2.68)$     $\leq .01$
†Objectives are listed in Inventory of Interest and Competency, Appendix K.

that there were changes in the mean scale values of interest. The high pre-program ratings (all greater than 7 from a possible 9) revealed the high interest levels of students who were entering the experimental program. There was little opportunity for upward change. Individual students did show changes in both directions, but these were not significant when a total student population was used except in the three cases discussed above.

Predictably, and fortunately, there were significant increases in mean scores of competencies perceived after the program, .01 levels on all items. Table 2 shows the results of student ratings of their own competencies in program objectives, pre- and post-program participation. (Negative numbers are shown in the "t's" because the larger post mean scores are subtracted from the smaller pre scores.) Students perceived themselves to have increased competency in every role-related objective. This was consistent with faculty evaluations of students' performance. Program results, then, were closely related

to program objectives for students who were prepared to serve as library media specialists.

Table 3 shows differences in student mean values on a Semantic Differential Scale (see Appendix L) before and after participation in the experimental program. Although the instrument originally included eighteen concepts and twenty sets of adjectives, it was determined that ten concepts were most likely to reveal change in attitude of students based on the content and methods used in the program. The scale administered after the program included only the ten concepts listed in Table 3.

Adjectives used in the scale remained the same for each concept and were divided into three groups. The first group of eleven showed evaluation and the next four revealed potency according to Osgood's study.[8] The last five adjectives were not used in either the sub-categories, evaluation and potency, or the total scale.

---

8. *The Measurement of Meaning.*

TABLE 3. DIFFERENCES BETWEEN STUDENT MEAN VALUES ON A SEMANTIC DIFFERENTIAL SCALE PRE- AND POST-PARTICIPATION IN THE EXPERIMENTAL PROGRAM

| TERMS | EVALUATION SCALE | | | | POTENCY SCALE | | | | TOTAL SCALE | | | |
|---|---|---|---|---|---|---|---|---|---|---|---|---|
| | PRE | POST | $t$ | P | PRE | POST | $t$ | P | PRE | POST | $t$ | P |
| Media | 6.14 | 6.40 | —1.405 | | 5.45 | 5.64 | — .815 | | 5.95 | 6.18 | —1.229 | |
| Learning Theory | 5.11 | 5.05 | .217 | | 4.42 | 4.39 | .108 | | 4.98 | 4.89 | .333 | |
| Communication | 6.43 | 6.31 | .706 | | 5.54 | 5.34 | .823 | | 6.21 | 6.05 | .969 | |
| Leadership | 5.72 | 5.79 | — .277 | | 5.28 | 5.06 | .843 | | 5.62 | 5.57 | .211 | |
| Research | 5.45 | 5.61 | — .635 | | 4.56 | 4.84 | —1.107 | | 5.21 | 5.41 | — .917 | |
| Human Behavior | 5.31 | 5.37 | — .261 | | 4.39 | 4.65 | —1.166 | | 5.07 | 5.18 | — .426 | |
| Nonprinted Materials | 6.00 | 6.35 | —1.861 | | 5.16 | 5.47 | —1.336 | | 5.78 | 6.06 | —1.474 | |
| Equipment | 5.68 | 5.95 | —1.222 | | 5.03 | 5.18 | — .551 | | 5.49 | 5.77 | —1.489 | |
| Design and Production | 6.29 | 6.07 | .843 | | 5.54 | 5.43 | .470 | | 6.08 | 5.89 | .819 | |
| Curriculum | 5.13 | 5.83 | —2.405 | * | 4.35 | 4.95 | —1.935 | | 4.98 | 5.96 | —3.636 | ** |

N = 24     df = 46     * = P (—2.012 $\leq t \leq$ 2.012) $\leq$ .05     ** = P (—2.685 $\leq t \leq$ 2.685) $\leq$ .01

One student's responses were incomplete and unusuable, making N = 24 for the analysis of the semantic differential.

Overall, student attitude did not change significantly during the program. An exception was the concept, curriculum. Students made a significant change in their evaluation and in their total response to curriculum as a concept. Although it was hoped that more change in attitude would occur, the relatively positive attitude at the beginning of the program made this less likely to happen. Curriculum development was a new program component and an important area of competency for the school library media specialist.

In addition to the objectives for school library media specialists, there were five stated objectives for the University. The first concerned an increase in interdisciplinary cooperation. Several results can be documented. Before the experimental program there were two courses joint-listed by the Schools of Library Science and Education, Literature for Children and Literature for Young Adults. Two additional courses for the program are now joint-listed by these schools, Design and Production of Media and Teaching with Media. Courses which were joint-listed were reviewed and approved by both schools, indicating a recognition of their importance to the programs of both. Another result of the interdisciplinary cooperation was the increased number of courses in the School of Education elected by library students. Before the program few library science students elected more than one education course at the graduate level. There is now an average of three or more courses per student enrolled in the experimental program. A third result was that the School of Library Science purchased media equipment and materials which were housed in the School of Education Building and used by education classes as well as by program faculty and students. Finally, the School of Educa-

tion agreed, when the program proposal was submitted, to provide space for all school library media program classes within their building, making it possible for greater access to media equipment and materials from the Educational Media Center.

The second University-related objective was concerned with holding seminars on use of media to increase productivity in teaching within the two schools mentioned above. One workshop on media utilization was held for the School of Library Science faculty in December 1971. However, operation of the program suggested a modification of this objective to allow for a more individualized approach to media utilization in teaching. Several campus-wide programs on media utilization were sponsored by CREE, Combined Resources for Educational Electronics, an organization of faculty members from various disciplines who have an interest in educational technology and its effective use.

A third objective concerned the provision for individualized learning within the Schools of Education and Library Science. There have always been opportunities for individualization of instruction through directed reading and research and, within courses, through choices of topics for projects, papers, and oral presentations. Nevertheless, the increased number of seminar courses for students in the experimental program, at least three for all students, and the development of the Self-Instructional Laboratory as a part of the Educational Media Center are indications of increasing opportunities for individualization. Students in the program were encouraged to elect the independent section of General Reference as a means of experiencing learner reactions to computer assisted instruction. The internship experience provided another opportunity for individualization as each student responded to the environment in an assigned school. Several students elected an additional field-centered directed study to initiate a project within the school setting. A module for independent study of the Dewey Decimal Classification was planned but was not completed.

Increased use of media facilities and collections, another objective for the University, was encouraged by a more lenient circulation policy in the Educational Media Center which allowed students to borrow nonprint media for use. Carrels and equipment for viewing and listening within the EMC were purchased and installed during the experimental program. The EMC extended its weekday hours through the evening until nine o'clock. This increased accessibility greatly and stimulated use of EMC facilities and collections. The Library Science Library increased its microform collection and has begun to provide other viewing and listening opportunities for its users. Slide and filmstrip viewers and cassette tape players were available for use with tapes of convocation speeches, sets of locally-produced slides assigned by library science instructors, and some commercial materials appropriate for a professional collection.

A final objective for the University was that of making available appropriate resources for the evaluation of the experimental program. The employment of a research assistant during the planning stages of the program and, subsequently, the use of various university staff members to develop questionnaires and to gather and compile data for a formative evaluation of the program were in support of this objective.

Modifications in the program and in the original objectives have been discussed throughout the report as they were appropriate to the topic. Some changes occurred in course content and method each term, generally in the directions of increasing use of media and greater student choice. This, however, was consistent with program objectives and not a modification of them.

As it happened, the first group of seven students had somewhat similar undergraduate preparation— liberal arts and a teaching certificate. Later, some students entered the program after completing an undergraduate major in library science or, in one case, after completing a master of arts degree in education. These students had a greater opportunity to gain depth in special competencies since they had already met some of the basic program requirements. Again, this was a modification consistent with the objective to provide for individualization of instruction.

## BY-PRODUCTS

A valuable by-product of the program was the media developed for use in classroom and in the Self-Instructional Laboratory. The media technician worked with a number of faculty members to produce slides, tapes, and transparencies for classroom presentations. Some of these materials could be used by more than one faculty member, e.g., slides of selection tools, and most items could be used in subsequent semesters with different students. Of long range instructional value were three trigger films produced for the experimental program by the Television Center. These will continue to be useful to stimulate discussion in classrooms and in other settings such as school service programs and professional workshops. Students produced media for classroom and self-instructional use primarily as a part of the seminar in media design and production. As interest in this seminar increases more students become involved as partners with faculty members in instructional design.

Another important by-product of the experimental program was the interest in nonprint media which grew among students outside the program. Persons whose professional goals were public, university, and special library work expressed interest in taking Media Design and Production, Seminar in Media for Children and Young Adults, and other experimental program courses. These students joined school library media program students in requests that the basic cataloging and classification course give greater consideration to nonprint media.

Participation in the experimental program brought opportunities for student as well as faculty involvement with persons from other institutions of higher education. Some students and faculty members attended national conferences and represented the University of Michigan program on discussion panels and in exhibit area booths. They interacted with participants from other School Library Manpower Project experimental programs and with interested people attending the conferences. On returning to campus, student and faculty conference participants shared their experiences with others at Knapp-sack lunches or seminars, and in the LSSO Newsletter. This involvement with other institutions was enriching to individuals and to the program as ideas were exchanged and program components compared.

Although fieldwork was explicitly included in program goals and objectives, the opportunity for increased communication with schools in the area might be viewed as a by-product of that component. The planning and implementation of visits, field projects, and internship experiences enriched classroom activities by making faculty members more familiar with current practices and conditions. Students involved in these fieldwork activities brought back to classroom discussion the ideas gained and problems identified in the schools. Another means of extending communication with the field was in the use of media specialists as resource persons and speakers in the classroom. An example is the use of the library media consultant from the University's Bureau of School Services in developing a case study of a school library media program.

Institutional support is a requisite for any experimental program. Happily, it can also be a by-product of such a program. In this case, the University's central administration, as well as the deans of library science and education, pledged support to continue the new positions created if grant funds were secured to begin the program. As the second and final year of funding ended, the University included in its budget request to the state legislature the school library media program. The legislature agreed to fund the school library media program as a new program for 1973-74. New programs funded in this manner become a part of the school's incremental budget thereafter. Thus, a very real by-product of the experimental program was the increase in the faculty of the School of Library Science from fourteen to sixteen and the permanent addition of a media technician to the School's staff.

In summary, there is evidence of progress in all program objectives although no controlled experimental research has taken place. Students perceived themselves to have gained competency in all role-related objectives. By-products of the program included media to be used in classroom and self-study, growing interest in all media by library science students outside the program, student and faculty involvement with persons from other institutions, increased communication with area schools, and continuing institutional support for the school library media program.

# Program Conclusions

The experimental program at the University of Michigan operated within the framework of a graduate, ALA-accredited library school in cooperation with a large, NCATE-accredited school of education. Utilizing the strengths of a graduate school faculty with a variety of expertise, while modifying the traditional library science core, the program sought to provide for the instructional needs of a special group of students, those preparing to be school library media specialists. These needs were identified and specified through a series of program objectives which listed competencies necessary for an effective school library media specialist. Objectives were fulfilled primarily through a series of courses, although some could be met by means of exemption examinations, records of previous academic work, or past experience.

Recognition of the widely diversified educational and experiential backgrounds of students, as well as their differing interests and career goals, resulted in individually planned programs developed through student-faculty conferences. Formal counseling sessions were held at least once each term, with the possibility of further sessions at the request of either the student or one of the faculty members. Informal counseling was frequent.

Interdisciplinary cooperation between the Schools of Library Science and of Education expanded as a result of the experimental program. Five persons with joint appointments in education and library science constituted the core faculty and a number of other persons from the School of Education were members of an Advisory Board to the program. Students took more graduate education courses within the program than any library science students at the Master's level have taken in the past. The School of Library Science purchased audiovisual equipment and nonprint media to supplement the resources of the Educational Media Center in the School of Education Building. All classes for the experimental program were held in that building to facilitate the use of media for instruction.

Curriculum, learning, and human relations competencies were achieved by students primarily through courses offered by the School of Education. Choice of courses in these fields of study depended not only on student background and interests, but also on availability of specific courses at times suitable for the student's schedule.

A sequence of courses in media design and production utilized a basic audiovisual methods course, or achievement of its objectives through the Self-Instructional Laboratory, as a prerequisite for two new courses in principles of design and practice in production skills. A third new course, Seminar in Media for Children and Young Adults, completed the sequence in selection and utilization of media. Other courses in that sequence included Literature for Children, Literature for Young Adults, and Teaching with Media. All these courses were restructured to utilize a multimedia approach in content and method.

In order to provide instructional media for program faculty and assistance for students in the media design and production laboratory sessions, the role of a media technician was defined and a competent person was employed. This position and two new faculty positions were added to the School of Library Science on a permanent basis as a result of the experimental program.

A field work component allowed for interaction between classroom and selected school library media centers. This component included visitations, field-centered projects, and an internship experience. In addition, professionals from the field helped in the formative evaluation of the program and served as resource persons and guest lecturers in some classes.

The group officially designated to guide the program faculty was the Advisory Board. Among its membership were leaders from education, librarianship, and representatives from students in the program. This Board met at least twice each year, beginning in spring of 1971, and it will continue to meet during the 1973-74 academic year. Each Board member also served on a sub-committee to advise on campus courses, the fieldwork component and program evaluation and dissemination.

Program elements noted in the preceding paragraphs were considered by the Director and core faculty to be keys to the success of this experimental program. Planners utilized faculty strengths, involved a variety of persons from the field, designed a series of courses and a fieldwork component through competency-based objectives, and counseled students into individually planned sequences of courses culminating in an internship experience. There were, however, some problems along the way.

Most of the problems were related to time as a limited resource. Planning and implementing a new program takes a great amount of time. The effective involvement of persons outside of the program's core faculty took more time. Added to this was the time needed to develop conference programs, brochures, slides, written reports and other devices for informing the public of the experimental program and the School Library Manpower Project. Designing in-

structional media for classroom presentations and for self-instructional programs took considerably more time than originally expected. The time problems involved in administering the fieldwork segment have already been noted.

Another major problem area the program faced was communication. The simple act of notifying the students in the experimental program of a special event or the need to complete a questionnaire was sometimes quite difficult. Invariably some students did not have telephones and others were hard to reach because of changing work and class schedules. Mailings took time and letters did not always reach their intended destination. Announcements in library science classes, the usual means of notification of school events, did not reach students taking classes outside the School of Library Science. Bulletin boards in the Library Science Library and the Educational Media Center were utilized, but on a large campus where needed facilities were highly decentralized some students missed these notices, especially if they were on campus only one or two days a week. Communicating between the Schools of Library Science and Education on such matters as scheduling of classes and laboratory space at times proved frustrating to both groups as well as to those students who had to make substitutions in their course elections. There was always a willingness by administrators of the two schools to reach agreement, but sometimes this did not happen before time schedules, used in counseling students, were printed.

In conclusion, the experimental program attempted to become more responsive to the needs of the profession and the users of school media centers, to the needs of individual students within the program, and to the potential resources for teaching and learning within the university. It initiated change within a large university without significantly altering the concepts of credit hours and courses. The major implications of the program for other institutions involved in library education are: (1) that such change was possible, (2) that it was difficult and required a greater commitment of time and resources than operating within the status quo, and (3) that innovation was rewarded as well as rewarding.

RECOMMENDATIONS

The writing of the final report has provided the opportunity for examination of the experimental program as it has operated through August. 1973. As a result of that examination the experimental program staff makes the following recommendations:

1. The program should continue to operate through-

out the 1973-74 academic year with modifications based on present and future formative evaluation. Major changes should take into consideration the results of Phase III of the School Library Manpower Project.

2. The Advisory Board should continue its review of the program throughout the 1973-74 year.

3. The Curriculum Committee of the School of Library Science and the faculty of the School should review this report and consider its implications for the School's total program.

4. The Dean of the School of Education and appropriate divisions, particularly the Teacher Education Division, should review this report and consider its implications for their programs.

5. The fieldwork component should be continued and every effort should be made to explore and resolve the issue of stipends for cooperating school library media specialists.

6. Consideration should be given to assigning the supervision of interns as part of the regular faculty load.

7. The School of Library Science should continue to expand its instructional design capability for members of the teaching faculty.

8. The School of Library Science should increase its efforts to obtain well-equipped classroom space designated exclusively for its use.

9. Consideration should be given to expanding the program to provide for greater competency in such areas as educational television, film making, and instructional design.

10. Student involvement in program planning and evaluation should be continued and expanded.

11. The study of certification for media specialists now being made in Michigan and other states should have access to this report and should utilize experiences of the experimental program.

Appendix A

QUESTIONNAIRE TO ALUMNI

THE UNIVERSITY OF MICHIGAN
SCHOOL OF LIBRARY SCIENCE


Name:_____


I.  Employment Record:

A.  What professional positions have you held since leaving library school?
    List current position last.

| Place | Position Title | From/To<br>(Month & Year) |
|-------|----------------|---------------------------|
|       |                |                           |
|       |                |                           |

B.  Present Position Description:  (check where appropriate)

____ District School Library Media Director

_2_ District Level School Library Media Specialist

_4_ Head, School Library Media Center

_7_ School Library Media Specialist

____ Other:  specify _____

C.  Level of Service:  (present position)

_7_ Elementary School

_1_ Middle School

_2_ Junior High School

_2_ High School

_1_ K - 12

____ Other:  specify _____

D.  Number of Persons Currently Supervised  (professional and non-
                                             professional adults)

    /2/ None              /_/ 3

    /4/ 1                 /2/ 4-5

    /2/ 2                 /3/ 6 or more

Appendix A (cont'd)

II. Using a rating scale ranging from 1 to 5, (1 = low – 5 = highest) indicate the value of your professional education in terms of your present position: (use NA if not applicable)  Place an x in the appropriate box.

A. **Library Science**

| | 1 | 2 | 3 | 4 | 5 |
|---|---|---|---|---|---|
| Book Selection | | 1 | 3 | 4 | 5 |
| Cataloging and Classification | | 1 | 4 | 2 | 5 |
| Children's Literature | | 1 | 3 | 1 | 6 |
| Curriculum Materials | 3 | 1 | | 2 | 4 |
| Field Experience | 3 | | 1 | | 2 |
| History of Children's Literature | 1 | | | 1 | 1 |
| Reference Materials | | | 4 | 2 | 5 |
| School Library Administration | 1 | 1 | 3 | 1 | 7 |
| Seminar in School Library Problems | 3 | 2 | | 1 | |
| Storytelling | 2 | | 1 | 1 | |
| Subject Bibliography | 4 | 3 | 1 | | 3 |
| Young Adult Literature | 1 | | 2 | | 6 |
| Other (specify) Library as Public Service Institution | 1 | 1 | | | |
| LC Cataloging | 1 | | | | |
| Library Public Relations | | | | | 1 |

B. **Education**

| | 1 | 2 | 3 | 4 | 5 |
|---|---|---|---|---|---|
| Audiovisual Methods | 2 | 1 | 1 | 4 | 5 |
| Curriculum Development | 2 | | 1 | 2 | 2 |
| Educational Psychology | 4 | 2 | 3 | 1 | 1 |
| Methods of Teaching (subject area) | 2 | 2 | 2 | 2 | 2 |
| Social Foundations of Education (Philosophy and/or Sociology) | 2 | 2 | 2 | 1 | 1 |
| Student Teaching | | | | 4 | 4 |
| Other (specify)  School Law | | | | 1 | |
| Fieldwork on School Libraries | | | | | 1 |

Appendix A (cont'd)

C. <u>Areas of Study Outside Library</u>
   <u>Science and Education</u>

| | 1 | 2 | 3 | 4 | 5 |
|---|---|---|---|---|---|
| Liberal Arts | | | 2 | 3 | 7 |
| Business (administration) | 1 | | 1 | | 1 |
| Communications | 1 | | 2 | 1 | 2 |
| Foreign Languages | 1 | 2 | 3 | 3 | 1 |
| Other (specify) Medical Technology | | | 1 | | |
| Printing | | | | | 1 |
| Typing | | | | | 1 |

III. What aspects of your education have you felt most valuable for your present professional library position?

_____

IV. What requirements of your present position or role were not covered in your educational program?

_____

V. Considering current developments and future trends in the school library media field, what skills and knowledge do you believe will be needed by a specialist in that field, but were not included in your own educational program?

_____

VI. List any workshops and institutes (credit or non-credit) which you have attended since receiving the AMLS degree. (Give topic, place, & dates).

_____

VII. What topics do you suggest for future workshops or institutes which might be sponsored by the University of Michigan?

_____

VIII. Which of the following courses, which have been added recently to the Library Science curriculum, would you be interested in taking at the Post AMLS degree level?

__5__ Contemporary Library Developments

__5__ Design and Production of Media

__3__ Introduction to Documentation and Information Retrieval

__5__ Seminar in Media Production

__10__ Seminar in Media for Children and Young Adults

Appendix A (cont'd)


IX.  If you were to take additional work in library science, which times would be most convenient for you?

_____ Extension Centers

_____ Evenings (7-9 p.m.)

_____ Late afternoons (4-6 p.m.)

_____ Saturday mornings

_____ Summer Sessions

Appendix B

THE LIBRARY SCIENCE EVALUATION FORM

THE UNIVERSITY OF MICHIGAN
SCHOOL OF LIBRARY SCIENCE

Summer Term -- 1973

Instructor_____ Course_____ Section_____

1.  Did the content and methodology meet the objectives of the course?

    Fully ____:____:____:____:____ Not at all

2.  Was the presentation of material appropriate to the intellectual level of the student?

    Appropriate ____:____:____:____:____ Inappropriate

    If inappropriate please comment or explain.


3.  Was the material presented in a well-organized fashion?

    Well-organized ____:____:____:____:____ Disorganized

4.  Did the instructor appear sensitive to attitudes and reactions of the class?

    Responsive ____:____:____:____:____ Unaware

5.  Did the instructor make students feel free to ask questions, disagree, express their ideas, etc.?

    Encouraged student ideas ____:____:____:____:____ Intolerant

6.  Was the instructor helpful when students had difficulty with course work?

    Actively helpful ____:____:____:____:____ Not helpful

7.  Did the instructor utilize class time effectively

    Effectively ____:____:____:____:____ Ineffectively

8.  Was the instructor able to clarify the subject matter?

    Always ____:____:____:____:____ Never

9.  Did the instructor stimulate thinking and encourage further study?

    Frequently ____:____:____:____:____ Never

10. Was the amount of work required appropriate for the credit received?

    Appropriate ____:____:____:____:____ Inappropriate

    If inappropriate check one:  a. ____too much work
                                 b. ____too little work
                                 c. ____other-comment

Appendix B (cont'd)

11. Were the tests relevant to the course objectives and course content?

Relevant ____:____:____:____:____ Not relevant  Does not apply ____

12. What features of this course (projects, term papers, speakers, etc.) did you consider most valuable?

_____

13. What were least valuable?

_____

14. What suggestions do you have to improve this course?

_____

15. Other Comments:

_____

Appendix C
STUDENT QUESTIONNAIRE

100% Return
N = 16

Date:  October, 1972

Number of hours this term:

Date of enrollment:

All percentages rounded to nearest integer

Information sought in this questionnaire will be used in the formative evaluation of the University of Michigan Experimental Program for School Library Media Specialists and in a report to the School Library Manpower Project.

Please read the questions carefully, and respond to each one as accurately as possible.  Consider responses on a 5 point scale ranging from very positive to very negative, and place a check mark on the blank beside the number that you consider most appropriate.  Do not write your name on this questionnaire.

1.  How would you rate the adequacy of the information about expected competencies of a media specialist that was made available to you before beginning the program?

    1._____  2.___6%____  3.___50%___  4.___38%___  5.____6%____
       Fully                                                Inadequate
       Adequate

2.  To what degree did you receive preinstruction information on the educational objectives outlines by your courses?

    1.___6%____  2.___50%___  3.___13%___  4.___31%___  5._____
       Fully Adequate                                    No Information
       Information

3.  If you did receive any explanation of course objectives, to what degree were these objectives explained in the context of behavioral terms to include description of desired behavior and of conditions under which the behavior should occur?

    1.___19%___  2.___44%___  3.___19%___  4.___19%___  5._____
       Fully Adequate                                    No Explanation
       Behavioral
       Explanation

4.  To what extent were performance measuring and testing procedures explained to you before your instruction began?

    1._____  2.___44%___  3.___31%___  4.___13%___  5.___13%____
       Full                                               No Explanation
       Explanation

5.  What is your opinion of the assessment procedures used in the program?

    1._____  2.___56%___  3.___31%___  4.___13%___  5._____
       Excellent                                          Poor

Appendix C (cont'd)

6. Do you have any suggestions for improving the current assessment procedures?

_____

7. How would you judge the effectiveness of the counseling that you have received?

1. __50%__  2. __19%__  3. __19%__  4. __13%__  5. _____
   Extremely                                      Ineffective
   Effective

8. Do you feel that student/advisor meetings are helpful in evaluating your progress, strengths, and weaknesses?

1. __60%__  2. __20%__  3. __7%__  4. __13%__  5. _____
   Extremely                                     Useless
   Helpful

9. Do you feel that advisors are accessible to you for help?

1. __63%__  2. __25%__  3. __13%__  4. _____  5. _____
   Always                                              Never

10. How effective are the instructional methods used in the program?

1. __6%__  2. __75%__  3. __19%__  4. _____  5. _____
   Extremely                                    Ineffective
   Helpful

11. Identify the instructional method or methods that you have found most effective.

_____

12. Identify other instructional methods which you would like to have seen used in the program.

_____

13. To what degree do you feel that you have an opportunity to evaluate and comment on your courses in the program?

1. __50%__  2. __44%__  3. _____  4. __6%__  5. _____
   Sufficient                                       None

14. Do you think that any comments and/or evaluations you make are used in a constructive manner as suggestions for possible improvements in the program.

1. __7%__  2. __64%__  3. __21%__  4. __7%__  5. _____
   Always                                        Never

15. Is the Educational Media Center in the School of Education Building used as an important instructional factor?

1. __19%__  2. __38%__  3. __31%__  4. __13%__  5. _____
   Always                                          Never

Appendix C (cont'd)

16. How effective do you find the Educational Media Center as a learning environment?

1.___6%___ 2.___56%___ 3.___25%___ 4.___6%___ 5.___6%___
   Extremely                                         Ineffective
   Effective

17. What suggestions would you make for increasing the effectiveness of the Center?

_____

IF YOU HAVE NOT HAD OR ARE NOT PRESENTLY ENROLLED IN AN INTERNSHIP, PROCEED TO QUESTION 20.

18. How would you evaluate the field experience opportunities (actual practice in a school library media center)?

1.___43%___ 2.___57%___ 3._____ 4._____ 5._____
   Excellent                                      Poor

19. Does the internship you have experienced indicate that the School of Library Science has fulfilled its commitment for opportunities of this nature?

1.___29%___ 2.___71%___ 3._____ 4._____ 5._____
   Completely                                   Not at all

20. Judging from your experience thus far, do you feel that the University of Michigan Experimental Program is fulfilling its educational objectives?

1.___6%___ 2.___75%___ 3.___19%___ 4._____ 5._____
   Completely                                   Not at all

THE UNIVERSITY OF MICHIGAN SCHOOL LIBRARY MEDIA PROGRAM

FACULTY QUESTIONNAIRE

Date:  October, 1972

All percentages rounded to nearest integer

Information sought in this questionnaire will be used in the formative evaluation of the University of Michigan Experimental Program for School Library Media Specialists and in a report to the School Library Manpower Project.

Please read the questions carefully, and respond to each one as accurately as possible.  The 5 point scale, when used, ranges from very positive to very negative.  Please place a check mark on the blank beside the number that you consider most appropriate.  Do not write your name on this questionnaire.

1.  To what extent have you used non-print media and its accompanying equipment in course instruction since January 1, 1972.

    a.  As much as possible.                42%
    b.  I would use it if it were available. 25%
    c.  It is not appropriate for my courses.
    d.  Never.                              25%
    e.  Other comments _____  8%

2.  Is this more than or less than or approximately the same amount that was used prior to January 1, 1972?

    more _17%_    less _____    approximately the same _83%_

3.  Please check the types of media you now use.

    Transparencies                 Filmloops (8mm)
    Slides                         Filmstrips
    Recordings (audio)             Microforms
    Video tape recordings          Books and other printed materials
    Films (16mm)                   Other _____

4.  Which of the above types would you use if suitable materials for your course were available?

    _____

5.  What suggestions do you have for improving conditions for use of media?

    _____

6.  Insofar as you know, are students given adequate information concerning expected end of course capabilities before beginning instruction?

    1._30%_  2._40%_  3._30%_  4._____  5._____
      Always                                  Never

Appendix D (cont'd)

7.  Insofar as you know, are students made aware of measuring/testing procedures
    before the beginning of each course?

    1.___50%___  2.___40%___  3._____  4.___10%___  5._____
       Always                                            Never

8.  Do you feel that student/advisor meetings are helpful in evaluating the
    student's progress, strengths, and weaknesses?

    1.___42%___  2.___17%___  3.___33%___  4.___8%___  5._____
       Extremely                                       Useless
       Helpful

9.  To what degree do the students have an opportunity to evaluate and comment
    on their courses?

    1.___67%___  2.___17%___  3.___17%___  4._____  5._____
       Sufficient                                        None

10. Do you feel that student comments and/or evaluations are used in a construc-
    tive manner as suggestions for possible improvements?

    1.___17%___  2.___25%___  **3.**___58%___  4._____  5._____
       Always                                              Never

11. To what degree do you feel free to make suggestions for improvements in
    the School Library Manpower Program?

    1.___55%___  2.___9%___  3.___27%___  4._____  5.___9%___
       Free                                             Restricted

12. Do you feel that faculty and staff suggestions constitute an important
    input to the program's direction?

    1.___40%___  2.___30%___  3.___20%___  4.___10%___  5._____
       Always                                           Never

13. To what degree are faculty members free to plan their own course outlines?

    1.___92%___  2.___8%___  3._____  4._____  5._____
       Free                                             Restricted

Appendix E

100% Return
N = %

THE UNIVERSITY OF MICHIGAN SCHOOL OF LIBRARY SCIENCE

CORE FACULTY QUESTIONNAIRE

Date:  October, 1972

All percentages rounded to integers

Information sought in this questionnaire will be used in the formative evaluation of the University of Michigan Experimental Program for School Library
Media Specialists and in a report to the School Library Manpower Project.

Please read the questions carefully, and respond to each one as accurately
as possible.  Consider responses on a 5 point scale ranging from very positive
to very negative, and place a check mark on the blank beside the number that
you consider most appropriate.  Do not write your name on this questionnaire.

1.  Have the students been given adequate information concerning expected end
    of program capabilities before beginning instruction?

    1.___20%___  2.___60%___  3.___20%___  4._____  5._____
       Always                                               Never

2.  To what degree have the educational objectives outlined by the School Li-
    brary Manpower Program been explained to the student prior to instruction?

    1.___60%___  2.___20%___  3.___20%___  4._____  5._____
       Satisfactory                                        No Explanation
       Explanation

3.  Have the program's objectives been accurately described in behavioral
    terms to include description of desired behavior and of conditions under
    which the behavior should occur?

    1.___40%___  2.___60%___  3._____  4._____  5._____
       Always                                               Never

4.  In your opinion, are students made aware of measuring/testing procedures at
    the beginning of each course?

    1.___20%___  2.___60%___  3.___20%___  4._____  5._____
       Always                                               Never

5.  How would you rate the program's procedures for identifying changes in
    media services which suggest curriculum changes?

    1.___20%___  2.___60%___  3.___20%___  4._____  5._____
       Excellent                                            Poor

6.  Do you feel that student/advisor meetings are helpful in evaluating the
    student's progress, strengths, and weaknesses?

    1.___80%___  2.___20%___  3._____  4._____  5._____
       Extremely                                            Useless
       Helpful

Appendix E (cont'd)

7.  To what degree does the opportunity exist for student/advisor conferences?

    1.___60%___ 2.___40%___ 3._____ 4._____ 5._____
    Many                                                No
    Opportunities                                       Opportunities

8.  How effective are the instructional methods used in the program?

    1._____ 2.___80%___ 3.___20%___ 4._____ 5._____
    Extremely                                           Ineffective
    Effective

9.  Identify the method or methods that you find most effective.

    _____

10. To what degree do the students have an opportunity to    aluate and
    comment on their courses?

    1.___60%___ 2.___40%___ 3._____ 4._____ 5._____
    Sufficient                                          None

11. Do you feel that student comments and/or evaluations are used in a
    constructive manner as suggestions for possible improvements?

    1._____ 2.___100%___ 3._____ 4._____ 5._____
    Always                                              Never

12. To what degree are faculty and staff members free to make suggestions
    for program improvements?

    1.___80%___ 2._____ 3.___20%___ 4._____ 5._____
    Free                                                Restricted

13. To what degree are faculty members free to plan their own course outlines?

    1.___75%___ 2.___25%___ 3._____ 4._____ 5._____
    Free                                                Restricted

14. Do you feel that faculty suggestions constitute an important input to
    program direction?

    1.___40%___ 2.___60%___ 3._____ 4._____ 5._____
    Always                                              Never

15. How would you rate the current field experience opportunities for the students?

    1.___25%___ 2.___75%___ 3._____ 4._____ 5._____
    Excellent                                           Poor

16. Does the field experience available indicate that the school has fulfilled
    its commitment for opportunities of this nature?

    1.___50%___ 2.___50%___ 3._____ 4._____ 5._____
    Completely                                          Not at all

Appendix E (cont'd)

17. How would you rate the effectiveness of the Educational Media Center in the School of Education Building as a learning environment?

1.___20%___ 2.___40%___ 3.___40%___ 4._____ 5._____
   Excellent                                              Poor

18. Is the Educational Media Center used as an important instructional factor?

1._____ 2.___100%___ 3._____ 4._____ 5._____
   Always                                                 Never

19. To what degree are the management and administrative requirements of the Experimental Program judged to be reasonable and capable of execution?

1.___40%___ 2.___20%___ 3.___40%___ 4._____ 5._____
   Reasonable                                            Unreasonable

20. What do you consider to be the major problems and limitations of the current management and administrative requirements?

_____

21. To what extent have you used non-print media and its accompanying equipment in course instruction?  (Within the past year.)

a. As much as possible.                    100%
b. I would use it if it were available.
c. It is not appropriate for my courses.
d. Never.
e. Other comments _____

22. Please check the types of media or equipment you now use in course instruction.

Transparencies                    Filmloops (8mm)
Slides                            Filmstrips
Recordings (audio)                Microforms
Video tape recordings             Books and other printed materials
Films (16mm)

23. Which of the above types would you use if they were available?

_____

24. What suggestions do you have for improving conditions for use of media?

_____

Appendix F

STUDENT QUESTIONNAIRE

Date: June, 1973

Number of hours this term:

Date of enrollment:

All percentages rounded to nearest integer (1/12 = 8.33%)


Information sought in this questionnaire will be used in the formative evaluation of the University of Michigan Experimental Program for School Library Meida Specialists and in a report to the School Library Manpower Project.

Please read the questions carefully, and respond to each one as accurately as possible. Consider responses on a 5 point scale ranging from very positive to very negative, and place a check mark on the blank beside the number that you consider most appropriate. Do not write your name on this questionnaire.


1.  How would you rate the adequacy of the information about expected competencies of a media specialist that was made available to you before beginning the program?

    1.____8%____  2.____58%____  3.____8%____  4.____8%____  5.____17%____
    Fully                                                    Inadequate
    Adequate


2.  To what degree did you receive preinstruction information on the educational objectives outlined by your courses?

    1.____33%____  2.____42%____  3.____8%____  4.____17%____  5._____
    Fully Adequate                                No Information
    Information


3.  If you did receive any explanation of course objectives, to what degree were these objectives explained in the context of behavioral terms to include description of desired behavior and of conditions under which the behavior should occur?

    1.____33%____  2.____33%____  3.____17%____  4.____17%____  5._____
    Fully Adequate                                No Explanation
    Behavioral Explanation


4.  To what extent were performance measuring and testing procedures explained to you before your instruction began?

    1.____17%____  2.____42%____  3.____25%____  4.____17%____  5._____
    Full                                          No Explanation
    Explanation


5.  What is your opinion of the assessment procedures used in the program?

    1.____8%____  2.____42%____  3.____33%____  4.____8%____  5._____
    Excellent                                    Poor

Appendix F (cont'd)

6. Do you have any suggestions for improving the current assessment procedures?

_____

7. How would you judge the effectiveness of the counseling that you have received?

1.____33%____ 2.____50%____ 3.____17%____ 4._____ 5._____
    Extremely                                        Ineffective
    Effective

8. Do you feel that student/advisor meetings are helpful in evaluating your progress, strengths and weaknesses?

1.____50%____ 2.____25%____ 3.____25%____ 4._____ 5._____
    Extremely                                        Useless
    Helpful

9. Do you feel that advisors are accessible to you for help?

1.____75%____ 2.____17%____ 3.____8%____ 4._____ 5._____
    Always                                             Never

10. How effective are the instructional methods used in the program?

1._____ 2.____75%____ 3.____17%____ 4._____ 5._____
    Extremely                                        Never
    Helpful

11. Identify the instructional method or methods that you have found most effective.

_____

12. Identify other instructional methods which you would like to have seen used in the program.

_____

13. To what degree do you feel that you have an opportunity to evaluate and comment on your courses in the program?

1.____58%____ 2.____42%____ 3._____ 4._____ 5._____
    Sufficient                                        None

14. Do you think that any comments and/or evaluations you make are used in a constructive manner as suggestions for possible improvements in the program?

1._____ 2.____75%____ 3._____ 4._____ 5._____
    Always                                        Never

15. Is the Educational Media Center in the School of Education Building used as an important instructional factor?

1.____17%____ 2.____42%____ 3.____8%____ 4.____33%____ 5._____
    Always                                        Never

Appendix F (cont'd)

16. How effective do you find the Educational Media Center as a learning environment?

1. __17%__  2. __33%__  3. __17%__  4. __25%__  5. _____
   Extremely                                      Ineffective
   Effective

17. What suggestions would you make for increasing the effectiveness of the Center?

   _____

IF YOU HAVE NOT HAD OR ARE NOT PRESENTLY ENROLLED IN AN INTERNSHIP, PROCEED TO QUESTION 20.

18. How would you evaluate the field experience opportunities (actual practice in a school library media center)?

1. __50%__  2. __25%__  3. _____  4. _____  5. _____
   Excellent                                       Poor

19. Does the internship you have experienced indicate that the School of Library Science has fulfilled its commitment for opportunities of this nature?

1. __8%__  2. __67%__  3. _____  4. _____  5. _____
   Completely                                     Not at all

20. Judging from your experience thus far, do you feel that the University of Michigan Experimental Program is fulfilling its educational objectives?

1. __17%__  2. __75%__  3. __8%__  4. _____  5. _____
   Completely                                     Not at all

Appendix G

U-M SCHOOL LIBRARY MEDIA PROGRAM

QUESTIONNAIRE ON THE INTERNSHIP EXPERIENCE

Please respond to the three questions below by checking the appropriate items.

1.  What was your role in the Internship Experience?
      X   (1) Student Intern
          (2) Cooperating Library Media Specialist

2.  Which term or terms have you been involved with the Internship Experience?
      X   (1) Fall, 1972
      X   (2) Winter, 1973
      X   (3) Spring, 1973

3.  What is the level of the school in which the Internship Experience took place?
      X   (1) Elementary
      X   (2) Middle or Junior High
      X   (3) High School

Items in the next portion of the questionnaire are taken from "Guidelines for Internship Experience" developed by a subcommittee of the Advisory Board for the U-M Experimental Program. Your responses are necessary for a formative evaluation of the Internship. For each item we wish to know:

      (1) Whether the activity was included in your program.
      (2) The relative value you place on the activity as
         part of an internship.

To respond to the latter, consider _1_ to indicate great value and _2_ to indicate little value.

N = 22 (Responding) In some cases total for an item is less than "N" because some persons did not respond to every item.

| Included | | Value | | Media Service Experiences |
|---|---|---|---|---|
| Yes | No | 1 | 2 | |
| 20 | 2 | 21 | 0 | 1. Cooperated closely and plan with the School Media Specialist. |
| 17 | 4 | 21 | 1 | 2. Consulted with and provide services and media to meet the needs of pupils, teachers, administrators, and the curriculum. |
| 12 | 9 | 16 | 3 | 3. Interpreted policies for effective utilization of the media center. |
| 14 | 8 | 17 | 1 | 4. Encouraged the use of media and the media center, publicized new media, et cetera. |
| 4 | 18 | 12 | 3 | 5. Implemented utilization of community resources. |
| 22 | 0 | 20 | 1 | 6. Maintained an atmosphere conducive to learning. |
| 21 | 1 | 21 | 0 | 7. Provided reference service. |
| 17 | 5 | 19 | 1 | 8. Contributed unique talents to special projects. |
| 10 | 12 | 13 | 3 | 9. Trained pupils and staff in the use of media equipment. |
| 15 | 7 | 20 | 0 | 10. Worked intensively with groups of pupils, i.e. storytelling, book talks, developing media research skills, working with student media assistants. |

Appendix G (cont'd)

| Included | | Value | | |
|---|---|---|---|---|
| Yes | No | 1 | 2 | Media Service Experiences (cont'd) |
| 14 | 8 | 16 | 1 | 11. Designed and produced media for special instructional needs. |
| 20 | 2 | 13 | 7 | 12. Supervised circulation and retrieval of materials and equipment. |
| 9 | 13 | 16 | 1 | 13. Evaluated and selected media in cooperation with pupils and staff. |
| 15 | 7 | 15 | 2 | 14. Attended in-service programs for faculty, when appropriate, suggesting creative and innovative uses of various media. |
| 9 | 12 | 15 | 3 | 15. Prepared or assisted with reports. |
| 11 | 10 | 14 | 2 | 16. Evaluated the media program and recommended improvements. |
| 12 | 10 | 15 | 6 | 17. Studied the selection, arrangement, and utilization of media center furnishings and equipment. |
| 11 | 11 | 18 | 2 | 18. Took inventory as a quality control factor - perhaps of one small part of the collection - analyze the strengths, weaknesses, and relevance of items in the collection in light of needs of the pupils, teachers, and curricular offerings. |
| 21 | 0 | 15 | 2 | 19. Observed and supported the administrative structure of the school media program. |
| 6 | 15 | 7 | 7 | 20. Cooperated with the school media specialist in the application of systems analysis to selected work procedure. |
| 8 | 14 | 13 | 5 | 21. Studied techniques of working effectively with sales representatives in the media field. |
| 19 | 2 | 19 | 1 | 22. Maintained and improved professional skills. |
| 12 | 10 | 13 | 5 | 23. Participated in professional organization activities or meetings. |
| | | | | Orientation Experiences |
| 20 | 1 | 16 | 3 | 1. Received orientation to the area and/or school district media program. |
| 12 | 8 | 14 | 3 | 2. Observed and/or participated in area and/or district level meetings for media personnel. |
| 13 | 8 | 13 | 4 | 3. Observed and/or assisted at a media processing center. |
| 19 | 2 | 18 | 0 | 4. Received orientation at the building level, including introduction to administrators, teachers, and students; community characteristics; school regulations and policies; media program status and needs. |
| 7 | 14 | 14 | 2 | 5. Attended school, departmental, subject area, grade level, or team faculty meetings in order to learn ways in which the media center might provide services. |
| 9 | 12 | 12 | 5 | 6. Attended the other special group meetings, i.e. curriculum study group sessions, special interest pupil groups, building PTO meetings, etc. |

Appendix G (cont'd)

What do you consider to be the most important project and/or activity in which the student intern participated?

_____

What are your suggestions for change in the internship experience?

_____

Was preinternship course work satisfactory as a preparation for this experience?

_____

Appendix H

U-M SCHOOL LIBRARY MEDIA PROGRAM

QUESTIONNAIRE ON THE INTERNSHIP EXPERIENCE

Please respond to the three questions below by checking the appropriate items.

1. What was your role in the Internship Experience?
    _____ (1) Student Intern
    __X__ (2) Cooperating Library Media Specialist

2. Which term or terms have you been involved with the Internship Experience?
    __X__ (1) Fall, 1972
    __X__ (2) Winter, 1973
    __X__ (3) Spring, 1973

3. What is the level of the school in which the Internship Experience took place?
    __X__ (1) Elementary
    __X__ (2) Middle or Junior High
    __X__ (3) High School

Items in the next portion of the questionnaire are taken from "Guidelines for Internship Experience" developed by a subcommittee of the Advisory Board for the U-M Experimental Program. Your responses are necessary for a formative evaluation of the Internship. For each item we wish to know:

    (1) Whether the activity was included in your program.
    (2) The relative value you place on the activity as
        part of an internship.

To respond to the latter, consider _1_ to indicate great value and _2_ to indicate little value.

N = 17 (Responding)  In some cases total for an item is less than "N" because some persons did not respond to every item.

| Included | | Value | | |
|---|---|---|---|---|
| Yes | No | 1 | 2 | Media Service Experiences |
| 16 | 0 | 16 | 0 | 1. Cooperated closely and plan with the School Media Specialist. |
| 16 | 1 | 15 | 2 | 2. Consulted with and provide services and media to meet the needs of pupils, teachers, administrators, and the curriculum. |
| 13 | 3 | 11 | 3 | 3. Interpreted policies for effective utilization of the media center. |
| 12 | 4 | 10 | 4 | 4. Encouraged the use of media and the media center, publicized new media, et cetera. |
| 4 | 12 | 7 | 5 | 5. Implemented utilization of community resources. |
| 15 | 1 | 16 | 1 | 6. Maintained an atmosphere conducive to learning. |
| 15 | 1 | 16 | 1 | 7. Provided reference service. |
| 15 | 2 | 16 | 0 | 8. Contributed unique talents to special projects. |
| 10 | 6 | 10 | 2 | 9. Trained pupils and staff in the use of media equipment. |
| 14 | 2 | 14 | 2 | 10. Worked intensively with groups of pupils, i.e. storytelling, book talks, developing media research skills, working with student media assistants. |

Appendix H (cont'd)

| Included | | Value | | |
|---|---|---|---|---|
| Yes | No | 1 | 2 | Media Service Experience (cont'd) |
| 9 | 8 | 11 | 2 | 11. Designed and produced media for special instructional needs. |
| 13 | 4 | 12 | 2 | 12. Supervised circulation and retrieval of materials and equipment. |
| 13 | 4 | 12 | 3 | 13. Evaluated and selected media in cooperation with pupils and staff. |
| 9 | 6 | 10 | 3 | 14. Attended in-service programs for faculty, when appropriate, suggesting creative and innovative uses of various media. |
| 9 | 7 | 13 | 1 | 15. Prepared or assisted with reports. |
| 11 | 6 | 13 | 1 | 16. Evaluated the media program and recommended improvements. |
| 9 | 9 | 8 | 5 | 17. Studied the selection, arrangement, and utilization of media center furnishings and equipment. |
| 7 | 10 | 11 | 3 | 18. Took inventory as a quality control factor – perhaps of one small part of the collection – analyze the strengths, weaknesses, and relevance of items in the collection in light of needs of the pupils, teachers, and curricular offerings. |
| 14 | 4 | 9 | 5 | 19. Observed and supported the administrative structure of the school media program. |
| 3 | 13 | 4 | 8 | 20. Cooperated with the school media specialist in the application of systems analysis to selected work procedure. |
| 3 | 15 | 5 | 7 | 21. Studied techniques of working effectively with sales representatives in the media field. |
| 16 | 0 | 16 | 0 | 22. Maintained and improved professional skills. |
| 11 | 6 | 10 | 3 | 23. Participated in professional organization activities or meetings. |
| | | | | Orientation Experiences |
| 16 | 0 | 13 | 1 | 1. Received orientation to the area and/or school district media program. |
| 12 | 4 | 8 | 4 | 2. Observed and/or participated in area and/or district level meetings for media personnel. |
| 7 | 10 | 10 | 4 | 3. Observed and/or assisted at a media processing center. |
| 16 | 1 | 14 | 1 | 4. Received orientation at the building level, including introduction to administrators, teachers, and students; community characteristics; school regulations and policies; media program status and needs. |
| 12 | 5 | 12 | 2 | 5. Attended school, departmental, subject area, grade level, or team faculty meetings in order to learn ways in which the media center might provide services. |
| 10 | 6 | 11 | 3 | 6. Attended the other special group meetings, i.e. curriculum study group sessions, special interest pupil groups, building PTO meetings, etc. |

Appendix H (cont'd)

What do you consider to be the most important project and/or activity in which the student intern participated?

_____

What are your suggestions for change in the internship experience?

_____

Was preinternship course work satisfactory as a preparation for this experience?

_____

Appendix I

UNIVERSITY OF MICHIGAN SCHOOL OF LIBRARY SCIENCE

WORKSHOP EVALUATION

1.  How would you rate the overall workshop?

| 0 | 1 | 2 | 3 | 4 | 5 |

very
poor

very
good

2.  Please evaluate the following elements of the workshop:    poor          good
    a. Contribution by trainer (Process Resource Person)    1  2  3  4  5

    b. Contribution by participants    1  2  3  4  5

    c. Value of training materials    1  2  3  4  5

    d. Overall organization    1  2  3  4  5

3.  What was the general atmosphere in the group?
    a. formal _____    informal _____

    b. competitive _____    cooperative _____

    c. hostile _____    supportive _____

4.  Quantity and quality of work accomplished:
    　　　　　　　　　　　　　　(high)    (low)
    a. accomplishment    _____    _____

    b. quality of production    _____    _____

    c. goals    _____    _____

    d. methods    _____    _____

5.  What did you like most about the workshop?

    _____

6.  What did you like least about the workshop?

    _____

7.  Other comments, suggestions, reactions:

    _____

See the following page for tabulation of responses.

Appendix I (cont'd)

## TABULATION OF THE WORKSHOP EVALUATION

| Scale | 0 | 1 | 2 | 3 | 4 | 5 |
|---|---|---|---|---|---|---|
| 1. Overall Evaluation | 0 | 0 | 0 | 2 | 25 | 7 |
| 2. a. Trainer | | 0 | 1 | 7 | 13 | 13 |
|    b. Participants | | 0 | 0 | 2 | 15 | 7 |
|    c. Materials | | 0 | 4 | 9 | 11 | 7 |
|    d. Organization | | 0 | 0 | 9 | 16 | 8 |

3. a.

| Formal | 1 | | Informal | 32 |
|---|---|---|---|---|
| Competitive | 3 | | Cooperative | 30 |
| Hostile | 2 | | Supportive | 31 |

| 4. Subject | High Response | Low Response |
|---|---|---|
| a. Accomplishment | 27 | 6 |
| b. Quality of Production | 27 | 6 |
| c. Goals | 29 | 3 |
| d. Methods | 26 | 5 |

APPENDIX J

THE UNIVERSITY OF MICHIGAN
SCHOOL OF LIBRARY SCIENCE
EXPERIMENTAL PROGRAM
SCHOOL LIBRARY MEDIA SPECIALIST

## Inventory of Interest and Competency

Use the self-appraisal scale to indicate for each statement: (1) its
interest to you personally, and (2) your present competence with respect
to it.  Select and place in the appropriate blank the number (1-9) which
best describes your degree of interest.  Then select and place in the
appropriate blank the number (1-9) which best describes your degree of
competence.

### Self-Appraisal Scale

| 1 | 2 | 3 | 4 | 5 | 6 | 7 | 8 | 9 |
|---|---|---|---|---|---|---|---|---|
| Of no interest | | | | Of some interest | | | | Of high interest |
| NO competence | | | | Some competence | | | | High competence |

| | Interest to you | Your present competence | |
|---|---|---|---|
| 1. | _____ | _____ | Communicate to faculty a knowledge of materials available and their appropriate use. |
| 2. | _____ | _____ | Communicate to faculty a knowledge and appropriate use of available equipment. |
| 3. | _____ | _____ | Communicate to students a knowledge of materials available and their appropriate use. |
| 4. | _____ | _____ | Communicate to students a knowledge and appropriate use of available equipment. |
| 5. | _____ | _____ | Contribute regularly to curriculum development through his knowledge of available materials. |
| 6. | _____ | _____ | Contribute regularly to curriculum development through his ability to analyze and use results of past institutional experiences and research data. |
| 7. | _____ | _____ | Communicate regularly with media staff in planning and interpreting media center programs and activities. |

Appendix J (cont'd)

|  | Interest to you | Your present competence | Inventory - page 2 |
|---|---|---|---|

8. \_\_\_\_\_ \_\_\_\_\_ Communicate regularly with faculty in planning and interpreting media programs and activities.

9. \_\_\_\_\_ \_\_\_\_\_ Communicate regularly with parents in planning and interpreting media center programs and activities.

10. \_\_\_\_\_ \_\_\_\_\_ Communicate regularly with the public library and other community agencies in planning media center programs and activities.

11. \_\_\_\_\_ \_\_\_\_\_ Interpret the content of any print materials selected at random from the media collection.

12. \_\_\_\_\_ \_\_\_\_\_ Interpret the content of any non-print materials selected at random from the media collection.

13. \_\_\_\_\_ \_\_\_\_\_ Provide and use suitable criteria for evaluation and selection of materials.

14. \_\_\_\_\_ \_\_\_\_\_ Provide and use suitable criteria for evaluation and selection of equipment.

15. \_\_\_\_\_ \_\_\_\_\_ Involve faculty and students in the evaluation and selection of materials.

16. \_\_\_\_\_ \_\_\_\_\_ Organize the media collection and equipment for easy accessibility and use.

17. \_\_\_\_\_ \_\_\_\_\_ Provide information needed by students and teachers through the reference collection or through resources outside the school library media center.

18. \_\_\_\_\_ \_\_\_\_\_ Recommend to students a wide range of materials suitable for their developmental levels.

19. \_\_\_\_\_ \_\_\_\_\_ Design media for instructional needs.

20. \_\_\_\_\_ \_\_\_\_\_ Produce media for instructional needs using available resources.

21. \_\_\_\_\_ \_\_\_\_\_ Arrange media facilities to meet functional objectives.

22 \_\_\_\_\_ \_\_\_\_\_ Create an environment conducive to learning.

23. \_\_\_\_\_ \_\_\_\_\_ Develop the media program.

24. \_\_\_\_\_ \_\_\_\_\_ Promote the media program.

25. \_\_\_\_\_ \_\_\_\_\_ Evaluate the media program.

Appendix K

SEMANTIC DIFFERENTIAL SCALE

Instructions given to the students:

On the following pages are lists of adjectives. There is a line
with seven spaces between each set of adjectives. You are to put a
check mark in the space that best describes your feelings in relation
to the heading on each page.

1.  Place checks in the middle of the spaces.

2.  Be sure to check every item.

3.  Be sure to make only one check per item.

4.  Mark each item quickly, your first impression is best.

5.  Sometimes the set of adjectives may not make sense. Even so,
    give your best answer.

The Semantic Differential Scale contains these eighteen concepts:
Media, Learning theory, Communication, Reading, Listening, Viewing,
Leadership, Design and Production, Research, Human Behavior, Student,
Faculty, School Administrator, Curriculum, Printed Materials, Non-
Printed Materials, Equipment, Freedom. The list of twenty sets of
adjectives used by the students to rate their feelings about each
concept remains the same for all eighteen concepts. (See sample on
following page.)

Appendix K (cont'd)

CURRICULUM

| Good | | | | | | | | Bad |
|------|---|---|---|---|---|---|---|------|
| Worthless | | | | | | | | Valuable |
| Pleasant | | | | | | | | Unpleasant |
| Clear | | | | | | | | Hazy |
| Untimely | | | | | | | | Timely |
| Pleasurable | | | | | | | | Painful |
| Meaningless | | | | | | | | Meaningful |
| Important | | | | | | | | Unimportant |
| Progressive | | | | | | | | Regressive |
| Negative | | | | | | | | Positive |
| Foolish | | | | | | | | Wise |
| Hard | | | | | | | | Soft |
| Strong | | | | | | | | Weak |
| Free | | | | | | | | Constrained |
| Constricted | | | | | | | | Spacious |
| Active | | | | | | | | Passive |
| Simple | | | | | | | | Complex |
| Interesting | | | | | | | | Boring |
| Unusual | | | | | | | | Usual |
| Sensitive | | | | | | | | Insensitive |

Date Due